WOMEN'S LABOR
IN THE
GLOBAL ECONOMY

WOMEN'S LABOR IN THE GLOBAL ECONOMY

Speaking in Multiple Voices

EDITED BY SHARON HARLEY

RUTGERS UNIVERSITY PRESS
New Brunswick, New Jersey, and London

Library of Congress Cataloging-in-Publication Data

Women's labor in the global economy : speaking in multiple voices / edited by Sharon Harley.
    p.   cm.
Includes bibliographical references and index.
ISBN-13: 978-0-8135-4043-6 (hardcover : alk. paper)
ISBN-13: 978-0-8135-4044-3 (pbk. : alk. paper)
    1. Minority women—Employment—Case studies.   2. Women alien labor.   3. Minority women—Economic conditions.   4. Minority women—Social conditions.   5. Globalization.
I. Harley, Sharon.
    HD6057.W66 2007
    331.408—dc22

                                  2006027315

A British Cataloging-in-Publication record for this book is available from the British Library

Manufactured in the United States of America

Contents

Preface

This book offers an insightful collection of cross-disciplinary essays by women of color scholars based in the United States and West Africa. These chapters address the myriad ways in which the work opportunities and experiences of women of color illustrate how gender, ethnicity, race, class, and nationality affect the power dynamics of the global economy. This represents the culmination of a collaborative research project between historians, sociologists, anthropologists, legal scholars, cultural critics, and artists intending to build upon the successes (and even occasional disappointments) of a preceding working group, "Meanings and Representations of Work in the Lives of Black Women" (BWW). Seeking new intellectual possibilities and challenges, the "Meaning and Representations of Work in the Lives of Women of Color" (WOC) research seminar explored ways to better understand how the work lives of diverse groups of women of color intersect and differ and, moreover, how globalization and immigration affect the life courses of women the world over—including our lives as scholars responding to these occurrences and attempting to affect social justice for impoverished and disempowered workers.

I would like to thank all of the "senior" and "junior" women scholars who participated in the Ford-funded "Women of Color and Work Research Seminar," from 2002-2006, and our Ford Foundation project officers, Irma McLaurin and Gertrude Fraser. Support from the Ford Foundation and recommendations from my University of Maryland (UMD) colleagues allowed me to invite as participants some of the most established female labor scholars in the United States whose research analyzes work in the lives of Afro-Cuban, Latina, Asian, Caribbean, African American, and white women. The inaugural meeting, hosted in 2002 by the African American Studies Department (AASD), at UMD's campus in College Park began like those of BWW, with expressions of shared gratitude for the still seldom opportunity for women of color scholars to gather for ongoing intellectual dialogue, and then was almost immediately followed by the sharing of personal narratives of discriminatory and unfair treatment in the hallowed halls of many American universities. While laughter followed stories of being mistaken for a member of the custodial staff or routinely being enlisted to serve in the role of nurturer rather than colleague, they also provoked sadness among us as the experiences proved common to the point of cliché. Nevertheless, such awareness that women of color (consistently more so than men and white women) continue to be underestimated and disrespected provided additional incentive for us to excavate the stories of women workers and to join with them to improve their work lives across occupations, economic strata, and geographical locations.

As to the political connotations of terminology, I must note that we embraced "women of color" as a shared identity that evokes and reflects a sense of intellectual and political solidarity despite the potential of the term and the tendency of traditional scholarship to conflate us as a monolithic group. Instead, "women of color" becomes a means to activate and acknowledge a shared political consciousness that includes the support and voices of white women routinely excluded by this terminology. Of course, personal backgrounds, ethnic/racial identities, disciplinary training, and political stances (although predominantly progressive and feminist) expose differences in our ranks, but we were ultimately united by our collective commitment to social justice, as well as through similarities in research areas, which helped to minimize most, but not all, conflicts among the seminar participants. Even then, conflicts in this environment prompted serious reflection and reconsideration of our analyses rather than the questioning of our self-worth as scholars. Lastly, without a predetermined theoretical framework, but with long careers of studying the labor and activism of individual and groups of women of color, we embarked upon a multi-year research seminar to situate our analyses of women's work in larger ethnic, racial, regional, and international contexts.

Under the direction of myself as project director and with the assistance of several project coordinators, including Francille Rusan Wilson, Caitlin Phelps, Nellie Pharr-Maletta, and Sara Irwin, as well as grant coordinator Valencia Skeeter and graduate research assistants Amelia Wong and Rebecca Krefting, in UMD's African American Studies Department, we met initially and most often on Maryland's campus. Other seminar members with administrative posts and/or access to logistical support co-hosted other seminar meetings on their home campuses: Vicki Ruiz co-hosted two meetings (with support from the History Department at Arizona State University and from the Chicano/Latino Studies Department at the University of California, Irvine), Carole Boyce Davies co-hosted at the African New World Studies Department at Florida International University, and Nancy Hewitt co-hosted a meeting at Rutgers University with support from the Institute for Research on Women and the Department of History. Although not a seminar member, noted activist and labor historian Michael Honey co-hosted another meeting, obtaining funding from the Evergreen State College Labor Education and Research Center and the Harry Bridges Center for Labor Studies at the University of Washington, Tacoma; he is affiliated with both institutions. Exemplifying how the professional and personal knit together in everyday life, exchanges began in formal meetings and continued over good food at an array of restaurants (Brazilian, Mexican, Indian-Chinese, and soul food, to name a few) in California, Florida, "Harlem, USA," Washington state, and the District of Columbia.

Each of these meetings and other opportunities for communication allowed us to workshop our research papers. We hope the readers of these essays will readily appreciate the extent to which our "theories" are driven by the voices, struggles, and daily realities of women we studied rather than obscuring and invalidating them with fixed theoretical models and academic jargon. This working method brought us back time and again to the distinctive experiences of women of color as workers and activists in specific locations and moments of time, while also enabling us to uncover multiple overlapping sites and struggles of the individuals and groups of women we studied.

Examining the lives of women in this fashion allowed us a personal vantage illumining how issues of immigration and globalization influence the work lives of many Latina, Caribbean, and Asian women—insights which then affected the discussions of our seminar. Consequently, seminar participant Lynn Bolles and I applied for and were awarded a grant from the Rockefeller Foundation to bring scholars from the Unites States, West Africa, Puerto Rico, and the United Kingdom together at the Bellagio Study and Conference Center in Italy. With additional support from the Ford Foundation, UMD's Provost's Office, and Office of the Dean of the College of Behavioral and Social Sciences, we were able to gather an international group of scholars whose research focuses on working women within and outside the United States—namely Ghana, Sri Lanka, Jamaica, Zimbabwe, and China—at Bellagio. As a result of this rich working environment, the contributors to this volume offer insights and critiques of the multiple ways in which the work lives of women intersect with the global marketplace—nearly each chapter describes how intimately tied seemingly small-scale occurrences are with those of a more obviously global scale.

The studies in this volume thus reveal how globalization is constantly being reconfigured to develop new sites and forms of exploitation while its most likely victims continue to be women, men, and children of color in the United States and in "developing nations" in Africa, Asia, and South America. Still, as activists or entrepreneurs, mothers or colleagues, the women of color documented in this book often reposition themselves as workers who engage in individual as well as collective actions to combat the elements of globalization that oppress them and optimize the economic rewards available to them to increase their likelihood for survival in a world of treacherous uncertainty. For this, I would like to dedicate this book to working women everywhere.

S.H.

WOMEN'S LABOR
IN THE
GLOBAL ECONOMY

Introduction

SHARON HARLEY

Women of color have historically adapted to changes in their local environments, social/familial orders, and relations of production. Recently, changes largely spurred by the machinations of globalization have required them to create new strategies for ensuring their daily survival. Globalization is reshaping the nature of women's work—*how* they work, in what conditions, in what capacities—and, in the process, creating economic systems that are not only gendered, but also raced and classed. Subsequently, women of color respond with innovation and tenacity in order to survive fluctuations in the market and its attendant social and cultural shifts. Though they may seem casual and quotidian, these are not innocuous actions; the concentration of women of color as laborers at the most basic and necessary level of economic capitalism—production—suggests how powerful they are as global actors. As implied by Evelyn Hu-DeHart in her chapter featured in this volume, their power is in numbers. It is the hope and aim of this anthology that increased exposure of the conditions of women of color's lives may spur greater resistance against the hegemonic powers that exploit them and all oppressed people.

It is important to note that the authors here recognize this world system of integrative economics *not as a new phenomenon*, but as one merely played out now with greater intensity, new technology, and more people. By surveying the many different forms of labor in which women of color and immigrant female laborers participate in the United States, the authors here draw parallels with the lives of women in newly industrialized countries, parallels that show how local/ global and legal/illegal divisions are not valid when studying their quality of life or opportunities. Deindustrialization of the United States in conjunction with industrialization in "developing countries," the advent of global free trade, and the intertwining of national economies have set a stage for women of color— whether they are in host or home countries—to serve as a racialized, gendered, and sexualized base of cheap labor that is indispensable to the maintenance of a system of global capitalism that also relies on manufacturing desire in order to sustain consumer interest in the notion of disposable goods.

In light of these complex power dynamics, this collection of chapters presents a critical lens through which to better understand the intersecting experiences, struggles, and lives of women of color as businesswomen, field laborers, care providers, factory workers, artists, and activists in the global political economy. It thus discusses women of color's paid work in different contexts and timeframes and in each case links them with larger issues of (in)equality, (dis)empowerment, and (un)freedom. Scholarship on this subject must also address how the forces that control global and transnational economies routinely reconceptualize gender, race, ethnicity, and the meaning of work to reap and hoard even larger profits for themselves. Consequently, the contributors recognize, both in their own lives and in the work lives of the women they examine, that the exploitation of workers, in this case mostly women of color, is critically tied to larger issues of (in)equality, democracy, and citizenship. In that sense, as women of color in academe we join forces with oppressed women workers around the globe to combat the most destructive forces of globalization and patriarchal domination as well as to acknowledge any existing benefits.

Part I: Laboring in Transnational Public Spheres

Traditional and dominant historical narratives typically confine women's work to the periphery—if they concede it as "work" at all. The chapters in this section seek to show the extent to which historical and contemporary patterns of global exploitation and male domination of women of color have been deliberately linked to the denial of female equality, full citizenship, and autonomy. Describing and thus confining women's movements as occurring within "private" spheres of influence (namely, the home) as opposed to the "public" spheres of labor and politics is one of the modes by which patriarchy accomplishes such oppression. However, while women, individually and collectively, have experienced limited political and social capital due to their gender, race, class, and immigrant status, some have openly contested their subordination, even when such political work negatively impacted their wage-paying work. The most fortunate ones saw their political activism channeled into paid work as they fought to expand notions of citizenship and obliterate the exploitation of workers at the bottom of the occupational hierarchy.

While discussing four African American women activists in the late nineteenth and early twentieth centuries, historian Sharon Harley's chapter, "Race Women: Cultural Productions and Radical Labor Politics," introduces a major theme of part I and this book: the resourcefulness of women of color as workers and activists navigating circumscribed roles and spheres to widen or resolve for themselves the limits of their experiences and identities. Through acts of doing, these women protest oppressive economic, cultural, and political practices by creatively manipulating social hierarchies of authoritative power in ways that challenge male political practices on behalf of the working and middle classes. Harley demonstrates how public space may be made more fluid and complicated because of the alternative ways these "race women" entered and used it as agents of change who wielded art and culture as political tools across an international stage.

With "Of Poetics and Politics: The Border Journeys of Luisa Moreno," Vicki Ruiz also gives us a piece that looks further afield than typical labor histories to flesh out her subject, in this case a union leader active in the first half of the twentieth century. By self-locating herself as an evolving historian and individual, Ruiz also integrates her own protest as a woman of color with Moreno's in a way that challenges typical scholarly approaches that often neglect international contexts and interdisciplinary research. Exploring Moreno's personal history, activism, and poetry with attentive and intimate knowledge, Ruiz delves into her willingness and ability to transform her life through assessment and conscious choice in order to champion her political and cultural beliefs about human equality.

Like the other pieces in this section, sociologist Evelyn Nakano Glenn's complicates and problematizes the perception of the public/private divide that Western patriarchal societies have used to devalue women's labor and, consequently, their claims to citizenship. "Caring and Inequality" interrogates how women's caregiving both historically and in the modern globalized community is conflated with notions of domesticity, virtue, and love. She highlights how labor becomes a gendered experience in order to expose how women and other oppressed people creatively navigate, expand, and protest their expected socioeconomic roles. Her evidence, which supports interclass and interracial cooperation, buoys her demand for social justice for the neglected, ignored, and underprivileged working populations of our world.

Finally, historian Nancy A. Hewitt's "Economic Crisis and Political Mobilization: Reshaping Cultures of Resistance in Tampa's Communities of Color, 1929–1939" offers a critical analysis of the multidimensional nature of African American and immigrant women's community organizing in a transnational setting. Like Harley and Ruiz, she investigates the cultural and creative production by women of color in order to reveal the true extent of their political doings among fellow workers of different races, genders, and nationalities. By exploring women's "care" work in the "private" social realm, Hewitt perceives how church organizations and mutual aid societies were platforms for political work.

Part II: The Global Politics of Labor

As illustrated by the chapters in part I, everyday actions are political when they seek to mitigate a system of oppression. The authors in part II take a close look at how women of color throughout the world today struggle to support themselves and their families in a global system of economics and politics that metes out uncertain futures.

Evelyn Hu-DeHart, a historian and ethnic studies scholar, offers an articulate and eloquent overview of the modern characteristics of globalization in "Surviving Globalization: Immigrant Women Workers in Late Capitalist

America." She details the structure of global capitalism, the way it functions through a web of contractors and subcontractors who decentralize authority and reinforce the exploitation of women of color with little legal recourse due to their often undocumented status and the temporary and transient nature of the low-skill, low-cost labor to which they are most often relegated. These patterns also reinforce female stereotypes of Third World women that deem them a docile and dexterous workforce that is considered secondary to men. However, the way they blur the lines between work and home places and formal and informal economies reveals that they exceed such passive stereotypes in their actual lives.

Drawing from her experience as a legal scholar, Maria Ontiveros considers in "Harassment of Female Farmworkers: Can the Legal System Help?" how the continual sexualization of immigrant female farmworkers in California, many of them Mexican, is not simply about sex or sexuality, but violates their whole identities. Facing sexual harassment (ranging from groping to rape) from many different corners, these women, documented or not, are held in limbo by an American legal system whose discursive structure fails to recognize or allow for their individual conditions as transnationals with a culture often misinterpreted by people trying to help them. Explaining first that Mexican women's identification as *campesinas* (a word that combines their locations of work, home, and nation) reflects how sexual harassment is an assault on their entire persons, not simply their female bodies, Ontiveros then shows how reinterpreting sexual harassment law so that it is more expansive and understanding of the trauma involved with this type of crime may improve legal redress not only for women of color laboring in fields, but for all Americans.

In "Caribbean Women, Domestic Labor, and the Politics of Transnational Migration," African diaspora and literary scholar Carole Boyce Davies reminds us that the impetus for women of color to migrate does not hinge solely on economics—a myopic focus taken by many researchers—but can include the desire to procure better treatment (e.g., medical care), to create opportunities for the success of future generations, or to distance oneself from an unsatisfying or abusive relationship. She seeks to expose the mitigating factors that provoke women's migration, their experiences as migrants, and migration's impact on families and personal identity. Using ethnography as a lens for examining the motives for migration among Caribbean women across two distinct generations, Boyce Davies, like many of the other contributing authors, finds it useful to draw conclusions from the study of women's life and work experience in order to make sense of how globalization is made operable—charting the local to illuminate the global.

Finally, sociologist Mary Johnson Osirim seeks to expand our understanding of gendered labor in sub-Saharan Africa and to enrich social science scholarship's exploration of one of the region's micro-enterprises: knitting and crocheting. Also using ethnography and employing a critical lens of feminist political economy theory, Osirim illustrates in "Creatively Coping with Crisis and Globalization: Zimbabwean Businesswomen in Crocheting and Knitting" how women entrepreneurs contribute to Zimbabwe's development through acuity and innovation in their crafts and businesses. We learn that these women employ informal women's networks to respond to the negative effects of Economic Structural Adjustment Programs and exhibit market savvy by adjusting to consumer tastes, including venturing into selling material culture traditionally reserved for men, and even selling and trading across national borders. In so doing, they place themselves as actors on the global stage, aware of and responsive to the world.

Part III: Surviving the Global Economy

The authors in the third section examine changes in the past thirty years that have dramatically transformed the nature and quality of women's work around the globe. These changes never operate uniformly, nor are received or applied uniformly; thus we see a wide range of economic and cultural responses, some positive and many negative, depending upon one's vantage point. The authors here discuss how Jamaicans experienced dramatic repercussions when their economy shifted from agricultural to industrial, Ghanaians' range of responses to major political and economic reforms, and how Sri Lankans dealt with massive agricultural reform. Despite bleak circumstances and often desperate conditions, these pieces reveal the varied nature of women's resistance, creativity, business acumen, and resilience.

Anthropologist Lynn Bolles, in "Of Land and Sea: Women Entrepreneurs in Negril, Jamaica," follows three women workers seeking to earn a living in an economy that relies almost exclusively on tourism. She conveys the vitality of women's contributions to the business sector—that the very success and sustainability of Jamaica as a tourist destination depends on these women "higglers" who buy, market, sell, and trade commercial goods. Her discussion considers the difficulties of this work as well as its potential benefits and also implicates the gendering of the tourist industry that is pivotal in determining women's work and worth in the economy and society.

Bolles's chapter anticipates Akosua K. Darkwah's analysis of a different group of women active in the tourist industry in "Work as a Duty and as a Joy: Understanding the Role of Work in the Lives of Ghanaian Female Traders of Global Consumer Items." In her examples of border crossings, women able to secure positions as successful traders have the opportunity to establish transnational relationships, access other world views, influence their own culture, and establish economic independence.

However, many other women in the world are unable to build enough capital to develop and sustain a successful trading operation. For these women other means of obtaining economic independence is available, but as sociologist

Akosua Adomako Ampofo explains in " 'My Cocoa Is between My Legs': Sex as Work among Ghanaian Women," they attain it at a high price. Using personal interviews from over two years of field research, Adomako Ampofo situates the women she studies both locally and globally because the increased demand for women's bodies as marketable commodities that is perpetuated by globalization and international sex tourism also resonates locally as communities adapt to new forms of commerce and women's role in them. Adomako Ampofo demonstrates, as do the other authors in part III, that women's work is mediated by the surrounding environment and conditions of the radical shifts seen in women's labor during sovereignty, colonization, modernity, and various phases of globalization. Current globalization practices are seen to further determine where women can find work and the value of that labor as Ghanaian women's financial well-being and survival have become largely dependent on the income of men in their families—a strikingly new phenomenon given cultural traditions that formerly fostered women's entrepreneurial skills in order to encourage their economic autonomy.

A similar pattern emerges in the writing of anthropologist Nandini Gunewardena, whose chapter, "Gendering Sugar: Women's Disempowerment in Sri Lankan Sugar Production," also brings to light a transition in women's treatment pre-dating modern globalization. She offers a compelling look at the sugar industry in Sri Lanka through a case study of the Pelwatte Sugar Corporation (PSC) and uncovers an exhaustive range of problems that women workers face under the new system of production, such as their depreciation in social and economic status. Specifically, the practices, policies, and ideologies espoused by PSC produce and reinforce women's subordination, devaluing their worth as laborers as well as their bodies. Local communities learn these hierarchical and patriarchal notions and, unfortunately, seem quick to follow suit, setting in motion a tendency to dismiss women's contributions to labor in both the public and private spheres.

Lamenting the relative absence of women of color in scholarship on labor and economic practices, particularly in a global context, the contributors to *Women's Labor in the Global Economy: Speaking in Multiple Voices* seek to rectify those omissions. Together, we suggest that globalization is not enforced or enacted neutrally, that gender inequities, racial/ethnic discrimination, and disparate allocation of resources are part and parcel of its construction, maintenance, and success. Transnational corporations profit hugely at the greatest expense of women of color, who in their vulnerable position at the bottom of the global labor hierarchy are the most likely to feel the negative impacts of globalization, but are just as likely to demonstrate resilience and ingenuity through shrewd negotiation, creativity, or subversion in their daily lives.

PART I

LABORING IN TRANSNATIONAL PUBLIC SPHERES

Race Women

CULTURAL PRODUCTIONS AND
RADICAL LABOR POLITICS

SHARON HARLEY

In 1884, five-year-old Nannie Helen Burroughs, her sister, and her mother, Jennie (Poindexter) Burroughs, left Orange County, Virginia, bound for Washington, D.C., then one of late nineteenth-century America's "Negro Meccas." It was the destination of single and married black women and men—especially those from the South—in search of better jobs, better educational opportunities for their children, and a place where racist physical attacks were more the exception than the rule. The long hours, hard work, and many personal sacrifices of her washerwoman mother enabled Burroughs to attend and graduate from M Street High School, at the time one of the most prestigious public schools in the United States. Graduating near the top of her M Street class was apparently not enough for Burroughs to overcome the social stigma of being the dark-skinned daughter of a washerwoman in class-conscious Washington colored society; she later maintained that the failure to be appointed as an assistant teacher (a position she believed she had been promised) in the highly competitive D.C. colored public school system was due to her dark skin color and lack of important social connections. However, the disappointment and hurt failed to permanently stifle Burroughs's ambitions for herself and for legions of other daughters of washerwomen as she set out on a life dedicated to aiding working-class women through organization and institution building as well as to reclaiming African American history and culture for the race, especially for its working class. So less than fifteen years after graduating from M Street High School in 1896, Burroughs was back in the nation's capital—as the president and founder of the National Training School for Women and Girls, a position which helped bolster her reputation as one of the most prominent "race women" of her time.

The daughter of a well-educated A.M.E. minister, Shirley Lola Graham studied in Paris and earned two degrees from Oberlin College; she joined the ranks of the race women of the twentieth century with a different familial, educational, and class background than Burroughs, although with shared experiences of prejudice that lead her to devote her life and work to fighting for social justice.

Her biographer, Gerald Horne, recounts an influential encounter with racism in Graham's early life, when she watched her father face down a white mob from the doorway of her childhood home with a "loaded gun on top of his Bible." His militant defiance, Horne reported, "provided her with the liberating idea that Jim Crow could be confronted"[1] as well as with the courage to do so. Later, the dramatic and musical productions she wrote throughout the 1930s bespoke the Pan-Africanism and radical class politics that would dominate her life, especially after the death of her first son, Robert, in 1944. She described the event as "the greatest tragedy of my life" that "gave me impetus and determination to change many things in our society."[2] Thus, she became, like Burroughs, an equally outspoken and courageous advocate for racial and social justice and women's causes in the United States and Africa, even if she occasionally wavered (unlike Burroughs) in her feminist stance both philosophically and personally.

In 1932, the year that Graham's Afrocentric opera, *Tom-Tom: An Epic of Music and the Negro,* premiered in Cleveland, Ohio, her radical compatriot Louise Thompson returned to her home in Harlem from a trip to the Soviet Union, where she had traveled to work with Langston Hughes and other Harlem Renaissance luminaries on an aborted film project about race relations in the United States. In her lifelong career as an activist for equality and justice on behalf of her race, women, and the working class, Thompson, like fellow race women Graham and Burroughs, often combined political and cultural work in her personal and professional lives, engendering creatively progressive space not only through organizations that employed her, such as the International Workers Order (IWO), but in her involvement with the Vanguard, "the left-wing cultural group" she co-founded with sculptor Augusta Savage and whose members included artists Romare Bearden and Aaron Douglas, its "primary goal [being] to spread interest in radical politics in artistic circles."[3]

Concurrently with Thompson on the Harlem scene, which by the 1920s was widely considered the epicenter of racial and cultural politics for blacks and bebop whites, was Billie Holiday, a self-designated race woman who weathered her own storms of racism and sexism as she struggled to make a living as a black singer in the era of Jim Crow.[4] While performing as a vocalist with the all-white Artie Shaw traveling band in 1938 throughout the southern United States, Holiday's race consciousness grew day by day as she was called various disparaging names, including "blackie" and "nigger," and was often forced to use outdoor toilets or to relieve herself on roadsides and stay in private black homes, whereas white male band members could use "public" indoor restroom facilities and hotels. Reportedly, Holiday proclaimed she preferred the bushes, rather "than [taking] a chance in the restaurants and towns" where her presence often caused an uproar.[5]

Although Thompson, Graham, and Burroughs may not have regularly crossed paths with Holiday in the night clubs, juke joints, and after-hours clubs of Harlem, they certainly shared an orbit with the singer, whose leftist political leanings brought her to occasionally perform at rallies for Communist candidates. It is unlikely that Holiday's fellow race women, including active church woman Burroughs, could not know of the songstress's riveting performance of the anti-lynching anthem "Strange Fruit": the song became her signature statement about challenging inequality and injustice in America after she began singing it in 1939.

Focusing on the cultural and political work of these four distinct black race women, this chapter seeks to examine the nexus of their cultural production and political activism both within and outside organized labor and political movements in order to expand on black men and women's long and ongoing struggle for economic equality and racial justice in the United States. Legal scholar and former Black Panther leader Kathleen Neal Cleaver has observed, "The visual record always documents the presence of women, but in the printed texts of academic accounts women's participation tends to fade."[6] As example, although Thompson Patterson, Graham Du Bois, and Burroughs were major political figures in their lifetimes, and thus were subject to intense contemporary media coverage, they are missing figures in most historical accounts of the communities and major movements to which they dedicated their lives (with a few recent exceptions). In a different sort of omission, the political voice of cultural icon Billie Holiday has been neglected by scholars in a way that diminishes understanding of the complexity of an individual and also the myriad ways in which black women protest social injustice. Expanding the historical record by delving into the methods such women used to engender a political voice, which has too often been unduly silenced, is to continue their struggles, addressing, as Buzz Johnson writes in the preface to Claudia Jones's biography, the same forces responsible for our oppression who "also seek to control what we know of the past and the present."[7]

My chapter thus falls within the current scholarly purview that recognizes most black women and men, especially of the working class, as engaged not necessarily in organized resistance, but in what labor historians Charles Payne, Tera Hunter, Robin Kelley, and others, including Holiday herself, have identified as "personal protests" against racial injustice. As documented by historians Hunter and Elizabeth Clark Lewis and articulated by Blanche White, the title character and black domestic in Barbara Neely's detective fiction, stories of domestic workers' acts of sabotage against unfair employers were widely shared as they rode buses to their places of work, signaling a race consciousness that was learned through both firsthand experience and observation of the daily, often unrecorded, personal struggles of independent and hardworking relatives and neighbors.[8] Each one of them could potentially have answered the same as Louise Thompson Patterson when scholar Margaret Wilkerson asked the activist what radicalized her. Without even a hint of hesitation, she responded, "Racism."[9]

For black women, discriminated against on the grounds of *both* race and gender, the patriarchy of otherwise progressive labor and political organizations denied most women an overt political voice in the form of high-level leadership positions, leading the most articulate and talented among them to turn to alternative sites for their political expression. To expose these female activists' ingenuity within a political space circumscribed by male dominance, scholars must look toward work too often neglected—that of cultural production. With the exception of an occasional labor song, play, or the unique cultural/arts recruitment strategies employed by the IWO, the role of art in political causes is too often dismissed by labor organizations and ignored in labor and activist scholarship, almost as if they represent polar opposites on the spectrum of human experience. Characteristic of Communist members and officials, even Louise Thompson Patterson's second husband, William Patterson, held firmly to the belief that art and politics should not be connected. Yet, the two are historically entwined in the African American experience. Since being violently separated from their African homelands, forced into slavery, and oppressed in post-emancipation communities, cultural expression was for Africans, and, over time, their African American descendants, the major and sometimes sole venue available to them for simultaneously articulating personal pain and resistance to their political oppression. As a result, it is critical to look for covert and subverted communications in addition to more overt ones when examining the political roles of blacks, particularly women and the working class, in U.S. history.

I selected Holiday, Burroughs, Thompson Patterson, and Graham Du Bois for this chapter because their work and lives suggest a fuller range of political and cultural voices within twentieth-century black communities than has been possible to uncover when only looking at the institutional actions of labor unions, dominant black political organizations, or even black women's secular and religious organizations. I explore their political and cultural work in an attempt to better understand how such activities can merge to advance similar goals, such as, in these cases, racial equality, working-class advancement, internationalism, and feminism. The work of these individuals exemplifies how many black women, known and unknown, married art and politics together in their political consciousness and daily lives.

Further, in being anointed with or claiming the title of "race women," they represent how black women in the late nineteenth and twentieth centuries exhibited race consciousness and resistance not only to the racial prejudice also addressed by "race men," but to gender prejudice within the arena of work. Looking at how these women employed cultural avenues as part of their political activism, often on behalf of the most oppressed of the black working class, affords a way to observe how they opened a space for all black women to speak out simultaneously about their racial and gendered identities. Their paths to a racialized gender identity known as "race woman" were not the same, but as I will show, they were each outspoken (some would say outrageous), courageous, and fearless as they blended their cultural and political work to fight for social and racial justice, women's equality, and better economic opportunities, especially for the working class.

The first half of the 1900s saw limited job choices available to black women, who—regardless of education, but especially someone with only up to a fifth-grade education, like Billie Holiday—were relegated to the ranks of domestic service and, in rare cases, teaching, a situation which often heightened their feminist race consciousness. Many black women (as did three of those in this chapter) worked themselves, shared homes with, or heard stories about grandmothers, mothers, and aunts who, as maids in white households, were often overworked, mistreated, and occasionally sexually abused. Even more so than was true for black men, courageous as well as talented black women were forced to pursue alternative career paths that afforded them a decent living but could also bar them from middle-class circles of respectability. Billie Holiday accepted that fact when she joined the nightclub/after-hours world of the jazz singer.

A year after Holiday's mother, Sadie Fagan (who adopted the Holiday name after two failed marriages), relocated to New York City to work as a maid for a white family, fifteen-year-old Eleanora Fagan joined her there and adopted the name Billie Holiday.[10] (Although a noted musical center in its own right, the Baltimore she left was no match for New York City, which was also the new home of her father, Clarence Holiday, and other jazz greats.)[11] Billie Holiday took New York City by storm, becoming one of the most talented jazz performers of the twentieth century, but she is just as renowned for her drug addiction and subsequent arrests. The noted songstress is less remembered for her political side, but her singing of the song "Strange Fruit" was public and graphic evidence of her race consciousness and abhorrence of racial violence.[12]

The potential power of the song lay not only in its provocative lyrics, "black bodies swinging in the Southern breeze, strange fruit hanging from the poplar trees . . . The bulging eyes and the twisted mouth," but in its delivery, which Holiday articulated in both her staging and phrasing of the song. David Margolick, *New York Times* law reporter/editor and author of *Strange Fruit: The Biography of a Song*, points out that to elicit the most profound effect and reaction from her audience, "Strange Fruit" always came at the end of her set: "Before she began, all service stopped. Waiters, cashiers, busboys were all immobilized. The room went completely dark, save for a pin spot on Holiday's face. When she was finished and the lights went out, she was to walk off the stage, and no matter how thunderous the ovation, she was never to return for a bow."[13] Margolick adds, "Holiday always left the stage after completion of the song, which added to the psychological weight and emotive drama of the composition. These methods of performing 'Strange Fruit' were techniques used by Holiday to command respect from her audiences for the social and *political* significance of the song."[14] He further maintains that the theatrical staging of this particular song was the idea of Bernie Jacobsen, owner of Café Society. However, Holiday made the performance and singing of "Strange Fruit" her own by continuing the practice in musical venues throughout the United States and Europe. On this point, Dawn-Wisteria Bates argues in her master's thesis that "the timing, emotional intensity, and sophisticated lyrical phrasing of Holiday's delivery of 'Strange Fruit' is [*sic*] undeniably a testimony of her artistic authority and *political* comprehension of the song."[15] From her own vantage point (as related to William Dufty in her "autobiography," *Lady Sings the Blues*)[16], Holiday claimed, "I worked like the devil on it because I was never sure I could put it across or that I could get across to a plush night-club audience the things that it meant to me."[17]

Despite the personal depression that allegedly accompanied each performance of the song, Holiday felt compelled—indeed, wanted—to sing it because, in part, she associated it with her father's death. Holiday allegedly asserted, "I have to keep singing it, not only because people ask for it but because twenty years after Pop died the things that killed him are still happening in the South."[18] Holiday reveals in *Lady Sings the Blues* that her father, Clarence Holiday, who had been exposed to poison as a soldier during World War I, had died after traveling some distance to the veteran's hospital in Dallas, Texas, after fearing denial of medical treatment for a bout of pneumonia in the rural southern community where he was performing. Holiday reportedly told Dufty,

> [It] wasn't the pneumonia that killed him, it was Dallas, Texas. That's where he was and where he walked around, going from hospital to hospital trying to get help. But none of them would even so much as take his temperature or take him in. That's the way it was.
>
> Pop finally found a veterans' hospital, and because he had been in the Army, had ruined his lungs and had records to prove it, they finally let him in the Jim Crow ward down there. By that time it was too late.[19]

While it is not clear how much of this account of Clarence Holiday's death is factual, the lack of access to medical and other public services generally available to whites was a commonly acknowledged negative aspect of life for southern blacks, a reality that Holiday experienced personally when performing in the South and, for that matter, in some northern venues.

John Hammond, the jazz producer and writer who is widely credited with having "discovered" Holiday in 1933 and who was one of the most vociferous and, indeed, imprudent critics of Holiday's performance and recording of "Strange Fruit," concluded that "artistically [it] was the worst thing" that could have happened to her. With perhaps a bit of hubris, Hammond allegedly claimed that it was "the beginning of the end for Billie" because "she became too studied, too concerned about becoming an *artiste*, a darling of leftist intellectuals."[20] Holiday seems to have been unconcerned with such criticism, as she continued to sing "Strange Fruit" and, around 1940, also began singing the equally provocative, Communist-associated "The Yanks Aren't Coming." Her choices attracted the attention of the Federal Bureau of Investigation, which maintained a file on her.[21] Although not active as a member of any twentieth-century organized labor or political movement, through her performance of "Strange Fruit," Billie Holiday was drawn into the orbits of both leftist and civil rights organizations, including the National Association for the Advancement of Colored People; she also attended political rallies in Harlem for black Communist Benjamin Davis. These instances and others provide a rich background as to why the singer identified herself as a race woman and invite scholars to take a closer look at an artist whose political consciousness has been wrongly overlooked.[22]

Thirty years before Holiday daringly sang "Strange Fruit" for the very first time, Nannie Helen Burroughs—"the black goddess of liberty"[23]—took a bold, courageous step in a different direction in displaying her race/political/feminist/class consciousness: she opened a school for young working-class black females from the United States, the Caribbean, and Africa.

From the National Training School for Women and Girls' founding in Washington, D.C., in 1909, Burroughs made the study of black culture and history an integral part of the curriculum for young women pursuing professional training in such fields as domestic service, printing, dormitory management, dressmaking, and home nursing, signaling her belief that studying black history and culture was not the sole privilege of the middle class. While serving as founding president of the National Training School (NTS), Burroughs also was an active life member of the Association for the Study of Negro Life and History, which was founded by Carter G. Woodson in 1915 to promote, research, and interpret African American and diaspora history. In addition, in 1912 she started and edited a monthly school newspaper aptly named *The Worker,* which promoted individual self-help and employment opportunities for women as well as racial advancement and improved race relations.[24] Also, like activist Shirley Graham Du Bois, Burroughs wrote plays, including *The Slabtown District Convention,* which was perhaps her most popular and continues to be performed today.

At the 1900 National Baptist Convention meeting in Richmond, Virginia, Burroughs delivered one of her earliest public denunciations of sexism within black community and church life. There she attacked the sexism that limited opportunities available to black women in a speech titled "How the Sisters Are Hindered from Helping." In *Slabtown,* Burroughs addressed that subject again by humorously depicting the congregation of officers, delegates, members, and visitors of the Tenth Annual Session of the Slabtown Woman's District Missionary and Educational Convention at fictional Happy Hollow Church. Burroughs's feminist race philosophy is clearly evident in the messages voiced by her characters. For instance, the president, after asserting, "We need [black] leaders, but our first duty is to prepare ourselves for [black women's] leadership,"[25] extols the virtue of independence for women as she advises her audience: "In choosing delegates to your annual meeting, get women with brains enough to think for themselves. It is a reflection on our intelligence and on our ability to manage our own organizations to have men sitting around, telling us when to rise and when to sit. Women who rise and sit to suit men are no women at all; they are tools."[26] Just as in her public speeches, Burroughs's play exhibits her characteristic disregard for the gender hierarchy that put black women at the bottom, and her candid words challenged black women to rethink their duties to the race. An unapologetically vocal race feminist and role model for black women who sought to defy conventional gender norms, Burroughs utilized her fictional delegates also to emphasize her regard for action over words:

> I have been sitting here watching everything that you all been doing. I got to go back home and make a report; and, to tell you the truth, I have not seen anything definite accomplished. . . . There is entirely too much getting happy and not enough every day living among professed Christians. If shouting and hollering "Amen!" will take you all to heaven you are in glory right now. But, sisters, that ain't going to take you nowhere. . . . [T]his Convention ought to send these women home with something definite to do. Suppose all of us decide as our Home Mission work for the year, that we are going to keep our homes spotless, that we are going to keep our children off the streets; and that we are going to keep them clean; and that we adopt as our Foreign Mission work the education of one African girl or boy, sending one box of new material for the industrial school near Monrovia, West Africa, and fifty dollars in money to carry on the work. That would be something worth while.[27]

Certainly, these lines underscore Burroughs's inclination toward *reform*, within a more traditional gender framework, instead of *revolution*, but its overall message is nevertheless one of female empowerment, encouraging black women to be productive as well as to think and do for themselves, their families, and their race, on the home front and in the diaspora.

Her race, feminist, and labor activism coupled with her calls for political action were undoubtedly influenced by her mother's hard work as a domestic worker, growing up in Reverend Walter Brooks's race-conscious Nineteenth Street Baptist Church, and the early disappointment of feeling she was denied a position she was qualified for because of her skin color and social standing. Such prejudice perhaps colored her attitude toward the primacy of hard work in the fight for equality, a belief she shared with Booker T. Washington, although she eschewed his public pro-segregationist stance. Burroughs called the NTS "the School of the 3 B's": "the bath [for cleanliness], the broom [respect of hard work and the most menial of jobs], and the Bible [religious teachings]." Believing in women's right to be independent and self-sufficient, Burroughs adopted as the NTS's first motto "work, support thyself, to thine own power appeal," a philosophy she firmly followed in her own life as a single, independent woman. While not necessarily well-versed in Marxist critiques of capitalism, Burroughs clearly and consistently challenged anyone who expressed contempt either for the working class or for "work." Burroughs meted out the harshest criticism toward those of her own race who "encourage[d] Negro women to loaf, rather than work at [domestic] service for a living." Indeed, she considered such persons to be "enemies to the race."[28]

Burroughs's commitment to black working women preceded and extended beyond her artistic productions and the founding of the National Training School and was reflected in, among other things, her active engagement in both secular and church women's projects to aid working-class women. While working in Louisville, Kentucky, in 1899 as the assistant to Louis G. Jordan, the corresponding secretary to the Foreign Mission Board of the National Baptist Convention, Burroughs aided women wage-earners, especially those who were young and newly arrived, in their search for a safe and wholesome place to live and work by forming the Woman's Industrial Club. In addition to helping women expand their employment opportunities, the organization, which operated for at least nine years, began offering free (and later fee-based) evening classes in millinery, bookkeeping, typing, cooking, sewing, and household chores. Around this same time, she also spearheaded the formation of the Woman's Auxiliary within the black National Baptist Convention (NBC) to promote women's leadership and equality in the Baptist Church and was elected its first corresponding secretary and later president. (Burroughs's dedication to her non-wage labor was shared by many black church and club women, but even Burroughs may have been an exception, recording that she had "worked 365 days, traveled 22,125 miles, delivered 215 speeches, organized 12 societies, written 9,235 letters, and received 4,820 letters" in her first year as corresponding secretary.)[29] Moreover, in November 1921, Burroughs served as founder and president of the National Association of Wage Earners (NAWE), an organization devoted to improving the lives of working women and men, although largely without condemning or even addressing the role of capitalism or even employers in the exploitation of the working class, especially that of black women, men, and children.

Decades before organizing the NAWE, Burroughs was active in the first truly national secular black women's organization, the National Association of Colored Women's Clubs (NACWC), serving on its board and as head of both its anti-lynching and business departments. The organization's efforts to politicize black women, especially following the ratification of the Nineteenth Amendment, which gave women the right to vote, agreed with Burroughs's long-held beliefs and advocacy of black women's political rights. Years before the women's suffrage

amendment, Burroughs had been an outspoken advocate of women's empowerment within and outside the black church.[30]

Armed with the right to cast her vote, Burroughs became active in the
Republican Party—"the party of Abraham Lincoln." In 1924, she joined with
other black club women in forming the National League of Republican Colored
Women and was elected its first president. Her gifts as a speaker and organizer
with a large, black female following, and her active and visible involvement in the
NACWC, the NAACP, the Urban League, and the NBC Woman's Auxiliary,
attracted the attention of Republican Party leaders. In the 1920s and early 1930s,
Burroughs delivered various political speeches on behalf of Republican candidates, especially at black churches, which she believed were critical sites for the
political mobilization of black working-class women and men. She also continued her public denunciations of racial inequality: this gifted orator publicly exco-
riated President Woodrow Wilson's administration for failing to condemn
lynching and fostering segregationist practices within the federal government
(claims which led to her placement under government surveillance)[31] and also
informed a large gathering at the Bethel African Methodist Episcopal Church in
1933 that "black people must give notice to the world that they were willing to die
for their rights."[32]

At first glance and taken out of historical context, Burroughs's more
reformist brand of activism might appear to be starkly different from that of such
race women as Louise Thompson Patterson and Shirley Graham Du Bois, whose
Communist-infused labor politics and cultural productions more obviously
marked them as "radical." While being one of the most active early twentieth-
century race women, it is true that Burroughs rarely ventured outside of the
more traditionally political venues of the black community, church, and women's
organizations and did not affiliate with any of the leftist movements that surfaced
in the United States in the 1920s and 1930s. Yet, when examined in the context of
that time period, Burroughs was one of the most outspoken black feminist
spokespersons and activists for the common woman and common man in the
Unites States and the diaspora, reflecting the radical tradition within the generally reform-minded traditional black institutions and organizations.

In the spirit and tone of radical politics, Burroughs took on black institutions
and their locally and nationally prominent black male and female leaders because
she appears to have cared little about how others viewed her or her "radical"
positions. For instance, in a 1906 speech at a meeting of the Metropolitan Literary
Society in Washington, D.C., she lambasted such famous black men as Booker T.
Washington, W.E.B. Du Bois, African Methodist Episcopal bishop Henry McNeal
Turner, and Howard University professor Kelly Miller. Reportedly, she claimed
that "'she had more brains' than them and 'all the men in Washington rooled
[sic] into one.'" In a letter describing this incident to Washington, Melvin Jack
Chisum, his "paid spy" and occasional "provocateur," proudly claimed to have

"brought the house down by flaying her in a nice sort of a way." Chisum's alleged public gentility did not persist long though, as he went on in the letter to refer to Burroughs as "a dangerous little *tramp*."[33] While Chisum's condemnation (minus the appellation) may have been shared by others subjected to her vitriolic criticism, it was inconsistent with the widespread support she had among the black working class and legions of black Baptist women for her courageous and very public denunciation of racism and class and skin-color hierarchy.[34] Among those she condemned were whites who supported racist practices, economic inequality, and job segregation and blacks who cowardly failed to decry such instances of injustice.

Functioning within the very traditional and often conservative black religious world, especially when it came to women's public roles and her outspokenness, Burroughs was probably perceived by black male leaders, within and outside black church circles, as even more radical than the left-leaning Louise Thompson Patterson and Shirley Graham Du Bois and entertainers like Billie Holiday, whose primary public realms were outside the piercing light of the black church and the watchful stares of churchgoers.[35]

Raised with no strong affiliation to the black church or other such influential institutions, Louise Thompson Patterson's life and work typified that of the more left-leaning labor and political activists of the mid-1920s and 1930s, especially as she affiliated with the Communist Party of the United States (CPUSA) and related groups. This Chicago native moved as a young child with her mother to California, Nevada, and Oregon. The consistency of racism, overt and otherwise, that Thompson witnessed—regardless of the region of the United States in which she lived—led to an early and deep resentment of racism and injustice in any form.

After earning a degree in economics from the University of California, Berkeley, in 1923 and being unable to find a professional position in her field of study, Thompson landed a series of jobs before becoming a teacher, first at Pine Bluff State College in Arkansas and then at Hampton Institute (Booker T. Washington's alma mater and now renamed Hampton University) in Virginia. Unlike many of her white and black colleagues, Thompson had not resigned herself to the conservative racial politics of the South that were evident at many black educational institutions in the first half of the twentieth century, where the boards and, indeed, administrations were largely composed of paternalistic (if not outright racist) white businessmen, church leaders, and national and local philanthropists. Most of her black colleagues may have (begrudgingly) accepted such a situation at Hampton for the opportunity to have one of the few professional jobs available to them in the Jim Crow South.

When Thompson turned to W.E.B. Du Bois, editor of *Crisis* magazine (the official organ of the NAACP) for publicity and support for the 1927 Hampton student protests, she clearly had to have known that her actions would be uncovered

(Du Bois not being known for keeping secrets) and that she would likely be ter-
minated. Her letter to Du Bois regarding the student-led strike, she asserted, was
"to give him the background of the Hampton Strike from the viewpoint of one
sympathetic to the aspirations of the students" because "[most] of the Negro
Press was giving *only* the viewpoint of the Administration of Hampton."[36] Du
Bois's almost verbatim referencing of her letter made it nearly impossible to hide
her identity as the faculty member responsible for writing the letter; as a consequence, she was forced to resign.

Thompson left Hampton and took up residence in the city that had always
been her ultimate destination—New York, which by all accounts had become a
major center of divergent black and leftist politics and cultural production by the
late 1920s, variously named the Harlem Renaissance, Jazz Age, and the New
Negro Movement. With Du Bois's support, Thompson secured an Urban League
fellowship. Eventually, she landed a job as a secretary and typist for poet and nov-
elist Langston Hughes and later also for writer and folklorist Zora Neale
Hurston, as part of the financial support provided them by white patroness
Charlotte Mason, whom the writers called "Godmother." (In her memoirs,
Thompson professed never to have referred to Mason by that title.)

The three shared a suburban rooming house in Westfield, New Jersey, just
across the Hudson River from Manhattan, where Thompson typed manuscripts
and helped the writers on the play *Mulebone*.[37] However, an internal squabble
between Hurston and Thompson led to Hurston's sudden departure, and soon
afterwards Hughes and Mason parted ways; Hughes reputedly considered her
too controlling. Howard University philosophy professor and essayist Alain
Locke allegedly blamed Hughes's rejection of Mason on Thompson's "radical"
influence on him.[38]

Thompson's involvement in Harlem's cultural scene extended beyond her
role as secretary to either Hughes or Hurston. At a time when many leftists questioned the political significance of cultural and literary texts, the intersectionality
of cultural and political interests was the impetus for Thompson's gathering of
members of the black literati—which she called "the Vanguard"—to her New
York apartment. There they engaged in wide-ranging and lively discussions of
artistic and political matters, the discussions frequently turning to the subject of
Marxism.

In 1932, Thompson traveled with a group of blacks—among them writers
Langston Hughes, Dorothy West, Henry Lee Moon, and Loren Miller—to the
Soviet Union to participate in a Soviet-sponsored film project meant to document the lives of African Americans in the United States, including the racist
practices they experienced there. However, the film, *Black and White,* was eventually canceled. Rather than returning immediately to the United States,
Thompson accepted, with Hughes, Miller, and others, the Soviet film company's
compensation (for the cancellation of the film) of a tour of the Soviet Union and

Central Asia. While traveling, she penned a series of letters to friends and news-papers to counter accusations being made by others in the film party who had already returned to the United States and who claimed that the Soviet Union was as racist as the United States. Thompson and a few other fellow travelers refuted that charge, asserting the film was not produced because of problems with the script and the difficulty of scheduling filming in a cold climate. Thompson's experiences in the Soviet Union led her to describe it as "the one country in the whole world which gives [blacks] complete equality."[39]

Back home in Harlem, with a fresh, new global commitment to economic equality, human rights, the working masses, and racial justice, Thompson resigned from her position with the interracial, reform-minded Congregational Educational Society and became instead the assistant secretary of the Communist-affiliated National Committee to Defend Political Prisoners (NCDPP). Her principal responsibility was to recruit African Americans to join the Free Scottsboro Boys Campaign. In May of 1933, three decades before King's march on Washington and nearly ten years before Randolph's threat to do so, Thompson organized the "Free the Scottsboro Boys March" in Washington, D.C.[40] Around this time, she also officially joined the CPUSA.

Her great talents as an organizer and public speaker, like Burroughs, led her to join the International Workers Order (IWO) as a representative. The IWO, a largely Jewish fraternal organization that defended worker's rights, provided life insurance policies and helped to preserve immigrant culture. This organization was an ideal fit for Thompson's mode of social justice work in that the IWO used cultural productions to present political ideas, recruit new members, and "provide . . . a way of developing members politically and translating political ideas to an audience that was wider than the party."[41]

Thompson rose through the ranks of this leftist organization after being cer-tified in 1934 as an organizer and representative. She went on to serve for seven years as an IWO national organizer, largely responsible for recruiting southern blacks, during which time she was also elected, in February 1936, as secretary of all English-speaking branches and, in 1938, national recording secretary; later, at the organization's fifth national convention held in New York City, Thompson was elected a vice president.[42]

While on a recruiting trip in Alabama she had the misfortune of visiting a northern white friend whose apartment had just been raided by Birmingham police for having links to the Communist Party. When Thompson knocked on her friend's door, she was greeted by the police, who determined that she "was not from around here," arrested her along with the five people already in the house, and accused her of being a Communist. She was eventually released. The circumstances surrounding her arrest became the subject of an article she penned, titled "Southern Terror," which was published in the November 1934 issue of Crisis.[43]

In 1938, with the IWO's financial backing, Thompson and Hughes established the Harlem Suitcase Theater. *Don't You Want to Be Free?*—the title of their first play (which Hughes wrote after Thompson's suggestion)—leaves little doubt about their understanding of the interconnectedness between cultural production and their progressive racial and class politics. Regardless of the IWO's philosophy about class (but not race) and cultural production, Thompson's personal interest in political and labor struggles centered around forming multinational and multiracial labor/political movements within and outside of labor unions. Following her marriage to openly acknowledged Communist William L. Patterson in 1940 and relocation to Chicago,[44] Louise Thompson Patterson was elected the Illinois state president of the IWO and became the Chicago branch's district organizer. In 1941 she established the Du Sable Lodge (#751) and in 1947 was elected to the IWO General Council and re-elected as a vice president at the Seventh General IWO Convention in June 1947. While the historical record gives fuller recognition to the political life of Thompson Patterson's husband, they were both active Communists. They both served as delegates to the 1937 world conference against racism and anti-Semitism in Paris. This "fiery" speaker drew large crowds to anti-fascist political rallies in Chicago and New York. An internationalist, Thompson Patterson frequently traveled and served with Paul Robeson and W.E.B. Du Bois on the Council of African Affairs. In April 1949, she became the council's director of organization.

Like Burroughs before her, Thompson Patterson devoted some of her incredible energy to a school, aiding her husband in keeping afloat the Abraham Lincoln School that he organized in Chicago.[45] For the "workers" as well as for "writers, and their sympathizers," this "broad, nonpartisan school" provided assistance to southern black migrants to the Midwestern metropolis.[46]

A final playwright who, like Burroughs, engaged in labor and political struggles, although in this case primarily through the Communist Party network, was Shirley Graham Du Bois. Before securing a position as a co-organizer and assistant field secretary of the NAACP (working with Ella Baker) and decades before her marriage to W.E.B. Du Bois, Graham made a name for herself with her cultural productions. She wrote and produced plays and masterful pageants that extolled the virtues of black culture in the United States, the Caribbean, and Africa, including *Dust to Earth, Elijah's Ravens,* the opera *Tom-Tom,* and a play about the Haitian Revolution, which she co-wrote.[47]

When *Tom-Tom,* "the first Negro opera," premiered in Cleveland, Ohio, in the summer of 1932, it made Shirley Graham famous. A description of the production appeared in the "Music" section of the August 1932 *Crisis* magazine. The author wrote: "The first act opens in an African jungle before 1619, the second indicates the African in America, the third and last act takes the Negro to Harlem. Running through and underlying all of the action from jungle to Harlem is the steady beat of the tom-tom, reminiscent of a similar practice in the 'Emperor

Jones.' "[48] The *Pittsburgh Courier's* lengthy article about *Tom-Tom* featured the bold caption, "Presentation Gives Stirring Portrayal of the Rise of a Race."[49]

In the late 1940s, she became increasingly active in leftist politics in the United States. Like Thompson Patterson a decade earlier, in 1947 Graham joined W.E.B. Du Bois in publicly criticizing the U.S. government for various human rights violations. When Du Bois was ousted from the NAACP in September 1948 for his critical remarks about the organization and being "associated" with the CPUSA, Graham organized a full-scale defense, exhibiting what her biographer Gerald Horne referred to as "a blackbelt in the art of verbal facility."[50] Among her caustic remarks, Graham accused the NAACP of having "fastened a cord around its own neck . . . that would [eventually] strangle it."[51] Three years after his ouster, on February 8, 1951, Shirley Graham and W.E.B. Du Bois married. The following day W.E.B. Du Bois was indicted for his peace activism as an agent of an unnamed foreign power (the Soviet Union). He was jailed, but eventually freed; however, the couple's U.S. passports were revoked, preventing them from traveling outside the United States.[52] Immediately after their passports were restored in 1958, Shirley and W.E.B. Du Bois departed the United States and traveled throughout Europe, the Soviet Union, and Asia. In 1961, they relocated to Ghana and became trusted advisors to Kwame Nkrumah's government.[53] Some of W.E.B. Du Bois's friends and associates allege that Graham Du Bois's affiliation with the Communist Party and other leftist causes was in part responsible for his becoming a member of the party. Indeed, one witness appearing before the House Un-American Activities Committee in 1955 declared that Graham Du Bois was the more radical of the two.

Each of the labor and race conscious women—Nannie Helen Burroughs, Billie Holiday, Louise Thompson Patterson, and Shirley Graham Du Bois—I have written about recognized that embedded in (white) male supremacy was both class and gender domination. Alone and outside of organized movements, or working within the confines of leftist organizations, each struggled to liberate women of color and the working class from white and black male sexism and white supremacist doctrines. Shirley Graham Du Bois, Louise Thompson Patterson, and other activist women of the pre-1960s women's movement took further steps to combat such racism and sexism when they founded and actively participated in one of the earliest self-identified multicultural, radical *feminist* organizations, the Sojourners for Truth and Justice (STJ). The stated goal of this "all–African American women's social protest organization"[54] was to "carry forward the tradition of Harriet Tubman and Sojourner Truth and give inspiration and courage to women the world over, the colored women of Africa and Asia who expect us to meet this challenge."[55] Inclusive and supportive of working-class women,[56] the group resolutely protested the government's willingness to recruit black men to fight in the Korean War—meanwhile accepting their second-class status at home—and its harassment of Communists like W.E.B. Du Bois,

Paul Robeson, William Patterson, and Claudia Jones. Further, the STJ participated in anti-apartheid protests and sought communication and collaboration
with female African activists.

My focus on the cultural production as well as the paid and political work of
Burroughs, Thompson Patterson, Graham Du Bois, and Holiday has been an
effort to capture race, labor, and feminist consciousness and activism in an early
twentieth-century political and public arena that largely excluded women from
most major political, organizational, and institutional leadership posts and from
subsequent historical accounts of those entities. Historically precluded from having an overtly political voice, black women turned to cultural traditions as old as
the African drums to express their race, class, and gender consciousness. Clearly,
they found additional avenues for their political expressions in cultural and artistic productions for both working-class and middle-class audiences that, while
often performed outside leadership positions, were nonetheless authoritative
proclamations about their complex identities as gendered, racialized, and politi-
cized race women.

NOTES

1. Gerald Horne, *Race Woman: The Lives of Shirley Graham Du Bois* (New York: New York
University Press, 2000), 40–41. Another black activist of this era, Trinidad-born U.S. resident
Claudia Jones, who was eventually deported for her "radical" politics, offered the following
observation: "My daily experiences as a Negro youth in the U.S.A. led me to search out political forces that were doing something about these things. Political forces who not only sought
on a day-to-day basis to alleviate these conditions, but who had a perspective as to a radical
solution to these conditions." (Claudia Jones, interview by George Bowrin, *Caribbean News*,
1956, cited in Buzz Johnson, *"I Think of My Mother": Notes on the Life and Times of Claudia Jones*
(London: Karia Press, 1985), vi.

2. Shirley Graham Du Bois to "My dear, dear Friend," April 13, 1967, Shirley Graham Du
Bois Papers, Amistad Research Center, Tulane University, New Orleans, quoted in Horne,
Race Woman, 26.

3. Erik S. McDuffie, "Long Journeys: Four Black Women and the Communist Party, USA,
1930–1956" (Ph.D. diss., New York University, 2003), 195.

4. Farah Jasmine Griffin, *If You Can't Be Free, Be a Mystery: In Search of Billie Holiday*
(New York: Free Press, 2001), 31.

5. Billie Holiday with William Dufty, *Lady Sings the Blues* (New York: Penguin Books,
1984), 76.

6. Kathleen Neal Cleaver, "Racism, Civil Rights, and Feminism," in *Critical Race Feminism: A
Reader*, ed. Adrienne Katherine Wing (New York: New York University Press, 1997), 36.

7. Buzz Johnson, *"I Think of My Mother": Notes on the Life and Times of Claudia Jones*
(London: Karia Press, 1985), vi.

8. See, for instance, historians Tera Hunter, *To 'Joy My Freedom: Southern Black Women's Lives
and Labors after the Civil War* (Cambridge: Harvard University Press, 1997); and Elizabeth
Clark Lewis, *Living In, Living Out: African American Domestics in Washington, D.C., 1910–1940;*
and Barbary Neely's series of mystery novels about Blanche White, beginning with *Blanche
on the Lam* (New York: St. Martin's Press, 1992).

9. Margaret B. Wilkerson, "Excavating Our History: The Importance of Biographies of
Women of Color," *Black American Literature Forum* 24, no. 1 (spring 1990): 81.

10. Her father, Clarence Holiday, called her "Bill" when she was child, but the name also connected her to film star Billie Dove, whom Holiday admired.

11. Clarence Holiday was himself an accomplished jazz musician. See Robert O'Meally, *Lady Day: The Many Faces of Billie Holiday* (New York: Da Capo Press, 2000), 68–75, for a fuller discussion of his musical career and influence on his talented daughter.

12. The courage it took to sing Lewis Allen's "Strange Fruit" as well as the divergent views about its impact on Billie Holiday's life and career are addressed in several publications. For discussion of the history and meaning of Holiday's performance of "Strange Fruit," see O'Meally, *Lady Day*, 133–140; Griffin, *If You Can't Be Free, Be a Mystery*; David Margolick, *Strange Fruit: The Biography of a Song* (New York: HarperCollins, 2001); and Holiday's "auto-biography," *Lady Sings the Blues*.

13. Margolick, *Strange Fruit*, 33–34.

14. Ibid., 38, emphasis added.

15. Dawn-Wisteria Bates, "Race Woman: The Political Consciousness of Billie Holiday" (MA thesis, Sarah Lawrence College, 2001), 20, emphasis added.

16. O'Meally and other scholars, as well as Holiday contemporaries, acknowledge the "book's exaggerations . . . [that] do convey a deep emotional truth." See O'Meally, *Lady Day*, 67.

17. Holiday, *Lady Sings the Blues*, 84.

18. Ibid.

19. Ibid., 68–69.

20. Hammond quoted in Margolick, *Strange Fruit*, 59.

21. She first began singing "The Yanks Aren't Coming" around 1940, and her first narcotics arrest was in 1947. The FBI file itself does not note the date it was opened, but everything in it is from 1949. See Stuart Nicholson, *Billie Holiday* (Boston: Northeastern University Press, 1995), 121.

22. Griffin, *If You Can't Be Free*, 31.

23. Nannie Helen Burroughs, "Up from the Depths," in *Rhetoric of Racial Hope*, ed. Roy L. Hill (Buffalo: University Press, State University of New York, 1976), 49.

24. See *The Worker*, Nannie Helen Burroughs Papers, Box 47, Library of Congress, Washington, D.C.; and Deborah G. Thomas, "Workers and Organizers: African-American Women in the Work Force and Club Movement, 1890–1930" (Ph.D. diss., Brown University, 1998). Also consult Floyd J. Calvin, "Pointing the Way to Better Womanhood: That's Nannie Burroughs's [sic] Job, and She Does It," *Pittsburgh Courier*, June 3, 1929, 6.

25. Nannie Helen Burroughs, "The Slabtown District Convention: A Comedy in One Act," 7th ed. (1926), 16. See the Nannie Helen Burroughs Papers, Container 46, Library of Congress Manuscript Division, Washington, D.C.

26. Ibid., 17.

27. Ibid., 38–39.

28. Nannie Helen Burroughs, *Proceedings of the Annual Sessions of the National Baptist Convention and Women's Convention* (Rochester, N.Y.: American Baptist Historical Society, 1915), quoted in "Nannie Helen Burroughs," by Evelyn Brooks Higginbotham, in *Black Women in America: An Historical Encyclopedia*, ed. Darlene C. Hine, Elsa B. Brown, and Rosalyn Terborg-Penn (Brooklyn, N.Y.: Carlson Publishing, 1993).

29. Higginbotham, "Nannie Helen Burroughs."

30. Evelyn Brooks Barnett, "Nannie Helen Burroughs and the Education of Black Women," in *The Afro-American Woman: Struggles and Images*, ed. Sharon Harley and Rosalyn Terborg-Penn (Port Washington, N.Y.: Kennikat Press, 1978), 97–108; and Sharon Harley, "Nannie Helen Burroughs: The Black Goddess of Liberty," *Journal of Negro History* 81 (1996): 62–71.

31. Higginbotham, "Nannie Helen Burroughs," 202.

32. Ibid.

33. Melvin Jack Chisum to Booker T. Washington, February 20, 1906, Booker T. Washington Papers, Library of Congress, Washington, D.C.; also in Thomas, "Workers and Organizers," 173–174, emphasis added.

34. Reportedly over 5,500 black people attended her funeral. See Higginbotham, "Nannie Helen Burroughs."

35. See Burroughs's publications and speeches, including "Unload the Leeches and Parasitic 'Toms' and Take Promised Land," *Black Dispatch*, n.d.; "Declaration of 1776 Is Cause of Harlem Riot," *Afro-American*, April 13, 1935; and "How the Sisters Are Hindered from Helping," in National Baptist Convention, *Journal of the Twentieth Annual Session of the National Baptist Convention* (held in Richmond, Va., September 12–17, 1900) (Nashville: National Baptist Publishing Board, 1900), 68, 196–197.

36. See Louise Thompson Patterson Papers, Container 19, Robert W. Woodruff Library, Emory University, Atlanta, Ga., original emphasis.

37. Arnold Rampersad, *The Life of Langston Hughes*, Vol. 1, *1902–1941: I, Too, Sing America* (New York: Oxford University Press, 1986), 184–185.

38. Later regretting this decision, Hughes practically groveled to get back in Mason's good graces and deep pockets. For a vivid account of these relationships, see Rampersad, *I, Too, Sing America*, chapter 8.

39. Louise Thompson, "The Soviet Film," *The Crisis* 40, no. 2 (February 1933): 37.

40. See, for instance, McDuffie, "Long Journeys," 132.

41. Roger Keeran, "National Groups and the Popular Front: The Case of the International Workers Order," *Journal of American Ethnic History* 14 (spring 1995): 28.

42. *Crisis*, September 1940, 288, 297.

43. *Crisis*, November 1934.

44. Thompson's involvement with the black literary scene had earlier led to a brief first marriage to the openly gay writer Wallace Thurman. In her unpublished memoirs, Thompson professes not to have known of Thurman's homosexuality when they married. His interest in marriage to a woman allegedly stemmed from a desire to have a child with the light-skinned and intelligent Thompson. Not surprisingly, the marriage ended abruptly. See Louise Thompson Patterson Papers.

45. Relying on her connections in the entertainment world, Thompson Patterson convinced the famous black singer, dancer, and actress Lena Horne to perform at one of the school's fund-raisers. In keeping with patriarchal traditions, the better-known Paul Robeson introduced Horne while the woman responsible for her appearance remained in the background.

46. Quoted in "Louise Patterson Dies at 97," *People's Weekly World*, September 7, 1999, http://www.hartford-hwp.com/archives/45a/140.html.

47. For a fuller discussion of Graham Du Bois's life and cultural productions, see Horne, *Race Woman*. During the last years of her life, she adopted various ideological stances from Ghana's socialist Pan-Africanism (articulated by Kwame Nkrumah), China's Maoism, Cairo's "Egypt-centrism," and the Black Nationalism of Southern Africa and the United States.

48. *Crisis* 39 (August 1932): 258. Also see the *Afro-American*, July 2, 1932, 15; and the *Pittsburgh Courier*, July 16, 1932, 28.

50. Horne, *Race Woman*, 12.

51. See Carol Elaine Anderson, "Eyes off the Prize: African Americans, the United Nations, and the Struggle for Human Rights, 1944–1952" (Ph.D. diss., Ohio State University, 1995), 128–131, quoted in Horne, *Race Woman*.

52. Horne, *Race Woman,* 134–137.

53. Ibid., 143–146, 164.

54. McDuffie, "Long Journeys," 441.

55. See Harley, "Nannie Helen Burroughs," 66. For the quote and other information about the Sojourners organization, see the Louise Thompson Patterson Papers, Emory University. Also consult McDuffie, "Long Journeys."

56. The opening meeting of the Sojourners for Truth and Justice took place in the Cafeteria Workers Union's hall in Washington, D.C. See McDuffie, "Long Journeys," for more information regarding the group's careful attention to working-class women.

Of Poetics and Politics

THE BORDER JOURNEYS OF
LUISA MORENO

VICKI L. RUIZ

Over a quarter of a century ago, between my first and second year of graduate school, I spent part of the summer in Guadalajara, Mexico, interviewing Latina labor and political activist Luisa Moreno.[1] Early one morning, we boarded a bus that took us to a poor, fairly isolated *colonia* outside the city. After walking a few blocks, we entered a plaza of sorts. We had come on market day, and women, dressed in traditional indigenous garb, were busy selling their wares—richly colored chiles, mangoes, other fruits, vegetables, and live poultry. As I followed Luisa as she made her purchases, I became entranced with the idea that I had gone back in time decades, perhaps centuries, into the world of an Indian market. Of course, we had not made it halfway through the vendors when my ears picked up chords of a familiar melody. No, it was not a traditional folksong—it was not even Mexican pop. Fleetwood Mac's "Dreams" was blaring from a boom box a few yards away amidst the chiles and the mangoes. My illusion shattered, I then began to muse (actually, "pontificate" is a better word) about the tentacles of U.S. consumer culture and its impact on the peoples of the Americas. Today I would have behaved differently. Instead of mouthing on and on about cultural hegemony, I would have approached the vendor with the boom box and attempted a conversation regarding what she liked about U.S. popular music, where she had purchased the stereo, and if she, or any relatives, had lived in the States (*al otro lado*). Certainly, I would exhibit a greater appreciation for the transhistoric, transnational market place I was privileged to encounter. Moreno teased me mercilessly on the way back to the city, laughing at my naïve polemics. What I had read of struggles for justice, she had lived. To her considerable credit and generosity, she continued to share her stories with me. Indeed, on the last day of my stay, I blurted out, "I know what I'm going to do for my dissertation. I'm going to write about you." She shook her head and said, "No, no. You are going to write your dissertation on the cannery workers in southern California. You find these women." I did and that's how my life work in history began.

Touching my scholarship at every turn, Luisa Moreno was an invaluable mentor for me, a woman of uncompromising principles, integrity, and honesty. Crafting her biography represents both a professional and personal challenge given the fragmentary nature of available archival evidence and my friendship with Moreno and later with her daughter. How does one narrate the life of another with any sort of speculative certainty? What degrees of revelation are necessary for the historical record? Where are the boundaries of discretion? I am reminded of the words of writer Tobias Wolff: "Memory is a storyteller and, like storytellers, it imposes form on the raw mass of experience. It creates shapes and meaning by emphasizing some things and leaving others out."[2] Mixing narrative and narrativity, I rely on the collective and individual memories of Moreno, her daughter, her close friends, and myself in chronicling and interpreting a life well-lived.

Luisa Moreno was one of the most prominent women labor leaders in the United States, comparable in stature to Mother Jones, Elizabeth Gurley Flynn, and, more recently, Dolores Huerta. From the maw of the Great Depression to the chill of the cold war, Moreno journeyed across the United States mobilizing seamstresses in Spanish Harlem, cigar rollers in Florida, beet workers in Colorado, and cannery women in California. The first Latina to hold a national union office, she served as vice president of the United Cannery, Agricultural, Packing, and Allied Workers of America (UCAPAWA), in its heyday the seventh largest affiliate of the Congress of Industrial Organizations (CIO). Moreno also served as the principal organizer of El Congreso de Pueblos de Hablan Española (the Spanish-speaking Peoples Congress), the first national U.S. Latino civil rights conference, held in Los Angeles in 1939. Her legacy, however, remains generally unknown outside of Latino studies. And even within this interdisciplinary field, scholars (myself included) have tended to mention her only within her U.S. trade union and civil rights work, paying scant attention to her background and activism outside the United States.[3] Relying extensively on oral interviews and Moreno's own writings, this chapter moves beyond the iconography of the labor heroine to interweave her poetry with her politics to render a more complicated understanding of this remarkable transnational organizer and intellectual, a courageous, totally human individual who made history. Indeed, while exceptional in many ways, Luisa Moreno embodied a quintessential transnational subject, given her movement across discordant spaces, physical and intellectual, where she invented and reinvented herself.

Born Blanca Rosa Rodríguez López on August 30, 1907, Luisa Moreno had an improbable upbringing for a fiery labor leader. The daughter of Ernesto Rodríguez Robles, a powerful coffee grower, and his socialite wife, Alicia López Sarana, Rosa grew up in a sheltered world of wealth and privilege in her native Guatemala. As an example of her family's opulent lifestyle, at the wedding reception for one of her siblings, the large fountain on the estate flowed with

French champagne, Veuve Cliquot, to be exact. Rosa Rodríguez received a boarding school education at the Convent of the Holy Names in Oakland, California. Dashing her father's hopes that she would enter religious life, she returned home at the age of thirteen. Fluent in Spanish, English, and French, Rosa attempted to pursue her studies beyond private tutors, but soon discovered that the doors to a university education in Guatemala were closed to women. Refusing to be dissuaded and taking matters into her own hands, she organized other well-heeled, ambitious young women into Sociedad Gabriela Mistral in order to push for women's rights, especially in the area of education reform. These adolescents gathered signatures on petitions and engaged in political lobbying, using their class status to affect concrete (and radical) institutional change. Members of Sociedad Gabriela Mistral also published a literary magazine and, as part of an evolving mission, they began to include like-minded men into their ranks. One Guatemalan history book, *La Patria de Criollo*, paid them tribute as "una generación que hizo historia" (a generation that made history). During the early 1920s as U.S. suffragists rejoiced in the passage of the Nineteenth Amendment that extended the franchise to women, Rosa Rodríguez and her compatriots celebrated their own feminist victory with Rodríguez herself admitted to the first entering class of university women. Yet, she never enrolled. Deciding to pursue her love of poetry and the arts in a more experiential fashion, she fled to Mexico City to join a burgeoning cultural renaissance taking place around the capital in the aftermath of the Mexican Revolution.[4]

Rejecting her family's wealth and no doubt the constrained gendered expectations it entailed, Rosa Rodríguez by the age of nineteen earned her livelihood as a newspaperwoman in Mexico City. She also belonged to the bohemian cultural avant-garde traveling in the same circles as Diego Rivera and Frida Kahlo. A Latina flapper, Rosa pursued her gifts as a poet and in 1927 published *El Vendedor de Cocuyos* [Vendor of the Fireflies]. Barely twenty when her book appeared in print, Rosa Rodríguez conveyed in her poetry youthful abandon, passion, and desire without artifice or pretense. Her poems have an elemental quality with trees and flowers as recurring metaphors. Reflecting her youth, the verses were often introspective, expressing personal emotion and self-awareness. One Guatemalan admirer considered her a bright light in women's literature both in her home country and throughout Latin America, even comparing her favorably with the legendary Gabriela Mistral. Like most writers, Rosa treasured her good reviews; throughout her many travels, she kept a small bundle of news clippings and correspondence. On the occasion of her twenty-second birthday, one newspaper article made reference to her beauty, poetry, and vanguard feminism.[5]

One of her poems, "Literatura," provides a sense of her dedication to craft as it captures the struggle of every obsessed wordsmith staring at a blank page (or in our day a computer screen). An excerpt follows in English translation:

> Literature, literature . . .
> I have succumbed to your madness
> and at your altar
> I have sought the expression
> of a love,
> a dream
> and a religion . . .
>
> . . .
>
> And still in my head
> There is a hunger for madness
> and all my road is
> shadowed by ghosts
> of not being able to say!
> not being able to say!
>
> Literature, literature . . .
> Bitter and sweet,
> Shadow and light . . .
> O great flowering mystery!
> In your madness
> I have sought the expression
> of a love,
> a dream
> and a religion.[6]

In November 1927, Rosa Rodríguez married Miguel Angel de León, a Guatemalan artist sixteen years her senior. From a prominent family, de León, as a young man, had also escaped their effete social world, but instead of running away to Mexico, he had joined the French Foreign Legion. When he met the young poet, he was well ensconced in the arts scene of Mexico City. Theirs would be a tumultuous marriage, and if her poems provide any indication, their courtship was marked by passion and pain. In "El milagro" (The Miracle), Rosa wrote, "And I have lived,/I have dreamed/held in the fire of your arms."[7] However, in "Tu amor," she revealed:

> I know
> that you are a tear in my life
> That your hands
> will strip off my petals
> and break my stem. . . .[8]

Soon after their marriage, the couple became expectant parents and suddenly and daringly decided to set sail, literally, on a new adventure far from their

Mexican cultural refuge. They boarded the SS *Monterey* and landed in New York harbor on August 28, 1928. In November, Rosa Rodríguez de León gave birth to her "Latin from Manhattan," a daughter, Mytyl Lorraine.[9]

Though fluent in three languages, including English, they found New York a difficult place to earn a living, especially with the onset of the Great Depression. Within months of Mytyl's birth, Rosa would find herself bending over a sewing machine in the garment sweatshops of Spanish Harlem. It is within this context that her political awakening occurred. The tragic death of a friend's infant (a rat had gnawed on the baby's face) spurred her to action. She joined Centro Obrero de Habla Española, a leftist community group in Spanish Harlem, and in 1930 the Communist Party, USA.

She also organized her *compañeras* into La Liga de Costureras, a small-scale garment workers' union. Reflecting on her days as a "junior organizer," she proudly related how at a time when only a few men's unions had "ladies auxiliaries," she had created a fraternal fund-raising group composed of male relatives and friends of Liga members. But making the union a family affair did not apply to her own. An absentee mother by circumstance and choice, Rosa Rodríguez de León also found in her radicalism an escape from a disintegrating marriage. In the midst of leftist political meetings, she struck up a friendship with Gray Bemis, a handsome young labor activist who had ventured far from his Nebraska farm boy roots. Drawn to him romantically, she refused to act on her emotions. "I liked him, but he was married and I was married. Although I was in a miserable marriage, I did not fool around with married men."[10]

In late 1935 Rosa Rodríguez de León made a momentous decision, actually several—she left her husband, New York City, and the Communist Party. She accepted a job with the American Federation of Labor (AFL) to organize African American and Latino cigar workers in Florida. Arriving by bus with her daughter, Mytyl, she chose yet another transformation—she became "Luisa Moreno."

Deliberately distancing herself from her past, she chose the alias "Moreno" (Dark), a name diametrically opposite her given name, "Blanca Rosa" (White Rose). I contend that Luisa Moreno conjugated her identity. "Conjugating identity" refers to an invention or inflection of one's sense of self, taking into account such constructions as race, class, culture, language, and gender. It represents a self-reflexive, purposeful fluidity of individual subjectivities for political action. Simply put, Moreno made strategic choices regarding her class and ethnic identification in order to facilitate her life's work as a labor and civil rights advocate. With her light skin, education, and unaccented English, she could have "passed"; instead, she chose to forego any potential privileges predicated on race, class, or color. Importantly, she made these changes in the Jim Crow South, where segregation and white domination was a way of life. Moreover, the first name "Luisa" could be interpreted as a political statement, perhaps homage to Puerto Rican labor organizer and feminist writer Luisa Capetillo, who had preceded her in

Florida twenty years earlier and whose legacy Moreno undoubtedly knew and built upon in organizing cigar workers.[11] Luisa Moreno was the professional persona. Her close friends called her Rosa, and as a graduate student conducting research, I quickly realized that identifying myself as a friend of Rosa's (not Luisa's) created an almost instant rapport with her *compañeros* in the labor movement. "Rosa" signified a level of intimacy and trust.

In Florida Moreno quickly grasped the challenges ahead. During her days as a labor organizer, Moreno penned two surviving poems in English.[12] With subtle tones, her poem "On the Road" revealed an awareness of African American life in the U.S. South:

> Unpainted gray boards
> formed the church
> by the poor Negro shacks.
> Voices sang in the evenings
> Hammock songs to the air.
> Hopeful words—hunger sounds:
> sorrow, love, and despair.
> And near by bled the trees
> in the forest of pines.
> Negro peons raised their arms,
> powerful arms to the skies,
> while the preacher's soft voice
> told the tale of a white man
> full of patience and love.
> And they dreamt of a new world
> in the turpentine country,
> as near by bled the trees
> in the forest of pines.[13]

With sympathy and irony, the images echo each other. African American turpentine workers bleed the trees while the white bosses bleed them.

On an immediate level, Moreno was cognizant of the role of the local Ku Klux Klan in suppressing labor militancy, including its involvement in the murder of Florida political activist and friend of labor Joseph Shoemaker in November 1935, just weeks before Moreno's arrival in early 1936. According to Moreno, her superiors believed that the Klan would think twice before harming a woman organizer. I would further note that her fair complexion, as well as her gender, afforded her added protection. Slender and under five feet tall, Moreno possessed a delicate beauty, but her physical appearance belied her brilliance and steely determination.

Given her fears about the Klan as well as the challenges and erratic schedules inherent in trade union work, Moreno decided to board her daughter with a pro-labor Latino family. From age seven until almost thirteen, Mytyl would live apart from her mother as she was shuttled from one informal foster family to the next from Florida to Pennsylvania to Texas. In some households, she received kind treatment, maybe even love, but in others she was molested—in Florida by the head of her very first foster family and later in Texas by an elderly neighbor. Decades later, Mytyl related these incidents with a rawness that had not abated with time. Moreno visited infrequently and to my knowledge remained ignorant of the abuse her daughter suffered. Mytyl Moreno carried a sense of profound loneliness throughout her life, always seeking a deeper spiritual connection with others initially through religion and later through political activism. Contemplating a childhood where she lived apart from her mother and lost all contact with her father, Mytyl recalled "having the feeling of being alone."[14]

Although she lived in Florida for less than two years, this is where Luisa Moreno honed her skills as a labor leader. Organizing "all races, creeds, and colors," she negotiated a solid contract covering thirteen thousand cigar workers from Ybor City to Lakeland to Jacksonville in 1936. When AFL officials revised the agreement to be friendlier to management, an infuriated Moreno urged the workers to reject it. As punishment for her insubordination, the AFL transferred her to Pennsylvania. In 1937 she resigned from the AFL to join its newly established rival, the Congress of Industrial Organizations (CIO), and a year later she joined the United Cannery, Agricultural, Packing, and Allied Workers of America (UCAPAWA-CIO). The union's commitment to rank-and-file leadership and to inclusion, recruiting members across race, nationality, and gender, resonated with Moreno. Indeed, as part of the UCAPAWA pledge, members swore "never to discriminate against a fellow worker because of creed, color, nationality, religious or political belief."[15]

Moreno's first assignment as a UCAPAWA representative in 1938 was to take charge of the pecan shellers' strike in San Antonio, Texas. The shellers earned miserable wages—less than two dollars a week in 1934—and in 1938 they had reached their limit, for as many as ten thousand workers went on strike. Their union, El Nogal, was an UCAPAWA affiliate, and their leader was the fiery secretary of the Texas Communist Party, a young native of San Antonio by the name of Emma Tenayuca. UCAPAWA's national president, Donald Henderson, sent Moreno to help solidify the local, to move it from street demonstrations to a functioning trade union. As an outsider from the East Coast and a Latina (not a Tejana or a *mexicana*), Moreno at first had to gain the strikers' trust; but rather quickly she organized them into a united, disciplined force that employers could no longer ignore. Five weeks after the strike began, management agreed to arbitration with a settlement that included recognition of the UCAPAWA local and piece-rate scales that conformed to the new federal minimum wage of twenty-five cents an hour. Tenayuca had stepped aside to give Moreno a wide berth, but she had done so very reluctantly and, as a result, the working relationship between these two legendary figures in Latino history was strained at best.[16]

After the settlement, Moreno next traveled to the Rio Grande Valley of Texas. While organizing Mexican migrants in dire straits, she too had few resources. She lived with farm workers, slept under trees, and shared her groceries with those around her. Moreno encountered what she termed a "lynch spirit" among rural white residents. Lynching affected both African Americans and Mexicans in Texas. According to historians William Carrigan and Clive Webb, 597 Mexicans died at the hands of vigilante mobs from 1850 to 1930, almost half of these murders (297) occurred in Texas. While 597 represented a mere fraction of the 3,386 recorded lynchings of African Americans for the same time period, this specter of mob violence was embedded in the lexicon of Tejano collective memory. Perhaps drawing on border folklore, *corridos* (ballads), and stories told in the migrant campus and influenced by the haunting lyrics of Billie Holiday's "Strange Fruit," Moreno made a stark reference to lynching with the line "a brown and gruesome form" in her unpublished poem "1939."[17]

His soul—a winter scene,
where thoughts
were leafless boughs
reflecting on the stream
a brown and gruesome form.

The earth was cold and quiet
the sky a plate of steel.
I waited for a word
a single word,
but nothing came.

The fallen leaves
went rolling by . . .
No more was there to say.
I gambled every claim
on a foolish dream.[18]

Composed during or immediately after her sojourn in South Texas, this poem raises several questions. Was this poem primarily about a deep disappointment or self-doubt? Was Moreno lamenting a lost romance, possibly with Gray Bemis? Or was the imagery of unrequited love simply a guarded metaphor for a feeling of abandonment by the national union or by the principles of the Communist Party?

When UCPAWA pulled her out of South Texas after only a few months in 1938, she took a leave of absence in order to organize a Latino civil rights conference. Traveling without Mytyl, she ended up in Los Angeles working with a small group of like-minded community and labor activists—Josefina Fierro, Eduardo

Quevedo, and Bert Corona. These four would form the leadership for the national convention.

On April 28 through 30, 1939, the first national civil rights conference for U.S. Latinos was convened—El Congreso de Pueblos de Hablan Española. Although the majority of the one thousand to fifteen hundred delegates hailed from California and the Southwest, women and men traveled from as far away as Montana, Illinois, New York, and Florida to attend the convention. Over three days, they drafted a comprehensive platform. Bridging differences in generational and ethnic background, they called for an end to segregation in public facilities, housing, education, and employment and endorsed the rights of immigrants to live and work in the United States without fear of deportation. While encouraging immigrants to become citizens, delegates did not advocate assimilation but rather emphasized the importance of preserving Latino cultures, calling upon universities to create departments in Latino studies. Despite the promise of the first convention, a national network of local affiliates never materialized. While Moreno had taken the lead in organizing the 1939 national meeting, Josefina Fierro was vital in buoying the day-to-day operations of the fragile southern California chapters. Fierro, a vibrant Los Angeles activist, descended from a long line of rebellious women as her mother and grandmother were staunch supporters of Juan Flores Magón during the Mexican Revolution. Fierro was married at the time to Hollywood screenwriter John Bright (later a member of the black-listed "Hollywood Ten"), and she used her celebrity contacts to raise funds for El Congreso and various *barrio* causes. Lifelong friends, Moreno and Fierro emphasized the dignity of the common person and the importance of grassroots networks, reciprocity, and self-help. As Fierro commented in an interview with historian Mario García, "Movie stars such as Anthony Quinn, Dolores Del Rio, and John Wayne contributed money, 'not because they were reds, . . . but because they were helping Mexicans help themselves.'"[19]

The stands taken by Moreno, Fierro, and El Congreso delegates must be placed in the milieu of the deportations or repatriations of the early 1930s. Between 1931 and 1934, an estimated one-third of the Mexican population in the United States (over five hundred thousand people) were either deported or repatriated to Mexico even though the majority (an estimated 60 percent) were native U.S. citizens. Viewed as foreign usurpers of American jobs and as unworthy burdens on relief rolls, Mexicans were the only immigrants targeted for removal. From Los Angeles, California, to Gary, Indiana, Mexicans were either summarily deported by immigration agencies or persuaded to depart voluntarily by duplicitous social workers who greatly exaggerated the opportunities awaiting them south of the border.[20] Thus, advocating for the rights of immigrants was a courageous course given the recent history of intimidation and removal. In Washington, D.C., Luisa Moreno spoke before the 1940 Conference of the

American Committee for the Protection of the Foreign Born, a national left-of-center political group that grew out of the American Civil Liberties Union in 1933. Her only surviving speech, "Caravans of Sorrow," bears witness to her power as an orator. An excerpt follows:

> Long before the "grapes of wrath" had ripened in California's vineyards a people lived on highways, under trees or tents, in shacks or railroad sections, picking crops—cottons, fruits, vegetables—cultivating sugar beets, building railroad and dams, making a barren land fertile for new crops and greater riches. . . .
>
> One can hardly imagine how many bales of cotton have passed through the nimble fingers of Mexican men, women, and children. And what conditions have they had to endure to pick that cotton? . . . Once a cotton picker told me . . . [that] she remembered so many nights, under the trees in the rain, when she and her husband held gunny sacks over the shivering bodies of their sleeping children—young Americans.
>
> These people are not aliens. They have contributed their endurance, sacrifices, youth, and labor to the Southwest. Indirectly, they have paid more taxes than all the stockholders of California's industrialized agriculture, the sugar beet companies and the large cotton interests that operate or have operated with the labor of Mexican workers.[21]

That same year (1940) Moreno accepted a desk job with UCAPAWA in Washington, D.C., serving as the editor of its Spanish-language newspaper. I contend that she took this post in an attempt to establish a relationship with her daughter, now almost a teenager. Moreno and Mytyl celebrated their first Christmas together in years—an East Coast holiday that Mytyl always recalled with great fondness.[22] A year later the duo would live in Los Angeles, where Moreno, newly elected vice president of UCAPAWA, took charge of consolidating the cannery locals there. She threw herself into this task, earning the nickname "the California Whirlwind." Capitalizing on the gendered networks on the shop floor, Moreno would harvest unparalleled success, as food-processing operatives under the UCAPAWA banner significantly improved their working conditions, wages, and benefits.

The California canning labor force included young daughters, newlyweds, middle-aged wives, and widows; 75 percent of cannery workers were women, 25 percent were men. Occasionally, three generations—daughter, mother, and grandmother—worked together at a particular cannery. Entering the job market as members of a family wage economy, they pooled their resources to put food on the table. "My father was a busboy," Carmen Bernal Escobar recalled, "and to keep the family going . . . in order to bring in a little more money . . . my mother, my grandmother, my mother's brother, my sister, and I all worked together at

Cal San." One of the largest canneries in Los Angeles, the California Sanitary Canning Company (Cal San), employed primarily Mexican and Russian Jewish women. Working side by side, they were clustered in specific departments—washing, grading, cutting, canning, and packing—and paid according to the production level. Standing in the same spots week after week, month after month, women workers often developed friendships crossing family and ethnic lines. Their day-to-day problems (slippery floors, irritating peach fuzz, production speed-ups, arbitrary supervisors, and sexual harassment) cemented feelings of solidarity. Cannery workers even employed a special jargon when conversing among themselves, often referring to an event in terms of when specific fruits or vegetables arrived for processing at the plant. For instance, the phrase "We met in spinach, fell in love in peaches, and married in tomatoes" indicates that a couple met in March, fell in love in August, and married in October.[23]

In 1939 Cal San employees staged a dramatic strike led by UCAPAWA organizer Dorothy Ray Healey. Wages and conditions improved at the plant as workers nurtured their union local, and they jealously guarded their closed shop contract. When Luisa Moreno arrived, she enlisted the aid of union members at Cal San in union drives at several Los Angeles–area food-processing firms. Workers organized other workers across canneries, ethnicities, generations, and gender. The result would be Local 3, the second-largest UCAPAWA affiliate in the nation. Moreno encouraged cross-plant alliances and women's leadership. In 1943 the southern California cannery women held twelve of the fifteen elected positions, with eight won by Mexican women. In addition to higher wages and improved conditions, they negotiated innovative benefits such as a hospitalization plan, free legal advice, and, at one plant, management-financed day care. In 1944, UCAPAWA became the Food, Tobacco, Agricultural, and Allied Workers of America (FTA). During an era when few unions addressed the concerns of women, UCAPAWA/FTA blazed a new path. By 1946, 66 percent of its contracts nationwide contained equal pay for equal work clauses. A fierce loyalty to the union developed as the result of rank-and-file participation and leadership. Four decades after the strike, Carmen Bernal Escobar declared, "UCAPAWA was the greatest thing that ever happened to the workers at Cal San. It changed everything and everybody." As an example of women's leadership, Moreno herself rose in the ranks of the California CIO, becoming the first Latina to serve on a state CIO council.[24]

Moreno's home life did not match her professional success. In 1941 she wed a local Los Angeles dry cleaner, but the marriage lasted only a few months. Mytyl was in no mood for a stepfather, and the friction within the household became intolerable. "I wanted my mother all to myself," her daughter explained: "She was nobody else's. She was mine." Mytyl grew into a rebellious teenager, ditching classes and cajoling sailors into buying her booze. Moreno worked behind the scenes raising money for the legal defense of the young Mexican American men unjustly convicted in the Sleepy Lagoon murder case, men the press had characterized as dangerous, zoot suit–wearing *pachucos*. However, she would not tolerate her own daughter dressing in *pachuca*-style clothing, personally taking a pair of scissors to one outfit. In 1945, Mytyl, just shy of her seventeenth birthday, eloped with returning veteran Edward Glomboske, the older brother of a girlfriend. During one of our interviews, Moreno remarked, "I had a choice. I could organize cannery workers or I could control my teenage daughter. I chose to organize cannery workers and my daughter never forgave me."[25]

The year 1945 would also mark Moreno's greatest professional challenge. She would organize cannery workers in northern California in a head-to-head battle with the International Brotherhood of Teamsters. In May 1945 the AFL national president turned over its northern California cannery unions to the Teamsters; as a result, disgruntled local leaders approached FTA. Directing an ambitious drive that extended from San José to Sacramento to Modesto, Moreno handpicked her organizing team, and within three months the team had collected fourteen thousand union pledge cards and helped to establish twenty-five functioning locals. Under Moreno's leadership, FTA decisively won the National Labor Relations Board (NLRB) election that covered seventy-two plants. In February 1946 the NLRB, under intense political pressure, rescinded the results of the 1945 election and called for a second tabulation. The Teamsters began a campaign of sweetheart contracts, red baiting, and physical assaults. Amazingly, Moreno and the FTA narrowly lost the second election. This Teamster victory marked the beginning of the end for FTA. In 1950, the union, battered by red baiting, was expelled from the CIO for alleged Communist domination.[26]

Luisa Moreno retired from public life in 1947 and married Gray Bemis. A naval officer recently divorced, Bemis rekindled his relationship with Moreno at a CIO dance held in San Francisco. Their devotion to one another was apparent to all who knew the couple. As her attorney and friend Robert Kenny wrote in a letter to Luisa after Gray's death in 1960, "Certainly the story of your marriage and devotion is a love story that most novelists would want to claim as their own creation."[27]

Their happiness in the United States would be short-lived. In 1948 she faced deportation proceedings. According to Moreno, she was offered citizenship in exchange for testifying against legendary Longshoremen union leader Harry Bridges, but she refused to become a "free woman with a mortgaged soul." Although high-profile journalists Carey McWilliams and Ignacio López chaired her defense committee and put forth a valiant effort, the result was almost a foregone conclusion. With Gray Bemis at her side, she left the United States in 1950, under terms listed as "voluntary departure under warrant of deportation," on the grounds that she had once belonged to the Communist Party.

In preparing for the Immigration and Naturalization Service hearings, Luisa Moreno clearly articulated her own legacy. "They can talk about deporting me . . . but they can never deport the people that I've worked with and with whom things were accomplished for the benefit of hundreds of thousands of workers—things that can never be destroyed." As retired California labor activist Doris Walker related in a memorial message in 1992, "Luisa Moreno has been an example for me ever since 1946, when she was a leader and I was a young green organizer. . . . Her indomitable courage and perseverance will continue in all of us who had the privilege of knowing and working with her."[28]

Luisa Moreno "died" when she crossed El Paso's Stanton Street Bridge into Ciudad Juárez on November 30, 1950. Rosa Rodríguez de Bemis would live on, participating in many activities associated with the progressive government of Guatemalan president Jacobo Arbenz. In particular, she organized a literacy campaign in the hinterlands, teaching basic reading, writing, and math skills to indigenous women. During the CIA-sponsored coup that the toppled the Arbenz government, Rosa Rodríguez de Bemis went into hiding; and although her brother had secured asylum for her in El Salvador, she and her husband fled to Mexico in their Studebaker. As a forty-seven-year-old woman in 1954, Rosa Rodríguez de Bemis would shift her identity once more as she began another round of travel and migration. From 1954 to 1960 she and Gray Bemis raised chickens in a radical American expatriate community near Mexico City. With Gray's death in 1960, she moved to Cuba, where she translated economic materials from English into Spanish. She missed her daughter and grandchildren and so returned to Mexico in 1963. The Immigration and Naturalization Service issued a "Look Out Notice for Luisa Moreno," stating, "since deportation, she has continued her communist activity in Latin America including service in Cuba as one of Castro's bodyguards." When I shared this document with her in 1984, she burst into laughter: "Imagine me, a big, bad bodyguard."[29]

In the mid 1960s she managed an art gallery in Tijuana. Dolores Huerta and César Chávez visited her on occasion as they sought her advice during their early days of organizing farm workers. Later on she settled in Guadalajara. In failing health and failing finances, she was denied entrance to the United States for medical treatment in 1984. Refusing to cross the border under any subterfuge, she had no choice but to move in with her brother and his family in Guatemala. Perceived as the prodigal sister, the woman with a radical past, she did not physically live with the family, but resided instead in the children's playhouse on the grounds of the estate.[30]

My last contact with Rosa revolved around her poetry. Through her close friend Elizabeth Eudey, I had received from her a gift—her sole copy of *El Vendedor de Cucuyos*. A few months later Eudey forwarded to me a copy of the poems in English, translated by Abbott Small, a Spanish teacher and published poet who had spent his boyhood in Mexico as part of the American expatriate community. His parents, Berthe and Charles Small, had known Rosa Rodríguez since her organizing days in Florida. María Lucia Gómez, a poet from Columbia, also took a turn at translating the verses. In 1991 Mytyl Glomboske carried both sets of translations along with a copy of the original poems to her mother in Guatemala. Although debilitated by a stroke, she asked her daughter to read each version aloud; and then after examining each text, she wrote simply "Rosa" by the translation she preferred.[31]

In retrospect, she had chosen politics over poetry, considering the latter a luxury she could no longer afford as a labor leader. Yet, it is precisely through her poetry that one can catch a glimpse of her passion, intellect, and spirit, hints of the woman (or women) she would become. Her gift of *El Vendedor de Cocuyos* signified not only a special trust between us but also a readiness to share Rosa Rodríguez, the poet and intellectual, alongside the very public Luisa Moreno. According to her daughter, she was thoroughly engaged in selecting the translations, though it required a great deal of stamina from an eighty-four-year-old woman in failing health. Possibly, she felt a sense of closure, of her life coming full circle. This dance of remembrance was captured by the poet herself in "La ausencia" (The Absence), written during her days as a feminist flapper:

When we are far apart
and I think of you,
the light of the memory of you
will open out in the night of absence,
like a fan of sunlight . . .
Distance,
watching over you in its black cape,
will not have the power
to separate us. . . .

And like the stars
spilling out on the dark thread of my life,
luminous waterfalls,
your eyes,
your mouth,
your whole body!
will open the dawn of enchantment
along all of my road. . . .

When we are far apart,
and from invisible censers there left
the golden spirals
Of memory. . . .[32]

Rosa Rodríguez de Bemis died on November 4, 1992. Several weeks later, I received a phone call from Mytyl Glomboske. She had in her possession a package from Guatemala. We talked as she unwrapped its contents. It was a blue suitcase, containing the remaining effects of her mother's life. She asked me to open the case with her the next morning and I readily agreed. We stared at the old suitcase for a moment before Mytyl pressed the metal latches. Inside there was an array of neatly packed items—two photo albums, assorted sheets of unpublished poetry and drafts of poems, correspondence and news clippings related to her poetry, Gray Bemis's death certificate and assorted business papers, and a hand-crocheted blue *rebozo* (shawl). The most surprising of all was a bundle of note cards. She had saved every letter and greeting card I had ever mailed to her (no matter how silly or inconsequential). And there at the bottom of the suitcase lay my dissertation. As an oral historian who tends to fret over issues of reciprocity, I to this day remain moved beyond words. Not only had Rosa Rodríguez (aka. Luisa Moreno) profoundly influenced my own life professionally and personally, but I had also mattered to her.

NOTES

I would like to express my deep appreciation to my sister scholars of the Meanings and Representations of Women and Work in the Lives of Women of Color Research Group, especially Nancy Hewitt and Lynn Bolles. I also thank Virginia Sánchez Korrol and Sharon Block for their careful comments. Most importantly, Valerie Matsumoto, my dear friend and critic, pushed and prodded, encouraging me to think about the poems in ways I had not imagined. I look forward to working with Albert Camarillo on our joint venture in crafting a full-fledged biography on Moreno. And thanks to my biggest fan, Victor Becerra, who never tires of my "Rosa" stories.

1. I use the term "Latina/Latino" as a U.S.-specific umbrella term, as a descriptor for all people of Latin American birth or heritage in the United States.

2. *New York Times*, April 28, 2001. My approach to biography has been profoundly influenced by the works of Mary Felstiner and Greg Sarris. See Mary Lowenthal Felstiner, *To Paint Her Life: Charlotte Salomon in the Nazi Era* (New York: Harper Collins, 1994); and Greg Sarris, *Mabel MacKay: Weaving the Dream* (Berkeley: University of California Press, 1994).

3. As an example, see Vicki L. Ruiz, *From out of the Shadows: Mexican Women in Twentieth-Century America* (New York: Oxford University Press, 1998).

4. "Data on Luisa Moreno Bemis," file 53, Robert W. Kenny Collection, Southern California Library for Social Studies Research, Los Angeles (hereafter referred to as the Kenny Collection); interviews with Luisa Moreno, August 4, 1984, and July 27, 1978, conducted by the author; "Handwritten Notes by Robert Kenny," file 53, Kenny Collection. Interview with Berthe Small, Alba Zatz, and Asa Zatz, September 28, 1996, conducted by the author; e-mail correspondence from Patricia Harms to the author, April 5, 2004. After the first references (which include the interviewer's name), all interviews will be cited by the last name of the interviewee and the year. Note: In a move that no doubt further disconcerted their elders, Sociedad members began to advocate for the rights of indigenous people. According to Latin American women's historian Patricia Harms, several Sociedad members would continue their feminist activities in Guatemala well into the 1940s.

5. Moreno interview, 1984; Rosa Rodríguez López, *El Vendedor de Cucuyos* (Mexico: Imprenta Mundial, 1927); letter from Guatemalan admirer (signature illegible) to Rosa Rodríguez, October 23, 1927; Marco Augusto Recinos, "El Vendedor de Cucuyos," *ALMAMÉRICA* (n.d.); "Cumpleaños," unidentified news clipping, ca. August 30, 1929. All referenced materials are in author's possession.

6. "Literatura," in Rodríguez López, *El Vendedor de Cucuyos*, 71–72. The original is as follows:

"Literatura, literatura . . ./Yo he succumbido a tu locura/y en tu altar/he buscado la expresión/de un amor,/un sueño/y una religión.

"Y todavía en mi cabeza/hay hambre de locura/y en todo mi camino/sombrean los fantasmas/¡de no poder decir!/¡de no poder decir!

"Literatura, literatura . . ./Amarga y dulce./Sombra y luz . . ./¡Oh gran misterio en flor!/ En tu locura/he buscado la expresión/de un amor,/un sueño/y una religión . . ."

All English translations courtesy of Abbott Small, poet and friend of Rosa Rodríguez.

7. Moreno interview, 1984; *Jacksonville Journal*, September 23, 1943; French Foreign Legion Handbook of Miguel Angel de León (in author's possession); interview with Luisa Moreno, August 5, 1976, conducted by Albert Camarillo; "Data on Luisa Moreno Bemis;" "El milagro," in Rodríguez López, *El Vendedor de Cucuyos*, 25. The original verse follows: "Y he vivido,/he soñado/en el fuego de tus brazos."

8. "Tu amor," in Rodríguez López, *El Vendedor de Cucuyos*, 33. The original verse follows: "Yo sé/que eres lágrima en mi vida./Que tus manos/deshojarán mis pétalos/y romperán mi tallo . . ."

9. "Data on Luisa Moreno Bemis"; interview with Luisa Moreno, August 12–13, 1977, conducted by Albert Camarillo; Moreno interview, 1976.

10. Moreno interviews, 1976, 1977, and 1984.

11. Ibid. This concept of conjugating identities derives from interviews with Luisa Moreno and her daughter, Mytyl Glomboske, as well as my reading of the scholarship of Rebecca Lester, Michael Kearney, Chela Sandoval, Stuart Hall, Paula Moya, and Ramón Gutiérrez. I also owe an enormous intellectual debt to all of my *compañeros* in the University of California Humanities Research Institute "Reshaping the Americas" Residency Group (spring 2002). Moreover, I thank Nancy Hewitt for bringing to my attention the importance of Luisa Capetillo's organizing in Florida to Moreno's efforts twenty years earlier. Note: I surmise that she left the Communist Party out of expediency, given her new position with the American Federation of Labor. Her commitment to Marxism never wavered.

12. If Moreno composed verses in Spanish as a labor leader, they did not weather her many travels,as all but one of the Spanish-language poems she saved during her lifetime appear to date from her youth in Mexico. Moreover, among her effects at her death were fragments of two scrawled poems she composed as an elderly woman.

13. Luisa Moreno, "On the Road" (unpublished poem, 1935, in author's possession).

14. Interview with Mytyl Glomboske, August 27, 2001, conducted by the author; "Handwritten Notes"; Small, Zatz, and Zatz interview, 1996; Moreno interviews, 1977, 1978. For more information on the radicalism of the Tampa workers, see Nancy A. Hewitt, *Southern Discomfort: Women's Activism in Tampa, Florida, 1880s–1920s.* (Urbana: University of Illinois Press, 2001); and for more information on the role of the Ku Klux Klan, see Robert Ingalls, *Urban Vigilantes in the New South: Tampa, 1882–1936* (Knoxville: University of Tennessee Press, 1988).

15. Moreno interviews, 1977 and 1978; Vicki L. Ruiz, *Cannery Women, Cannery Lives: Mexican Women, Unionization, and the California Food Processing Industry, 1930–1950* (Albuquerque: University of New Mexico Press, 1987), 44.

16. Moreno interviews, 1976, 1977, 1978. For more information on the pecan shellers' strike, see Zaragosa Vargas, "Tejana Radical: Emma Tenayuca and the San Antonio Labor Movement during the Great Depression," *Pacific Historical Review* 66 (1997): 553–580; and Ruiz, *From out of the Shadows*, 79–80.

17. William D. Carrigan and Clive Webb, "Muerto por Unos Desconocidos (Killed by Persons Unknown): Mob Violence against African Americans and Mexican Americans," in *Beyond Black and White: Race, Ethnicity, and Gender in the U.S. South and Southwest*, ed. Stephanie M. Cole and Alison M. Parker (College Station: Texas A&M Press, 2003), 65–66. For information on lynching in Tejano collective memory, see Américo Paredes, *With Pistol in His Hand: A Border Ballad and Its Hero* (Austin: University of Texas Press, 1958); Julian Samora et al., *Gunpowder Justice* (Notre Dame: University of Notre Dame Press, 1979); María Eva Flores CDP, "The Good Life, the Hard Way: The Mexican American Community of Fort Stockton, Texas" (Ph.D. diss., Arizona State University, 2000). On the resonance and meanings of the song "Strange Fruit," in American memory and popular culture, see Angela Y. Davis, *Blues Legacies and Black Feminism: Gertrude "Ma" Rainey, Bessie Smith, and Billie Holiday* (New York: Pantheon, 1998).

18. Moreno interviews, 1977, 1978; Luisa Moreno, "1939" (unpublished poem in author's possession).

19. Moreno interviews, 1977, 1978; interview with Josefina Fierro de Bright, August 7, 1977, conducted by Albert Camarillo; Carlos C. Larralde and Richard Griswold del Castillo, "Luisa Moreno: A Hispanic Civil Rights Leader in San Diego," *Journal of San Diego History* 14 (1995): 284–310. For more information on El Congreso, see David G. Gutiérrez, *Walls and Mirrors: Mexican Americans, Mexican Immigrants, and the Politics of Ethnicity in the Southwest, 1910–1986* (Berkeley: University of California Press, 1995); George J. Sánchez, *Becoming Mexican America: Ethnicity, Culture, and Identity in Los Angeles, 1900–1945* (New York: Oxford University Press, 1993); Albert Camarillo, *Chicanos in California* (San Francisco: Boyd & Fraser, 1984); Mario García, *Mexican Americans: Leadership, Ideology, and Identity, 1930–1960* (New Haven: Yale University Press, 1981). Quote is from García, *Mexican Americans*, 158.

20. Camarillo, *Chicanos in California*, 48–49; Abraham Hoffman, *Unwanted Mexican Americans in the Great Depression* (Tucson: University of Arizona Press, 1974), 43–46; Francisco Balderrama, *In Defense of La Raza: The Los Angeles Mexican Consulate and the Mexican Community, 1929–1936* (Tucson: University of Arizona Press, 1982), 16–20. The most comprehensive survey of the Mexican deportations and repatriations during this period is Francisco Balderrama and Raymond Rodríguez, *Decade of Betrayal: Mexican Repatriation in the 1930s* (Albuquerque: University of New Mexico Press, 1995).

21. Luisa Moreno, "Caravans of Sorrow: Noncitizen Americans of the Southwest," in *Between Two Worlds: Mexican Immigration in the United States*, ed. David Gutiérrez (Wilmington, Del.: Scholarly Resources, 1996), 120, 122.

22. Moreno interview, 1976, 1977, 1979; Glomboske interview, 2001.

23. See Ruiz, *Cannery Women*, 21–39.

24. This discussion is taken from Ruiz, *From out of the Shadows*, 80–82; and Ruiz, *Cannery Women*, 69–85.

25. Carey McWilliams, "Luisa Moreno Bemis" (August 1949), file 53, Kenny Collection; "Data on Luisa Moreno Bemis"; "Handwritten Notes"; Glomboske interview, 2001; Moreno interview, 1984.

26. Ruiz, *Cannery Women*, 103–107.

27. Moreno interview, 1984; Small, Zatz, and Zatz interview, 1996; Glomboske interview, 2001; Robert W. Kenny to Luisa Bemis, February 11, 1950, file 56, Kenny Collection.

28. Ruiz, *Cannery Women*, 113–118; "The Case of Luisa Moreno Bemis," Labor Committee for Luisa Moreno Bemis pamphlet (in author's possession); U.S. Department of Justice, Immigration and Naturalization Service, "Closing INS Report (Los Angeles District) on Luisa Moreno," December 6, 1950; Steve Murdoch, *Our Times*, September 9, 1949, file 53, Kenny Papers; letter from Doris Walker to Luisa Moreno Memorial Committee, November 29, 1992.

29. Moreno interviews, 1976, 1977, 1979, 1984; Small, Zatz, and Zatz interview, 1996; U.S. Department of Justice, Immigration and Naturalization Service, "Look Out Notice for Luisa Moreno," July 15, 1965 (cancellation date August 1977).

30. Moreno interview, 1984; Glomboske interview, 2001.

31. Unfortunately, this bilingual volume remains unpublished.

32. "La ausencia" in Rodríguez López, *El Vendedor de Cucuyos*, 51–52. The original is as follows:

"Cuando estemos lejos/y piense en ti,/se abrirá en la noche de la ausencia,/como abanico de sol,/la luz de tu recuerdo . . .

"La distancia,/velándote en su capa negra,/no tendrá la fuerza/de apartarnos . . .

"Yo como estrellas,/vertiendo en el hilo oscuro de mi vida,/cascadas luminosas,/tus ojos,/tus manos/y tu boca,/¡tu cuerpo entero!/abrirá la aurora del ensueño/en todo mi camino . . .

"Cuando estemos lejos,/y se alcen de invisibles pebeteros/los dorados espirales/del recuerdo . . ."

Caring and Inequality

EVELYN NAKANO GLENN

The following words from two caregivers serve as a prologue to this chapter.

"I live a treadmill life and I see my own children only when they happen to see me on the streets when I am out with the [employer's] children. . . . You might as well say that I'm on duty all the time—from sunrise to sunrise, every day in the week. I am the slave, body and soul, of this family. And what do I get for this work? . . . The pitiful sum of ten dollars a month! And what am I expected to do with the ten dollars? With this money I'm expected to pay my house rent, which is four dollars per month, for a little house of two rooms just big enough to turn round in; and I'm expected, also to feed and clothe myself and three children."[1]

"You're working the minute you open your eyes until the minute you close your eyes. You keep your strength and your body going so that you will finish your work. . . . You keep waiting on your employers until they go to sleep because, although you finish your work, for example you finish ironing everything, putting the children or the elder person to bed, even if you put them to bed at ten o-clock, there are still other members of the family. So you keep on observing, 'Oh, can I sleep or maybe they will call me to give them food or to given them a yoghurt.' And even if you are sleeping you sometimes feel you are still on duty."[2]

As we settle somewhat uncomfortably into the twenty-first century, a spate of recent books and articles has announced that the United States and other developed nations face a so-called crisis in care. According to these accounts, the number of people needing care—children, but also many elderly, ill, and disabled persons—has grown, while simultaneously the ranks of those who have traditionally *provided* care, stay-at-home wives and mothers, has shrunk. As Mona Harrington describes the situation in a recent popular treatment of the situation in the United States, "We have patchwork systems, but we have come nowhere near replacing the hours or quality of care that the at home women of previous generations provided for the country."[3]

One reason that the crisis has become a public issue is that it is severely affecting relatively affluent middle-class families—a politically influential class that once had the luxury of having stay-at-home wives and mothers. In addition to the growing need for two incomes in middle-class households, new ideals about women's right to seek fulfillment in jobs and careers have made two-earner households the norm even among professional and corporate elites. The increase in women's employment has occurred without any reduction in the average workweek, a reduction that might make it more possible for workers to meet caring responsibilities. American workers put in more hours than workers in all other industrialized nations. Thus today's affluent families are experiencing a "time bind" in their efforts to meet the dual demands of careers and caring. To make matters worse, Barbara Ehrenreich and Arlie Hochschild note, "The down-sized American—and to a lesser degree, western European—welfare state has become a 'deadbeat dad.'" Unlike the rest of the industrialized world, the United States does not offer public child care for working mothers, nor does it ensure paid family and medical leave."[4]

In fact, however, this supposedly new crisis in care is nothing *new* for working-class families or families of color. Women in these families have always been stretched thin, contributing income through outside employment and production in the home while also bearing the brunt of unpaid caring work. The miserable mines and mills of Marx's day were notorious for failing to pay for the costs of reproducing the labor force. Some of the gap was filled by women's unpaid labor, but even with unremitting efforts, infant and child mortality was high and adult workers were used up and worn out long before old age. Essentially, workers were not able to sustain themselves on a daily basis or to create a new generation of workers. Instead, the industrial labor force had to be continually replenished by migrants from rural areas.

In a similar fashion, today's global capital is clearly *not* paying for the costs of maintaining the current labor force, nor for nurturing the next generation of workers, nor for caring for those who have worked for many years and can no longer produce. These burdens are borne largely by two groups: by women in the family—wives, mothers, and daughters—who provide unpaid nursing and other care for family members and by low-paid service workers, such as care technicians, nursing aides, nannies, and child-care workers, who provide care in settings such as private homes, nursing homes, and day-care centers.

A *New York Times* article in 1999 reported that an estimated 26 million Americans were providing nursing services, such as administering medication and checking vital signs for sick or dependent relatives, putting in an average of eighteen hours per week. A survey by the National Family Caregivers Association in 2000 found that more than a quarter of the sampled population was caring for a family member or friend or had done so during the previous year. As for *paid* care workers, a large proportion is made up of immigrant women. Immigrants are an especially cheap source of labor because neither capital nor citizens pay for *their* reproduction, maintenance, or education. In most cases, they arrive as able-bodied adults, and when they get too old to work or are incapacitated, they receive few social benefits.[5]

The historical continuities in links between caring and inequality are the focus for this chapter. My purpose is to highlight the embeddedness of caring labor in the larger political economy. This embeddedness has been obscured by cultural constructions of caring. Caring has been mythologized as love, rather than labor, as a private family matter, and as an activity natural to women. Characterizing caring work in these ways serves the interests of capital by defining this form of labor as separate from and outside the political and economic systems. By denying that caring serves to maintain the labor force and therefore the productive processes, these conceptions help corporations and their investors evade responsibility for paying the costs of sustaining workers and their families. It need hardly be pointed out that it also serves the interest of men as a class by defining caring work by women as part of a natural order and therefore immutable.

It is frequently asserted that caring is more than labor; it is also about love and relationships. However, the love versus labor opposition is itself an ideological construct, a product of capitalism. Recall that Marx's conception of human labor—that is, labor in its non-alienated form—was activity in which individuals transformed an object from nature into something completely new and useful. The process of transformation began with a vision of what was to be created and continued with the investment of thought, feeling, and purposive activity. Labor was ultimately a form of self-expression. Through labor, individuals also connected to the world of things and other people.[6] Marx's definition of unalienated labor corresponds closely to our notions of good caring labor, which can be defined most simply as the activities involved in creating and recreating people as physical, emotional, and social beings, on a daily basis and intergenerationally. It entails intellectual, physical, and emotional labor. And, just as labor under capitalist relations of production becomes alienated, so caring under certain conditions can become alienated labor.

Once we clear away some of the ideological smoke, we can see that for well over two hundred years caring work in the United States has been carried out under conditions of unfreedom and dependency. As a consequence, those who do caring work have been denied full citizenship—that is, they have not been recognized as fully independent and responsible members of the community, entitled to civil, political, and social rights. The other side of the coin is that those who *already* lacked full citizenship rights, namely, slaves, indentured workers, colonial subjects, immigrants, and women, have been relegated the tasks of caring. The structures maintaining coercion and the groups assigned to different types of caring labor have varied historically, but the overall conditions of coercion and denial of full citizenship have persisted. The connection between caring labor and inequality has remained deeply embedded in political-economic systems and the myths and ideologies that justify them.

Historical Roots: Unpaid Caring as Obligatory Labor

Several aspects of caring have historically been used to exclude caregiving and caregivers from the realm of free labor and citizenship: First is the public-private divide. Caring has been defined by capital as an activity that goes on in the private realm of the family rather than as a public activity or a form of "real labor." As part of the "private" arena, it is supposedly governed by emotion, particularity, subjectivity, and concrete relations. In contrast, the "public" arena of citizenship is thought to be governed by rational thought, universality, objectivity, and abstract principles. Traditionally, those relegated to the private realm and associated with its values—women, servants, and children—were excluded from civil and political citizenship.

By being conceptually bracketed within the private sphere, caring work has not been recognized as a public societal contribution comparable to employment in the labor market. As Judith Shklar has pointed out, *earning* has long been valorized as the source of the independence necessary to make reasoned choices in the market and in the political realm. It was on the basis of being "free workers" that white working men demanded universal white manhood suffrage in the nineteenth century. Earning has also been treated as an *obligation* of citizens. Earners were viewed as fulfilling their responsibilities as full members of the community and therefore as deserving of social rights. Social entitlements such as old age pensions, unemployment insurance, and health and safety protection are all tied to paid employment. In contrast, unpaid family caregivers were seen as carrying out strictly private responsibilities and not as fulfilling broader citizenship responsibilities. Hence, they were not accorded entitlements comparable to those given to wage earners. Instead, they were defined as dependents. If they were married to a wage earner, they might gain indirect—usually lesser— entitlements, for example, survivor benefits. Though nominally recognized as citizens, they did not have *substantive* standing as citizens.[7] Thus care workers were caught in a vicious circle: their work was not paid, so they were not independent; and since they were not independent, they could not be earners.

Another reason why caring labor has had a negative relationship with citizenship is that historically it lacked conditions of choice and freedom. The ability to act freely and make choices has been viewed as a qualification for citizenship since classical times. In the Aristotelian tradition, citizens, free from their individual, concrete, material interests, came together to make decisions on behalf of the general welfare. This formula depended on strict separation of *polis* from *oikos* (the private, material realm of people and things). In the Roman/Gaian tradition, the citizen was one who was free to act by law, to ask and expect the law's protection. In contrast to the Aristotelian ideal of leaving the world of things behind, the Roman formulation made the capacity to *act* on things the central attribute of human beings. Although Greek and Roman formulations differed, in both traditions independence was a necessary condition for exercising citizenship; independence was established by family headship, ownership of property, and control over wives, slaves, and other dependents. In essence, the citizen was one who was *free* of caring labor by virtue of having dependent wives and slaves to perform this labor.[8]

In British common law, which was carried over into the American colonies, married women did not have a separate legal identity. According to the doctrine of coverture, a woman's legal identity became merged with that of her husband upon marriage. (Paraphrasing Blackstone's famous formulation, husband and wife were one and that one was the husband.) A woman's labor was not her own to sell, since it belonged to her husband. Women could not enter into contract on their own account; any earnings belonged to their husbands. Under the doctrine of marital service, a wife was obligated to provide domestic services, including nursing and personal care. Caring work was thus defined as a woman's marital duty and therefore was not part of the free labor system. In essence, wives were put in a position of forced dependence, required to provide care in exchange for economic support—the level of which was determined by their husbands.

Revolutionary-era rhetoric justified overturning the old hierarchical order on the basis of equality and natural rights. Yet the same men who claimed the right to overthrow their overlords assumed the continuing exclusion of women from political participation. According to Linda Kerber, American revolutionaries resolved this contradiction by refashioning the doctrine of baron and *feme*, which defined men as masters over their wives' persons and property, to make it consistent with republicanism. Women's traditional labor for husbands and families was recast as the duties of "republican motherhood." As republican mothers, women were thought to play an entirely different political role than men. The new myth posited that women served the republic not by taking up arms, voting, or holding office, but "by their refusal to countenance lovers who were not devoted to the service of the state," and by raising "sons who were educated for civic virtue and for responsible citizenship."[9] The concept of republican motherhood helped to assert white women's moral worth and to valorize their contributions to the republic. Simultaneously, however, it helped to keep women consigned to the domestic sphere.

The early decades of the nineteenth century saw further polarization of the public-private dichotomy and the separation between men's and women's spheres. With rapid social change and mobility came a variety of social ills, which came to be associated with industrialism and urbanization. The public realm no longer could be associated with virtue. The private sphere came to be viewed as morally superior, and women, as mistresses of the hearth, as its guardians. The elevation of the domestic sphere did not promote women's independence; rather it underlined the importance of coverture—the fiction of merged interests—to maintain family harmony.[10]

In the nineteenth century, *white* women made substantial gains in the area of civil citizenship, including expanded parental, property, and divorce rights. Starting in 1839, states began passing married women's property laws, which allowed women to retain rights over property they brought into marriage. In the 1860s states started adding earnings statutes to give women the right to contract their own labor and ownership of earnings from work they performed on their own account. However, husbands continued to have the right to control and manage their wives' property, including collecting fees and rents. Also, until late in the nineteenth century, earnings and property obtained during marriage still belonged to the husband. In ruling after ruling involving women's property rights, courts cited the necessity of women's dependence to maintaining the patriarchal family, the cornerstone of American values.[11] In cases involving private contracts in which a husband agreed to transfer property or to leave a share of his estate to his wife in exchange for her providing extensive and often extraordinary nursing care, courts refused to recognize such contracts, maintaining that wives were obligated by reason of marriage to provide nursing and other care and could not be "paid" for such services.[12]

Married women's obligation to care was also the basis to deny women other rights. One major test case involved a woman's right to pursue an occupation, which might be assumed to be a fundamental right of citizenship. In a precedent-setting judgment in *Bradwell v. Illinois*, in 1873, the U.S. Supreme Court upheld the right of Illinois to bar women from practicing law, rejecting the well-qualified Myra Bradwell's claim that the law deprived her of privileges and immunities of citizens under the U.S. Constitution. While the majority opinion firmly centered on the right of states to confer the right to practice law, a concurring opinion signed by three justices went much further in curtailing rights solely on the basis of women's marital duties, stating in part:

> The harmony, not to say identity, of interests and views, which belong, or should belong, to the family institution is repugnant to the idea of a woman adopting a distinct and independent career from that of her husband. . . . It is true that many women are unmarried and not affected by any of the duties, complications, and incapacities arising out of the married state, but these are exceptions to the general rule. The paramount destiny and mission of women are to fulfill the noble and benign offices of wife and mother. This is the law of the Creator, and the rules of civil society must be adapted to the general constitution of things, and cannot be based upon exceptional cases.[13]

Passage of the Nineteenth Amendment in 1920, more than forty-two years after its first introduction, was a long-delayed victory for women's political citizenship. Still, it did little to alter the common law and myriad statutes that circumscribed women's civil citizenship by assuming women's dependence and husbands' prerogatives over wives' labor and income. In the absence of specific laws specifying otherwise, courts continued to hold that women were subordinate to their fathers and husbands and that men held property rights over the labor of daughters and wives. A 1904 Supreme Court ruling held that husbands had "personal and exclusive" right of sexual intercourse with their wives, a right upon which "the whole social order rests." Women still could not bring suit against husbands for assault and battery, nor could they have citizenship in a different state than that in which their husbands held citizenship unless a court found that it was necessary for their protection. Women's domestic obligations also continued to trump their obligations as citizens. Thus, as late as 1965, only twenty-one states made women eligible for jury duty on the same basis as men. The other twenty-nine either excluded women or granted special exemptions based on their domestic responsibilities.[14]

Historical Roots: Paid Caring as Coerced Labor

Alongside the history of excluding mostly white women from citizenship on the basis of their responsibility for caring labor has been a long history of *extracting* caring labor from women of color as part of a larger system of coerced labor, including chattel slavery, indentured servitude, and colonial labor regimes. The story of African American women in the antebellum south performing all manner of caring work for slave-owning families, including wet-nursing white infants, is well known enough not to require elaboration. And even after slavery was abolished, black women continued to perform domestic labor, being prevented from other options by strict color lines in employment. Up until World War I, 90 percent of all southern black women not employed in agriculture worked in some branch of domestic service, as laundresses, cooks, housecleaners, maids, and child nurses. In the North also, black women were shut out of non-domestic employment, even if they had other skills. An African American woman living in Philadelphia described her plight in a letter to the editor, November 1, 1871:

> Sir:
> Being a constant reader of your valuable paper, I take the liberty of asking you to explain to me why it is that when respectable women of color answer an advertisement for a dressmaker, either in families or with a dressmaker, [they] are invariably refused, or offered a place to cook or scrub, or to do housework.[15]

Given the lack of options it is perhaps not surprising that more than three-fourths of all non-agriculturally employed African American women were employed as servants and laundresses throughout the last third of the nineteenth century and the first third of the twentieth. With the great migration north after World War I, African American women became the mainstay of the domestic labor force in northern cities. In 1920, servants and laundresses accounted for almost two-thirds of all gainfully employed African American women in the North.[16]

In other regions of the country, the Southwest, the West, and Hawaii, other groups, Mexican Americans and Japanese Americans, were the main caring labor force. The economies of these so-called peripheral regions of the country were based on extraction of raw materials, such as coal and metal mining, and agricultural production, such as growing cotton, sugar, fruits, and vegetables for the more developed parts of the country. Land and capital were heavily concentrated in the hands of a few corporations or a small class of individuals who exerted almost total economic and political control over the lives of workers. The labor systems in these regions were racially stratified and coercive in nature.

Even after the abolition of chattel slavery and indenture, employers were able to employ coercive means to compel labor. Debt bondage was commonly used to keep workers of color immobile. Black farmers were locked into sharecropping arrangements in which they had to repay landowners for moneys and supplies advanced to them after the crop was harvested and sold. Landowners kept the books and also calculated the worth of crops, and tenants had no recourse against landowner fraud. Thus, the sharecropper frequently was left with either no profit or a debt at the end of season. Southern vagrancy laws were used to round up blacks. Unable to pay the fines for their so-called crimes, black prisoners were forced to work for any private individual who came to pay the fine. Men, women, and children convicted of minor offenses could be leased to private individuals and corporations under a quasi-slave system.[17]

In the southwestern coal industry it was common practice to pay workers in scrip that could only be redeemed for full value at the company store. Workers were paid at the end of the month and were forced to charge fuel, food, tools, and other necessities to get by until payday. Often the whole month's pay was eaten up servicing the previous months' debts.[18] Women of color in these regions were also subjected to coercive labor. Black women in the South, Mexican women in the Southwest, and Japanese women in Hawaii were tracked into two main types of labor, fieldwork or domestic service, including baby and childcare. They were frequently inducted into domestic service as children. Particularly in the case of African American women, even those with skills and training were shut out of other types of employment. An African American domestic explained the situation to an interviewer: "I'll tell you the way white people used to be a long time ago. They would say, 'Well if your mother used to work for me, you grow up, and then after she got too old, the children will work for me.' They would just keep it coming on down from generation to generation. I say, it's going to stop right there! My daughter she won't need to think she need to do that day's work for a living."[19]

Andrew Lind noted a similar practice during the same period in Hawaii for tracking young Japanese American women into service: "It has been a usual

practice for a department head or a member of the managerial staff of the plantation to indicate to members of his work group that his household is in need of
domestic help and to expect them to provide a wife or daughter to fill the
need. . . . Not infrequently, girls have been prevented from pursuing a high
school or college education because someone on the supervisory staff has
needed a servant and it has seemed inadvisable for the family to disregard the
claim."[20] Throughout the first half of the twentieth century, poor single women
of color were denied any welfare relief under "employable mother" rules
enforced by local officials. A local observer noted: "The number of Negro cases
[on Aid to Dependent Children] are few due to the unanimous feeling on the part
of staff and board that there are more work opportunities for Negro women and
to their intense desire not to interfere with local labor conditions. . . . There is a
hesitancy on the part of the lay boards to advance too rapidly over the thinking
of their own communities which see no reason why the employable Negro
mother should not continue her usually sketchy seasonal labor or indefinite
domestic service rather than receive public-assistance grants."[21]

In the depths of the Great Depression in the 1930s, southwestern officials of
the Works Progress Administration (WPA) referred Chicana applicants to domestic jobs exclusively. WPA and Youth Project Administration representatives in
Colorado advocated household training programs for Chicanas, since in the opinion of the assistant director of WPA for Colorado, "The average Spanish
American girl on the NYA [National Youth Administration] program looks forward to little save a life devoted to motherhood often under the most miserable
circumstances."[22]

African American women in the South were routinely excluded from government work by local boards that wanted to ensure that they would be available
for field labor or domestic service. Lula Gordon, a black woman living in San
Antonio, wrote an appeal to President Roosevelt after applying for a job under
the Works Progress Administration and being offered only a domestic service
job: "My name is Lula Gordon. I am a Negro woman. I am on the relief. I have
three children. I have no husband and no job. I have worked hard ever since I was
old enough. I am willing to do any kind of work because I have to support myself
and my children. I was under the impression that the government or the W.P.A.
would give the Physical [sic] fit relief clients work." However, upon applying at
the courthouse, Gordon continued, "Mrs. Beckmon told me to phone a Mrs.
Coyle because she wanted some one to clean house and cook for ($5) five dollars
a week. Mrs. Beckmon said if I did not take the job in the Private home, I would
be cut off from everything all together. She said she was taking people off of the
relief and I have to take the job in the private home or none."[23]

The Great Depression also hit northern blacks hard as black men and women
were the first to lose their jobs and the number of stable domestic positions
plummeted. "Slave markets" arose in most northern cities where black women

congregated to wait to be hired for a day's work. An estimated two hundred such markets existed in New York City, most located in the Bronx and Brooklyn. One writer observed: "They come as early as seven in the morning, wait as late as four in the afternoon with the hope that they will make enough to buy supper when they go home. Once hired on the 'slave market,' the women often find after a day's backbreaking toil, that they worked longer than was arranged, got less than was promised, were forced to accept clothing instead of cash, and were exploited beyond human endurance. Only the urgent need for money makes them submit to this routine daily."[24]

The bracketing of women's unpaid caring labor in the family from the realm of citizenship and rights also extended to paid caring labor. Domestic workers were denied recognition as real workers. Thus, they were explicitly excluded from legislation that granted entitlements and protections to other types of workers. During the Progressive era, when state legislatures enacted maximum hour laws for women workers, domestic workers (as well as agricultural workers) were specifically excluded. They were also excluded from New Deal federal programs, including Social Security, and denied protection under the Fair Labor Standards Act of 1938, which established a maximum workweek, over-time pay, and minimum wages. Domestic workers were also specifically excluded from the provisions of the Occupational Health and Safety Act.[25]

In a major overhaul of the Fair Labor Standards Act in 1974, many types of domestic service, such as housecleaning, were finally included in its provisions. However, during hearings several members of Congress expressed their discomfort with treating the private home as a workplace and the domestic care provider as a worker rather than as a member of the family. The eventual compromise was to exclude baby-sitters and those who provided "companionship services" as long as neither service was performed by "trained personnel" such as a registered nurse, practical nurse, or licensed vocational nurse. Companionship services were defined as "those services which provide fellowship, care, and protection for persons who, because of advanced age or physical or mental infirmity, cannot care for their own needs. These services may include household work related to the care of the aged or infirm person such as meal preparation, bed making, washing of clothes, and other similar services. They may also include the performance of general household work, provided that such work is incidental, i.e., does not exceed 20 percent of the total weekly hours worked."[26] Through this label and definition, the work of hundreds of thousands of home-care workers, many of them paid through state stipends to disabled and elderly individuals, was effectively invisiblized—rendered into "companionship" rather than physical, mental, and emotional labor.[27] Thus, the ideology of caring work not being real work and therefore not deserving of protection and entitlements was continued and, indeed, formalized by U.S. legal and regulatory structures.

Transnational Extraction of Caring Labor
in the Twenty-first Century

Unfortunately, little has changed to the present day in how caring work is viewed or protected. A disproportionate share of care work in the United States, Canada, and Western Europe is still performed by unpaid female family members and by workers who lack citizenship rights and who consequently are subject to restrictions on their freedom, namely, immigrants from the global south, especially Latin America, Africa, and Southeast Asia. As noncitizens, many of them undocumented, they are denied rights and protections.

Contemporary patterns of the treatment of caring labor in the United States are a direct function of the composition and character of the current political economy. Accelerated economic globalization in the past three decades has seen production processes being further removed from the United States and other industrialized nations and exported to lower-wage areas of the so-called global south. At the same time, financial control and management remain concentrated in metropolitan centers of the global north. Consequently, the labor market in the United States is increasingly bifurcated between high-level professional, technical, and managerial jobs, on the one hand, and lower-level, low-paid service jobs, on the other. The two segments are interdependent in that individuals in the professional, technical, and managerial sectors "require" a large number of services to maintain their lifestyles and to relieve them from more onerous tasks of housecleaning, child care, and care for elders and disabled family members.

The demand for care labor in metropolitan centers is matched by the growing "availability" of Third World labor that has been displaced by the same global economic developments. Global economic integration has led to the disruption of agriculture and other traditional economies. As a result, farmers and other small producers have been displaced from their accustomed means of livelihood. Structural adjustment programs (SAPs) imposed by the International Monetary Fund, World Bank, and other international financial institutions controlled by the United States have increased poverty while reducing spending for even meager safety nets. Lacking other options, displaced workers have turned to migrating abroad for jobs that can help them support their families. Because of the demand for female caring labor in North America, Europe, and more prosperous parts of Asia and the Middle East, a high proportion of these migrants are women. Women immigrants have found positions performing care work both in private households as housekeepers, nannies, and home-care workers and in institutional settings as attendants and nursing aides.

The drive for profits has heated up as capitalism has become ever more unfettered by globalization. Industries that arose to provide commodified services, such as health care and elderly care, are undergoing pressure to increase profitability. They have done so by a two-fold strategy of reorganizing the labor process in order to transfer more of the work onto lower-paid workers and at the same time sloughing off (i.e., transferring) parts of the labor altogether by shifting it back to the consumer in a sort of return to pre-twentieth-century practices.[28] The health industry in particular has been undergoing a continuing round of cost-cutting in response to pressures from other sectors of capital to reduce both insurance and government payments for medical care.

As this happens, hospital and nursing home stays have been shortened so that patients are released earlier, before they can take care of themselves. Although much of the care is being taken up by relatives, particularly wives and daughters as unpaid work, some of the gap is being filled by home health aides, who work for minimum wage and without benefits. Many are employed by state-funded programs under the rubric of "in-house support services." Although funded by the state, these programs nonetheless save enormous amounts over the cost of nursing home care. A home health care aide provides housekeeping services, including cleaning, laundry, shopping, and cooking, as well as hands-on care by assisting with bathing, dressing, grooming, medication, and exercise. The U.S. Bureau of Labor Statistics (BLS) projects this field to be among the fastest growing occupations through the year 2006. The BLS also admits that it is highly demanding, low paid, and offers little opportunity for advancement.[29]

One major source of low-paid care workers for the United States and other industrialized nations is the Philippines. Although the actual number of workers is unclear because of the large number of migrants who evade official channels, estimates range up to 4.5 million workers in 120 countries. Taking only official labor migrants, those deployed through the Philippine Overseas Employment Administration, seven hundred thousand contract migrants were going abroad each year in the late 1990s. Some 55 percent of these contract workers were women, of whom over two-thirds were employed as domestic workers, nannies, housekeepers, or maids in middle- or upper-middle-class homes in the United States, Europe, the Middle East, Japan, Hong Kong, and other parts of Asia. In many countries they are "guest" workers and are allowed to remain in their host countries only as long as they stay in their jobs and do not move into other positions.[30] The Kanlungan Center Foundation, an advocacy organization representing Filipina domestics, notes: "We do not migrate as totally free and independent individuals. At times, we have no choice but to migrate, to brave the odds. . . . Even from the very start, we are already victims of illegal recruitment, victims of our government's active marketing of our cheap labor. . . . [S]uffering the backlash of states that fail to provide adequate support for childcare services, we enter First World countries that seek to preserve patriarchal ideology."[31]

In the United States, because of greater opportunities for mobility and due to the availability of Latina immigrant women for domestic work, Filipinas are more often concentrated in nursing, nursing aide, and home health care work than in private caring work. As Rhacel Parrenas has discovered from interviewing Filipina immigrants in Rome and Los Angeles, Filipina workers tend to be relatively well educated. Indeed, they are so over qualified that they are considered the "Mercedes-Benz" of maids and nannies. Typically, Filipina workers have left their own children behind; because of the lower standard of living in the Philippines, a Filipina maid in Rome or a home health aide in Los Angeles can afford to pay an even poorer Filipina to care for her own family back home. Economic globalization has thus transformed the historic racial division of female caring labor into what amounts to a transnational transfer of caring labor from South to North.[32]

Conclusions

In summary, we may ask who directly benefits from the current organization of caring labor. We can clearly identify two beneficiaries: global capital, which maximizes profit by not paying for "reproduction," and men as a class, who on average carry less of the burden and enjoy more of the benefits of caring work. Programs and policies to "correct" the present situation thus have to grapple with the vested interests of both capital and men.

Despite some loss of control due to globalized management and internationalization of finance, the state is still the only large-scale institution that has the capacity to affect redistribution in three areas: the resources to pay for social reproduction, the division of caring labor between men and women, and the rewards and costs of engaging in caring work. Obvious solutions such as universal health care and a more generous social safety net seem unlikely given the current U. S. political climate. Still, we should not stop striving to achieve these goals. Modest approaches, such as workplace reforms, workweek reduction, meshing schedules of employing organizations with those of schools, and equality of paid care leave for men and women, would make it easier for employees to meet both work and caring responsibilities. Tax policies also need to be revised. The breadwinner nuclear family model currently built into tax codes has shored up the gender division of caring work and the dependency of the caregiver. The current tax system allows for joint filing with deductions for dependents, which favors households with a primary breadwinner and a spouse who specializes in unpaid caring labor. If taxes were levied on individual income regardless of marital status or presence of dependents, the penalty for two-earner households in which both earners also engage in caring would be removed.[33]

Comparing the conditions of the caring labor force with those of the agricultural labor force over the last seventy years, we can see that they both started out being excluded from protections by New Deal legislation. The agricultural labor force had the benefit of charismatic leadership from Cesar Chavez and others who were able to mobilize a movement that garnered substantial support for improved labor conditions. The caring labor force today needs a comparable movement to mobilize public support for much needed reforms and to counter still prevalent myths about the "natural responsibility of women."

Care workers themselves are taking action to improve their wages and working conditions. Despite the difficulties of being scattered in disparate work sites, not having their right to organize recognized by the National Labor Relations Act, and being ignored by mainstream unions, domestic workers have a long history of forming worker organizations. In the 1930s, domestic workers in New York City formed the Domestic Workers Alliance, and in Washington, D.C., they organized the Domestic Workers Union. Other cities where domestic workers organized included Chicago, Philadelphia, Milwaukee, Oakland, and Newark. In contemporary Los Angeles, Latina housecleaners and nannies organized the Domestic Workers' Association (DWA) in 1990.[34] The DWA continues not only to advocate for domestics, but also to provide collective space to foster pride and identity and to run workshops and seminars and other activities to empower workers and develop their leadership skills.[35] As part of the upsurge of unionization among service workers, close to 350,000 personal-care attendants and home health care workers have joined the Service Employees International Union (SEIU), while about 60,000 are members of the American Federation of State, County, and Municipal Employees (AFSCME). In addition to negotiating with employers to obtain better wages, benefits, and working conditions, they also form coalitions with other organizations to gain public support and to influence legislators.[36]

As academics and researchers, we can play a part in the struggle to improve the lives of care workers by developing compelling language and conceptions that will enable broader social understanding of caring work as real labor and as an integral part of the political economy. By offering counter-hegemonic discourses, we can help to dispel the myths that keep caring work and caring workers confined within the realm of dependency and unfreedom.

NOTES

1. "More Slavery at the South," by a Negro Nurse, *Independent* 72, no. 3295 (January 25, 1912): 198.

2. Quote from a Filipina domestic in Athens, in Bridget Anderson, *Doing the Dirty Work? The Global Politics of Domestic Labour* (London: Zed Books, 2000), 41.

3. Mona Harrington, *Care and Equality: Inventing a New Family Politics* (New York: Knopf, 1999), 2.

4. Barbara Ehrenreich and Arlie Hochschild, eds., *Global Women: Nannies, Maids, and Sex Workers in the New Economy* (New York: Metropolitan Books, 2002), 9.

5. Abigail Zuger, "Arming Unsung Heroes of Health Care," *New York Times*, November 3, 1999; National Family Caregivers Association, *Caregiver Survey—2000* (Kensington, Md.: NFCA), www.nfcacares.org/survey.html; Anderson, *Doing the Dirty Work?* While an earlier NFCA 1997 survey found that 75 percent of those caring for elderly relatives were women, their 2000 survey of one thousand households found that women constituted 56 percent of family caregivers.

6. Harry L. Braverman, *Labor and Monopoly Capital* (New York: Monthly Review Press, 1980).

7. Judith Shklar, *American Citizenship: The Quest for Inclusion* (Cambridge, Mass.: Harvard University Press, 1991). Women who lacked a relationship with a male earner were excluded from entitlements. Whatever social benefits they received were considered charity, not entitlements.

8. J.G.A. Pocock, "The Ideal of Citizenship since Classical Times," in *Theorizing Citizenship*, ed. Ronald Beiner (Albany: State University of New York, 1995), 30–32, 34–36.

9. Linda Kerber, *No Constitutional Right to Be Ladies: Women and the Obligation of Citizenship* (New York: Hill and Wang, 1998), 146.

10. Alexis de Tocqueville, *Democracy in America*, ed. J. P. Mayer, trans. George Lawrence (New York: Perennial Library, 1988), 600–603; Mary P. Ryan, *Cradle of the Middle Class: The Family in Oneida County, New York, 1790–1865* (Cambridge, England: Cambridge University Press, 1981), 179–181; Carl Degler, *At Odds: Women and the Family in America from the Revolution to the Present* (New York: Oxford University Press, 1980), 332–333; Mary Beth Norton, *Liberty's Daughters: The Revolutionary Experience of American Women, 1750–1800*, with a new preface (Ithaca, N.Y.: Cornell University Press, 1996), 242–250, 272–287.

11. According to some legal historians, the laws were passed not out of conviction that women were equal, but as a response to increases in family separation and market transactions in a mobile and expanding society. Women's title to family property needed to be clarified so as to facilitate transactions of property in cases where men deserted wives and children to migrate west. The laws were more often invoked by couples to shelter their assets from outside creditors than by women to protect their individual rights. Such reforms were viewed as necessary to protect dependent women and were not intended to promote women's independence within marriage. See Elizabeth Bowles Warbasse, *The Changing Legal Rights of Married Women, 1800–1861* (New York: Garland Publishing, 1987), 287–291; and Richard H. Chused, "Married Women's Property Law: 1800–1850," *Georgetown Law Journal* 71 (June 1983): 1398–1426.

12. Evelyn Nakano Glenn, "The Legal Obligation to Care," unpublished paper, 2005.

13. Jo Freeman, "The Revolution for Women in Law and Public Policy," in *Women: A Feminist Perspective*, by Jo Freeman, 4th ed. (Mountain View, Calif.: Mayfield, 1995), 371, citing *Bradwell v. Illinois* 83 U.S. (16 Wall.), 130, 141–42 (J. Bradley, concurring).

14. Freeman, "Revolution for Women," 372.

15. Dorothy Sterling, ed., *We Are Your Sisters: Black Women in the Nineteenth Century* (New York: Norton, 1984), 423.

16. Joseph A. Hill, *Women in Gainful Occupations, 1870–1910*, United Sates Department of Commerce, Bureau of the Census monograph (Washington, D.C.: Government Printing Office, 1929), 115.

17. Evelyn Nakano Glenn, *Unequal Freedom: How Race and Gender Shaped American Citizenship and Labor* (Cambridge, Mass.: Harvard University Press, 2002), 98–106.

18. Sarah Deutsch, *No Separate Refuge: Culture, Class, and Gender on the Anglo-Hispanic Frontier in the American Southwest, 1880–1940* (New York: Oxford University Press, 1987), 88–93; Mario Barrera, *Race and Class in the Southwest: A Theory of Racial Inequality* (Notre Dame, Ind.: Notre Dame University Press, 1979), 41.

19. Told by "Zelda Greene," in Susan Tucker, *Telling Memories among Southern Women: Domestic Workers and Their Employers in the Segregated South* (Baton Rouge: University of Louisiana Press, 1988), 204.

20. Andrew Lind, "The Changing Position of Domestic Service in Hawaii," *Social Process in Hawaii* 15 (1951): 77.

21. Mary S. Labaree, "Unmarried Parenthood under the Social Security Act," *Proceedings of the National Conference of Social Work* (1939): 454.

22. Deutsch, *No Separate Refuge*, 183.

23. Julia Kirk Blackwelder, *Women of the Depression: Case and Culture in San Antonio, 1929–1939* (College Station: Texas A & M University Press, 1984).

24. Louise Mitchell, "Slave Markets in New York City," in *Black Women in White America: A Documentary History*, ed. Gerda Lerner (New York: Vintage, 1973), 230.

25. Alice Kessler-Harris, *In Pursuit of Equality: Women, Men, and the Quest for Economic Citizenship in Twentieth-Century America* (New York: Oxford University Press, 2001), 32, 105–106.

26. Fair Labor Standards Act of 1974, 29 CFR 552.6.

27. Evelyn Nakano Glenn, *The Legal Obligation to Care*, unpublished paper.

28. Nona Glazer, *Servants to Capital* (Philadelphia: Temple University Press, 1989).

29. U.S. Bureau of Labor Statistics, "Homemaker-home health aides," *Occupational Outlook Handbook* (Washington, D.C.: Government Printing Office, 1998).

30. Linda Basch, Nina Glick Schiller, and Christina Szanton Blanc, "Different Settings, Same Outcome: Transnationalism as a Global Process," in *Nations Unbound: Transnational Projects, Postcolonial Predicaments, and Deterritorialized Nation-States*, ed. Linda Basch, Nina Glick Schiller, and Christina Szanton Blanc (Langhorne, Pa.: Gordon and Breach Publishers, 1994), 225–265; Jonathan Karp, "A New Kind of Hero," *Far Eastern Economic Review* 158 (1995): 42–45.

31. Kunlungan Center Foundation, "A Framework on Women and Migration," prepared for NGO Forum, 1995, quoted in Grace Chang, *Disposable Domestics: Immigrant Women Workers in a Global Economy* (Cambridge, Mass.: South End Press, 2000), 136.

32. Rhacel Salazar Parrenas, *Servants of Globalization: Women, Migration, and Domestic Work* (Stanford, Calif.: Stanford University Press, 2001).

33. Nancy Folbre, *The Invisible Heart: Economics and Family Values* (New York: New Press, 2001).

34. Peggie R. Smith, "Organizing the Unorganizable: Private Paid Household Workers and Approaches to Employee Representation," *North Carolina Law Review* 45 (2000–2001): 45–110.

35. Pierrette Hondagneu-Sotelo, *Domestica: Immigrant Workers Cleaning and Caring in the Shadow of Affluence* (Berkeley: University of California Press, 2001), 221–229.

36. "Direct Care Workers Speaking out on Their Own Behalf," *Better Jobs Better Care Issue Brief* 2 (January 2004): 2–3.

Economic Crisis and Political Mobilization

RESHAPING CULTURES OF RESISTANCE
IN TAMPA'S COMMUNITIES OF COLOR,
1929–1939

NANCY A. HEWITT

The Great Depression of the 1930s shattered the economies of countries around the world. Individuals, families, and communities already living on the economic margins were devastated as hard won jobs, homes, and security were swept away in the currents of global collapse. The devastation that followed upon the economic crisis inspired a range of social and political movements, from fascist regimes to leftist insurgencies. This chapter focuses on a single city in the United States—Tampa, Florida—to explore the effects of the Depression on community organizing among African American and immigrant women.

Tampa offers a valuable window into Depression-era activism among women of color, locally and internationally. The city, located on the Gulf Coast some 250 miles north of Key West, developed as a cigar-manufacturing center in the late nineteenth century. Lodged at the intersection of global movements of capital and labor, it was also marked by the severe racial segregation that defined the post–Civil War South. Thus, African American efforts to claim first-class citizenship developed alongside of, but distinct from, traditions of radicalism carried to Tampa by Cuban, Italian, and Spanish immigrants. Together, these groups fueled a range of political movements from the 1870s through the 1920s. It was these diverse movements, and the women who sustained them, that were tested in the cauldron of the economic crisis.

Tampa was unusual, but not unique, in its racial demographics and political alignments. Many areas of the western United States and urban centers throughout the country were home to tri-racial and multi-ethnic communities in the early twentieth century. Even in the segregated South, such communities—including American Indians, Mexican Americans, Chinese Americans, and/or Caribbean immigrants—thrived in parts of Texas, Oklahoma, Louisiana, Mississippi, and North Carolina as well as Florida. Texas not only shared Florida's complicated ethnic and racial mix, but also a history of radical activism among immigrant workers, mainly Mexican and Mexican American, that drew women and men into Socialist, anarcho-syndicalist, and Communist insurgencies.[1]

These tri-racial communities disrupted but never displaced the biracial order of southern society and politics. Moreover, at least in South Florida, the radical politics embraced by ethnic minorities were counterbalanced by more main-stream approaches to organizing among African Americans. While African Americans in a few southern locales—most notably rural Alabama and some of the tobacco towns of North Carolina—joined forces with Socialist and Communist organizations during the 1930s and 1940s, they generally allied them-selves with native-born white rather than immigrant radicals.[2] In Tampa, African Americans rejected imported radicalism in favor of mutual aid societies, volun-tary associations, and reform organizations nurtured in the United States.

While Tampa was typical of most southern cities in the modes of activism chosen by African Americans, immigrant activists in the Cigar City shared much in common with their counterparts in Cuba, Puerto Rico, and U.S. cities with large Caribbean populations.[3] In these locations, radical organizing among Latin workers incorporated women and men, black and white, and drew on Socialist, anarcho-syndicalist, and Communist principles. In addition, at least some more affluent Caribbean immigrants supported their working-class neighbors, particu-larly those who viewed labor activism as part of the wider historical struggle for national independence in their homelands. In some cases, Italian and Spanish rad-icals also allied themselves with these circles of Latin insurgency. The African Americans who were drawn to such alliances—in Tampa, New York City, and elsewhere—almost all came via the Universal Negro Improvement Association, a Pan-Africanist organization founded in Jamaica by Marcus Garvey in 1914.[4]

During the late 1920s and throughout the 1930s, African American and immi-grant activists, whether radical or mainstream, were confronted with the daunt-ing task of continuing their political efforts in the face of the greatest economic crisis the world had ever experienced. In Tampa, the responses developed by women of color drew on a long history of activism in both African American and Latin communities. In the face of severe financial shocks, did these women of color sustain the organizations and movements forged in earlier decades? And, if so, how did the economic crisis reshape their political work and activist alliances?

The thousands of immigrants who settled in Tampa from the 1880s on had been drawn primarily by the booming cigar industry, established in the city in 1886. They had also sought escape from repressive regimes in their homelands. Indeed, many Cubans were forced to flee to South Florida after a failed effort to overthrow Spanish rule in the 1870s and the resurgence of revolutionary activity in the 1890s.[5] These immigrants were racially diverse with self-identified Afro-Cubans constituting some 15 percent of the island's emigres.[6] In the early 1900s, growing numbers of Italians joined Spanish and Cuban immigrants in the ethnic enclaves of Ybor City and West Tampa, both of which bordered the city proper. Their native-born white neighbors often categorized Cubans, many of whom were of mixed racial ancestry, as black; many Anglos also considered Spanish and Italian immigrants not quite white—though certainly not African American. Together these diverse immigrant groups forged a distinct Latin community in which residents spoke a mix of Spanish and Italian, worked in the cigar industry or in surrounding shops and restaurants, and embraced anti-clericalism and radical politics borne of battles against repression and for independence in their homelands.

Although the term "Latin" sounds peculiar to modern ears, it was a term of choice in the early twentieth century. The racial categories of this period included Anglo-Saxon, African, Germanic, Asiatic or Oriental, and Mediterranean or Latin. While some of these terms, like "Oriental," were imposed on immigrant groups by Anglo-Americans, Tampa's Spanish, Italian, and Cuban communities embraced a shared identity as Latins. Organizers for the radical Industrial Workers of the World, who recruited immigrants in Tampa in the 1910s, also used the word "Latin" to describe the various combinations of Spanish, Mexican, Italian, and Caribbean workers who labored in the southwestern and southeastern United States. And among a wide range of groups in the United States the term would have been familiar thanks to Rudolf Valentino, who was known as the "Latin Lover" in the early twentieth century.[7]

One of the unique features of Florida's Latin enclaves was their lack of sharp racial and ethnic divides. Drawing on alliances forged during the Cuban independence struggle of the late nineteenth century, white Cubans and Afro-Cubans embraced cultural and political visions that highlighted ethnic solidarity.[8] The Spaniards who settled in Tampa came mostly as cigar factory owners or managers, relying on Cuban workers to assure their success. The Italians, mostly peasants who had been victims of landlords and government authorities at home, arrived en masse at the turn of the century. Self-interest and pre-migration experiences thus converged to create a community with shared economic goals and political visions. This was no multicultural utopia, of course, but compared to most areas of the South at the time, Tampa's Latin communities were havens of racial and ethnic tolerance.[9]

At the same time, English-speaking immigrants from the Bahamas and the Canary Islands settled in predominately African American neighborhoods in downtown and West Tampa and soon intermarried with native-born blacks.[10] As in the Latin community, those who identified as African American in Tampa— whether native or foreign born—generally shared religious beliefs, political ideals, and language. Eschewing the anti-clericalism of their Cuban, Spanish, and Italian neighbors, African Americans viewed churches as critical sites for spiritual, social, and political development. Moreover, few had experiences with the Socialist and anarchist ideologies that inspired labor militancy and revolutionary activities in the Latin enclaves. Instead, they challenged native-born white Americans to live up to the ideals defined by the U.S. Constitution.

By 1900, Tampa was comprised of three relatively distinct communities—native-born whites (or Anglos), African Americans, and Latins—each comprising roughly one-third of the city's nearly sixteen thousand residents. Although the term "immigrant" in this chapter refers to Latins, all three groups included foreign-born members or their descendants. Irish and German settlers had inter-married with native-born white Tampans in the mid to late nineteenth century, just as Afro-Bahamians and Canary Islanders integrated themselves into the African American community in the early twentieth century. At the same time, the Latin enclaves in Ybor City and West Tampa were racially diverse, with Afro-Cubans, white Cubans, Italians, Spaniards, and ethnically and racially mixed resi-dents sharing neighborhoods, factory floors, and union halls. The colorful spectrum of Latin Tampans complicated any simple division of local residents into the bifurcated categories of black and white demanded by Jim Crow segre-gation. Since the children and grandchildren in each group often retained the lan-guage, religious affiliation (or disaffiliation), and activist traditions of their forebears, Anglo, African American, and Latin identities in Tampa were sustained into the 1930s, when Tampa housed some one hundred thousand residents.[11]

From the 1880s to the 1920s, Latins challenged Tampa's factory owners and civic authorities through a series of strikes and protests. At the same time, African Americans demanded economic, educational, and political rights. In both communities, women were central to activist efforts.[12] During the decade preced-ing the onset of the Great Depression, African American and Latin women honed their organizing skills and traditions. In 1920, some thirteen hundred African American women in the city took advantage of the passage of the Nineteenth Amendment to the U.S Constitution granting women suffrage and voted. That same year, Latin women joined an industry-wide strike and took over leadership roles when male union leaders were imprisoned or deported. By 1921, white civic leaders had defeated the strike and closed the loopholes that had allowed black women to cast ballots, but they could not contain the women's enthusiasm for activism. In the 1920s, Latin women increased their numbers in the cigar workforce and in union ranks. Simultaneously, they expanded their labor within the various ethnic mutual aid societies as African American women extended their earlier organizing efforts by founding or helping to found the Tampa Urban League (TUL), the Helping Hand Day Nursery, the Women's Community Center, and the Central Nurses' Registry.[13]

Yet despite decades of activism, women of color in Tampa faced a variety of problems and constraints in the years immediately preceding the Depression. Latin cigar workers failed to gain union recognition in the strike of 1920–21, and mechanization of the cigar industry—occurring worldwide—complicated hopes for further labor organizing. Machines also transformed the workforce, increasing women's employment both absolutely and proportionately even as the size of the overall labor force declined.[14] At the same time, African Americans struggled to sustain their political and economic leverage as growing class differences exacerbated ongoing conflict over strategies and goals within the community. When Atlanta activist Benjamin Mays took over as executive secretary of the TUL in 1926, he was shocked by the paternalistic character of race relations among native-born white and black elites, by the degraded conditions faced by working-class and poor African Americans, and by the level of anti-black violence that plagued the city and the state.[15]

In the midst of these struggles, in 1926 through 1927, a severe economic crisis gripped South Florida as the first hints of the national and international depression to come appeared amid tropical breezes. Over the next decade and a half, immigrants and African Americans faced dire economic circumstances. At the same time, racial discrimination and racist violence intensified. Indeed, violence remained a critical barrier to racial advancement, and both locally and nationally, native-born whites wielded it against African Americans and immigrants.[16] For Latin residents, the rise of fascism in Spain inspired grave concern, while attacks on radicals and labor organizers in Tampa suggested that such threats also existed close to home. Moreover, with the onset of the Depression, the precarious economic existence of Afro-Cubans and African Americans inspired large numbers in each group, but especially Afro-Cubans, to migrate north.[17]

Despite the obstacles faced by Latins and African Americans, people of color organized on a wide range of fronts during the 1930s. Women in particular expanded and reshaped their efforts to advance their individual and collective interests. Both Latin and African American women focused on economic issues, including housing and healthcare as well as jobs, and both sustained traditions of mutual aid through the Depression. However, Latin women continued to wield strikes and protests to dramatize their plight, while African American women worked through more mainstream political, religious, and voluntary associations. In addition, Latin women were more concerned with the rise of fascism abroad, while African Americans continued to focus on racism at home. Finally, in both communities, the establishment of New Deal employment and assistance programs by the federal government from 1934 on redirected some of women's efforts, even as activists continued to hone earlier organizing traditions.

Carrying on these traditions, African American women organized both alongside men and separately as women to counteract the effects of the Depression on their community. Initially, they worked within existing institutions, such as the TUL and the Helping Hand Day Nursery, to provide aid to needy families, child care for working mothers, and medical care for the sick. Yet they also established new organizations and extended statewide networks. The New Deal especially inspired dozens of black residents to appeal directly to federal officials for assistance and spawned efforts to assist African Americans in navigating the local bureaucracy in charge of federally funded programs. Such activities pale in comparison to the initiatives of African American tobacco workers in Winston-Salem, North Carolina, and sharecroppers in Alabama, who organized for racial and economic justice in company with radical unions and/or the Communist Party.[18] Yet they were certainly more typical of African American activism across the South in the 1930s. And such mainstream organizing in the midst of the Depression did sustain institutions and networks that would form the foundation for later struggles on behalf of racial equality. In Tampa, for instance, the local NAACP (National Association for the Advancement of Colored People) chapter, which had languished in the early 1920s, gained a new charter in 1929 and expanded its activities throughout the 1930s.[19]

Women were active in both the original and the revitalized NAACP. In the 1930s, teachers, many with experience in women's clubs and the TUL, joined in substantial numbers. Mary E. Potter, co-publisher with her husband of the *Tampa Bulletin*, the major black newspaper in the city, sat on the board of directors. Marion Rogers, a Bahamian immigrant who settled in Tampa in the 1890s, helped found the first NAACP chapter in the city and became a charter member of the second.[20] These women pushed the organization to agitate around economic rights as well as racist violence, responding to events locally and nationally. In 1931, in the infamous Scottsboro case, nine young African American men were falsely accused of rape by two white women and arrested in Alabama. They were tried, convicted, and sentenced to hang. Campaigns for their release, launched by the national NAACP and the Communist Party, mobilized groups throughout the United States and the world. Rogers was among the Tampa NAACP members who raised funds for the Scottsboro Nine.[21] She was engaged as well in campaigns for economic justice in which the local NAACP was joined by the Florida State Teachers Association and its affiliates. In October 1930, the Florida West Coast Negro Education Association, chaired by clubwoman and local Superintendent of Colored Schools Blanche Armwood Beatty, met at the newly opened Booker T. Washington High School in Tampa. That conference focused on interracial harmony through education, but members also joined the state organization's campaign for salary equalization with white teachers in Florida, which it pursued throughout the 1930s.[22] In addition to Beatty and Rogers, Emma Bryant, who participated in a range of missionary and reform efforts in the early 1900s, Marion Anderson, a leader in the Helping Hand Day Nursery, Frankie Berry, active in a range of women's clubs, and dozens of other women supported NAACP and educational initiatives.

Other civic organizations also inspired African Americans to push forward despite the economic crisis. In January 1932, a number of local women's clubs and fraternal organizations combined their resources to bring Oscar DePriest, the first African American elected to Congress (from Chicago in 1916), to speak. Appearing at the St. Paul A.M.E. Church, DePriest packed the hall with an enthusiastic crowd that spilled out into the streets. Men, women, and children all attended the event and embraced, at least briefly, a sense that change was possible.[23] With a similar focus on the future, the City Federation of Colored Women's Clubs, led by long-time activist and hairdresser Clotelle Williams, continued to hold the annual Lincoln-Douglass Ball during the early 1930s. The ball not only provided momentary respite from the problems of the day, but also raised much-needed funds for community organizations and programs.[24]

The material needs of local residents were critical in shaping the programs offered and advocated by African American civic organizations. For example, in 1932, the TUL opened a sewing room under the auspices of the Tampa Cooperative Unemployment Council, providing work for impoverished black women before federal employment projects were established. The TUL, in collaboration with African American clubwomen, also persuaded the city government to take control of the privately run Clara Frye Hospital, the only facility devoted wholly to black health care in Tampa. In the late 1930s, with the help of federal funds, the Tampa Negro Hospital was built, which provided not only care for those in need, but also employment for black nurses and physicians.[25] To advance, publicize, and fund these activities, middle-class African American women wrote articles, designed posters, organized meetings, sewed, and cooked.

Churches and schools continued to offer services to local African Americans as well. Beulah Baptist, the oldest black church in Tampa, provided ongoing assistance to its congregants throughout the 1930s, and also built a large, new sanctuary that opened in 1935. The Helping Hand Day Nursery continued to educate younger members of the race, moving to a new location in 1933. Drawing on every resource available, including the cooking and sewing skills of teachers and administrators, the nursery expanded the number of children cared for and organized a wide range of community events that brought black residents together from different neighborhoods, churches, and classes, including a growing number of Afro-Cubans from Ybor City. St. Paul A.M.E. Church also hosted a variety of programs, and its various women's circles and societies offered material as well as spiritual comfort to those in need.[26]

Other organizations were founded in the midst of the Depression to provide critical services to African Americans. The Lily White Pallbearers Temple, established in 1935 and later renamed the Lily White Security Benefits Society, assured dignified funerals for its members. Women and men were among the charter members, including teacher Corinne Alexander and seamstress Bessie Barefield.[27] The National Council of Negro Women, founded by Mary McLeod Bethune, opened a branch in Tampa in 1937. That same year, the local NAACP chapter petitioned the national office for a youth council to bring young women and men into the organization's work.[28]

Yet it was clear by the mid-1930s that local efforts alone could not meet the growing needs of an impoverished community. The federal government's promise of a New Deal thus offered some hope as community resources dwindled. Still, as many scholars have documented, New Deal legislation and its state and local implementation were deeply marred by race and gender discrimination with women, immigrants, and African Americans receiving far fewer benefits than native-born white men. The problems in Tampa were especially severe for a number of reasons. City politics were notably corrupt before the Great Depression, and vigilante violence had long served as a means by which native-born white civic and industrial leaders maintained control.[29] These traditions assured that relief efforts would be tainted and that those who protested invited physical reprisals.

Evidence abounded of the corrupt character of New Deal programs in Tampa, inspiring outrage among needy whites as well as African Americans and Latins. Dozens of local residents wrote to federal officials, voicing their concerns. A letter from Mrs. Daniel Fager, a native-born white Tampan, was typical of many. In October 1935, she complained to Harry Hopkins, head of the Federal Emergency Relief Administration: "The politics are so vile here in Tampa. It [*sic*] is controlled by a man who is a notorious importer of narcotics and aliens. Where are the Federal men that they don't do something about this? Everyone knows that these conditions exist, but they are all afraid of their jobs and don't dare say anything."[30] Local union leaders, organizers for the Workers' Alliance (a national organization of the unemployed allied with the Socialist Party), and leaders of the TUL also complained to state and federal officials on a regular basis, but generally to no avail.[31]

For African American residents, corruption was exacerbated by racism. Throughout the South, the implementation of New Deal programs threatened many whites, who feared the loss of cheap black labor. Tampa physician William Rowlett wrote to Democratic U.S. senator Claude Pepper of Florida, complaining that African American girls made more in sewing rooms opened by the Works Progress Administration (WPA) than as maids. "How long," he asked, "will the solid south remain solid when the negro is permitted to insult our white citizens believing that they have the backing of the government?"[32] In her December 1936 report, Frances A. Ewell, the executive assistant for the Women's and Professional Division of the WPA in Florida, noted, "Colored [sewing] centers have been closing down in a number of counties where continued complaints came to the local or state office that the colored women were refusing jobs in private industry as cooks and maids."[33] Where programs existed, white administrators, including women, attempted to circumvent the government's intent in order to maintain racist traditions. Thus, despite protests from the local NAACP, Tampa WPA administrator Marion Mickler set aside only one day a week to interview black clients. There was only one office, she explained, and African Americans could not sit in the waiting room with whites.[34]

While African American men in Tampa were repeatedly denied skilled jobs as carpenters, electricians, and plasterers, black women often faced even worse conditions. Most were only considered for unskilled work to begin with, and many lost those positions as more and more white women sought employment in any available job. As Mabel T. Adams, a resident of nearby Plant City, wrote to Mrs. Roosevelt in April 1939, "I am a colored woman with a family to support. . . . We don't have a project in this town [for African American women] but we have (4) four W.P.A. projects for white[s]. . . . And no help whatever as they laid off every one of us Negro[es]."[35]

The racism that fueled discrimination against African Americans also inspired violence. In January 1934, Robert Johnson, a forty-year-old native-born black man, was arrested in Tampa for questioning in the assault of a white woman. He was released from jail due to a lack of evidence, but was let out in the middle of the night and immediately kidnapped, driven to a deserted area, and shot four times in the head and once in the body. No one was ever indicted for the crime.[36] In a more widely publicized case in North Florida, African American Claude Neal was stabbed, mutilated, and shot before being hung from a tree after being arrested on little evidence for killing a young white girl. Despite national attention, no one was ever punished for the crime.[37] The Ku Klux Klan rallied in Tampa throughout the 1930s, targeting both African Americans suspected of "inappropriate" behavior and labor organizers suspected of Communist or Socialist sympathies. Indeed, in 1937, the American Civil Liberties Union (ACLU) "branded" Tampa "as one of the worst 'centers of repression' in the United States" and directly linked this fact to evidence that the city government was "under the control of public officials dominated by the Ku Klux Klan."[38]

The long history of anti-labor violence and lynching in Tampa and statewide helps explain why African American workers in South Florida failed to see labor organizing as an effective means of addressing racial injustice. Yet such limits on radical activities may have fostered the growth of more mainstream cross-class organizations. Immediately after federal passage of the National Recovery Act in 1934, local clubwomen organized an "educational mass meeting" to advise African American residents across the class spectrum of the opportunities made available to them by the program.[39] Inspired by this same legislative initiative, Blanche Armwood Washington (formerly Beatty) organized the Golden Rule Alliance in 1934 "to secure for Negroes of Tampa and vicinity some of the superior benefits enjoyed" by residents of other Florida cities. Anticipating the problems of implementation by racist white officials, the alliance asked for "a Negro Executive" to work under the supervision of the local administrator of federal programs to ensure the "prompt and correct interpretation" of federal policies, to secure opportunities for African Americans in vocational education and other programs, and to "interpret the needs of Negroes" to federal and local administrators "who otherwise fail to do the most effective work with and for Negroes."[40]

Although organized by middle-class and affluent African Americans, the Golden Rule Alliance recruited working women to serve on a variety of committees, including a hairdresser and a dressmaker on the executive committee. Moreover, individuals from a wide range of occupations chaired subcommittees, with women clerical workers, maids, cooks, teachers, dressmakers, and hairdressers overseeing programs in their own fields of labor.[41] Given the class divisions that fractured African American efforts at community organizing in the 1920s, the inclusiveness of the alliance is all the more impressive. And it did mitigate some of the racism in local New Deal programs and helped gain federal and county support for a second high school for black students in the city.[42]

African American women also extended their reach further into the ethnic enclaves. Afro-Cubans were especially hard-hit by the Depression, and hundreds left Tampa to seek work in northern cities. Those who remained, however, forged closer ties with their African American counterparts. Such collaboration had begun in the 1920s, when the TUL and the Helping Hand Day Nursery invited Afro-Cubans to participate in their work. By then, younger Afro-Cubans had learned English and interacted with African Americans in Tampa's segregated schools, restaurants, and parks. The economic crisis strengthened these bonds, recasting the definition of black Americans in Tampa to include individuals from both English-speaking and Spanish-speaking communities.[43]

Yet Afro-Cubans also organized alongside other Latin women in the face of the deepening Depression. Concerned with both the difficult conditions in Tampa and the rise of right-wing political regimes in their homelands, Cuban, Italian, and Spanish women and men mobilized throughout the 1930s. A major site for such efforts remained the factory floor, including efforts to retain the tradition of *los lectores* (readers). Since the late nineteenth century, readers had been hired and paid by the workers to provide information and entertainment during the workday. Owners and managers viewed readers as agitators since, through their work, they spread news about political events and working-class struggles at home and abroad.[44] During the late 1920s and early 1930s, however, decreases in production and pay were just as important in fueling workers' militancy. Between 1930 and 1940, the cigar labor force in Tampa declined sharply from 11,222 to 6,300; and by 1935, women outnumbered men, 4,828 to 3,811.[45] The threat of dismissal, with no severance pay and little chance of new employment, encouraged many Latin workers to join the Tobacco Workers Industrial Union (TWIU), a Communist-affiliated organization, when it began a campaign in Tampa in 1931. Throughout the summer and fall, TWIU organizers, including African American and white union representatives, sought unemployment relief, protested evictions, staged plays and rallies, and attracted significant support among women and men cigar workers. During a November 7 rally in Ybor City, violence erupted and the leaders of the meeting were arrested. Although many of the workers claimed that the police initiated the violence, Tampa authorities accused seventeen TWIU activists, including the leading woman organizer, Carolina Vasquez, of unlawful assembly, rioting, and assault to commit murder.[46]

Then, over the Thanksgiving holiday, owners tore down the readers' chairs. When employees returned to the factories on November 27, they immediately staged a massive walkout to protest this latest affront to their rights. Planning to return to work after a three-day peaceful protest, workers found themselves locked out by employers, who collaborated with a newly formed Citizens Committee created "to help cigar manufacturers 'wash the red out of their factories.'" [47] With the support of a federal injunction against the TWIU, the cigar factories reopened, allowing about 70 percent of workers to return, but dismissing women and men whom they considered agitators, Communists, and union leaders. Protests from the CMIU and other labor organizations had little effect given the powerful combination of legal and extra-legal forces brought to bear on the situation and the dire economic straits of most of the workers. [48]

Fifteen of the TWIU leaders were found guilty of unlawful assembly and served more than a year in prison before the Florida Supreme Court overturned their convictions. At the same time, the courts imposed injunctions against mass meetings, and vigilantes continued to attack radical leaders. Although the Communist Party protested the situation, their efforts were constrained by limited resources. Moreover, legal rulings and official protests had little impact on the continued use of violence to quell radicalism in Tampa. In 1935, vicious assaults on four Socialist organizers in the city heightened concern among Latin cigar workers still bent on unionization and intensified fears among African Americans in the wake of Robert Johnson's murder. One of the Socialists, Joseph Shoemaker, collapsed after being whipped, tarred, and feathered; he was hospitalized but died nine days after the beating. This time, public outrage over the death of a white man, pressure from a range of national organizations, including the AFL and the ACLU, and concerns about the city's national reputation led to the arrest of eleven men, including several local policemen with ties to the Ku Klux Klan. Still, although seven men were tried for kidnapping and five for murder, no one was ever punished for these crimes. [49]

The defeat of the 1931 strike, the prosecution of the TWIU leaders, and the murder of Joseph Shoemaker certainly discouraged some Latin residents from participating in further union activities. Yet these events also made clear that new alliances were possible, particularly with native-born white Communists and Socialists, who considered the severe Depression an opportunity for working-class organizing across racial and ethnic lines. [50] Indeed, some Latin labor activists raised funds for the Scottsboro Nine in this period, embracing a cause critical to African Americans. Moreover, despite the dangers and difficulty of holding mass meetings, CPUSA organizers arranged gatherings in individual homes and lauded local residents for their willingness to participate. Organizer Mike Bradford claimed he was "especially impressed by the Spanish [sic] women and children," who demonstrated courage in the face of the "terror and intimidation prevailing in real southern fashist [sic] manner." Bradford claimed that children of three and four years old sing the "Internationale"; housewives hang "the red flag"; students "defy the teachers and young fellows paint the hammer and sickle on the sidewalks."[51]

Given the hostile atmosphere in Tampa, the AFL threatened to cancel its national convention, scheduled to be held in the city in fall 1936, unless local authorities responded effectively to Joseph Shoemaker's murder earlier that year. Assured (falsely, as it turned out) that justice would be done, some twelve hundred AFL members gathered in Tampa that November. The convention provided a financial boost to the city and a morale boost to local workers. The Tampa Symphony Orchestra played twice for the AFL delegates as did "three colored bands." In addition, the Latin unit of the Federal Theater Project, based in Ybor City, presented a musical comedy, *Eva,* for the participants.[52] Just as importantly for Latin workers, Luisa Moreno appeared as a featured speaker at the 1936 convention. Born in Guatemala, Moreno moved to Mexico City and then New York City in the 1920s. Forced to work in a garment factory in Spanish Harlem during the Depression, she soon organized her sister workers into a union. In 1935, the AFL hired Moreno as an organizer, and a year later sent her to Florida to organize cigar workers. Her presence in Tampa signaled the AFL's revitalized concern for Latin workers in South Florida.[53]

Both before and after Moreno's visit to Tampa, Latin women remained central to workplace and community efforts. Their participation in factory labor and in WPA projects, such as sewing rooms, proved critical to family survival; and their work in mutual aid societies and other voluntary organizations grew more important as economic hardship and the growth of fascism threatened the community.[54] For example, the women's auxiliaries of the various mutual aid societies supported a wide range of theatrical events during the Depression to raise funds and provide entertainment. More than a dozen plays were staged as part of the Federal Theater Project's Spanish-language program in Ybor City. Although short-lived, nearly fifty thousand individuals, most of them Latin, attended the fifteen funded shows, which ranged from comedies to musical revues to political dramas like *Esto no lo Pasara Aqui* (It Can't Happen Here).[55]

Still, Latin women and men faced enormous obstacles. Some five thousand cigar workers were unemployed by 1935; large numbers left Ybor City and West Tampa, moving back to Cuba or north to New York City. Nonetheless, Latin women who remained in Tampa wielded their traditions of solidarity and militancy to demand benefits from New Deal programs at home and to protest the rising threat of fascism abroad.

Events in Spain inspired local Latins to mobilize on the international front. During the early 1930s, Cubans and Italians viewed the rise of right-wing dictatorships in their homelands with grave concern, while Spanish immigrants applauded the emergence of a democratic republic. Within a few years, however, divisions within the new regime, combined with the worldwide depression, left the Spanish Republic on the brink of collapse. Immediately following the election of 1936, in which a coalition of Republicans and Socialists won a narrow victory, acts of violence increased across Spain and rumors of a military overthrow spread. By July, civil war erupted with General Francisco Franco leading the right-wing forces against the Republican government and its allies. Although the U.S. government refused to intervene, American defenders of the Spanish Republicans, many of them labor activists, Socialists, and Communists, organized relief missions and military units.

Tampa's Latin immigrants leapt to the Spanish Republic's defense. While only a small number headed to the battlefront in Spain, thousands of women and men mobilized on the home front to provide funds, food, weapons, and other resources to sustain the fight. In 1937 Spanish immigrants formed the Democratic Popular Committee to Aid Spain, which attracted support from Latin labor unions as well as mutual aid societies. Once again, men were officially designated as leaders of the organization, but women were active in fund-raising, organizing rallies, and collecting goods for Spanish families and Republican soldiers. More than one thousand women—Spanish, Cuban, and Italian—joined the Antifascist Women's Committee, which served as a sort of women's auxiliary to the Popular Committee. Among the leaders was Elisa Moris, a cigar maker who devoted her time and her skills to *"el retroguardia de Tampa,"* the rearguard of the Spanish Republican cause.[56]

In November 1937, the Tampa Popular Committee shipped six thousand pounds of clothing to the Spanish Red Cross. Most of this clothing was made or mended by members of the Women's Committee, who met after a day's work at home or in the factory to sew for the cause. Some forty aid workers, a third of them women, posed on the dozens of boxes stacked for shipment at one of the local mutual aid societies.[57] By the end of the war, Latin immigrants in Tampa shipped some twenty tons of clothing to Spain. In December 1937, responding to an urgent appeal from the Spanish Red Cross, the Tampa committees sent thirty tons of beans and a thousand cans of milk to the Republicans.[58]

Women cigar workers participated in efforts at the factory as well as at home. Men and women cigar makers labored on Sundays for free to produce cigars for the Republican soldiers, and women sewed some twenty thousand tobacco pouches to include in the shipment. Women workers also contributed to the weekly collections made at each cigar factory, a custom that reached back to the 1890s and the Cuban War for Independence. Following the bombing of Guernica by Hitler's forces in April 1937, women at the Garcia and Vega factory organized a march to protest the slaughter of noncombatants. Led by women, the massive march proceeded from the Labor Temple in Ybor City to city hall, where the Popular Committee presented Tampa's mayor with a resolution protesting the "ruthless killing of women and children by Franco's forces."[59]

Latin women used their power as consumers to support the Republican cause as well. They led boycott campaigns against products imported from a range of fascist powers, including Germany, Italy, and Japan, and against stores that failed to contribute to the Popular Committee. Movies that were viewed as critical of the Republic were boycotted as well, as were films that included actors support-ive of Franco. Families also removed hundreds of children from Catholic schools, since the Spanish Catholic Church backed Franco.[60]

Finally, women joined men in more traditional political efforts. They peti-tioned and lobbied the president of the United States, Congress, and the State Department to change the U.S. policy of neutrality toward Spain. Women accompanied men to Washington, D.C., when they presented the Popular Committee's demands in person. They also sent letters and telegrams from Tampa, urging change. Men, women, and children marched in Labor Day parades in the city dressed as Spanish *milicianos* and carried American flags to tie the cause of democracy in Spain to democratic traditions in the United States. Women also hosted a visit by Isabel de Palencia, part of a delegation sent by the Spanish government in 1936 to persuade U.S. audiences of the need to support the Republic. She addressed a crowd of three thousand at a mass meeting in Plant Park and spoke as well to women delegates to the AFL convention.[61]

Fears over the rise of fascism abroad absorbed much, but not all, of Latin women's energy during the late 1930s. More immediate problems at home also inspired collective protest. Although WPA projects had seemed a godsend when Tampa first acquired them, their implementation caused grave concerns, espe-cially for needy women. Hoping to spark a general walkout of relief workers in the county, women employed at an Ybor City sewing room in collaboration with the Workers Alliance instigated a strike in July 1937.[62]

WPA projects were often construction related, employing largely men. Women comprised only 12 to 18 percent of WPA workers nationwide, and most of the jobs involved sewing or other handicraft work. In areas like Ybor City, where women comprised more than a quarter of all employed labor before the Depression and the primary employer was the cigar industry, the lack of jobs and the focus on sewing proved especially problematic. The local sewing projects were decentralized, with 200 to 300 women employed at each site. Although sewing-room jobs were not the most desirable by any means, they at least provided some work. Yet when funds ran low, sewing rooms were usually the first projects to be closed down, and workers were laid off until new funds were received. When the rooms were reopened, not all of the former employees were rehired.[63]

These problems sparked an uprising at the WPA sewing room in Ybor City, which was housed in the former La Flor de Cuba cigar factory. Nearly 500 native-born white and Latin women were employed there, including Mabel Hagen, a white organizer for the Workers' Alliance. The sewing-room insurgency res-onated with Latin labor traditions, but it was modeled on the December 1936 sit-down strikes at the General Motors plant in Flint, Michigan. The Workers' Alliance initiated the action in hopes of increasing relief funds and instituting some form of job security for relief workers. Hagen, joined by Adela Santiesteban and Elsie Seth, gained the support of the WPA forewomen at the site, most of whom were Latin, and a majority of the workers joined the sit-down on July 8.[64] After the WPA district supervisor and the local sheriff negotiated with the women for several hours, however, the sheriff demanded that all women who wished to leave be allowed to do so. Nearly three-quarters of the workers went home, but some 100 to 130 stayed.[65]

While the Workers' Alliance urged other WPA workers to walk out in support of the women, families and friends crowded around the building, fearing that local authorities would physically remove the women. However, the sewing room was a federal project, and local police were more wary than usual of intervening in the labor situation. Supporters brought guava pastries, bread, cookies, and coffee, and the women sang labor songs and smoked cigars before they bedded down for the night. According to La Gaceta, Tampa's largest Spanish-language paper, those who stayed included "girls of eighteen and grandmothers of sixty-five, most of them of Latin descent and most of them wearing yellow Workers' Alliance badges."[66]

Despite the solidarity shown by the striking Latin women, the sewing-room sit-down never led to a wider movement. Most native-born white workers abandoned the sewing room as soon as the sheriff offered them the opportunity to leave. Only 250 of 3,500 other WPA workers in the county walked off their jobs in solidarity with the women; and the Workers' Alliance raised only $150 to support the effort. The police, moreover, by showing restraint in this case, kept the sit-down strikers isolated. Finally, a WPA regulation that allowed strikers to be released from their jobs if they stayed away for more than four workdays brought the sit-down strike to a climax on Tuesday evening. Then, ninety-six women left the building without incident; the families of the remaining strikers convinced the Workers' Alliance to call off the strike later that night. The strike leaders lost their jobs immediately, and many of the Latin women were let go two months later when the U.S. Congress barred "aliens" from WPA employment.[67]

The sit-down strike revealed more than the limits of labor organizing in the midst of the Depression. It also made visible the fault lines among Tampa women. First, it made clear that even in the midst of economic crisis Latin women could not depend on most of their Anglo sisters to join them in challenging civic authorities. Certainly, dozens of white women complained individually to federal officials about working conditions and bureaucratic corruption in Tampa's New Deal programs. Still, with the exception of those like Mabel Hagen and Elsie Seth, who joined the Workers' Alliance, they did not demonstrate solidarity through collective action. Even more importantly, African American women, too, failed to find common cause with the Ybor City sit-down strikers.

In the midst of the strike, sixty-four African American women were laid off from a black sewing project in the city, yet they failed to ally with their Latin counterparts. Indeed, a WPA report claimed that some African American women "chanted derisively" when news of the strike reached them. They supposedly adopted a refrain from a popular black movie: "Lawd no, I cain't sit down. I just got to heaven and I got to look around. No lawd, I just cain't sit down."[68] Of course, WPA administrators may have sought to sew seeds of suspicion between African American and Latin relief workers.[69] Yet they had every reason to believe that such suspicions were already well entrenched. There is little evidence beyond the efforts of a few Afro-Cuban and African American women activists in the TUL and Helping Hand Day Nursery of solidarity among women of color in Tampa before or during the Depression. Even those alliances reflected more about the ways that racism and economic exploitation had come to constrain the lives of Afro-Cubans than about common perspectives or goals among Latins and African Americans more generally.[70] The historic divide among Latins and African Americans institutionally, ideologically, and organizationally in Tampa made it difficult to find common ground in the midst of economic crisis.

This chapter demonstrates that, despite the economic devastation wrought on communities of color, both Latin and African American women organized throughout the period. Rarely, however, did they join forces. Many Cuban, Italian, and Spanish immigrants continued to focus on workplace issues, embracing radical unions and political movements. In the late 1930s, they also committed themselves to the Republican, anti-fascist cause in Europe. African Americans sought change largely on the domestic front and mainly through the proliferation of mutual aid, fraternal, and reform organizations. Despite traditions of radical working-class activism in Tampa, African Americans did not engage in the type of interracial labor politics that occurred in Winston-Salem, North Carolina; rural Alabama; and a scattering of other southern locales. If anything, the tradition of Latin labor militancy seems to have limited the possibilities for local African Americans to join in the kinds of radical struggles for economic and social justice that scholars have highlighted elsewhere in this period.

Both African Americans and Latins did fight for equal treatment in the numerous federal assistance programs launched during the 1930s, and in these battles both confronted Tampa's traditions of political corruption and vigilante violence. Yet even in areas of mutual concern, Latins and African Americans wielded distinct organizing traditions. Only Latins, for instance, embraced strikes to pressure the local administrators of federal assistance programs, and the array of radical organizers in Tampa—Socialists, Communists, and anarchists—recruited far more Latins than African Americans to their cause. Despite these differences, many women of color in Tampa drew on traditions of mutual aid and collective action during the Depression, joining international battles for racial and economic justice and fighting discrimination in programs to assist those in need at home. In each case, women of color engaged in politics as work, devoting time, energy, and their skills as laborers and organizers to address the material and political needs of their communities in Tampa and beyond.

Although African American and Latin women rarely found common cause, each group was critical to developments in its own community, assuring that people of color throughout Tampa would sustain the cultures of resistance forged in more hopeful times. In this way, they carried traditions of mutual aid, solidarity, and political work through the Great Depression and into the civil rights movements of the World War II era and beyond.

NOTES

1. On tri-racial communities in the South, see Neil Foley, *The White Scourge: Mexicans, Blacks, and Poor Whites in Texas Cotton Culture* (Berkeley: University of California Press, 1997); and Sarah Deutsch, "Being American in Boley, Oklahoma," in *Beyond Black and White: Race, Ethnicity, and Gender in the U.S. South and Southwest*, ed. Stephanie Cole and Alison M. Parker, Walter Prescott Webb Memorial Lectures Series (College Station: Texas A & M University Press, 2004), 97–122. On radical organizing among Mexican Americans, see Vicki Ruiz, *From out of the Shadows: Mexican Women in Twentieth-Century America* (New York: Oxford University Press, 1998).

2. Language and cultural differences help to account for the absence of alliances among radical immigrants and African Americans. On militant organizing among working-class African Americans, including women, in the South, see Robert Korstad and Nelson Lichtenstein, "Opportunities Found and Lost: Labor, Radicals, and the Early Civil Rights Movement," *Journal of American History* 75 (December 1988): 786–811; Robin D. G. Kelley, *Hammer and Hoe: Alabama Communists during the Great Depression* (Chapel Hill: University of North Carolina Press, 1990); and Robert Korstad, *Civil Rights Unionism: Tobacco Workers and the Struggle for Democracy in the Mid-Twentieth-Century South* (Chapel Hill: University of North Carolina Press, 2003).

3. See Bernardo Vega, *Memoirs of Bernardo Vega: A Contribution to the History of the Puerto Rican Community in New York*, ed. Cesar Andreu Iglesias (New York: Monthly Review Press, 1984); Winston James, *Holding Aloft the Banner of Ethiopia: Caribbean Radicalism in Early Twentieth-Century America* (New York: Verso, 1998); and Ivette Marie Rivera-Giusti, "Gender, Labor, and Working-Class Activism in the Puerto Rican Tobacco Industry, 1898–1924" (Ph.D. diss., State University of New York at Binghamton, 2003).

4. See James, *Holding Aloft the Banner of Ethiopia*, esp. 4–5 and chapter 5; and Nancy A. Hewitt, *Southern Discomfort: Women's Activism in Tampa, Florida, 1880s–1920s* (Urbana: University of Illinois Press, 2001), 267–68.

5. On the history of Tampa's development, see Gary Mormino and George Pozzetta, *The Immigrant World of Ybor City: Italians and Their Latin Neighbors in Tampa, 1885–1985* (Urbana: University of Illinois Press, 1987), chapter 1; and Hewitt, *Southern Discomfort*, part I.

6. On Afro-Cubans in Tampa, see Susan D. Greenbaum, *More Than Black: Afro-Cubans in Tampa* (Gainesville: University Press of Florida, 2002).

7. On the use of the term "Latin" by the Industrial Workers of the World, which organized in Tampa in the 1910s, see James Barrett and David Roediger, "In Between Peoples: Race, Nationality, and the New Immigrant Working Class," *Journal of American Ethnic History* 16 (spring 1997): 25. On Latin identity, see also Linda Gordon, *The Great Arizona Orphan Abduction* (Cambridge, Mass: Harvard University Press, 1999), esp. 99–105.

8. On racial categories and race relations in Cuba at the turn of the twentieth century, see Aline Helig, *Our Rightful Share: The Afro-Cuban Struggle for Equality, 1886–1912* (Chapel

Hill: University of North Carolina Press, 1995), esp. 3–7; and Ada Ferrer, "Rethinking Race, Nation, and Empire," *Radical History Review* 73 (winter 1999): 22–46.

9. On the particular experiences of distinct racial and ethnic groups and tensions as well as commonalities between groups, see, for example, Mormino and Pozzetta, *Immigrant World of Ybor City*, chapter 8; and Greenbaum, *More Than Black*, chapter 2.

10. On the multi-ethnic composition of the African American community in Tampa, see Nancy A. Hewitt, "Becoming Black: Creating a Shared Identity among African Americans and Afro-Cubans in Tampa, 1880s–1920s," in *Black Women's History at the Intersection of Power and Knowledge*, ed. Janice Sumler-Edmond and Rosalyn Terborg-Penn (Acton, Mass. Tapestry Press, Ltd., 2000), 101–113.

11. On demographics, see Mormino and Pozzetta, *Immigrant World of Ybor City*, chapters 2 and 3; on formation of Latin and African American communities, see Hewitt, *Southern Discomfort*, part I.

12. On Latin radicalism, see Gerald Poyo, *"With All, and for the Good of All": The Emergence of Popular Nationalism in the Cuban Communities of the United States, 1848–1898* (Durham, N.C.: Duke University Press, 1989); and Robert P. Ingalls, *Urban Vigilantes in the New South: Tampa, 1882–1936* (Knoxville: University of Tennessee Press, 1988). On Latin women specifically, see Joan Marie Steffey, "The Cuban Immigrants of Tampa, Florida, 1886–1898" (MA thesis, University of South Florida, 1975); and Hewitt, *Southern Discomfort*. On traditions of African American activism, including women, see Kathleen S. Howe, "Stepping into Freedom: African Americans in Hillsborough County, Florida, during the Reconstruction Era," *Tampa Bay History* 20 (fall/winter 1998): 4–30; and Rowena Ferrell Brady, *Things Remembered: An Album of African Americans in Tampa* (Tampa: University of Tampa Press, 1997).

13. Nancy A. Hewitt, "In Pursuit of Power: The Political Economy of Women's Activism in Twentieth-Century Tampa," in *Visible Women: New Essays on American Activism,* ed. Nancy A. Hewitt and Suzanne Lebsock (Urbana: University of Illinois Press, 1993), 199–222; and Hewitt, *Southern Discomfort*, chapters 5 and 8.

14. Mark J. Prus, "Mechanisation and the Gender-based Division of Labour in the US Cigar Industry," *Cambridge Journal of Economics* 14 (1990): 63–79; and Jean Stubbs, *Tobacco on the Periphery: A Case Study of Cuban Labour History, 1860–1958* (Cambridge: Cambridge University Press, 1985); Mormino and Pozzetta, *Immigrant World of Ybor City*, 289–291; Ingalls, *Urban Vigilantes*, 149–150.

15. Benjamin Mays, *Born to Rebel: An Autobiography* (New York: Charles Scribner's and Sons, 1971), chapter 7.

16. On lynching in Florida, see James R. McGovern, *Anatomy of a Lynching: The Killing of Claude Neal* (Baton Rouge: Louisiana State University Press, 1982). On vigilante violence in Tampa, see Ingalls, *Urban Vigilantes*.

17. On Afro-Cuban migration northward during the Depression, see Greenbaum, *More Than Black*, 231–32.

18. See note 2 above.

19. Robert W. Saunders Sr., *Bridging the Gap: Continuing the Florida NAACP Legacy of Harry T. Moore* (Tampa: University of Tampa Press, 2000), 29 and 14–19.

20. Ibid., 28; Greenbaum, *More Than Black*, 245.

21. Saunders, *Bridging the Gap*, 28. On the Scottsboro case more generally, see James Goodman, *Stories of Scottsboro* (New York: Random House, 1994).

22. "West Coast Teachers Meet in Tampa," *Florida Sentinel*, October 25, 1930, Education: Miscellaneous File, box 2, Armwood Family Papers, Special Collections, University of South Florida, Tampa, Florida.

23. Saunders, *Bridging the Gap*, 32.

24. Clipping, *Tampa Weekly World*, n.d. [1934], Education: Miscellaneous File, box 2, Armwood Family Papers.

25. Brady, *Things Remembered*, 77; Paul Diggs, "Clara Frye Hospital," Federal Writers' Project Report, Florida Negro File, November 1938, typescript, Special Collections, University of South Florida.

26. See Andrew J. Ferrell Sr., "The History of St. Paul AME Church," in Brady, *Things Remembered*, 179–199.

27. Brady, *Things Remembered*, 103.

28. Papers of the National Association for the Advancement of Colored People, Part II, Youth File, 1919–1939, Microfilm, Reel 3, 0709, New York Public Library, New York.

29. On political corruption, see Mormino and Pozzetta, *Immigrant World of Ybor City*, 280–286; on use of violence by Tampa officials and citizens' committees, see Ingalls, *Urban Vigilantes*, passim.

30. Mrs. Daniel Fager to Harry Hopkins, October 17, 1935, RG 69, WPA Central Files: States, Florida, 1935, Works Progress Administration Papers, National Archives, Washington, D.C. (hereafter cited as WPA Papers, D.C.).

31. See, for example, "Blood Money of the Public Works Administration," pamphlet, RG 69, WPA Central Files: States, Florida, July 1937–July, 1938; David Lasser (National President, Workers' Alliance) to Aubrey Williams, August 12, 1937, RG 69, WPA Central Files: States, Florida, 1938; David L. Clendenen (Workers' Defense League)to Harry Hopkins, July 13, 1937, WPA Central Files: States, Florida, 1937; all WPA Papers, D.C. See also "WPA Head to Probe Charges of Favoritism," *Tampa Morning Tribune*, August 16, 1940.

32. W. M. Rowlett to Claude Pepper, November 2, 1938, RG 69, WPA Central Files: States, Florida, 1938, WPA Papers, D.C.

33. Frances A. Ewell, Narrative Report, Women's and Professional Division, WPA, December 1936, 2 and 27, Works Progress Administration Papers, P. K. Yonge Library, University of Florida, Gainesville.

34. Michael Lazarus to Alfred E. Smith, November 25, 1938, RG 69, WPA Central Files: States, Florida, 1938. See also letters to Tampa Urban League executive secretary, Cyrus T. Greene to Franklin Delano Roosevelt, June 17, 1935, and November 20, 1937, RG 69, WPA Central Files: States, Florida, 1935 and 1937; all WPA Papers, D.C.

35. Mabel T. Adams to Eleanor Roosevelt, April 26, 1939, RG 69, WPA Central Files: States, Florida, 1939, WPA Papers, D.C. See also Mabel Adams et al. to Manager, WPA Headquarters, April 11, 1939, WPA Papers, D.C.

36. Ingalls, *Urban Vigilantes*, 166–168.

37. Saunders, *Bridging the Gap*, 16; and McGovern, *Anatomy of a Lynching*.

38. Quote from ACLU, *Eternal Vigilance!* 13, in Ingalls, *Urban Vigilantes*, 200.

39. "NRA Program at St. Paul," clipping, Miscellaneous File, box 3, Armwood Family Papers.

40. "Golden Rule Alliance," clipping, n.d. [1934], Miscellaneous File, box 3, Armwood Family Papers.

41. Tampa Golden Rule Alliance, letterhead and clipping, n.d. [1934], Organizations File, box 3, Armwood Family Papers.

42. Brady, *Things Remembered*, 93.

43. See Nancy Raquel Mirabel, "Telling Silences and Making Community: Afro-Cubans and African Americans in Ybor City and Tampa," in *Between Race and Empire: African Americans and Cubans before the Cuban Revolution*, ed. Lisa Brock and Digna Castañeda Fuertes (Philadelphia: Temple University Press, 1998), 49–69; and Hewitt, "Becoming Black."

44. On readers, see Gary Mormino and George Pozzetta, " 'The Reader Lights the Candle': Cuban and Florida Cigar Workers' Oral Tradition," *Labor's Heritage* 5 (spring 1993): 4–27.

45. See Ingalls, *Urban Vigilantes*, 248, n. 214; and "Reports, Studies, and Surveys: The Cigar Industry," 7, RG 9, National Recovery Administration Records, National Archives, Washington, D.C. Ingalls notes that production dropped 17 percent and the cigar industry payroll 30 percent between 1929 and 1931 (Ingalls, *Urban Vigilantes*, 149–153).

46. Ingalls, *Urban Vigilantes*, 153–158.

47. Ibid., 154.

48. Ibid., 156.

49. Robert P. Ingalls, "The Tampa Flogging Case: Urban Vigilantism," *Florida Historical Quarterly* 56 (July 1977): 13–27.

50. See, for example, Mike [Bradford] to Comrade Weinstone, January 11 [1932], Communist Party U.S.A. Papers (hereafter cited as CPUSAP), Microfilm, Reel 233., Delo 3017, Frames 19–20; and Hy Gordon to Comrade Mills, July 3, 1932, CPUSAP, Reel 233, Delo 3017, frames 160–163, both in Tamiment Library, New York University, New York City.

51. Mike [Bradford] to Weinstone.

52. On AFL Convention, see Rolla A. Southworth, Narrative Report, November 1936, Women's and Professional Division, Works Progress Administration, WPA Papers, P.K. Yonge Library.

53. On Moreno, see Ruiz, *From out of the Shadows*, especially 95–96.

54. A. M. de Quesada, *Images of America: Ybor City* (Charleston, S.C.: Arcadia Publishing, 1999), 55, 56, 58, 61

55. Mormino and Pozzetta, *Immigrant World of Ybor City*, 182–183.

56. Ana M. Varela-Lago, " '!No Pasaran!': The Spanish Civil War's Impact on Tampa's Latin Community, 1936–1939," *Tampa Bay History* 19 (fall/winter 1997): 5–35; and William F. Garcia, "Tampa Does Not Forget Elisa Moris," *Volunteer* (summer 2000): 4.

57. Photo, Armentina M. Macias, used in promotional flyer for exhibit on "The Spanish Civil War Remembered," Centro Asturiano, Tampa, Florida, November 1997, in author's possession.

58. Varela-Lago, " '!No Pasaran!' " 16–17.

59. Ibid., 15–16; quote from *Tampa Daily Times*, May 7, 1937.

60. Varela-Lago, " '!No Pasaran!' " 17; and conversation with Delia Sanchez, March 16, 2005, Tony Pizzo Memorial Lecture, Tampa, Florida.

61. Varela-Lago, " '!No Pasaran!' " 18–19, 22.

62. James Tidd, "Stitching and Striking: WPA Sewing Rooms and the 1937 Relief Strike in Hillsborough County," *Tampa Bay History* 11 (spring/summer 1989): 5–21; and Elna Green, "Relief from Relief: The Tampa Sewing Room Strike of 1937," manuscript in author's possession.

63. Tidd, "Stitching and Striking," 10–11.

64. Ibid.; and Green, "Relief from Relief," 1–9, 11–12.

65. *Tampa Morning Tribune*, July 9, 1937; and Green, "Relief from Relief," 14–17.

66. *La Gaceta*, July 9, 1937, quoted in Tidd, "Stitching and Striking," 13.

67. Tidd, "Stitching and Striking," 16–17, 18.

68. WPA Narrative Report, July 1937, quoted in Tidd, "Stitching and Striking," 15.

69. Green, "Relief from Relief," 22–23.

70. On the convergence of Afro-Cuban and African American activism, see Greenbaum, *More than Black*, chapter 7; and Hewitt, "Becoming Black."

PART II

THE GLOBAL POLITICS OF LABOR

Surviving Globalization

IMMIGRANT WOMEN WORKERS IN LATE CAPITALIST AMERICA

EVELYN HU-DEHART

Rosario Jocha, forty-nine, stands at the corner of Eighth Avenue and Thirty-seventh Street in Manhattan, in the heart of the fashion district, hoping to be picked up for a day's work. She said she had recently grabbed at the chance to cut threads from jackets for $5.75 an hour, twenty-four cents below New York State's minimum wage. The man who offered the job was a Chinese immigrant subcontractor who said he could not pay more. "What else is there to do if you have nothing to eat?" Rosario lamented, adding, "I've been here eleven years, and I still have not found a stable, steady job." Like Rosario, an immigrant from Ecuador, Rosa Yumbla supports four children left at home. She said, "We suffer the changing weather throughout the year, the heat of the sun and cold in winter, because where we wait to be picked up is on the street." And Nellie, thirty-two, also from Ecuador, pulls out a picture of the three children she left behind under her sister's care while she tries to earn enough money as a contingent worker doing casual work for the heart operation needed by her son, the youngest child. "The little I make here I send to him," she said. "Many times I just want to go to be with him, but I don't have the money to do so. It gives me a desperate feeling."[1] Immigrants waiting at urban street corners hoping to be picked up for a day or two of work at minimum wage or less is no longer just a male phenomenon, as the *New York Times* recently discovered; it is fast gaining a female dimension that can no longer be ignored.

Meanwhile, on the other coast in San Francisco, police broke up in early July 2005 a sex-trafficking operation that supplied Korean women for brothels and massage parlors in the Bay Area. All over Southern California, in cities like Santa Monica, Los Angeles, and Rodondo Beach, hundreds of South Korean women worked as prostitutes, having also been smuggled into the country. These prostitutes were managed by an underground network of Korean "taxi" services that coordinated the prostitutes' daily schedules, working closely with brothel operators to deliver the women to their clients. The operators even arranged to fly prostitutes to work in Las Vegas, Dallas, New York, and Boston.[2]

These women are among the newly revealed faces of globalization moving from the Third World periphery or global South straight to the belly of the beast of the global North or core, the United States. This chapter summarizes the considerable research on the system of global production and the role of immigrant women workers in the formal or visible economies, such as electronics and garment, while prying open the window on the less well studied and less visible informal economies of globalization, such as home, nursing, and elderly care; housecleaning; child care; sex work; and street vendoring. While many of these immigrant women workers came as part of the massive legal immigration flow, many others form part of the estimated 10 million undocumented workers in the United States.

De-industrialization and Globalization

De-industrialization in the global core, the United States, was the other side of the coin of a restructured international economy, where an innovative development strategy called export-based industrialization (EBI) was adopted by the global periphery, the newly developing Asian countries soon dubbed NIC's (newly industrializing country); that is, Taiwan, Hong Kong, Singapore, South Korea, followed by Thailand, Indonesia, and Vietnam. Japan was there at the beginning, but the sleeping communist giant, the People's Republic of China, would not get on the radar screen until later. And for reasons beyond the scope of this chapter to explore, the highly populous India did not immediately join the switch from import-substitution industrialization to this new export-based industrialization, perhaps because, after hundreds of years of British colonial rule, and being more committed to establishing democracy than most of its neighbors, the ruling Congress Party did not relish the idea of being overwhelmed by foreign investment and consequent foreign control that inevitably accompanied this new development strategy. Essentially, the Asian NIC's agreed to a new international division of labor with the United States by accepting large doses of U.S. investment to set up light manufacturing in jerry-built factories located on specially designated lands appropriately named "export processing zones" (EPZ) or "free trade zones" (FTZ). Here, the largely authoritarian, staunchly anti-communist governments, some military in nature, offered the advanced, capitalist, multi- or transnational corporations cheap Third World labor to assemble finished products from materials supplied by first world investors, for export back to the first world nations.[3] Electronics, toys, athletic shoes, and apparel represent the majority of products in these EPZ factories. "The removal of barriers to free trade and the close integration of national economies," according to economist Joseph Stiglitz, is a good definition of globalization.[4]

Although many of these export zones are located on the Asia Pacific Rim, the prototype was the Border Industrialization Project (BIP), established in 1969 on the Mexican side of the U.S.-Mexican border, which gave rise to thousands of assembly plants called *maquiladoras* (or *maquilas,* for short), now transitioned into the backbone of the North American Free Trade Agreement (NAFTA) between Canada, the United States, and Mexico. During the past decade, maquilas have also moved well beyond the northern border zone deep into the heart of Mexico, all the way south to the Yucatán to take advantage of the cheap labor of indigenous Mayan women. In addition, EPZ's have also proliferated all over Central America, in countries like Honduras, Guatemala, El Salvador, Nicaragua, as well as the Caribbean.[5] In addition to North Americans, other big corporate maquila investors come from Japan, South Korea, Taiwan, Hong Kong, and assorted European countries such as Germany.[6] The "giant sucking sound" that pierced Ross Perot's ears was that of jobs flowing southward to Mexico, the Caribbean, and Central America, and eastward across the Pacific as the United States eliminated industrial jobs. During this de-industrialization phase in the global core, the United States simultaneously experienced a rapid rise in service employment at both the high- and low-skilled end. In this country, the non-manufacturing labor force came to constitute 84.3 percent of the total (measured in hours) by 1996, or a growth of almost 30 million jobs since 1979.[7] In time, some Asian countries that had prospered from early export-based industrialization—notably Japan, Singapore, Taiwan, and Hong Kong (before re-integration with China)—themselves became exporters of finance capital, setting up assembly plants in poor and densely populated Asian countries such as Indonesia, Thailand, and China, as well as in Mexico, Central American, and the Caribbean, as noted above. In sum, globalization in late capitalism changes relations of production, marked by a labor strategy that stresses minimizing cost and maximizing flexibility. It is characterized by a shift from a Fordist or vertically integrated (characterized by the assembly line) system of production to a leaner and fragmented production process, with greater "spatial mobility" for both capital and labor.

The Global Sweatshop: Subcontracting and Outsourcing

Amazingly, global capital and production, in continuous and relentless search for cheap labor, manufacturing flexibility, and spatial mobility, have come full circle: the global assembly plant employing low-skill, low-cost female labor can now be found in abundance in the global core, the United States itself, in the form of hundreds of electronics assembly plants in the Silicon Valley of Northern California as well as factories in the apparel industry of Southern California, the San Francisco–Oakland area, and in and around New York's garment district and Chinatowns (in Manhattan and Queens). Although clothing manufacturing has constituted a mainstay of the Mexican maquilas and fly-by-night assembly plants set up in EPZ's all over Asia itself, fast-changing designs and fluctuating market demands of the garment business have dictated the need to produce certain styles and quantities close to the retailers (big department stores), manufacturers (labels), and consumers in the United States.

Central to global production is the subcontracting system, a pyramid-shaped hierarchy consisting of a small number of U.S.-based manufacturers and retailers at the top, several thousand Third World–based contractors in the middle, and massive numbers of Third World workers at the bottom, most of them women. The exact same system is adapted to conditions in the United States, where outsourcing is localized, and subcontractors and workers co-exist in the same crowded urban space. Intense competition in this business has revitalized the garment sweatshop—defined as factories that fail to meet minimum wage, labor, and safety standards according to the law and state and local regulations—in New York and California. Mostly young female immigrants from Asia, Mexico, and Central America (legal and undocumented) have quickly filled the labor needs of hundreds of subcontractors operating small factories and sweatshops, doing the same work they would in their home countries had they not migrated to the Unites States.[8] Immigrant entrepreneurs, especially Koreans and Chinese, increasingly fill the ranks of subcontractors in New York and California.

While hidden for years from the American consuming public and the media, the revived American sweatshop is no longer a secret, its exposé helping to fuel the anti-globalization movement. The raid on the El Monte (California) underground sweatshop in August 1995 freed seventy-two Thai workers (sixty-seven women, five men) smuggled into the country by the Thai-Chinese owners, who contracted with several well-known U.S. brand-name manufacturers. Paid only $1.60 per hour, these workers were kept in a modern version of indentured servitude, denied their freedom to leave the barbed-wire compound, forced to pay off their passage, threatened with rape and retribution against family members back home if they disobeyed their captors. In January 1999, the media exposed another shameful sweatshop situation that resembled El Monte. Hundreds of sweatshops owned by Asians and Asian American subcontractors were found in the U.S. Pacific territory of Saipan, where workers, predominately young women from the Philippines, China, Thailand, and Bangladesh, worked twelve hours daily, seven days weekly, living seven to a room in "dreary barracks surrounded by inward-facing barbed wire."[9]

The Electronics Industry: Prototype of the Global Sweatshop

An early form of the global sweatshop was actually not about clothes or shoes, but accompanied the rise of the U.S. electronics industry, based on revolutionary new technology of the 1960s and 1970s. Labor relations patterns established in this industry would re-appear later in other industries that relied heavily on immigrant, particularly immigrant women, labor. Renewed immigration from the Third World in the mid-1960s coincided with the postwar rise of the electronics/semiconductor industry, centered in the Silicon Valley of Santa Clara County, south of San Francisco and down the road from Stanford University, where much of the new technology was incubated. Its highly sophisticated technology notwithstanding, the semiconductor industry retained a component that is very labor intensive and requires "hand-eye coordination" in assembly work that is difficult to automate.[10] From the very beginning, much of this work was subcontracted out to export zones in Asia and Mexico, where docile, patient, manually dexterous, and, best of all, cheap labor, provided by young, unmarried "girls," was in abundance. As it turned out, the largely married and older women of the newly settled Asian immigrant communities in the emerging Silicon Valley proved equally adept and eager for this kind of work, in the absence of better paying jobs for new immigrants with little or no English skills.[11] Feminization of localized assembly plants occurred rapidly: in San Jose, from just 6,900 in 1966, the number of women workers rose to 18,288 by 1978.[12] For the entire Silicon Valley, some 70,000 women made up the bulk of the production workforce in the 1980s and held close to 90 percent of "operative" and "laborer" jobs on the factory floor. Of these women, 45 to 50 percent were Third World immigrant women, including undocumented ones from Mexico and Central America,[13] while white women moved into clerical and white-collar positions. From 1966 to 1978, Latina and Asian women in the workforce doubled, from 23 percent to 45 percent. During this period, the $4.91 hourly wage they earned fell behind the $5.69 blue-collar wages in other industries.[14] So while electronics production was being internationalized, the lowest-paid, least-skilled, most dead-end, highest turnover, least stable jobs were held by the same Third World women, whether they worked in the Third World itself or as immigrants to the United States.

Ironically, notes economist Linda Lim, "it is the *comparative disadvantage* of women [italics in original] in the wage labor market that gives them a *comparative advantage* [italics added] vis-à-vis men in the occupations and industries where they [women] are concentrated." These women-dominated niches became known as "female ghettos of employment," the jobs as "women's work."[15] By characterizing assemble-type manufacturing thus, the clear suggestion is that such jobs are somehow naturally or inherently more suited for women, or that women are innately more suited for the work, given their natural patience, dexterity, docility, discipline, and other similar traits. Further debasing and undervaluing women's work, managers in the Silicon Valley often suggested that the immigrant women workers were only "temporary" and their incomes "secondary," next to their spouses, and that they were, by choice, "mothers" first. Thus these women workers were deemed not "career-minded" and hence did not mind dead-end jobs with few advancement possibilities.[16] Furthermore, if these workers were induced to think of themselves as "temporary," and were seen by others as such, then they would not likely seek unionization, nor would unions be interested in them. Thus, a perfectly designed, segregated, segmented, and secondary labor market has been created for the downgraded manufacturing sector of the otherwise high-tech industry.[17] In the next section, we will see how critics expose these arguments as constructed or manufactured rationalizations for exploitation of immigrant women's work.

If most of the assembly jobs in the electronics industry were shifted overseas early, why did any have to remain in the Silicon Valley, where the mental and creative work of design and innovation is done? The reason is similar to why the garment industry also created production capacities closer to home: an ongoing need for "quickly available prototypic and short term products" in this fast-changing technological field.[18] But if it were not for the arrival of Third World immigrant women, Silicon Valley industries might not have been able to afford building a parallel assembly infrastructure right at home, given competition from cheap wages in the Third World. As it were, Silicon Valley, in fact, was able to replicate at the *core* a domestic version of the stratified system—by race, sex, and class—that has been euphemistically termed an "international division of labor" at the *periphery* of the restructured global economy.

The Underside of Globalization

The maquiladoras in Mexico, the export-processing factories in Asia and Central America, the electronic assembly plants and garment sweatshops in the United States—these are the unattractive public faces of globalization in late capitalist or de-industrialized America, appropriately and rather ominously dubbed by President George W. Bush as the New World Order. Do sweatshops represent the trickle-down dividends of globalization by creating jobs, as global boosters would have us believe,[19] or do they represent "lurid examples of random inhumanity," as critics such as William Greider charge?[20] Or, as Stiglitz alleges, U.S.-driven globalization has not only *not* reduced poverty around the world, but exacerbated the gap between rich and poor nations.[21]

There is now considerable research and published literature that supports Greider's and Stiglitz's observations and conclusions, especially when globalization is viewed from the perspective of immigrant women at the global periphery (Asia, Latin America, the Caribbean), many of whom, driven by growing poverty at home, have been moving to the global core (the United States). What follows is a discussion of what can be termed the underside of globalization—or globalization and its discontents, to borrow a term from Stiglitz—and how this perspective reframes the points raised above around subcontracting and outsourcing, immigration, free trade, and exploitation of female labor, especially in the informal sector.

Race to the Bottom

Corporate-led globalization depends on intense exploitation of labor, exacerbated by the subcontracting system that answers to the logic of a race to the bottom of the wage scale. To win a contract, the subcontractor must submit the lowest bid; he then squeezes the workers to make his profit. Third world women at home and immigrant women from these countries in the United States bear the brunt of this brutal logic. They are constantly fearful of losing their jobs to even more vulnerable women somewhere in the world who would work for even less wages under even more abysmal conditions. As Bonacich and Appelbaum conclude, "We believe that the current system of globalized, highly flexible production creates a new kind of labor regime and labor discipline. Workers are kept under control by the mobility and dispersal of the industry. This system, which constantly threatens job loss, and severely inhibits labor struggles, keeps workers toiling at breakneck speed for long hours and low wages. They do not require coercive oversight to achieve the desired effect."[22]

Third world women workers in their home countries and Third World immigrant women in the United States form one continuum in the same gendered and transnational workforce which lies at the base of globalization and its international subcontracting system. Whether they work in a Nike plant subcontracted to a Taiwanese factory owner in Indonesia or Vietnam or as contract workers in an Asian-owned Saipan factor, or in an unregistered, underground sweatshop in Los Angeles operated by a Korean immigrant, or in a union shop in New York's Chinatown owned by a newly naturalized Chinese American, they may well be sewing the same style for the same manufacturer, affixing the same label on the finished garment. Given this, labor activists and immigrant rights advocates must adopt a globalized strategy of resistance to combat abuses in the workplace.[23]

Rationalizations for Low Wages

"Nimble fingers" and "bootstrap" myths have emerged to justify this intense exploitation of Third World women on the global periphery and immigrant women in the global core as natural, inevitable, and even desirable. These women are characterized as inherently, innately, and naturally suited for the kind of low-skill labor needed in light manufacturing, whether in Third World export-processing factories or in U.S. electronic assembly plants and sweatshops. Critics charge that this is nothing less than rationalization for low wages, not to mention justification for the perpetuation of the notion of Third World women's cognitive inferiority. It is not just the gendered quality of the division of labor that is so problematic, but that the gendered division is inferred and inscribed in a permanent hierarchy that is further reinforced by race, class, and nationality differences, as well as denial of immigration and citizenship rights in the case of the smuggled and undocumented.

What is so inherent about poor Third World women that should render them into "cheap and docile labor," cultural critic Laura Hyun Hi Kang pointedly asks, "as if depressed wages and workplace discipline were ontological properties unique to Asian women rather than historically specific, culturally dictated, and closely managed conditions." Can it be that the preponderance of young women employed in EPZ's is less the result of a "natural supply" than "a consciously pursued strategy" on the part of transnational corporations (TNC) and authoritarian governments alike? "The mobilization of disproportionate numbers of young Asian women in these TNC factories is thus revealed to be the modus operandi of corporate managers and not a sign of their innate fitness for these jobs," Kang concludes.[24] In short, we must begin to disabuse ourselves of believing in the inevitability of the grossly inequitable and exploitative gendered division of labor in the global assembly line, one in which the gendered position is fixed and immutable and usually not a transition to some better condition. More than just protesting abuses in the system, we must begin to question its rationality and logic in the first place.

Another kind of frequently voiced rhetoric rationalizing exploitation of immigrant women is the bootstrap myth: that sewing jobs are steps leading to the American dream, there for the ambitious Mexican women to grasp. As one Southern California manufacturer puts it in direct, no-nonsense terms: "We provide entry-level jobs for women, for Mexican women. These women have no other options; they can either do this or become dish washers. Working in a garment factory requires learning some skills. Maybe they are being taken advantage of, but they have a choice. No one is holding a gun to their heads. They come in at minimum wage, get some training, and can then put their children through college. It is the great American Dream!"[25] For a handful of Korean garment workers who immigrate with some capital and first enter the factory to learn the business, then quickly move on to being a subcontractor, the American dream may come true. But the reality for the vast majority of immigrant, particularly Latina, workers is closer to that of the thirty-five-year-old single mother Salvadoran garment-machine operative who worked in the same garment factory for fourteen years without ever receiving a raise.[26]

Not surprisingly, garment manufacturers are also stridently anti-union, advancing a logic similar to that employed to argue the bootstrap myth. Union drives by UNITE (Union of Needletrades, Industrial, and Textile Employees),[27] they argue, "may unwittingly serve to break the back of an industry that has been one of the key routes of upward mobility for immigrant entrepreneurs and workers"; and if union drives succeed, they warn, the LA garment "miracle" would become a "nightmare," with "tens of thousands of workers thrown into the street."[28]

The Rich Get Richer

Increased trade spurred on by decreased regulation and removal of all barriers does not necessarily produce better jobs. If anything, removal of regulations only serves to increase the power of wealthier nations (the North) over poorer ones (the South). Thus, unregulated global free trade will disproportionately benefit the already wealthy nations to the great disadvantage of the poor nations, enabling a few corporations and individuals to become fabulously, obscenely rich while deepening the misery of the world's multitudinous poor. Many new studies have demonstrated the growing gap *between* and *within* nations, with the

United States a notable example of both kinds of inequalities.[29] As some critics have pointed out, contrary to the World Bank's bald assertion that accelerated globalization has produced greater world equality, the rising tide of globalization, far from lifting all boats, is "only lifting yachts!"[30] Today, the world's richest two hundred individuals have more wealth than 41 percent of the world's humanity.[31] Growing impoverishment in the global South is driving a "globalization of migration"—men, women, and children leaving for the global North in search of jobs and livelihood. In this context, immigration is not merely a simple matter of individuals or families making decisions to move and relocate, but becomes a de facto survival strategy. In the words of sociologist Arlie Hochschild, "migration has become a private solution to a public problem."[32]

Immigrants Are Indispensable

Immigrants are not only *not* a drain on the U.S. economy, but an absolute necessity, especially women immigrants, who comprise half or more of new immigrants to the United States. Immigrant labor is indispensable for the labor-intensive, service-dependent, restructured economy of the United States, as well as for the resurgent light manufacturing sector, captured at its worst by the image of the garment sweatshop.[33] Lately, well-educated and professionally trained immigrant labor is also in great demand in the computer programming sector of the Silicon Valley.[34] The role of the INS (since September 11, 2001, removed from the Justice Department and absorbed into Homeland Security as ICE, Immigration and Customs Enforcement) is not to stop the flow of immigration to the United States so much as to regulate the level of that flow and to control the type of immigrants who come in at any given time.[35] When demand for new workers surges in any critical sector of the economy, as periodically happens in the high-tech industry of places like Silicon Valley or in the low-tech industries of agriculture in the West, meatpacking in the Midwest,[36] and poultry in the South,[37] the government is perfectly capable and willing to "look the other way."[38] In the booming economy of the Clinton years, with unemployment at just 4 percent and a strong demand for people to take jobs paying $8.00 an hour or less, which were 25 percent of all jobs, mostly immigrants—both legal and undocumented—made up the pool of applicants for these jobs.[39] Is U.S. immigration policy just an undetected contradiction or part and parcel of another unspoken logic in global capitalism, alongside the manic logic of the subcontracting system? Until very recently, even the U.S. labor movement subscribed to the arbitrary line invented by the government to differentiate between legal, thus good, immigrants and illegal, thus bad, immigrants. That colossal canard was finally laid to rest when the Service Employees International Union (SEIU) led its eighty-five hundred janitors, many of them "illegal aliens" from Mexico, Central America, and Asia, on successful strikes in downtown Chicago and Los Angeles, where they cleaned high-rise office buildings.[40] In the face of this new reality of globalized labor,

AFL-CIO's leader, John Sweeney, finally proclaimed at the dawn of the new millennium a "new internationalism" for American unions.[41]

Informalization of Labor

Informalization of labor is a growing phenomenon under globalization, both in the global core (the United States) and the periphery (Mexico, Central America, the Caribbean, and Asia). Even more than other jobs, work in the informal economies mainly engages immigrant women, usually the poorest or most recent arrivals among them. Underground sweatshops, such as the infamous El Monte noted above, only scratch the surface of this hidden or invisible aspect of globalized labor. In fact, much of the work in informal economies is above ground and visible to anyone who cares to look and acknowledge benefits from the labor of those who toil in this sector. Hidden in plain sight, immigrant women workers are, indeed, everywhere, because for the most part, informal economies exist side by side with formal economies and are often different sides of the same coin. They are income-generating or income-substituting activities that hover under the radar screen of our collective consciousness.

In the informal economy, wages are paid in cash and thus not reported and not taxed. Employers own and operate very small enterprises, such as factories with ten or fewer workers. Work hours are flexible, and no labor, occupational health, or safety laws are observed. There are, of course, no benefits and no unions and no government oversight. In short, there is no contractual relationship between capital (employer) and labor (worker). Workers work "off the books" and are paid "under the table." Various types of the self-employed, like independent contractors and small business owners, can also be found in abundance in informal economies. Distinguished from criminal and illicit activities, such as drug running, they are, in fact, similar economic activities performed or produced in the formal sector but under conditions described above.[42]

In the garment industry, sweatshops, particularly underground sweatshops such as the notorious El Monte and Saipan examples, represent the informal sector of this economy because they flaunt wage and labor laws and other regulations. But while sweatshops have been exposed and denounced, there are other less visible instances of informal labor in garment and electronics assembly work. Called "industrial home work" when women workers moonlight after a regular workday in the plant by taking more work home, this is the most invisible kind of informal labor because it is performed in the privacy of the home. It is usually paid at piece rate, that is, by the number of completed tasks. In garment work, home work tasks usually entail finishing touches, such as cutting loose threads or sewing on buttons, tasks to which children can and do contribute.

In electronics, home work entails fusing components onto electronic boards or repairing and modifying older boards. Children and other family members, such as the elderly, often participate in speeding up production at home in order to maximize earnings, but unwittingly also share in the exposure to toxic chemicals from which they have no protection. For pregnant women who accept electronics home work for obvious reasons, the health consequences can be very severe. These low-tech and manual tasks of informal labor occur at home, alongside the highly automated assembly-floor jobs that pay regular wages. In fact, subcontractors recruit and sub-subcontract work to home workers; they deliver and collect work from the homes.[43]

To be sure, for some women, home work is one way to increase their income, an option they exercise along with job-hopping and working overtime. For those who have to juggle child care and other household duties, home work gives them more flexibility and perhaps a sense of greater control over their work. For other women who feel alienated from the oppressive environment on the job floor, home work may give them a chance to feel "independent," to earn what they want and work when they want, away from the prying eyes of supervisors. Of course, piece rate pay usually translates into less than minimum wage, no overtime, no breaks, no benefits, thus further downgrading the work of women for the industries. It means that they work at jobs, sometimes dangerous and toxic ones, totally eluding the scrutiny of government inspectors. Meanwhile, for managers and subcontractors, home work affords them a more flexible strategy to meet production goals and deadlines, reasons why they embrace the practice.[44] When home becomes a site for the global market under these totally unregulated conditions, immigrant women and families find themselves in a work situation not unlike a sweatshop.[45] Workers not only exploit themselves by speeding up work to earn more, but may need to exploit their family members, including children, without adequate remuneration.

Another category of informal labor can be grouped under the rubric of social reproductive work. If industrial home work is largely secluded and invisible, social reproductive work permeates the lives of middle- and upper-class families in America, especially when women of these families—mothers and wives—also work outside the home. While industrial home work is performed in the privacy of the worker's home, social reproductive labor is usually conducted in the client's space and delivered personally, sometimes intimately, and often emotionally. Whether working as nannies or housekeepers, in child care or elder care, for the sick or the young, as cooks or nurses, and as prostitutes, in massage parlors, even as mail-order brides, Third World immigrant women providing these services are not just making a living in low-paying, low-status occupational niches that require little English or few skills. In a very crucial way, they too are part of the new transnational division of labor, their paid labor replacing the previously unremunerated responsibilities of first world women in the social reproduction of daily and family life, in the renewal of intimacy and conveyance of emotional love. On a daily and intergenerational basis, they relieve professional first world women of much of the burden of the "second shift." Such social reproductive labor has always been associated with women's work and continues to be debased and devalued when industrialized or commodified, that is, performed for payment by Third World immigrant women for their largely white, first world "sisters" in a racial division of labor.[46] Barbara Ehrenreich has very aptly dubbed this kind of work "outsourcing the work of the home."[47]

Increasingly, American middle-class working women have joined upper-class women to access other women for social reproductive labor, with women performing such labor overwhelmingly Latina and Asian. The 1990 U.S. census recorded 28,859 domestics working as maids, housekeepers, and child care providers in private homes; over 80 percent identified as "Hispanics."[48] Because of the informality of such work, the actual numbers are probably many times higher. In sum, "most white middle class women could hire another woman—a recent immigrant, a working-class woman, a women of color, or all these—to perform much of the hard labor of household tasks" as they fulfill themselves in careers outside the home.[49] The "private sphere" responsibilities of class-privileged women are thereby transferred to racially and socially subordinate women.[50] Even immigrant women who find domestic employment through co-ethnic brokers remain largely informal or contingent workers, as they have little job security, irregular hours, and no benefits, can be hired or fired instantly, and are paid hourly or by the job.[51] Many of these maids and home caregivers, whether caring for children or the elderly, are undocumented; for them, informal work is their only option.[52]

This discussion on informal immigrant labor would not be complete without acknowledgment of sex work, perhaps the most contingent of informal labor. Asian women as preferred sex partners—paid or even unpaid in the case of military wives and mail-order (now Internet) brides—for some American men dates back to the days of America's serial military involvement in Asia, from World War II through the Korean War and the Vietnam War. "Militarized prostitution" developed around all the army bases in Asia, while American soldiers on furlough for "rest and relaxation" stimulated the development and growth of sex tourism to countries far beyond the battlegrounds, such as to Bangkok.[53] Just as American transnational capital has constructed Third World women, whether "over there" or after migration to the United States, as particularly adept at electronics and garment assembly work, so American men have imagined these same women as particularly seductive as girlfriends, attentive and submissive as wives, and, best of all, not "corrupted" by Western feminist ideas and values.

Some sex workers are self-employed in small businesses, such as massage parlors. Structurally, the massage parlor operates like an agency, with workers as "independent contractors" working with their own clients, sometimes off the books. Typically, masseuses are not paid a wage, nor guaranteed work, but provided with space at the parlor to meet their clients, with whom they negotiate desired services. The women pay the massage parlor owner a cut of their take from each customer.[54] U.S. morality laws criminalize sex workers by arresting them after sweeping streets or raiding massage parlors. Criminalization drives sex workers further underground to avoid detection and exposure, thus intensifying the already informal nature of sex work, making it even more difficult to address their right to be considered like other working people, deserving of decent wages and safe and humane working conditions.[55] Furthermore, criminalization adds another layer of oppression to the already multilayered system under which immigrant women labor, condemning them as noncitizen, criminal, and morally corrupt.[56]

Many types of self-employment can be found in informal economies, one of which has become well known as a Latino/Latina niche in Southern California. These are the street vendors—mostly Mexican and Central American women—who hock their food and other wares on freeway entry or exit ramps, in the center island divides of major boulevards, and on sidewalks of ethnic neighborhoods. They complement formal-sector food businesses such as supermarkets, restaurants, and bakeries.[57]

Informality is already highly feminized. It is likely to become more gendered and more likely to proliferate, spreading out from places like the U.S.-Mexican border, where it has always been prevalent and known, indeed, as the "Mexican solution."[58] To escape poverty, people on the border pursue multiple strategies with multiple earners in a household, sometimes straddling both sides of the border, often with one foot planted in a wage job and the other dallying in an informal economic activity. Many on the Mexican side may eventually choose migration as the ultimate solution, cross the border, and basically continue what they and so many other Mexicans have always done to survive globalization, pursuing the elusive *casa de mis sueños* (house of my dreams).[59]

Conclusion: The Evolving Logic of Globalization

We began this chapter with an emblematic story of contingent workers in an increasingly familiar kind of work associated with immigrant women, slowly unmasking the invisibility surrounding informal labor. We close with the next big story on the global horizon, one that has already taken the United States by storm, leaving much of the public perplexed and worried about their well-being. I am referring to the exporting of information-based service-sector jobs, previously thought immune to elimination from the American workscape under the logic of globalization.

This is a transnational story, like so many under globalization, but with a novel twist. On one side of the global divide, welfare recipients in Kansas, Arizona, Alabama, and Tennessee dial their usual toll-free number to inquire about their next check. Welfare mothers from New Jersey are especially anxious as they have been notified their checks will soon be cut off because they should be getting jobs. On the other side, in far off Bombay, India, a soft voice identifying herself as

Megan takes the calls. "How can I help you?" she asks in her mild southern drawl as she attempts to answer questions about benefits and food stamp balances, patiently waiting out angry tirades, quietly listening to the sobs of stressed-out young single mothers at rope's end.

Megan is really Manisha Martin, twenty-seven, a worker at an Indian call center. Her employer is a subcontractor for a company based in Scottsdale, Arizona, which is in turn the subcontractor for various state welfare agencies to handle calls from their welfare recipients. Her training included learning a clearly identifiable American accent, hence the southern drawl, and learning to be vague about her location or other personal data if asked. Martin and others doing similar work earn about two hundred dollars a month, less than what the American welfare recipients receive but much higher than the five hundred dollar average yearly income in India. The over-educated Indian college graduate undoubtedly appreciates her significant economic uplift, but the problem is that the New Jersey welfare mother forced off the rolls and ordered to get work just saw one of the few jobs she was likely qualified to do slip away.[60] While one poor woman survived globalization, the other did not; ironically, the one who fell through the threadbare safety net lives in the United States, heart of the global core, very likely a woman of color herself.

On the other side of the U.S.-Mexican border, high-tech data work called "informatics" has also been outsourced from the United States. In these maquiladoras, as at similar sites in the Caribbean, China, the Philippines, South Korea, Sri Lanka, Malaysia, and Ghana, young women hunch over computer keyboards, "fingers flying" as they digitize U.S. and European market research surveys, insurance claims, airline tickets, package delivery invoices, credit card applications, even books, New York City parking tickets, U.S. medical doctors' scribbles, and a myriad of other data-processing work made possible by rapidly developing new satellite and telecommunications technology.[61] Again, these are jobs that U.S. women of color and immigrant women already here can perform, but Third World women can do them just as well and for much less. Will these jobs stem the tide of women pouring into the United States from India, China, the Philippines, and other parts of Asia and from Mexico? Probably not, as free trade continues to push more Mexicans deeper into poverty, and jobs are not created fast enough in India.[62]

NOTES

1. Nina Bernstein, "Invisible to Most, Immigrant Women Line up for Day Labor," *New York Times*, August 15, 2005 (online edition).

2. Jason Van Derbeken and Ryan Kim, "Alleged Sex-Trade Ring Broken up in Bay Area," *San Francisco Chronicle*, July 2, 2004, A1 and A9.

3. Swasti Mitter, *Common Fate, Common Bond: Women in the Global Economy*. (London: Pluto Press, 1986); Helen I. Safa, "Runaway Shops and Female Employment: The Search for Cheap Labor," *SIGNS: Journal of Women in Culture and Society* 7, no. 2 (1981): 418–433; David A. Smith,

"Going South: Global Restructuring and Garment Production in Three East Asian Cases," *Asian Perspectives* 20, no. 2 (fall–winter 1996): 211–241; Saskia Sassen, *The Mobility of Labor and Capital. A Study in International Investment and Labor Flow* (New York: Cambridge University Press, 1988); Saskia Sassen-Koob, "Notes on the Incorporation of Third World Women into Wage Labor through Immigration and Off-Shore Production," *International Migration Review* 18, no. 4 (1983): 1144–1167; Paul Ong, Edna Bonacich, and Lucie Cheng, "The Political Economy of Capitalist Restructuring and the New Asian Immigrants," in *The New Asian Immigration in Los Angeles and Global Restructuring*, ed. Paul Ong, Edna Bonacich, and Lucie Cheng (Philadelphia: Temple University Press, 1992): 3–43; Gary Gereffi, "Global Sourcing and Regional Divisions of Labor in the Pacific Rim," in *What Is in a Rim? Critical Perspectives on the Pacific Region Idea*, 2nd. rev. ed., ed. Arif Dirlik (Lanham, Md.: Rowman & Littlefield, 1997), 143–161.

4. Joseph E. Stiglitz, *Globalization and Its Discontents* (New York: Norton, 2002), ix.

5. Evelyn Hu-DeHart, introduction to *Across the Pacific: Asian American Formations in the Age of Globalization*, ed. Evelyn Hu-DeHart (Philadelphia: Temple University Press, 2000), 1–28; Evelyn Hu-DeHart, "Asian Women Immigrants in the U.S. Fashion Garment Industry," in *Women and Work in Globalising Asia*, ed. Dong-Sook S. Gills and Nicola Piper (London: Routledge, 2002), 209–230; Annette Fuentes and Barbara Ehrenreich, *Women in the Global Factory* (Boston: South End Press, 1983); Mary Beth Sheridan, "Riding Ripples of a Border Boom," *Los Angeles Times*, June 9, 1996, A1, A8; Leslie Kaufman and David González, "Labor Progress Clashes with Global Reality," *New York Times*, April 24, 1999, A1, A10; Elizabeth Becker, "Central American Deal Ignites a Trade Debate," *New York Times*, April 6, 2002, C1, C4.

6. Anthony DePalma, "Economic Lessons in a Border Town," *New York Times*, May 23, 1996, C1; Kelly Her, "Mexico's Leading Taiwan Investors," *Free China Journal*, September 13, 1995, 8; Barbara Stallings and Gabriel Szekely, eds., *Japan, the United States, and Latin America: Towards a Trilateral Relationship in the Western Hemisphere* (Baltimore: Johns Hopkins University Press, 1994).

7. Robert Brenner, "The Economics of Global Turbulence. A Special Report on the World Economy, 1950–98," *New Left Review* (special issue) 229 (1998): 204–205.

8. Hu-DeHart, "Asian Women Immigrants."

9. *Sweatshop Watch Newsletter*, http://sweatshopwatch.org, 1995 to 1999; Steven Greenhouse, "Janitors, Long Paid Little, Demand a Larger Slice," *New York Times*, April 28, 1999, A12.

10. June R. Keller, "The Division of Labor in Electronics," in *Women, Men, and the International Division of Labor*, ed. June Nash and María Patricia Fernández-Kelly (Albany: SUNY Press, 1983), 345–373.

11. Susan S. Green, "Silicon Valley's Women Workers: A Theoretical Analysis of Sex-Segregation in the Electronics Industry Labor Market," in Nash and Fernández-Kelly, *Women, Men, and the International Division of Labor*, 273–331.

12. Robert Snow, "The New International Division of Labor and the U.S. Work Force: The Case of the Electronics Industry," in June and Fernández-Kelly, *Women, Men, and the International Division of Labor*.

13. Naomi Katz and David S. Kemnitzer, "Fast Forward: The Internationalization of Silicon Valley," in Nash and Fernández-Kelly, *Women, Men, and the International Division of Labor*, 332–345.

14. Snow, "The New International Division of Labor."

15. Linda Y. C. Lim, "Capitalism, Imperialism, and Patriarchy: The Dilemma of Third-World Women Workers in Multinational Factories," in Nash and Fernández-Kelly, *Women, Men, and the International Division of Labor*.

16. Lim, "Capitalism, Imperialism, and Patriarchy"; Karen J. Hossfield, "Their Logic against Them: Contradictions of Sex, Race, and Class in Silicon Valley," in *Women Workers and Global Restructuring,* ed. Kathryn Ward (Cornell: School of Industrial and Labor Relations (ILR) Press, 1990), 150–178.

17. Sassen, *The Mobility of Labor and Capital.*

18. Hossfield, "Their Logic against Them."

19. Jeffrey Sachs and Paul Krugman, "In Principle: A Case for More 'Sweatshops,'" *New York Times,* June 22, 1997 (Week in Review).

20. William Greider, *One World, Ready or Not: The Manic Logic of Global Capitalism* (New York: Simon & Schuster, 1997).

21. Stiglitz, *Globalization and Its Discontents.*

22. Edna Bonacich and Richard P. Appelbaum, *Behind the Label. Inequality in the Los Angeles Apparel Industry* (Berkeley: University of California Press, 2000), 198.

23. Kim Moody, *Workers in a Lean World: Unions in the International Economy* (London: Verso, 1997).

24. Laura Hyun Hi Kang, "Si(gh)ting Asian/American Women as Transnational Labor," *Positions* 5, no. 2 (fall 1994): 403–437.

25. Bonacich and Appelbaum, *Behind the Label,* 121.

26. Ibid., 182.

27. In 2004, UNITE merged with H.E.R.E., Hotel Employees and Restaurant Employees Union, to become UNITE HERE. Both unions represent low-paid, low-skilled service workers, who are largely immigrant and heavily women.

28. Bonacich and Appelbaum, *Behind the Label,* 124.

29. William Macklin, "Making Them Sweat: Students Step up Pressure to Hold Colleges Accountable for Apparel," *USA Today,* April 13, 2006, 19; Mary Williams Walsh, "Latinos Get Left out of Economic Boom," *Boulder Daily Camera,* March 25, 2005, 14A (from the *Los Angeles Times*); Stiglitz, *Globalization and Its Discontents.*

30. "Global Monoculture," *New York Times* (paid advertisement), November 15, 1999, A7.

31. Robert L. Borosage, "The Battle in Seattle," *Nation,* December 6, 1999, 20–21.

32. Arlie Russell Hochschild, "Love and Gold," in *Global Woman: Nannies, Maids, and Sex Workers in the New Economy,* ed. Arlie Russell Hochschild and Barbara Ehrenreich (New York: Metropolitan Books, 2001), 24.

33. Harold Meyerson, "Liberalism with a New Accent: Immigrants Are Helping to Create a Dynamic, Globally Focused Movement," *Nation,* October 11, 1996, 15–20.

34. William Branigan, "Visa Program, High-Tech Workers Exploited," *Washington Post,* July 26, 1998, A1; Marc Cooper, "Class War at Silicon Valley," *Nation,* May 27, 1996, 11–16.

35. James D. Cockcroft, *Outlaws in the Promised Land: Mexican Immigrant Workers and America's Future* (New York: Grove, 1986).

36. Louise Lamphere, Alex Stepick, and Guillermo Grenier, eds., *Newcomers in the Workplace: Immigrants and the Restructuring of the U.S. Economy* (Philadelphia: Temple University Press, 1993); Jane Slaughter, "Welcome to the Jungle," *In These Times,* August 22, 1996, 5–6.

37. Raymond A. Mohl, "Globalization, Latinization, and the Nuevo New South," *Journal of American Ethnic History* 22, no. 4 (summer 2002): 31–66.

38. Louis Uchitelle, "INS Is Looking the Other Way as Illegal Immigrants Fill Jobs," *New York Times,* March 9, 1998, A1.

39. Uchitelle, "INS Is Looking the Other Way"; John Markoff, "Influx of New Immigrants Found in Silicon Valley," *New York Times*, January 10, 2002, C2; Louis Freedberg, "Borderline Hypocrisy: Do We Want Them Here, or Not?" *Washington Post*, February 6, 2000, B1.

40. Greenhouse, "Janitors, Long Paid Little."

41. David Bacon, "Labor's About Face," *Nation*, March 20, 2000, 6–7; William Greider, "Time to Rein in Global Finance," *Nation*, April 24, 2000, 13–20.

42. Marta López-Garza, "A Study of the Informal Economy and Latina/o Immigrants in Greater Los Angeles," in *Asian and Latino Immigrants in a Restructuring Economy: The Metamorphosis of Southern California*, ed. López-Garza, Marta Díaz, and David R. Díaz (Stanford: Stanford University Press, 2000), 144–145.

43. Tran Ngoc Angie, "Transnational Assembly Work: Vietnamese American Electronic and Vietnamese Garment Workers," *Amerasia Journal* 29, no. 1 (2003): 4–28.

44. Katz and Kemnitzer, "Fast Forward: The Internationalization of Silicon Valley."

45. Angie, "Transnational Assembly Work."

46. Evelyn Nakano Glenn, "From Servitude to Service Work: Historical Continuities in the Racial Division of Paid Reproductive Labor," *SIGNS: Journal of Women in Culture Society* 18, no. 1 (1992): 1–43; Thanh Dam Truong, "Gender, International Migration, and Social Reproduction: Implications for Theory, Policy, Research, and Networking," *Asian and Pacific Migration Journal* 5, no. 2 (1992): 27–52; Milyoung Cho, "Overcoming Our Legacy as Cheap Labor, Scabs, and Model Minorities: Asian Activists Fight for Community Empowerment," in *The State of Asian America*, ed. Karin Aguilar San Juan (Boston: South End Press, 1994), 253–273; Sassen-Koob, "Notes on the Incorporation of Third World Women"; Bridget Anderson, "Just Another Job? The Commodification of Domestic Labor," in Hochschild and Ehrenreich, *Global Women*, 104–114; Rhacel Salazar Parreñas, *Servants of Globalization: Women, Migration, and Domestic Work* (Stanford: Stanford University Press, 1998); Pierrette Hondegneu-Sotelo, *Doméstica: Immigrant Workers Cleaning and Caring in the Shadows of Affluence* (Berkeley: University of California Press, 2002); Mary Romero, *Maid in the U.S.A.*, 10th anniversary ed. (New York: Routledge, 2002); Grace Chang, *Disposable Domestics: Immigrant Women Workers in the Global Economy* (Cambridge: South End Press, 2000); Charlene Tung, "The Cost of Caring: The Social Reproductive Labor of Filipina Live-in Home Health Caregivers," *Frontiers. A Journal of Women Studies* 21, nos. 1 and 2 (1997): 61–82; Kristine M. Zentgraf, "Through Economic Restructuring, Recession, and Rebound," in *Asian and Latino Immigrants in a Restructuring Economy: The Metamorphosis of Southern California*, ed. Marta López-Garza and David R. Díaz (Stanford: Stanford University Press, 1998), 46–74.

47. Barbara Ehrenreich, "Maid to Order," in Hochschild and Ehrenreich, *Global Women*, 85–103.

48. Grace A. Rosales, "Labor behind Front Door: Domestic Workers in Urban and Suburban Households," in López-Garza and Díaz, *Asian and Latinos Immigrants in a Restructuring Economy*, 169–187.

49. Glenn, "From Servitude to Service Work," 7.

50. Parreñas, *Servants of Globalization*.

51. Kristen Hill Maher, "Good Women 'Ready to Go,' Labor Brokers and the Transnational Maid Trade," *Labor* 1, no. 1 (spring 2004): 55–76.

52. Tung, "The Cost of Caring."

53. Alexandra Suh, "Militarized Prostitution in Asia and the U.S.," in *States of Confinement: Policing, Detention, and Prisons*, ed. Joy James (New York: St. Martin's Press, 1996).

54. Suh, "Militarized Prostitution."

55. Kamala Kempadoo and Jo Doezema, *Global Sex Workers: Rights, Resistance, and Redefinition* (New York: Routledge, 1994).

56. Suh, "Militarized Prostitution."

57. Normal Stoltz Chinchilla and Nora Hamilton, "Doing Business: Central American Enterprises in Los Angeles," in López-Garza and Díaz, *Asian and Latino Immigrants in a Restructuring Economy*, 188–214; Clair M. Weber, "Latino Street Vendors in Los Angeles," in López-Garza and Díaz, *Asian and Latino Immigrants in a Restructuring Economy*, 217–240.

58. Kathleen Staudt, *Free Trade? Informal Economies on the U.S.-Mexico Border* (Philadelphia: Temple University Press, 1997).

59. Peri Fletcher, *La Casa de Mis Sueños: Dreams of a Home in a Transnational Mexican Community* (Boulder: Westview, 1999).

60. Amy Waldman, "More 'Can I Help You?' Jobs Migrate from U.S. to India," *New York Times*, May 11, 2003, International Section, 4.

61. Debbie Nathan, "Sweating out the Words," *Nation*, February 21, 2000, 27–28.

62. Mary Jordan and Kevin Sullivan, "Very Little Trickles Down: Free Trade Has Failed to Lift Mexicans out of Poverty," *Washington Post National Weekly Edition*, March 30–April 6, 2004, 15; Amy Waldman, "Low-Tech or High, Jobs Are Scarce in India's Boom," *New York Times*, May 6, 2004, A3.

Harassment of Female Farmworkers

CAN THE LEGAL SYSTEM HELP?

MARIA L. ONTIVEROS

In the 1990s, California Rural Legal Assistance contacted the Equal Employment Opportunity Commission seeking to have the U.S. federal government come to the aid of female farmworkers in California's central valley. For years, these women had been the victims of a barrage of sexual harassment, ranging from groping and propositions to forced sex in the "field de calzon" or "field of panties," so named because "so many supervisors raped women there."[1] The question posed for all concerned was what, if anything, did the federal antidiscrimination laws offer this group of women, given their particular situation and concerns. This chapter examines the sexual harassment of female farmworkers in California and how the law of sexual harassment can best be interpreted to address that problem. The first section of the chapter describes this sexual harassment in the lives of female farmworkers in California, with an emphasis on what makes their experience unique from other female workers. The second section briefly discusses the legal doctrine of sexual harassment and analyzes the best way to interpret sexual harassment law to address the experience of female farmworkers. The final section discusses the implication of this interpretation for other workers.

The law looks at sexual harassment in isolation—as an incident of workplace discrimination that needs to be remedied. Further, the law focuses on a determination of whether the harassment occurred "because of her sex." For female farmworkers, the reality is more complex than that. The reason that the harassment occurs, the way in which it is experienced, and the woman's response to the harassment are all shaped by the unique circumstances of her life. In order to end the harassment, the law must be responsive to all these factors which affect her ability to achieve equality in the workplace. Interpreting federal antidiscrimination law to do so would better serve all victims of sexual harassment, as well as victims of other types of discrimination.

Sexual Harassment in the Lives of Female Farmworkers

Between five hundred thousand and seven hundred thousand farmworkers live and work in California. Most of them (90 to 95 percent) were born in Mexico, and many maintain a residence there. Few speak English, and most are illiterate.[2] The great majority are "undocumented," which means that they do not have the legal right to be in the United States.[3] Without proper work or residency authorization, farmworkers constantly face the risk of job loss and deportation. If they are deported, many will attempt to return to the United States because they view themselves as being residents of both the United States and Mexico. They view themselves as transnationals. They maintain a Mexican identity and residence, while work, homes, communities, and families in the United States simultaneously pull them northward. Returning to the Untied States, via an illegal border crossing, entails a great deal of danger. According to one source, "over 1,870 border deaths have been recorded since 1994, of which 387 were in the last year."[4] Most of the deaths occur from exposure, and the number has increased as the federal border policy known as Operation Gatekeeper has closed the least dangerous, most visible migration corridors and forced immigrants into the extreme cold of mountain ranges or the extreme heat of desolate deserts.[5] In addition, *coyotes, polleroes,* or *pateroes* (the names given to guides paid to arrange an illegal border crossing) may swindle immigrants out of their money and abandon them.[6]

California's agricultural economy offers a variety of different jobs and employment structures to farmworkers. Farmworker jobs include planting, weeding, cultivating, harvesting, and processing food. About 40 percent of farmworkers engage in temporary or seasonal work. Most of these seasonal workers work for farm labor contractors. The farm labor contractor signs an agreement with a grower to provide a certain amount of labor for a lump sum. The contractor, not the grower, recruits and hires the labor. The contractor alone controls the rate of pay, job assignments, and job tenure for these workers. Contractors operate at the edge of the legal system. Farmworkers who work for contractors are often paid below the minimum wage, do not receive legally required work benefits, and have fewer guaranteed and less stable work hours. In addition, contractors often act in an arbitrary and abusive manner. The remaining 60 percent of farmworkers tend to work directly for growers and have the opportunity to work year-round. They are generally paid more and treated better because the grower sees them as his employees.[7]

Most farmworkers work long hours yet still live in poverty. In 1997, the median annual income for agricultural workers was about nine thousand dollars.[8] About 60 percent of all farmworkers are married, and most have children with them. They live in shared housing, garages, tool sheds, automobiles, labor camps, or "under the trees."[9] They have disproportionate rates of chronic health conditions, infant mortality, and workplace injuries and have short life expectancies.[10]

Current estimates suggest that about 30 percent of farmworkers are women. In addition to fieldwork, women work inside the home, too. As one female farmworker described it,

> After working in the fields, you come home exhausted. As a woman, when you get home, you don't lay down and rest or turn on the television or drink

a beer like the men do. You have to keep on working. When you get back home, you have to do all the housework—cleaning, sweeping, washing dishes, and cooking. Sometimes you have to keep on working until late at night. Then, you hardly have time to sleep before you have to wake up in the morning and do it all over again—making lunch for everyone, preparing things for the family, and going back to work. That's the experience that thousands of farmworker women live through every day.[11]

It is within this world that female farmworkers experience sexual harassment. Almost all (90 percent) female farmworkers view sexual harassment as a major problem. [12] As one farmworker described it, "A lot of times, the contractors and the *mayordomos* [supervisors] take advantage of women who work in the fields, especially single women, widows, and women without working papers. They tell them that if they don't have sex with them, they won't give them a job. Many women working in the fields are afraid. They're afraid to complain. They're worried that if they say anything, then they'll be fired. If they lost their job, then how would they support their children?"[13] The U.S. Equal Employment Opportunity Commission (EEOC) staff eventually concluded that "hundreds, if not thousands, of women had to have sex with supervisors to get or keep jobs and/or put up with a constant barrage of grabbing and touching and propositions for sex by supervisors."[14]

Immigrant women also face sexual harassment and abuse in other parts of their life. During illegal border crossings, women are often forcibly raped by *coyotes* or given the "choice" of having sex with them or being abandoned.[15] Human Rights Watch, the American Friends Service Committee, and court cases have all documented rapes and sexual assaults committed by officers of the U.S. Border Patrol against migrating women.[16] Domestic violence is also a reality for one out of three female farmworkers.[17]

Given the context of a female farmworker's life, the sexual harassment she experiences differs from that of most women in the United States in significant ways: the extremity of the consequences she faces if she does not comply with the harassment; the structural difficulties in the reporting of and response to these incidents of sexual harassment; the sexualization of migrant women; the cultural factors that influence the harassment; and the fluidity of her workplace. In several cases, these unique features of the female farmworkers' experience parallel the experiences of other immigrant women workers. Recognizing this link and incorporating the academic work done regarding their experiences can contribute new insight to the legal literature on sexual harassment.

If a farmworker refuses sexual advances or objects to sexual conduct, she faces unusually dire consequences. For an undocumented woman, the consequence may be deportation with attendant loss of family and community, including separation from her children if she decides they will be better off staying in California. When she chooses to return to the United States, deportation means facing another risky border crossing, during which she could be raped, abandoned, or killed. Even without the threat of deportation, her job alternatives are extremely limited. If she has a direct-hire job, the alternative of work with a job contractor is significantly worse. Alternately, for the typical farmworker family with limited income, job loss can push a family already on the edge of poverty into subsistence.

In these regards, the sexual harassment raises issues similar to those raised about "consent" in trafficking discourse and around "survival sex" in human rights literature. In trafficking discourse, feminists and policy makers have experienced a great deal of difficulty in defining illegal trafficking because of the felt need to define "consent" with regard to movement and with regard to sexual activity, such as prostitution or marriage.[18] With regard to human rights literature, a variety of international treaties and conventions protect women and children against sexual exploitation and abuse.[19] Similar to human rights cases dealing with rape as a war crime, cases often look to whether or not sex has been "forced." Given the precarious nature of refugee women, scholars have begun to argue that so-called consensual sex, when it is the result of economic exploitation or engaged in for survival, is also a human rights violation.[20]

Second, for undocumented Latinas, unique structural difficulties make reporting harassment difficult and the response from the legal system problematic. A typical employee begins the legal process by filing an administrative charge with the EEOC or a parallel state agency. Although an employee may file the charge on her own, most employees are assisted by an attorney. The EEOC then decides whether the government will pursue the claim or leave the employee to go forward on her own. In attempting to find an attorney or get the support of the EEOC, female farmworkers are hampered because, to a large extent, the antidiscrimination laws were not originally conceived to deal with this group. Race discrimination was thought of as a black-white issue, and sex discrimination dealt with the issues confronting white women in more traditional workplaces. As William Tamayo, regional attorney for the EEOC, stated, "Despite the size of the industry, there were very few EEOC cases in agriculture. Additionally, there were not sexual harassment cases filed in court until September 1998. . . . The lack of involvement reflects in part the Commission's traditional focus on the discrimination issues of African Americans in urban areas, with much less attention given historically to the concern of Latinas/os and Asian Americans."[21] In order for the EEOC to respond effectively, it needed bilingual attorneys or community workers to overcome the language barrier. More importantly, it needed bicultural help, especially on issues of credibility and communication with victims of sexual assault. Without such training, many of the attorneys viewed behaviors such as fidgeting and lack of eye contact as indicators of prevarication, instead of trauma.[22]

In addition, the legal system faces structural problems in protecting the rights of undocumented workers. Although labor and employment laws protect employees, as employees, regardless of immigration status, the law still penalizes undocumented workers in several ways. A few courts have argued that since the worker does not have the legal right to take a job, she should not be protected at all. The U.S. Supreme Court, in *Hoffman Plastic Compounds, Inc. v. National Labor Relations Board,* recently limited the types of remedies available to undocumented workers.[23] The law generally provides workers with reinstatement and payment of the wages they would have earned had they not been illegally fired. These remedies encourage workers to report violations and discourage employers from violating labor laws. In *Hoffman,* the Court found that neither of these remedies could be awarded to an undocumented worker because they could not legally be re-employed or legally earn wages. This ruling makes discrimination against undocumented workers less costly to employers and makes undocumented workers less likely to file complaints.

To a large extent, the legal system also structurally excludes coverage for agricultural workers. The law considers those who work for labor contractors as contractors, not employees, and so excludes them from coverage. In addition, under the policy of "agricultural exceptionalism," many federal workplace laws—such as those governing minimum wage, the right to organize, and overtime—have excluded agricultural workers.[24] The policy of agricultural exceptionalism has been traced to a desire to protect the growers of food,[25] concern over Congress overreaching into farm activity that did not affect interstate commerce,[26] and a compromise, reached by the New Deal architects, that "preserved the social and racial plantation system in the south—a system resting on the subjugation of blacks."[27] Regardless of its origin, clearly some of the most brutal forms of workplace governance—including slavery, sharecropping, and the bracero program—have involved agricultural work performed by people of color.

Historically, agricultural labor has been commodified to a larger extent than most other labor. Under slavery, workers were literally bought and sold. On Hawaiian plantations, "filipinos" were listed on the supply list right in between "fertilizer" and "fuel."[28] In modern times, the commodification of agricultural labor is undoubtedly made easier because, like slaves, those performing the work have been dehumanized. These immigrant workers are seen as "aliens," rather than members of the community. As such, their workplace conditions are regulated by the market, rather than by the system of workplace laws that we have established to protect the human rights of workers.

Third, as a migrant woman of color, a female farmworker may be seen as especially sexually available. Men who employ or supervise her in a "work" relationship may feel that they "own" her. This feeling of ownership often goes beyond the idea of owning her labor, to that of owning her body and, especially, her sexuality. In their minds, they may justify the sexual relationship they impose upon her as being part of the natural, normal, or expected part of the relationship.

This dynamic is similar to that experienced by other immigrant women and women of color. Professor Adrienne Davis pioneered work on how slavery was a "sexual economy" where white men extracted "forced sexual and reproductive labor from enslaved women" as part of the labor institution of slavery.[29] More recently, scholars have described the way in which sex has become part of the job requirement of migrant domestic workers. As Raul Manglapus, former secretary of Foreign Affairs for the Republic of the Philippines, "joked," "If rape is inevitable, relax and enjoy it."[30] Annelise Orleck describes this as the "colonization" of the brown body.[31] A similar dynamic is at play when U.S. Border Patrol officers rape migrating women in an attempt to maintain patriarchal and racial control, as a form of national security, in the militarized border zone. [32]

Fourth, a variety of unique cultural factors affect and influence the harassment. When the harasser is a member of her own ethnicity (such as a coyote, labor contractor, or field supervisor), the abuse may be affected by the harasser's relative lack of power. He lives in a world where he lacks status and privilege relative to white men, and there are simply no other women over whom he may exercise such power. The harasser also knows that, because of the dire consequences associated with her refusing sex and losing a job or being abandoned on the border, she is particularly vulnerable and unlikely to object.

In addition, cultural considerations can make the woman less likely to object, refuse, or file a complaint. In her culture, she may have been taught that, when someone is raped, it is the woman's fault. Others in her community, sharing this view, may be quick to shun her or justify the harassment because "she asked for it." If she brings a claim, she may be seen as one who is bringing not only dishonor to the community, but also the probing eyes of the state, including the Immigration and Naturalization Service. The presence of the state puts many in the entire community at risk of deportation.

Finally, the fluidity of a farmworker's workplace makes her experience unique. The world of the farmworker is a place where it is hard to draw borders or boundaries. Many other workers can draw a sharp line between the workplace and home. For farmworkers, it is different because their "home" in the United States is inextricably linked to their workplace. For migrant workers, their home is mobile; it moves to follow the growing season. Others may live in a farm labor camp that is on the employer's property and have conditions controlled by the employer. Many workers routinely share living space with other farmworker families. Outside their home, they live in tight-knit communities that are made up of other farmworkers. The fluidity extends internationally, as many farmworkers create lives in both the United States and Mexico. Because of migration patterns, a farmworker community in the United States will often be comprised of the same families that live in one community in Mexico. Besides the physical fluidity of the workplace, there is also a fluidity in identity as well. Female farmworkers identify themselves not in separate categories—woman, farmworker, Mexican—but as a "campesina," a term embodying all those aspects as once.

This fluidity makes her experience with harassment unique because its impact strikes at all aspects of her identity, not just her identity as a woman or as a worker. It affects her not just at her workplace, but also in her home and in her community. It affects her in both her homeland and her adopted country, as well as during the time of migration/border crossing. From one perspective, she experiences the harm at the very core of who she is. From another perspective, her subordination is defined by all these dimensions. In her case, the harassment is much more than just *sexual* harassment. Contextualizing the current law of sexual harassment to fit female farmworkers is thus necessary.

Title VII of the Civil Rights Act of 1964 prohibits employers from discriminating on the basis of certain protected categories: race, color, sex, national origin, and religion. The statute obviously prohibits employers from making hiring, discharge, or promotion decisions on these bases. During the 1970s and 1980s, women began to theorize and eventually bring complaints alleging that various sexual behaviors in the workplace also violated this statute. Over time, courts began to recognize two types of "sexual harassment" that are prohibited by Title VII: quid pro quo harassment and hostile work environment. Quid pro quo harassment prohibits situations where an employer requires an employee to comply with a sexual request in order to receive a tangible work benefit. Under the hostile work environment theory, employers may not allow verbal or physical conduct of a sexual nature that creates a hostile work environment for women.

In order for a woman to bring a claim under the statute, she has to prove four things: first, that she was harassed "because of her sex," and second, that prohibited conduct occurred. For quid pro quo harassment, the conduct is usually a request for sexual favors. For hostile work environment, it is traditionally verbal or physical conduct of a sexual nature. Third, the woman must show that the conduct was "unwelcome." Finally, she must show either that the response to the conduct affected a tangible aspect of employment (quid pro quo harassment) or that it was sufficiently severe and pervasive that it altered her work environment (hostile work environment).

A typical case of sexual harassment might involve a female accounts manager whose boss and co-workers constantly tell sexual jokes and "joke" that she only generates business because she sleeps with her customers. Her boss may touch her and, if she objects, tell her that she better "loosen up" around him or that she better go out with him if she wants more and better accounts. To state a claim of sexual harassment, she will argue that this conduct occurs because she is a woman, that sexual conduct and propositions occurred, that she objected to the conduct, and that it either resulted in fewer good accounts or a hostile work environment. She could satisfy all four elements of a claim.

Recently, the first two elements—harassment because of sex and propositions or conduct of a sexual nature—have become the subject of significant changes in legal doctrine and feminist debate. Traditionally, courts found that the first element was met anytime sexual behavior was involved because of an assumed heterosexual norm that men would only behave sexually toward women (and vice versa). Some feminist theorists supported this argument because they argued that heterosexual conduct is inherently subordinating for women. Recently, both courts and commentators have revisited this conclusion for a variety of reasons. A number of cases have been brought by men and women who have been harassed by members of their own sex. These same-sex cases seem objectionable under the old approach because they involve sexual conduct, but they fall outside the traditional framework because (when there is not a homosexual harasser) the conduct is not seen as occurring "because" of the target's sex. Similarly, cases appeared where an employer harassed both men and women. These "equal opportunity harasser" cases again seem objectionable because of their sexual nature, but fall outside a framework that requires a plaintiff to show that the harassment would not have occurred to someone of the opposite sex.

In a recent case of same-sex harassment, the U.S. Supreme Court seemed to move away from a "sexual behavior" standard and toward a "but for" standard, which requires that the plaintiff show that the same action would not have been taken against someone of the opposite sex.[33] The Court expressed concern that, under the traditional sexual-behavior approach, Title VII could become a civility code for the workplace. It shifted its focus to whether the plaintiff would have been harassed "but for" his sex. It suggested that a plaintiff in a same-sex case could satisfy this requirement by showing that the behavior was motivated by sexual desire; that it involved sex-specific, derogatory terms evidencing hostility toward the plaintiff's sex; or through direct comparative evidence of how the harasser treated members of the opposite sex.

Meanwhile, feminist commentators have also been reconsidering an approach that focuses on the sexual nature of the conduct. Professor Vicki Schultz objects that this approach leaves out nonsexual harassment, such as ostracism and insults, which she identifies as the biggest problem facing female workers today.[34] She argues that most harassment is targeted at pushing women out of certain types of jobs and that, as long as courts cling to a sexual-conduct approach, these nonsexual behaviors (even when they are targeted at women "because of their sex") will receive different treatment and be disaggregated from the sexual harm suffered by a plaintiff. Other feminist commentators argue for the prohibition of harassment that seeks to reinforce gender roles, even if the harassment is not inherently sexual or directed at someone because of sexual desire.[35] They argue that this is a form of sexual discrimination because, by reinforcing gender roles, it replicates a patriarchal system that disempowers women.

The biggest problem with the doctrinal shift away from a sexual-conduct standard is the simultaneous shift toward a very narrow construction of the purpose of Title VII. A narrow focus on whether harassment is solely "because of sex" will never deal with the key doctrinal problem for female farmworkers. Although the harassment is because of their sex, it is also influenced by a variety of other personal identity factors. Thus, an interpretation of Title VII which emphasizes discrimination against members of a protected class instead of workplace equality will be less effective. Female farmworkers' harassment must be contextualized. The harassment could just as easily be characterized as because of their national origin or because of their immigration status or occupation. Although the first type of claim (national origin) is actionable under Title VII, the other two (immigration status and occupation) are not. Within Title VII jurisprudence, some courts recognize claims that incorporate a combination of protected classes (i.e., a woman from Mexico) or the combination of a protected class with an unprotected characteristic (i.e., an undocumented woman). Other courts, however, reject such claims and insist on a narrow focus on whether the workplace conduct was because of sex or national origin or some other protected factor. The dominant trend in courts is to only recognize combination claims when they involve a protected characteristic and a fundamental right (i.e., the claims of married women would be protected, but not those of undocumented women) or combinations that describe well-known, unique discriminatory biases (i.e., claims by African American women but not by female agricultural workers).

For Title VII to be meaningful to farmworkers, the courts must recognize claims that implicate more than one personal identity factor. The concern that courts will not recognize harassment claims by female farmworkers arises from the history of the EEOC's focus on black-white relationships, the history of agricultural exceptionalism, the policy limiting recovery for undocumented workers, and the narrow "but for" construction of the term "because of sex" in Supreme Court doctrine. Contextualizing the doctrine of sexual harassment presents the opportunity not only to broaden the definition of "because of sex," but also to focus on the broader purpose of Title VII. One way to approach Title VII is to focus on employer conduct and measure whether it discriminates because of a protected characteristic. An alternative approach is to view it as a statute designed to guarantee workplace equality. The experience of female farmworkers makes clear that to achieve workplace equality the law must take into account much more than a single workplace action and a single protected category.

The feminist debate on the requirements of "because of sex" and "sexual conduct" can also be enhanced by considering the experience of female farmworkers. First, conduct of a sexual nature is exactly the problem faced by female farmworkers and must be protected in feminist theory.[36] Female farmworkers are too often viewed as the sexual property of their employers. Like domestic workers and female slaves, sexual availability and sexual conduct remain a core factor in defining their subordination. It dehumanizes them and prevents them from claiming their rights. This is especially true because of the fluidity of their lives and the multiple loci of their sexual abuse and exploitation (in the home, at the border, in the workplace, and in their community). Thus, feminist theory must continue to recognize sexual conduct as inherently discriminating against women.

In addition, the focus of theorists on "nonsexual" harassment does not offer much help to female farmworkers because their condition is much more extreme than that. On the other hand, theorists who focus on gender roles do offer a way to contextualize sexual harassment for female farmworkers because this theory allows for the unique cultural ways that harassment operates to be given full consideration.

Feminists have found the third element of the sexual harassment claim—the plaintiff must show that the conduct was unwelcome—problematic for several reasons. Some argue that no woman would ever welcome conduct that constituted a sexual barter for a tangible job advantage or that was sufficiently severe that it created a hostile work environment. To others, it replicated the anti-woman requirements for proving rape and put the target of harassment on trial, to determine if her behavior invited the harassment. On the other hand, several commentators argue that the unwelcomeness requirement is necessary because people do engage in consensual romance in the workplace, and these relationships can be beneficial to individuals and society. Others argue that prohibiting all sexual conduct robs women of their sexual agency and the ability to decide for themselves how sexual to be in the workplace.

The experience of female farmworkers offers several insights into this discussion. First, they do not have much to lose by prohibiting all sexual conduct. For them, the social good of "romance in the workplace" does not make much sense because of the fluid nature of their workplace, which blends with their home and community. In addition, most female farmworkers live with a husband, as part of a family unit. Third, the protection of sexual agency is not really a concern for female farmworkers because they are already over-sexualized. The way to give them control over their sexuality is to focus on issues of sexual exploitation, survival sex, and domestic violence, not by arguing that they could, indeed, welcome sexual contact in the workplace. Although female farmworkers do not lose much with the elimination of the unwelcomeness requirement, its retention creates serious problems. Because of the cultural issues that make it difficult for female farmworkers to object to and report harassment, they may not be able to find evidence to support their claim that the conduct was, in fact, unwelcome.

The final element for a sexual harassment claim—that the conduct was sufficiently severe and pervasive to create a hostile work environment—must also be contextualized in the case of female farmworkers. Courts have generally required that the harassment be both objectively and subjectively severe. In crafting the objective part of the test, most of the debate has focused on whether courts should use the perspective of a reasonable man or a reasonable woman in a given situation. A few commentators have advocated that issues of race or class also need to be included in this analysis. As the case of female farmworkers makes clear, whether sexual activity makes a work environment hostile turns on a whole variety of factors. Because of their unique situation, it is virtually impossible to craft an objective test that makes any sense.

Contextualizing the Doctrine of Sexual Harassment: Implications for Other Workers

A central theme of this chapter has been that the doctrine of sexual harassment fails to adequately understand and respond to sexual harassment in the lives of female farmworkers because the harassment is influenced by a variety of factors, not just their sex. Although the specific combination of factors which affect female farmworkers is unique to them, the fact that the harassment is affected and influenced by a variety of complex, interrelated factors is not.

The sexual harassment of every woman is influenced and affected by a variety of factors that need to be understood by courts and the judicial system in applying the doctrine of sexual harassment. The context for a sixteen-year-old, working-class waitress holding her first job, for example, is different than the experience of a well-credentialed white woman surgeon who is the first woman seeking tenure at a prestigious medical school. Both can experience sexual harassment which deserves to be remedied. The current law, however, may end up denying both of their claims. The waitress, for example, may be told by the restaurant owner that occasionally having sex with him is simply part of the job. Although she may not want to, she may be too young, inexperienced, and poor to object. As a result, she may not be able to prove that the harassment was unwelcome. The surgeon may be insulted, patted, and shunned. Although these types of activities may discredit her in front of patients and senior faculty, making tenure impossible, a court may find that this type of activity is simply good-natured horseplay in the hospital and not sufficiently severe to constitute a hostile environment.

A second major critique offered in this chapter is that Title VII fails to serve the needs of female farmworkers because of its focus on discrimination due to membership in a protected class, rather than a focus on overall equality. Broadening the scope of Title VII helps farmworkers, but it also helps all workers. As the composition of the workforce changes and the structure of the workplace evolves, equality for all workers can no longer be accomplished by merely focusing on discrete employer acts and asking if they discriminate on the basis of a protected characteristic.

NOTES

1. William R. Tamayo, "The Role of the EEOC in Protecting the Civil Rights of Farm Workers," *UC Davis Law Review* 33 (2000): 1075, 1080.

2. California Agricultural Labor Relations Board, *The Agricultural Labor Relations Board in the 21st Century—A Needs Assessment of the ALRB's Ability to Meet Its Statutory Obligations* (Sacramento: California Agricultural Labor Relations Board, 2001), 8. Estimates are that only 15 percent are more than "marginally literate" in any language.

3. California Agricultural Labor Relations Board, "The Agricultural Labor Relations Board," 8. Estimates range from 42 percent to 70 percent.

4. Don Villarejo, "Are Migration and Free Trade Appropriate Forms of Economic Development? The Case of Mexico and U.S. Agriculture," *UC Davis Journal of International Law & Policy* 9 (2003): 175, 191 (citing California Rural Legal Foundation Web site www.stopgatekeeper.org).

5. American Friends Service Committee, "Deportee Monitoring Project Part II" (2000), at www.afsc.org. See also Bill Ong Hing, "The Dark Side of Operation Gatekeeper," *UC Davis Journal of International Law & Policy* 7 (2001): 121.

6. Maria L. Ontiveros, "Lessons from the Fields: Female Farmworkers and the Law," *Maine Law Review* 55 (2002): 158, 165.

7. See sources gathered in Ontiveros, "Lessons from the Fields," 162–164.

8. Villarejo, "Are Migration and Free Trade Appropriate Forms," 199.

9. Ibid., 199–200.

10. Ontiveros, "Lessons from the Fields," 170–171.

11. Daniel Rothenberg, *With These Hands—The Hidden World of Migrant Farmworkers Today* (New York: Harcourt Brace, 1998), 55.

12. Maria M. Domingues, "Sex Discrimination & Sexual Harassment in Agricultural Labor," *American University Journal of Gender & Law* 6 (1997): 231, 255; see also Richard Kamm, "Extending the Progress of the Feminist Movement to Encompass the Rights of Migrant Farmworker Women," *Chicago-Kent Law Review* 75 (2000): 765, 774–775.

13. Rothenberg, *With These Hands,* 55.

14. Tamayo, "The Role of the EEOC," 1080.

15. Rothenberg, *With These Hands,* 130.

16. Eithne Luibhéid, *Entry Denied: Controlling Sexuality at the Border* (Minneapolis: University of Minnesota Press, 2002), 121–127.

17. Pat Swift, "Labor Official Will Reach out to Female Farmworkers," *Buffalo News,* September 9, 2000, 7C; see also Mary Ann Dutton et al., "Characteristics of Help-Seeking Behaviors, Resources and Service Needs of Battered Immigrant Latinas: Legal and Policy Implications," *Georgetown Journal Poverty Law & Policy* 7 (2000): 245.

18. Janie Chuang, "Redirecting the Debate over Trafficking in Women: Definitions, Paradigms, and Contexts," *Harvard Human Rights Journal* 11 (1998): 65.

19. In particular, the United Nations Convention on the Rights of the Child, G.A. Res. 44/25, U.N. GAOR, 44th Sess., Supp. No. 49, Annex, at 167, art. 34, U.N. Doc. A/44/49 (1989) (entered into force September 2, 1990); Declaration on the Elimination of Violence against Women, G.A. Res. 48/104, U.N. GAOR, 48th Sess., Supp. No. 49, at 217, U.N. Doc. A/48/49 (1993).

20. Royce Bernstein Murray, "Sex for Food in a Refugee Economy: Human Rights Implications and Accountability," *Georgetown Immigration Law Journal* 14 (2000): 985.

21. Tamayo, "The Role of the EEOC," 1078.

22. Ibid., 1081.

23. *Hoffman Plastic Compounds, Inc. v. Nat'l Labor Relations Board* (2002), 535 U.S. 137.

24. Guadalupe T. Luna, "An Infinite Distance? Agricultural Exceptionalism and Agricultural Labor," *University of Pennsylvania Journal of Labor and Employment Law* 1 (1998): 487.

25. Ibid., 489.

26. Peggie R. Smith, "Organizing the Unorganizable: Private Paid Household Workers and Approaches to Employee Representation," *North Carolina Law Review* 79 (2000): 45, 63 n.81.

27. Marc Linder, "Farm Workers and the Farm Labor Standards Act: Racial Discrimination in the New Deal," *Texas Law Review* 65 (1987): 1335, 1336.

28. Ronald Takaki, *Pau Hana: Plantation Life and Labor in Hawaii* (Honolulu: University of Hawaii Press, 1983), 23–34.

29. Adrienne Davis, "'Don't Let Nobody Bother Yo' Principle'—The Sexual Economy of American Slavery," in *Sister Circle-Black Women and Work,* ed. Sharon Harley et al. (New Brunswick, N.J.: Rutgers University Press, 2002), 103.

30. Dan Gatmayan, "Death and the Maid: Work, Violence, and the Filipina in the International Labor Market," *Harvard Women's Law Journal* 20 (1997): 229. See also Joy M. Zarembka, "America's Dirty Work: Migrant Maids and Modern-Day Slavery," in *Global Woman: Nannies, Maids, and Sex Workers in the New Economy,* ed. Barbara Ehrenreich and Arlie Russell Hochschild (New York: Metropolitan Books, 2003), 146.

31. Annelise Orleck, "Wage-Earning Women," in *Companion to American Women's History,* ed. Nancy A. Hewitt (Walden, Mass.: Blackwells Ltd., 2002), 264 (summarizing the work of Judy Yung, Huping Ling, Evelyn Nakano Glenn, Susan Tucker, and Tera Hunter).

32. Sylvanna Falcon, "Rape as a Weapon of War: Advancing Human Rights for Women at the U.S.-Mexico Border," *Social Justice* 28 (2001): 31. See also Luibhéid, *Entry Denied,* 129–130 (arguing that these rapes are used as tools of cultural and sexual supremacy by constructing women's bodies as something over which men, not women, have control and that rape is a technology for (re)producing hierarchical social relationships and borders).

33. *Oncale v. Sundowner Offshore Services, Inc.* (1998), 523 U.S. 75.

34. Vicki Schultz, "Reconceptualizing Sexual Harassment," *Yale Law Journal* 107 (1998): 1683.

35. Kathryn Abrams, "The New Jurisprudence of Sexual Harassment," *Cornell Law Review* 83 (1998): 1169; Katherine M. Franke, "What's Wrong with Sexual Harassment?" *Stanford Law Review* 49 (1997): 691.

36. Adrienne D. Davis, "Slavery and the Roots of Sexual Harassment," in *Directions in Sexual Harassment Law,* ed. Catherine A. MacKinnon and Reva B. Siegel (New Haven, Conn.: Yale University Press, 2004), 47.

Caribbean Women, Domestic Labor, and the Politics of Transnational Migration

CAROLE BOYCE DAVIES

The large-scale migration of Caribbean people to the United States from the 1960s onward is a visible identification of the presence of U.S. imperialism, in much the same way that the migration to the United Kingdom in the immediate pre-independence period (1940s–1960s) was a formal manifestation of access to the seat of the Euro-colonial empire. Ransford Palmer identifies "the emigration in search of job opportunities . . . as an enduring feature of the economic history of the region" and linked to various capital flows between the United States and the Caribbean.[1] The migration of Caribbean women within the larger Caribbean migration flow has also caught the attention of researchers in the field. Caribbean women's migration into the U.S. labor pool and their labor exploitation in the context of home domestic work and factory work become other instances of a particular linkage of gender and race and labor mobility.

Recent analyses of globalization and imperialism reveal that the new imperialism is U.S. imperialism and that corporate globalization works with the United States functioning as an ensurer of global capitalist interests as it facilitates capital mobility networks at home and abroad.[2] In 1958 Caribbean feminist, activist, political thinker Claudia Jones provided an early reading of U.S. imperialism which is worth recalling. In "American Imperialism and the British West Indies," she takes an analytical, Marxist-Leninist, anti-imperialist position, clear about U.S. corporate interests in the Caribbean as they related to or were distinct from British versions.[3] She identifies this development as visible since 1942 with the creation of the Anglo-American Caribbean Commission, which facilitated the seizing of natural resources by American monopolists—the oil and bauxite industries, but also agriculture and banking. She identifies the failure of the West Indian Federation as linked to U.S. imperialism, for a unified West Indies would have meant the rise of an economic power in the Caribbean region.

Thus, what resulted was a few countries gaining independence and, since the early 1960s, no definite transition to full independence anywhere. Rather, the result was a range of exploitable locations, negotiated with local political and business elite, and the parallel migrating subjects, operating within and against U.S. imperialist interests. Thus, the people themselves, migrating and returning, purposefully operate, nevertheless contradictorily, within the logic of transnational flows.

Caribbean Women as Migrating Subjects

The research on the largely female migration to the United States in the 1960s and 1970s, ranging from 58 percent to 78 percent female, first came to the attention of many through the collection *Female Immigrants to the United States: Caribbean, Latin American, and African Experiences,* edited by Delores Mortimer and Roy S. Bryce-Laporte. Indeed, some of the major contributors to this collection, such as Saskia Sassen, Palmira Rios, A. Lynn Bolles, and Monica Gordon, have gone on to produce significant work of their own. Lynn Bolles's piece in that early collection, "Going Abroad: Working-Class Jamaican Women and Migration," asserts that "most of the younger women in her sample are not concerned with what kind of job they would find in the United States, or what it would pay, but to just get one. It is a consensus of opinion among working class Caribbeans that any job in the United States would have to be better in terms of working conditions and wages than what they had then. They knew too that their labor would be more exploited than native American workers because of their immigrant status (especially if illegal), but they saw this situation as temporary."[4]

But it is perhaps Judith Burgess and Meryl James-Gray's "Migration and Sex Roles: A Comparison of Black and Indian Trinidadians in New York City" that may be directly beneficial to an understanding of differences within the migration pool, this time based on ethnicity. Economic advancement and access to specialized education that can lead to upward mobility at home were identified as the primary indicators for this group. Many interviewees tended to be employed before leaving home, in a range of occupations. The study concluded that "the women expressed the view that they had greater 'independence' not only because they have more money of their own, but also because it is possible to purchase a variety of consumer goods and to invest in the advancement of their own education."[5]

Monica Gordon's "Dependents or Independent Workers? The Status of Caribbean Immigrant Women in the United States" still offers for many one of the most careful delineations of the issue of Caribbean women's migration and their status once they arrive in the United States. Using 1980s census data in her assessment, Caribbean women, as the "principal aliens" in migration to the United States, provide the contexts of gender and migration as their own dynamic. One of her assertions is that "migration confers not only economic opportunities but also opens new options for social growth and self-definition, which may have unanticipated consequences for familial and other relationships existing prior to their immigration."[6]

Studying the individual life experiences of a number of women is a useful approach to contemplating issues of globalization and women's work. Additionally, one has to differentiate between islands as between race and ethnic identification. While Saskia Sassen is perhaps the most known for her work on migration, labor, and capital flows, there are a range of other studies which flesh out the contours for these larger conclusions.[7] Sassen's work, nonetheless, has served to denaturalize migration and to link it deliberately to particular economic statuses between countries, particularly linked to foreign investment and military interventions. Sassen also identifies the shift in the nature of work done on the various islands, often linked to high-tech industries. Each island and its home economy and, therefore, its relationship to the global economy allow different readings of the experiences of migration and work in the United States. Still, under Sassen's model, a buoyant local economy does not deter migration. Carla Freeman's *High Tech and High Heels in the Global Economy* reveals the fine distinctions that must be made in the home context in terms of the various types of workers now made desirable under global capitalism—the pink collar workers for whom dress as uniform signals a differentiation in terms of groups located differently in the local economy—while yet engaging in service work.[8]

Some answers to the open question—concerning why Caribbean women become migrating subjects—reside in an analysis that looks at the sexual division of labor.[9] A number of scholars have pursued this discussion and offer helpful analyses on the migration circuits,[10] globalization and capital mobility,[11] and work on domestic labor in a global context.[12] In the home context, studies done on the Caribbean provide the historical backdrop to contemporary migration of women. One example is *Women and the Sexual Division of Labor in the Caribbean*; Rhoda Reddock's "Historical and Contemporary Perspectives: The Case of Trinidad and Tobago" and Dorian L. Powell's "Women's Domestic Labor: Paid and Unpaid" have provided important readings of the history of Caribbean women's labor.[13] According to Reddock, the sexual division of labor, while an old process, was exacerbated in the Caribbean through the colonial agencies which had actual policy in place to keep women from access to employment outside of the service sphere and male dominance in the workplace. Additionally, from the period 1891 to 1960, there was a general "housewifization" process which saw women's participation in the wage employment and the general workforce declining from 73.0 percent in 1891 to 23.8 percent in 1960. And it is only in the period bracketing post-flag independence that one sees a new increase in women in the workforce. In the period between 1891 and 1960, most women were employed in the service industries. Still, the majority of domestic servants tended to be largely from Grenada and St. Vincent, while Trinidadian women tended to be employed in the "pink-collar sector" or in agricultural work, government service, dressmaking, teaching, nursing, and clerical work.[14]

In my view, the issue of women desiring a means of escaping unsatisfying relationships as they simultaneously control the fruits of their own labor and improve their own and their children's lives has been less articulated than the issue of economic reasons for migration. Additionally, it becomes clear that as a number of women enter the workforce, a variety of them search elsewhere for more advanced economic remuneration. The pull to the United States via more liberal immigration legislation provides additional opportunities for migration.

So, how did women who were not able to earn a decent wage, had aspirations for more developed futures, were leaving unsatisfying relationships, or wanted to educate their children abroad unhook themselves from these Caribbean conditions which stagnated their desires? Migration and the shifting working relationships in the United States provided an avenue largely for working-class and lower-middle-class women, as Gordon found in her study. The various rationales behind these moves have been already identified in a great deal of the research on this pool of largely female Caribbean women who migrated in the 1960s. Still, very little ethnographic work has been done on the women themselves in the post-1980s period. Analyses of the most recent census data will no doubt provide additional interpretations. Questions like, What happens after they come to the United States? remain to be more fully explored?

Some of the angles taken in studying Caribbean migrants in New York, in Mary C. Waters's *Black Identities: West Indian Immigrant Dreams and American Realities,* provide additional information. Waters concludes, for example, that "the realities of persistent, blatant racial discrimination," as it manifests itself in inadequate housing, inadequate city services, high crime rates, and inferior public schools, "undermine their hopes for their children's future as low wages and poor working conditions are no longer attractive for their children, who use American and not Caribbean standards to measure success."[15] These research findings are consistent with a study done in Miami in 2000 by the Caribbean Research Group, headed by Marcia Magnus, which found that the same issues that plague African Americans also plague Caribbeans: police brutality, housing, education, salary scales.[16]

And what happens when they return to the Caribbean still remains an open research question. In particular, the aging group of women of that 1960s generation is still in need of studying. Additionally, the September 11, 2001, terrorist actions in the United States have led to redefinition and tightening of immigration into the United States. Significant among these changes has been the combining of data bases, such as the link between social security numbers and immigration offices. This makes it harder, though not impossible, for some women to find work that pays them formally, as earlier happened through domestic employment agencies. This chapter gestures toward the need for a full-scale sociological study on this topic.

In pursuing my own project, following the publication of my book, *Migrations of the Subject* (1994), I conducted interviews and conversations with twenty-five women during the period 1995 to the present. In that group, I noticed that two generations began to emerge: the generation that migrated in the 1960s and the younger generation of women migrating in the 1980s and 1990s, the former retired, the latter still operating fully in the process. Of course, as is usual, many of the women felt that their lives had nothing to contribute and so rejected formal interviews in favor of conversations. Still, I was able to raise the major questions prominent in this study: What were the reasons for migration? What was the nature of the process? What is the relationship to families back home? And what are the plans for the future and the possibility of return? This is an ongoing project, and I have included for the purposes of this chapter five sample migration narratives, and I note that more studies of the second generation are warranted.

Caribbean Migration Narratives

Marva

In preparation for a forthcoming marriage in 1996, Marva, a twenty-eight-year-old mother of a four-year-old daughter, came to the United States to do domestic work and earn some money in order to organize the event, shop, and get enough money for a down payment on her home in the Caribbean. Marva, who is close to six feet tall, did some light modeling in her home country in the Caribbean, doing enough to have some photographs in the local newspaper. She has a high school certificate and some dressmaking skills and has been employed seasonally. Visiting the United States first for about three months and spending that time with her sister, who has lived in the United States since the late 1970s, she actually went, on the insistence of her sister, to some modeling agencies in New York, hoping for a big break. Strikingly beautiful, but not exactly what they were looking for at that time, perhaps older than the age at which models are recruited, she settled on some light domestic work, largely because she did not have legal papers to do any thing else. She worked for about six months with a family as a child minder, taking care of an infant and doing light live-in housework as well for an upper-middle-class professional/corporate couple. At the end of the time, when she was scheduled to return home, she told the family the truth, that she was getting married and wanted to return home. Surprisingly, the woman she worked for excitedly helped her with shopping for her wedding, gave her presents, reluctantly let her go, but indicated that, if she wanted to return, they were so satisfied with her work that they would re-hire her. Her fiancé came to the United States, and together they both shopped for the wedding reception, returned home together, and had a lavish event. About a year into the marriage, Marva realized that she was very unhappy in that situation; she was used to having her own income and freedom and decided to try to return to the United States to work again, this time planning that she would stay a few years and then decide what to do about her marriage, or time would take care of the uncertainty. Fortunately, she had kept a pleasant relationship with the family; they now had two children and the wife was trying to return to work but would only do so if she could find someone really reliable. She trusted Marva, who had helped mind the first baby. Marva found this to be great fortune; they paid her transportation and arranged her papers. Four years later, Marva, at thirty-three-years-old, was still in the United States and had settled into being a domestic worker for the time being, with Sundays off and a half day on Thursday. I saw her once at her workplace. I had gone with her sister, who lives in the same state and works as an executive secretary, to take an item to her. Her appearance was meant to camouflage all of her physical attractiveness (sweats, scarves, hair pulled back). On another occasion, in her sister's home, in preparation for a night out, she was stunningly beautiful by contrast, and I wondered what it meant to that family to have a woman of that physical attractiveness in their home working as a domestic. Her seven-year-old daughter from a premarital relationship is going to school in the Caribbean and lives with her maternal family, and Marva spends a lot of money sending things home in the customary "barrel." Her plan is still to work long enough to set up her home in the way she wants, not to bring her daughter to the United States but to keep her in school in the Caribbean and make a life for them there. Her daughter still lives with the extended family, and as a result her money goes to assist in the smooth maintenance of the entire family. Her marriage is for the time being on autopilot, with both of them clearly free to do whatever they want to in terms of other relationships. She shops and returns to the Caribbean whenever she can and plans to live at home once she has raised enough money and perhaps gotten some educational credentials. Her sister encourages her to make the break and get a job and an apartment, but Marva is never ready and indicates that she is preparing to go to nursing school eventually.

Esther

Esther came to the United States through Canada in 1982. She traveled to Canada on vacation with the full intention of trying to get into the United States. After spending a few weeks in Canada just before the local Caribana, in a prearranged situation, she traveled to the United States, crossing the border one night by lying flat on the back floor of a car under the legs of two or three men who were occupying the back seat, all of whom had legal papers to be in the United States. She describes the experience as scary but relatively easy as the border guard asked few questions that night. Instead of going the route of domestic work, which she hated, Esther, who had hairdressing skills in the Caribbean, worked in a beauty shop and developed a clientele of her own. Because she was very enterprising and talented as a hairdresser, within a few years she got a male friend to help her invest in her own hairdressing shop, which she still owns; it is a thriving business in Brooklyn. Throughout all of this, Esther never secured her residence visa but has been able to travel in and out of the United States for family and social reasons by using various forms of disguise (age, gender) and the passports of friends. She has been technically eligible for the various amnesties, and when I asked her why she has not bothered to regularize her papers, she surprisingly expressed fear that, if she does, it will alert the INS to her illegal status and she will be sent home. During this period she has been able to bring her daughter to the United States and send her to middle school and then high school. The biggest problem she has faced is that because she worked long hours her daughter remained unsupervised and gradually became part of the urban youth culture, became sexually active, and did not make her way through school as her mother had intended. Instead, she has left home, lived with boyfriends, and now has a young child. Esther, now a very attractive fifty-one-year-old, meanwhile, continues to thrive, runs her business, helps out people looking for work when it is possible, travels to the various U.S. Caribbean carnivals, takes boat rides and Atlantic City trips, lives well, and has a healthy social life. Fliers and posters for various local Caribbean events are available in her shop, which is one of those centers for Caribbean people in Brooklyn. She was planning a Mother's Day concert with one of the popular calypso singers when I last talked to her and was thinking of getting some other educational certification as she did not want "to do hair for her entire life."

Velma

Velma is a forty-five-year-old police officer who recently built a house in the Caribbean. When I met Velma she was about to move into the house; she talked with pride about having gone through the process of acquiring the land and beginning construction of the house and was waiting for it to be completed. Located in a fairly residential area now, the three-bedroom house is sparingly furnished. I stayed with Velma for about three days last year, and the conversations were conducted during that time. Because of her police service, Velma had amassed about six months' leave, which she decided to use to go to New York to work to furnish her house. She thought about working as a security guard because of her police training but decided that a live-in domestic job would provide accommodation and food and thus maximize what she could save. Through her sister in Brooklyn, she found a job in New Jersey and was assigned to take care of an aging white woman who had little connection with her family. Velma said that the woman was very rebellious, did not want to bathe, was particular about what she ate, and also had a wound on her leg from a fall; she was not attending to the wound. Velma indicated that under her care the wound healed. She detailed, with pride, the steps she took to make the woman's life better: she insisted that the woman bathe and made her eat balanced meals. Taking it on as any other project she would see well to the end, as a trained police officer, she felt great pride on cleaning up this old woman's life and indicated that she actually felt great pity for her. She said as well that upon the end of the six-month stay she felt great sadness and guilt at leaving. Rather than prolong the departure, she decided to simply not go back after the long weekend and called the agency on Sunday night to say that she needed to be replaced as she had a family illness which necessitated that she return home. She felt that since this was in part true she was justified, because her twelve-year-old daughter's father, with whom she had an on-again, off-again relationship, had been in an accident. Though he lived at home with his mother, she wanted to be there for him if he needed her. Back home when we talked last year, she was awaiting the furniture which she had shipped, had a nice collection of household appliances, and she and her daughter were always well dressed. She also sends her daughter routinely to the United States to spend time with her cousins in New York during the summer months. She is well respected, likes her job in the Caribbean, has returned to her police service work, and is studying for a promotion to a higher rank. Only close friends and family know how she spent her leave time.

Nancy

The Richardson extended family lived for years in a decrepit shack in an area not far from one of the branches of the University of the West Indies. The mother and one daughter and her children inhabited the front and main house, another daughter erected a lean-to shack on the same property behind the main house. The other houses in that neighborhood are well kept in an otherwise clearly upwardly mobile neighborhood. It would not be unfair to say that their style of living must have been an eyesore to the other neighbors. Once the grandmother died, the two daughters and their now grown daughters and their children, who shared the space, realized that the land had been left to them. One daughter, now in her early sixties, decided to go to the United States and work for as long as she could and amass some money to put with what she already had accumulated at home. From the United States she made plans to begin the erecting of a massive two-story house, with about four bedrooms on each level. The initial money that she had was enough to erect the frame and to enclose one or two rooms in the bottom floor. Subsequent trips (about three in number) to the United States and short periods of employment there facilitated additional work on the house: to enclose the rest of the house and to include windows on the top floor. Her plan when we talked was subsequently to return to the United States for work again and to complete the house, but she did not have any anxiety about this and felt when the opportunity arose (God willing) she would travel. If not, something else would work out. When I talked to her again in early 2004, she indicated that she is older, in her seventies now, and has done as much as she could; but as it stands now, she does not plan to return to the United States to work and feels that her children have gotten a good start and that it is up to them to do the rest. The part of the house in which she lives is well kept with pretty curtains; her grand-children are part of her household. She is active in her church, has distinguished herself as one who prays with dynamism, visits with the sick, and is otherwise an active member of her community. One of her daughters recently came to New York to live with the New York branch of the family and to get work. Not long after that, her male friend and father of her two children followed her to the United States and proposed to her in a very romantic way, and they got married in Brooklyn. Interestingly, she is seeking hairdressing work in the United States as this is her training, and for years she had maintained a small beauty shop at the front of her family home and was able to make a fairly good living that way. Life in the United States without the official papers is one of hustle. She plans to send as much home as she can but feels that the house was her mother's project, and while she may help, she has to establish something for herself now. The house is almost completed as some of her children contribute when they can, in particu-lar, one of her sons, who drives a taxi in the Caribbean and lives on the first floor with his wife and two sons, in a partially enclosed area. The other sister of the family still lives in the same old house toward the back of the property, is a well-known baker of sponge cakes, which she sells or gives to friends and family, and has not done much to alter her home's condition, nor does she express any desire to migrate.

Mary

Mary came to the United States first in 1965, at age fifty-four, and spent three months with her son, leaving her daughter, who was taking her final exams, in the care of her cousin, who was a school teacher and ran a day-care center. Mary had spent most of her adult life as a primary school teacher, beginning at age fourteen as a "pupil teacher" in the government schools. A pregnancy cut short her ability to stay in this service, and after that she took her teaching skills and worked in the private school circuit, developing some still thriving schools in neighborhoods wherever she lived. Her first visit to the United States was com-pletely a social visit. Not satisfied with the arrangements for her daughter, she returned home from the United States, though she could have stayed longer and her friends told her she was crazy not to have done so. Instead, she decided to see her daughter through school. Struggling with the end of a difficult marriage, she endured for another year or so while she made plans to go to the United States, this time permanently. She left home in 1967 with her daughter, settled her in a university, and then headed off to Brooklyn to join the larger Caribbean commu-nity there and find work. She got a certificate as a nurse's aid and started training as a LPN. Her days were spent working as a nurse's aid to geriatric white women, providing in-home care, and sporadically training for her LPN certificate. Her employment history was checkered as she often went home in the winter months, not wanting to deal with the cold, and spent time with her older sister, who needed companionship and later care. Eventually, after fifteen years of inconsistent work in the United States, now sixty-nine, she returned home for good and declared herself retired. She lived on inheritance and some other pension money but had not put in enough social security time to earn a check if she did not live in the United States. She traveled annually to the United States to retain her green card, but after a while did not bother anymore and let the grace period at which one can stay out expire. Eighty-five now, an ailing diabetic, and confined to a wheelchair, she lives on a pension and remittances from her children abroad. Her health is not good and sometimes she laments not living anymore in the United States, saying that the services would be better. Two local women are employed to take care of her mornings and evenings, and their services are paid for by her daughter abroad. The early phase of her return, though, she describes as a lot of fun, filled with social activities with her peers. One woman formed a senior citizens organization to help the old folks meet each other and to provide social interaction, but it tended to be dinners and parties rather than craft work, and largely when they were still in their comparatively mobile sixties and seventies. The transition to the eighties has meant the death of many in the group, and infirmity and advanced aging and nursing-home living have cut down on the activity and travel to the United States. Many of that group had provided care services for elders abroad and are often dissatisfied with the service they get at home.

Philomena

Philomena lived for years with a man much older than she and in the interim had six daughters with him. She traveled to the United States in 1966, when she was in her mid-fifties, settled in Brooklyn, and easily found work as a live-in servant to a quite famous differently abled woman who painted with her feet and who frequently appeared in local newspapers for her work. Philomena spent at least ten years doing hard domestic service and spent all her free time either working extra time on her days off or shopping for furnishings for her home. These furnishings she took down in crates and mailed from time to time, everything from toilets and matching sinks to furniture, lighting fixtures, and appliances, planning to finally have her ideal home in the Caribbean. In the meantime, she went home and made sure that she got married to her children's father, the owner of a substantial piece of land, since other women were attempting to move in on an otherwise healthy man living in a house by himself. Philomena spent the next five years or so sending all her money home to improve the house, with the plan to return home after all her children were settled and happy in the United States. She oversaw her last unmarried daughter's college education, graduation, marriages, first babies, and returned to Brooklyn occasionally to shop. She returned home finally in 1992 and happily settled into her life at home in a nicely organized and decorated home. However in 1996, at age seventy-five, she returned to Brooklyn and while at her daughter's house had a stroke which left her badly brain damaged and living only on life-support systems. In the end, the family made a determination that she could not survive anymore and allowed the doctors to disconnect the support systems; she died shortly after. She was buried in her rural village in the Caribbean, eulogized by her family. The home she struggled for remains empty except for occasional visits by relatives from the United States who want to spend time at home and a family friend who lives in makeshift quarters adjacent to the house.

These narratives reveal some identifiable patterns. First of all, the economic impetus for migration is clear in all the narratives, whether it is for short-term benefit, such as money to build or furnish a house, or to educate a child. The knowledge that in the United States one has greater access to resources becomes part of the fueling mechanism which propels migration. This bears out all the analyses which underscore the economic and "life improvement" motives for migration.

Among the older women, the logic of temporariness and, thus, the desire and practice of returning to the Caribbean are clear. We get no intention from these narratives that any of them planned to make the United States their home. The younger women, by contrast, seem to be caught, once they are in the United States, in a series of life decisions which relocate them in the United States more permanently than intended. The options then become further study and certification and the move to more professional employment like nursing and clerical work or the other more remunerated professions through earning degrees like MBA's. It may be that the older women, who migrated as already middle-aged women, had a shorter but more intense work periods in the United States and a different expectation of retirement than women who enter the United States earlier in their lives. This is perhaps one area which deserves further study, though it is evident that women, like Velma, who already have a pretty certain pattern of professional advancement make different decisions than those who have only occasional work or no employment commitment of consequence in their home countries.

The Caribbean Woman as Domestic Worker

> Women Have Time
> Women have time
> To breast feed,
> Raise children
> Clean house
> Wash, iron,
> Fold clothes
> Carry water,

Gather wood.
Plant, weed, harvest,
Bake bread,
Make sauce,
Brew beer,
And more:
Do their hair,
Kohl their eyes,
Add makeup,
Dress and undress.
Women have time
For a day at the office
And then to shop
For breakfast, lunch and dinner
That they prepare.

Women have time.
Men, have no time. [17]

I have used poetry deliberately here for a few reasons. One of them is that this chapter is being written by someone whose primary field is literary criticism. But more importantly, because poetry offers succinct commentary on some of the ideas that appear in any discussion of this issue: the first, about the exploitation of women's labor and women's time; the second, about agency in leaving exploitative situations, one of the fundamentals of women's migration.

I have also selected two stories from two different generations and one other narrative which spans both generations. At the center of each narrative is the need for economic well-being and the centrality of acquiring a home and/or a better life. In some cases, it is the physical building itself; in others, it is the accouterments of a good home or education for one's children. Migration, then, is linked to the globalization of the economy and the absence of certain opportunities for women of working-class origin if they do not follow the route of mobility through education. Family connections are the other central feature in each case: the need to see the family advance and the grandchildren cared for in a much better way. Thirdly, the return home, successful or not, is a feature which is ever present. It moves from dream to reality, though the reality is often not borne out in a positive way. In some cases age and infirmity preclude full enjoyment; in others the economic gains are minimal in a relative way—cheap furniture and U.S. fittings.

Having written about the issue largely through literature, as in "Writing Home: Gender and Heritage in the Works of Afro-Caribbean/American Women Writers" and, subsequently, in *Migrations of the Subject* (1994),"[18] and with social science literature as a rich background, I find it interesting to locate these ethnographies in those two larger contexts. Interdisciplinary work aids well in this process. Recent work such as Patricia Pessar's *Caribbean Circuits* (1997), for example, identifies that the migration is circuitous, that it is never one-sided, and that a series of movements back and forth perhaps more closely identifies this migratory pattern. This study affirms the earlier conclusions of Bryce-Laporte and Mortimer (1976) and Gordon (1990) as it affirms Pessar's more recent conclusions.

In understanding the larger dynamics of migration, the Caribbean context for these historical and contemporary convergences are developed further in "Imperial Geographies and Caribbean Nationalism: At the Border between 'A Dying Colonialism' and U.S. Hegemony."[19] In both cases, we argue, the older imperialist formulations prefigure contemporary notions of globalization as, therefore, always already economic, but also always assuming control of space. The modern version of imperialism is clearly marked as U.S. imperialism and includes the extensive role of the U.S. armed forces, the extending U.S. business monopolies, and the assumptions of open markets for U.S. products as well as the development of new technologies of communication.[20]

In *Spaces of Hope* (2000), David Harvey's discussion of contemporary globalization as a process consistently linked to capitalist labor flows presents some allied positions. For Harvey, in terms of "contemporary globalization," four recent shifts are identifiable: (1) financial deregulation which began in the United States in the early 1970s and moved from a hierarchical system controlled by the United States to a more decentralized system of international finance with power blocks; (2) the waves of profound technological change and product innovation; (3) the media and communications systems and the ultimate "dematerialization of space" which had its origins in the military apparatus now controlled by the financial institutions and multinational corporations; and (4) the cost and time of moving commodities and people. These were accompanied by (1) geographical dispersal and fragmentation of production systems which transcend national boundaries and produce commodities globally; (2) doubling of the world wage-labor force, bringing women largely into the market and a parallel exploitation; (3) a global population on the move; (4) hyper-urbanization; (5) a re-territorialization of the world on the backs of the nation-states but operating at the supra-national level, and parallel environmental and social problems.[21]

The women represented here all have as primary reasons for migration the search for a "better life" linked to family advancement and, in comparison, often not with the full range of U.S. African American class positions, but measured against the success of their cohorts back home. It also identifies the temporariness of some of these movements as the "translocal movement" or "commuter nation," definitions of Puerto Rico. Puerto Ricans represent one important model that the United States has employed in its "misuse" of Puerto Rico and its creation of "surplus citizenship."[22] The assumption of the "commuter nation" or the "translocal nation" across borders, in which Puerto Ricans take part, mimics the same actions of capital between Puerto Rico and the United States as it shadows the same relationship with African American poor who similarly become "surplus citizens" within the United States. Similar points can be made about Mexico and the use of Mexican migrant labor within the United States, and particularly along its borders in the legendary *maquiladoras*. The result is that other Caribbean countries, like Trinidad, Tobago, and Barbados, become other versions of the same as they face either incorporation into an American zone of economic domination or the wrath of the United States, as Cuba has for forty years for daring to choose another path.[23]

The proximity of the United States to the Caribbean means that there is a much quicker passage between the two locations, as opposed to the United Kingdom, where preparations for return home, even now, are much more planned. Still, economic well-being of self and family and educational and professional advancement leading to a measure of comfort and happiness are primary motivating factors in the drive to self-empowerment.

The "super-exploitation" of the black woman, as outlined by Claudia Jones, is worth recalling here in the context of this chapter's concerns. Jones had early asserted that the black woman, as "mother, as Negro," occupies a particular position in terms of defense of the black family and that this then is what renders her so pivotal to struggles as it explains her possibilities for militancy. Jones's approach was not a romanticized view of motherhood as some sort of essential identity, but an analysis of the role of super-exploitation in black women's lives. Her larger point is that the United States boasts that American women possess "the greatest equality" in the world, yet this cannot hold up when one identifies the actual location of black women in American society: "Not equality, but degradation and super-exploitation."[24] So, Jones, in the 1940s and 1950s, made a point that still can be argued through a number of surveys of women's rights internationally today: while the United States boasts a certain superiority over other nations at a number of levels, in the way that it treats and locates women of color, this cannot hold up. Using economic statistics and indicators of her time, such as Department of Labor Statistics, Jones is able to identify the wage rates of black women in relation to other women and men and finds them at the lowest end of the pay scale, as all other contemporary studies and analyses in the 1980s up to the present have also found. She concluded that "Negro women are still generally confined to the lowest paying jobs" in 1948.[25]

Since black women are often heads of households, then the poverty of black communities is assured if the black women stay underpaid and super-exploited. Jones's analysis of Department of Labor Department statistics also revealed that black women workers are employed primarily in private families as domestics, as cooks and waitresses, and in a range of other service industries, agricultural work, and clerical work. Professional black women remained the minority.

Importantly, as well, she identified domestic work as the kind of "catch-all, fall-back" profession for black women and, in the postwar period, the job made to seem most desirous for black women. Again, she correctly identified media representations of black women as one of the sources for maintaining this identification of black women in service roles.

Rhonda Williams's "If You're Black, Get Back; If You're Brown, Stick Around; If You're White, Hang Tight: A Primer on Race, Gender, and Work in the Global Economy" provides more contemporary tables and analyses of some of these issues of occupational status according to race and class and identifies the decline in manufacturing, the de-emphasis on unionized employment, the relocation of women from welfare roles to lower-income employment, and the exportation of jobs. The recognition that "their jobs were exportable and the historic emergence of the global manufacturing economy puts these workers in direct competition with some of the poorest working women in the world." Since "job competition is race and gender specific, we expect that politically weaker and less numerous race-gender groups will bear most of the costs of competition," she concludes.[26]

In 2001, this position seems to have remained largely unchanged despite the advances of some women into the middle class.[27] Recent census data reveals a similar disparity: according to U.S. Department of Labor Statistics, women's annual earnings are only still 72 percent of men's, and women of color earn 65 percent of white men's earnings.[28] The lower-paying jobs are still in the service area, where women still tend to be congregated.

The sexual division of labor as expressed in feminist political economy is necessarily recalled here. Besides a segmented pattern of labor based on gender and class, assumptions are made about the value and availability of women's work. In particular, the labor of women of color is assigned lower remunerative value while it is multiply extracted and linked, therefore, precisely to that same history of imperialist exploitation.[29] Essentially, then, migration of Caribbean women for reasons of work, allowing some mobility and personal satisfaction within a larger context, suffers from that tension within the larger construct of transnational labor market flows. So, while one may finally have a "leaving" strategy, is there ever an "elsewhere" that is completely untouched by all of these machinations at the political and economic level?

Clearly, more study is warranted on this subject. This particular analysis simply confirms many of the earlier findings but provides a preliminary analysis of generational differences. More contemporary sociological and economic analyses on Caribbean women and migration are being undertaken by Monica Jardine at SUNY-Buffalo, looking at women in the professional sector, and Linda Carty at Syracuse University, looking at working-class women, largely domestic workers.

From my own analyses, however, I can conclude that migration for the second generation is not seen as mandatory for economic success, as it was for the

1960s generation, but as one option in a series of possibilities. In this context, and in both cases, the United States is used as a work space, a factory of sorts, a learning site as well, and home is linked to fun, relaxation, family commitments, connections, and, therefore, a more healthy social life.

The contestation of U.S. boundaries, legislation, policies, and rules of conduct is fundamental and almost instinctive. Many indicate that the policies are ridiculous given U.S. government and its people's mobility throughout the Caribbean, and they therefore assume the same right to enter in and work in the United States. The supplying of financial remuneration is a fixed feature of the monthly expenditures, i.e., not an option but the same as paying a bill or one's rent. Remittances become, as in Ransford Palmer's study, another aspect of capital counter-flow and part of the circular movement of labor and capital. Migration is thus linked to access to resources which are, in regional terms, plentiful and unbalanced in the United States. There is then an assumption of mobility which spells a certain resistance to fixity in intimate relationships and in economic and social life.

NOTES

This chapter is dedicated to my mother, Mary Boyce Joseph, who recently made her transition (February 10, 2005) to the realm of the ancestors. My years of trying to make sense of her various migrations and experiences have led me to this study. Her story is included here under the ethnography titled "Mary." I thank Monica Jardine as always for important information and useful discussion on Caribbean migration. Thanks also to the various readers and commentators of the Work in the Lives of Women of Color Working Group on this chapter in its various stages.

1. Ransford Palmer, ed., *In Search of a Better Life: Perspectives on Migration from the Caribbean* (New York: Praeger, 1990), 1.

2. See, for example, Stuart Hall, "The Local and the Global: Globalization and Ethnicity," in *Culture, Globalization, and the World-System,*" ed. Anthony King (London: Macmillan, 1991), 19–39. Hall indicates that this "new kind of globalization is not English, it is American" (ibid., 27). See also Zygmunt Bauman, *Globalization: The Human Consequences* (New York: Columbia University Press, 1998).

3. Claudia Jones, "American Imperialism and the British West Indies,"*Political Affairs* (April 1958): 9–8. See my "Claudia Jones, Anti-Imperialist, Black Feminist Politics," in *Decolonizing the Academy: African Diaspora Studies,* ed. Carole Boyce Davies et al. (Trenton, N.J.: Africa World Press, 2003), 45–60; and further discussion in my *Left of Karl Marx: The Politics and Poetics of Claudia Jones* (Durham, N.C.: Duke University Press, forthcoming).

4. Lynn Bolles, "Going Abroad: Working-Class Jamaican Women and Migration," in *Female Immigrants to the United States: Caribbean, Latin American, and African Experiences,* ed. Delores Mortimer and Roy S. Bryce-Laporte (Washington, D.C.: RIIES, Smithsonian, 1976, 1981), 66.

5. Judith Burgess and Meryl James-Gray, "Migration and Sex Roles: A Comparison of Black and Indian Trinidadians in New York City," in Mortimer and Bryce-Laporte, *Female Immigrants to the United States,* 101.

6. Monica Gordon's "Dependents or Independent Workers? The Status of Caribbean Immigrant Women in the United States," in Ransford Palmer, *In Search of a Better Life,* 131.

7. Saskia Sassen's work—such as *The Mobility of Labor and Capital: A Study in International Investment and Labor Flow* (New York and Cambridge: Cambridge University Press, 1988); *The Global City: New York London Tokyo* (Princeton, N.J.: Princeton University Press, 1991); *Globalization and Its Discontents: Selected Essays 1984–1998* (New York: New Press, 1998); *Guests and Aliens* (New York: New Press, 1999)—has in many ways spearheaded the development of a subfield of migration and the global economy.

8. Carla Freeman, *High Tech and High Heels in the Global Economy* (Durham and London: Duke University Press, 2000).

9. See my *Migrations of the Subject* (London: Routledge, 1994) for discussion of the mobile subject with agency. According to Foucault, there are two meanings of the word "subject": (1) subject to someone else by control and dependence and (2) having one's own identity by a conscience of self-knowledge. See also Kelvin Santiago-Valles, *"Subject People" and Colonial Discourses* (Albany: SUNY Press, 1994).

10. I have found the following helpful in providing the background information on the political economy of Caribbean women and have attempted to locate migration in that context: Patricia Pessar, *Caribbean Circuits: New Directions in the Study of Caribbean Migration* (New York: Center for Migration Studies, 1997).

11. See especially Saskia Sassen, *The Mobility of Labor and Capital*.

12. See, for example, Grace Chang, *Disposable Domestics: Immigrant Women Workers in the Global Economy* (Cambridge, Mass.: South End Press, 2000).

13. Keith Hart, ed., *Women and the Sexual Division of Labor in the Caribbean* (Kingston, Jamaica: Canoe Press, University of the West Indies, 1989/1996); Rhoda Reddock, "Historical and Contemporary Perspectives: The Case of Trinidad and Tobago," in ibid., 50–71; and Dorian L. Powell, "Women's Domestic Labor: Paid and Unpaid," in ibid., 139–147. See also the special issue "Rethinking Caribbean Difference," *Feminist Review* 59 (summer 1998).

14. Reddock, "Historical and Contemporary Perspectives," 59–60, 61–63.

15. Mary C. Waters, *Black Identities: West Indian Immigrant Dreams and American Realities* (Cambridge and London: Harvard University Press, 2001).

16. Study published in Miami *Caribbean Today,* March 2001, 3.

17. Poem by Reesom Haile, in her *We Invented the Wheel* (Trenton, N.J.: Red Sea Press, 2001). The inclusion of this poem is dedicated to the memory of Reesom Haile, one who left us to soon. *"One Love! One heart!"*

18. Carole Boyce Davies, "Writing Home: Gender and Heritage in the Works of Afro-Caribbean/American Women Writers," in *Out of the Kumbla: Caribbean Women and Literature,* ed. Carole Boyce Davies and Elaine Fido (Trenton, N.J.: Africa World Press, 1990); Davies, *Migrations of the Subject.*

19. Carole Boyce Davies and Monica Jardine, "Imperial Geographies and Caribbean Nationalism: At the Border between 'A Dying Colonialism' and U.S. Hegemony," *New Centennial Review* 3, no. 3 (fall 2003): 151–174.

20. See Carole Boyce Davies, "Beyond Unicentricity: Transcultural Black Intellectual Presences," *Research in African Literatures* 30, no. 2 (summer 1999): 96–109.

21. David Harvey, *Spaces of Hope* (Edinburgh, Scotland: Edinburgh University Press, 2000), 53–72.

22. In the Caribbean/U.S. domestic context as it relates to labor exploitation and citizenship rights, see Miriam Muniz of the University of Puerto Rico, Rio Pedras, formulation of USA citizenship as it pertains to Puerto Rico, as *"usar*—to use" citizenship is also applicable, her presentation at Binghamton University Coloniality Working Group Conference, March 2000.

23. This is Monica Jardine's argument in our "Imperial Geographies and Caribbean Nationalism."

24. Claudia Jones makes this argument in several articles, but it is available in part in her essay "An End to the Neglect of the Problems of the Negro Women," *Political Affairs* (June 1949), reprinted in vol. 53 (March 1974): 29, 28–42. See my "The Super-Exploitation of the Black Working-Class Woman: Women's Rights, Workers' Rights, Anti-Imperialism," in my forthcoming *Left of Karl Marx*.

25. Jones, "An End to the Neglect of the Problems of the Negro Women," 30.

26. Rhonda Williams, "If You're Black, Get Back; If You're Brown, Stick Around; If You're White, Hang Tight: A Primer on Race, Gender, and Work in the Global Economy," working paper, the Preamble Center, University of Maryland, May 2000, 27, 33.

27. Census data allow similar conclusions. United States Department of Labor, 2002, Bureau of Labor Statistics, Occupational Employment Statistics, Washington, D.C., http://www.bls.gov (accessed September 18, 2006).

28. Average annual earnings listed in the 1998 National Occupational Employment and Wage Estimates from Occupational Employment Statistics, U.S. Department of Labor, Bureau of Statistics, http://www.dol.gov/dol/ (accessed September 18, 2006).

29. U.S. Census Bureau, "United States Census, 2000," http://www.census.gov/ (accessed September 18, 2006).

Creatively Coping with Crisis and Globalization

ZIMBABWEAN BUSINESSWOMEN IN
CROCHETING AND KNITTING

MARY JOHNSON OSIRIM

Work is central to the lives and identities of sub-Saharan African women. During the past two decades, social science research on gender and work in sub-Saharan Africa has grown exponentially.[1] Feminist social scientists on both sides of the Atlantic have played a critical role in examining women's status in labor markets throughout the continent, the diversity of tasks in which they are engaged, as well as the gender stratification that persists in nearly all sectors of the economy in African states. Over the past decade, most studies of African women and work by gender researchers have focused on women's participation in the microenterprise (informal) sector of the economy.[2] Feminist scholarship, in particular, has focused on this sector since this is the second largest area of income-earning for women after agriculture on the continent and because women's participation in this sector has substantially increased as a result of increasing globalization, especially with the establishment of structural adjustment programs.[3] Further, in some African nations, such as Zimbabwe, women own the majority of businesses in the microenterprise sector (64 percent of such businesses in Zimbabwe), which includes the production of many gendered goods and services among other items. This chapter will explore the business activities of one group of women entrepreneurs in the microenterprise sector in urban Zimbabwe, crocheters and knitters, as well as the impact of structural adjustment on the operation of their businesses and their contributions to development.

Crocheting and knitting are the activities in the microenterprise sector that are most unique to Zimbabwe and most directly tied to the colonial enterprise. As part of the colonial project of domesticating African women, white women taught these crafts to individual black Zimbabwean women, as well as to black women in urban women's clubs and schools. For example, the African Women's Club, founded in 1937, taught knitting, crocheting, and other crafts to its members, including some black women.[4]

Overall, however, very little attention has been paid to knitting and crocheting as part of Zimbabwe's microenterprise sector, and this remains an understudied area in the literature on southern African women and work. Through an examination of in-depth interviews with fifty-seven crocheters in urban Zimbabwe, this chapter breaks new ground and shows that women in this sector have exhibited strong business acumen, demonstrated their creativity, and contributed to material culture as well as to local and national development. By their ingenuity and strategic decision-making, they are managing to maintain their households and their businesses beyond the level of simple survival in the midst of severe economic crisis. I will begin this analysis with an explication of the theoretical framework that informs this work. Next, the chapter will briefly discuss the demographic characteristics of the sample and the establishment and operation of their enterprises. Finally, this study will discuss the impact of one aspect of globalization—the Economic Structural Adjustment Program (ESAP)—on the operation of their firms and the coping strategies that black women have employed in responding to this program.

Making Sense of African Women's Status in the World of Work: Feminist Political Economy and the Zimbabwean Microenterprise Sector

In attempting to understand women's position in labor markets in contemporary northern and southern nations, the feminist political economy paradigm provides us with a useful set of tools. This perspective is important not only in comprehending women's status in the formal and microenterprise sectors of societies around the world, but in also understanding the opportunities and challenges that women face related to globalization.[5] Further, this theory enables us to understand how gender, racial, ethnic, class, age, and sexuality status (among other factors) either provides entrance to, mobility in, or blockage from labor markets.

Feminist political economy draws on world systems theory and comparative political economy in the sociology of development.[6] Precisely because an understanding of political economy at the national and global levels is so central to this paradigm, I have chosen to call this a feminist political economy perspective as opposed to simply a gender analysis. Feminist political economy supercedes the world systems perspective in arguing not only that an international division of labor exists, but that one exists and operates based on gender.[7] Building on world systems analysis, this theory maintains that both internal factors (such as specific problems within states) and external factors (the relations that exist between states in the global South, the northern hegemonic powers, and the international financial institutions) must be considered in charting a nation's prospects for development. Thus, the global capitalist system in combination with domestic factors creates and reinforces inequality between the rich and the poor as well as between women and men. In this process, some nations become the producers of certain goods and services, with the proceeds from this labor accruing to either women or men, but generally not both. For example, women, especially young women, have become the major laborers on many global assembly lines for electronics and textiles found in East and South Asia, particularly given the persistence of stereotypes about women's quick, nimble fingers. Moghadam points out that while we are witnessing increased rates of labor force participation for women, this growth is occurring largely in low-level manufacturing and service positions.[8] Men tend to be more major beneficiaries of higher-paying, higher-status managerial positions in multinational corporations (MNC's).

The feminist political economy perspective also considers how gender and class affect the lives of women of color around the globe and how race, capitalism, colonialism, and patriarchy are interlocking systems of oppression for women in such areas as southern Africa.[9] In societies such as Zimbabwe and South Africa, for example, race-based systems of stratification were established during the colonial regime and maintained by modern capitalism. Feminist political economy enables us to see how in a society with a class-color hierarchy, colored women in such societies could occupy roles as both oppressors and oppressed. In the labor market, for example, colored women often held lower-level clerical positions in the formal sector. When they returned home, however, these same colored women often occupied the role of oppressors frequently in their hiring and treatment of black domestic workers. Therefore, this paradigm reveals the multiple roles that individuals can occupy simultaneously, as well as the factors that converge in the lives of women of color and intensify the discrimination they experience.

Feminist political economy further acknowledges women's agency in their families, their communities, and their nations, as well as their acts of resistance to colonial and post-colonial states and to globalization.[10] This perspective enables an analysis of such issues as poor women's responses to globalization, particularly to structural adjustment programs (SAP's). Globalization has disproportionately affected poor and low-income populations in the South, most notably women and children, through state policies strongly encouraged or mandated by international financial institutions (IFI's) such as the World Bank and the International Monetary Fund (IMF), which reduce government spending on social service programs. These IFI's established conditions that poor, indebted nations needed to meet in order to receive future loans, including the adoption of the liberal economic model (the free market), reductions in state expenditures, and devaluation of the local currency. These mandates suggested economic conformity with the North and further integration into the world capitalist system. Under such conditions, many lower-echelon civil servants in the South lost their jobs and were often encouraged by their governments to start small enterprises and microenterprises to support their families. Drastic cuts in state expenditures for education, health care, and transportation led many market women, for example, in SAP-conforming nations to call for general strikes and to openly resist the state for the toll that it was taking on them.[11] Feminist political economy also enables us to study the coping strategies that women develop in response to globalization, such as Zimbabwean crocheters engaging in cross-border trade with South Africa.[12]

This paradigm has been most useful in my work on the development of women's entrepreneurship in the microenterprise sector in many ways. First, it enables us to explore how Zimbabwe's mode of incorporation into the world system and the establishment of a race-based system of stratification limited the development of the colonial state and society and restricted black women's status to that of legal minors. Zimbabwe (Rhodesia) entered the capitalist world system as a colony of Britain. It was incorporated into this system as a supplier of primary products, namely, tobacco, maize, coffee, tea, gold, nickel, tin, copper, and coal. Although Zimbabwe under colonialism also developed light industries, development was significantly curtailed by the subordinate position through which it entered the world system. A system of "internal colonies" was developed in which blacks were subordinate to whites and forced to live within the Tribal Trust Lands (the poorest land in the country) while the most arable land in the nation was reserved for whites.[13] As the colonial patriarchal state developed, the British developed a system of taxation, which forced black men to sell their labor to white-owned cash-crop farms or to light manufacturing industries or mining.[14] The lowest status in society was reserved for black women, who were expected to eke out a living in subsistence agriculture in the Tribal Trust Lands.[15]

In all areas of possible status attainment, black women were relegated to the lowest rungs on the ladder. With respect to the colonial education system, since black men were expected to serve the white colonial state in more formal-sector positions, they generally received more education than black women. Those black Zimbabwean women who lived on or near missions were likely to receive about four years of primary school.[16] This education, however, was highly gendered and usually included basic reading, writing, and arithmetic, with an emphasis on domestic skills, such as cooking, sewing, and sometimes crocheting and knitting.

The first post-independence decade in Zimbabwe was marked by economic growth and the state's commitment to promoting equality for women and men with the establishment of the Ministry of Community and Cooperative Development and Women's Affairs in 1981 and the passage of the Legal Age of Majority Act in 1982.[17] This positive period was quickly reversed with the downturn in the economy and the adoption of the ESAP in late 1990.[18] The feminist political economy approach further enables us to understand how poor and low-income black women disproportionately bore the costs of the economic crisis and adjustment. These women were particularly vulnerable given the legacy of colonialism as it is reflected in their low levels of educational attainment and blockage from formal-sector positions. Since many men lost formal-sector positions under ESAP, women found that they had to find work, if they were not already income-earners, and increase their financial contributions to their families, particularly given the skyrocketing food costs and the re-establishment of primary school fees. During this period, low-income women entrepreneurs also faced growing competition from men, who increasingly entered areas like market trade to earn a living. Due to the persistence of patriarchal forms of domination, their generally higher incomes, and the strength of their social networks, especially with respect to formal institutions, men generally out-performed women even in the small enterprise and microenterprise sector and had greater long-term prospects. Men were particularly more likely to obtain business loans, since their higher levels of educational attainment (when compared with their female counterparts) combined with their significant social capital meant that they had more connections with those in business, banking, government, and the non-profit sector. Further, they often had more capital to invest initially in their enterprises as well as more assets and, when considered in conjunction with their greater educational achievements and their gender, were considered the safer credit risks.[19]

Given the history of colonialism, the conditions under which Zimbabwe was incorporated into the world economy, the class-color hierarchy, and the persistence of patriarchy, there is little wonder that most black Zimbabwean women still occupy positions at the lowest levels of society. Although they are disproportionately found in low-status positions, black Zimbabwean women have made and continue to make very important contributions to the development of their families, their communities, and their nation. The feminist political economy perspective is the best framework for providing a comprehensive analysis of black women's current position—the successes and problems that they have experienced as well as the challenges that remain. With this theory as a backdrop, the chapter will now examine why and how many black Zimbabwean women have become entrepreneurs in the microenterprise sector.

Profile of the Entrepreneurs: The Decision to Become Crocheters and Businesswomen

During fieldwork visits to Harare and Bulawayo, the two largest cities in Zimbabwe, in 1991, 1994, and 1997, in-depth interviews were conducted with fifty-seven crocheters at their worksites located at or near various shopping centers in these cities.[20] The ethnic distribution of this sample is very similar to the overall distribution of the major ethnic groups in the country. Seventy percent (forty) of the crocheters were Shona, the largest ethnic group in Zimbabwe, which comprises about 80 percent of the population, and 18 percent (ten) were Ndebele, the second largest group in the country, with about 16 percent of the overall population. In addition, some crocheters were members of ethnic groups based in other nations in southern Africa, such as in Zambia and South Africa. Approximately 12 percent (seven) of this sample were members of non-Zimbabwean ethnic groups. This diversity points to the significant movement of populations throughout the southern African region.

The mean and median age of participants in this sample was thirty-eight years. Nearly all of the crocheters had received some formal education, with "completion of primary school" constituting the largest single category of educational attainment (about 42 percent of the sample). Approximately 26 percent (fifteen) of the respondents had received some secondary education, while another four crocheters had successfully completed their "O-level" examinations and thus completed the first level of secondary school.[21] One entrepreneur in this sample did receive some post-secondary education at a technical college, although she did not attain her O-level certificate. At the lower end of the educational spectrum, 21 percent (twelve) of the businesswomen received less than six years of primary schooling. Only one crocheter had not received any formal education.

During their childhood and adolescence, the vast majority of these entrepreneurs wanted to become nurses. Other businesswomen expressed desires to enter other gender-typed occupations, such as becoming a teacher or a flight attendant. Although two women mentioned that they wanted to become seamstresses or crocheters since their childhoods, for the most part, these respondents were not interested in the world of business. A few women did differ from the norm of gender-typed occupations and mentioned that they wanted to become doctors or policewomen, perhaps in the latter case because of the power and authority that seemed to accompany such positions. Further, all of these positions were likely viewed as desirable since they were believed to provide a good, regular salary. Although they had high aspirations for educational attainment in their youth, these businesswomen were unable to realize these dreams for several reasons. First, the vast majority of these women were blocked from entering formal-sector jobs because they lacked the requisite number of O-level passes on their secondary school examinations, the first criteria to obtain professional, managerial, clerical, and sales positions in the formal sector. The fact that these women were largely from poor backgrounds and generally had many domestic and child-care responsibilities throughout most of their youth left little available time for them to devote to their academic pursuits. Compared to their brothers of similar ages, young girls, especially secondary-school-aged girls, would be saddled with many more daily responsibilities for the preparation of meals, dishwashing, laundry, and child care. While young men did have household tasks assigned to them, these tended to be jobs such as car washing and home repairs, which were not always daily responsibilities.[22] Coming from poor backgrounds also meant that their families did not possess the resources to provide private tutoring or extra books to facilitate their educational experience. Thus, it does not come as a surprise that the majority of respondents did not pass five O-level examinations and thus did not receive their certificates for completion of lower secondary school. Students who wished to retake the examinations had to re-enroll in school and thus pay tuition and any additional costs associated with school attendance to take the examinations again. Such possibilities were generally out of reach for poor families. Without this credential, these women were barred from obtaining formal-sector positions. Second, many of these young women did not come from families who could afford to provide secondary education for all their children. In fact, when resources were so scarce, decisions were most often made to educate sons over daughters since the former remain a part of a father's family until death and continue to have obligations to support their family, while young women most often marry and join their husbands' families.[23] Third, female high school students who became pregnant while they were enrolled in school were forced to terminate their formal education. Many crocheters experienced these problems and, therefore, were unable to complete secondary school and obtain formal-sector jobs:

> [I] was raised to work hard and not to borrow to pay for what I can't afford or don't need. I wanted to go to school and pass well, and learn to be a doctor or a nurse or even be an air hostess. I really wanted to be an air hostess, but there was not money for school. (Interview with Maidei Mwambo, Harare, 1994)

> Yes, I wanted to be a teacher, but I got pregnant and had to leave school. Later on, I became too ill to continue my education. (Interview with Tsitsi, Harare, 1994)

> Wanted to become a teacher. . . . Could not pursue this because my father had no money for me to go to school beyond standard four. (Interview with Lisamiso, Bulawayo, 1997)[24]

Although receiving the O-level certificate was out of reach for the vast majority of participants in this study, many of the crocheters did gain additional knowledge and skills through training programs and other forms of informal education. Forty-seven percent of these entrepreneurs (twenty-six) supplemented their primary or secondary school education with training in evening schools, community centers, churches, and local clubs. Five of these businesswomen enrolled in academic courses that they had initially failed in secondary school in an attempt to gain their secondary school certificates. Most of these respondents were either unsuccessful in their attempts or were, at the time of these interviews, still enrolled in such programs. A few businesswomen had pursued secretarial courses, which included instruction in typing, shorthand, and, sometimes, bookkeeping. On the other hand, most women who continued to receive education beyond their formal schooling were receiving instruction in domestic science. Included among the skills that they acquired were sewing, crocheting, knitting, and embroidery. Needless to say, these latter skills either directly benefited these women in their current enterprises and/or provided them with a few options for other types of work they might pursue in the microenterprise sector. In fact, during periods of economic crisis, it was not unusual to see women engaged in multiple occupations to maintain themselves and their families. Thus, crocheters involved in cross-border trade in South Africa also frequently sold dresses or other items of women's clothing that they or a friend had made.

In addition to the roles of formal schooling, evening schools, clubs, and other training programs, learning to crochet and knit were skills that were mainly transmitted through women's networks. While crocheting and knitting were part of the primary school curricula in some cases and were also taught in community centers, churches, and clubs, most women learned these skills from friends and female relatives, especially their mothers, sisters, and aunts. In fact, women's social capital remains a very important factor in acquiring such skills and negotiating subcontracting arrangements in crocheting enterprises, since women often rely on their relatives and close female friends and neighbors to assist them in making large crochet items, such as tablecloths and bedspreads. Women who help in making these items are generally compensated on a piece-rate basis.

All in all, while women entrepreneurs experienced severe structural barriers with respect to educational attainment and acquiring formal-sector positions, they manifested a high level of commitment to education and skills development over the life course. Unfortunately, the heavy demands of maintaining their households and their commitments to their extended families and to their enterprises, coupled with their lack of capital and the economic crisis, make it extremely difficult for them to successfully complete a course of study that could lead to enhanced socioeconomic mobility. Their dedication and belief in the power of education to transform lives, however, remains quite strong and is a value they have fostered in their children.

Fifty-six percent (thirty-two) of these businesswomen held other positions prior to their current roles in crocheting. As would be expected given their levels of educational attainment, most of their earlier work experience was also in the microenterprise sector. Many of these entrepreneurs were previously involved in sales as produce or clothing vendors or cashiers in small shops. Such sales experience is likely to serve as a valuable asset to these women in their current positions as entrepreneurs in the microenterprise sector. Some of the crocheters also had prior experience as domestic workers, laundresses, or farmers. Three of these entrepreneurs had worked as temporary teachers or teacher trainers before starting their current businesses.

About 40 percent (twenty-three) of the respondents are currently supplementing their earnings from crocheting and knitting with sales in other areas. Most of these women are selling stone carvings, the indigenous Shona art form that is widely associated with Zimbabwe. The carving of stone figures remains within the purview of men, but as the economic crisis intensified, women were increasingly found to sell these carvings, often alongside men.[25] Crocheters, particularly those located at some of the major tourist shopping centers, such as Newlands in Harare, recognized the demand for such items among tourists and attempted to respond to this demand by providing items which Europeans and Americans generally identified as more "uniquely African" than most of the other crocheted and knitted items made by these entrepreneurs. Other businesswomen in this study tried to augment their earnings through the sale of produce or women's clothing that they had made.

Women in this study began crocheting enterprises and engaged in other activities in the microenterprise sector to assist in the support of their families. Women in Zimbabwe view their responsibilities to their children and to their extended families as major dimensions of their identities. Due to the blocked opportunities that prevented them from entering formal-sector occupations, these women began businesses in crocheting based on the skills that they had acquired in schools, clubs, and training programs and/or from their female relatives. These entrepreneurs were most often encouraged by relatives to establish crochet businesses:

> I had wanted to be a nurse, but I failed O-levels and didn't have the marks to continue. Don't think I learned anything in school; well, they taught me to sew, read, write, cook, and plow. Because it was dull at school, I wanted to be a housewife. School was hard for me. I wanted to be a housewife because it's the only thing I thought I'd be able to do. My mother taught me how to knit. My mother-in-law later helped by giving the money and advice. She told me to start this business so I can have money. She found the space for me where I now sell. She is in the same type of business and has two ladies working for her. (Interview with Joyce, Harare, 1997)

> I went to school for seven years and passed grade seven. . . . My aim was to go further in school, but I failed because my parents didn't have the money. My aunt taught me how to crochet doilies, and I learned to sew tablecloths in school. I wanted to be a teacher. I started this business because I know my only talent is crocheting. My aunt, because she also crocheted, she encouraged me. (Interview with Maube, Bulawayo, 1997)

Many women commented on the difficulties their husbands were experiencing in trying to provide for their families and saw starting a business as a way to help. There is no doubt that material needs provided a major incentive for starting these enterprises and that these women had few viable options:

> I saw that what my husband was earning was not enough to support us. . . . I would knit for the family, and they never paid me back, so I decided that if

I did it professionally, I would get paid. (Interview with Maidei Mwambo, Harare, 1994)

I would like to help my husband because his money was too little and short. To do something like dressmaking, I would have to go for training, and I did not have enough money. (Interview with Kusyedza, Harare, 1997)

How did these businesswomen in crocheting and knitting operate their enterprises? What particular challenges did the economic crisis and adjustment pose? This chapter will next explore how these women operated their enterprises and creatively responded to the demands of the changing market and the dilemmas posed by the economic crisis.

The Operation of the Firm

Women who own crocheting businesses are clearly entrepreneurs—first and foremost, because they established their enterprises and are responsible for their operation. In addition, they are clearly engaged in innovation and in the production of material culture. Further, they reinvest profits in their firms and in the development of human capital, and they diversify production to meet market demands. Their business activities and commitments to the future development of their enterprises demonstrate that they have moved beyond the level of simple survival in their firms. They are actively working toward the growth and expansion of their businesses and, in the process, they are contributing to their families, their communities, and national development.

Crocheting enterprises in this sample had a mean and median age of eight years. The largest single source of start-up capital was the personal savings of these businesswomen (in 39 percent of all firms). As stated above, many women earned their money from previous work as traders of food and/or clothing, domestics, or casual laborers. Husbands were the second largest single source of initial capital for crocheting establishments. Approximately 26 percent (fifteen) of the crocheters obtained all of their funding from their husbands. Female relatives were twice as likely as their male counterparts to provide the initial capital for crocheters. About 21 percent (twelve) of the businesswomen received their funding mainly from their mothers and sisters, compared to 11 percent (six) of the crocheters who received money from their fathers and brothers. As previously stated, mothers and sisters were also very salient in teaching the respondents how to crochet and knit. They also encouraged these entrepreneurs to begin these enterprises and frequently gave them advice regarding how to sell their goods. Finally about 3 percent of the sample obtained their initial investments from a combination of sources which most often involved the crocheters pooling contributions from several relatives. These cash outlays were largely a combination of gifts and loans from their families.

Employment creation is one lens through which the contributions of cro-cheters to community and national development can be assessed. While individ-ual small enterprises and microenterprises in the North and the South have historically provided small numbers of jobs, they are collectively most important in both hemispheres for creating the largest number of positions. Social scientists who study small enterprise and microenterprise development have frequently argued that employment generation is a major indicator of success (growth) for these firms and one factor that separates the successful firms from survival activ-ities.[26] Crocheters did provide employment in their firms. In fact, unlike the majority of occupations in the microenterprise sector in Zimbabwe, crocheters most often provided income-earning opportunities to other women through sub-contracting arrangements. In the few cases where women were employed on a regular, full-time basis to crochet or knit goods, entrepreneurs generally paid these workers Z$120–400.[27] As opposed to the development of the microenter-prise sector in other regions of the world, such as East Asia or Latin America, where subcontracting arrangements have been significant as large local and/or multinational firms outsourced work to smaller establishments in an effort to increase profits, subcontracting has been very rare in sub-Saharan Africa.[28]

Crocheters in this study, however, engaged in subcontracting arrangements within the microenterprise sector of the economy. Fifty-three percent (thirty) of these businesswomen provided an average of two positions per firm mainly through subcontracting arrangements with other women who did not work out-side of the home or who held other jobs in the microenterprise sector. Business-women in this study sought to increase efficiency in their enterprises by subdividing large tasks among several women. For example, the task of crochet-ing large tablecloths and bedspreads was largely given out to a few women who would each crochet dozens of squares (of possibly three inches by three inches) which were later stitched together by the entrepreneur to make a finished prod-uct. Women who crocheted the individual squares were paid on a piece-work basis, sometimes averaging about Z$.50 per square in 1994. Businesswomen were most likely to subcontract out all or part of their work in crocheting and knitting during the busiest seasons of the year: during the winter (June through September) and the Christmas holiday season. During the busy season, cro-cheters would also subcontract out the knitting of some sweaters, paying women approximately Z$30 per sweater. Such subcontracting of sweaters advanced the innovation noted in firms since each knitter created her own designs and, coupled with the sweaters made by the entrepreneur, ensured that each sweater had a unique pattern. Such distinctive handmade goods were most appealing to tourists and South African dealers.

Not only did subcontracting demonstrate an entrepreneur's attempts to increase efficiency in her firm, but this form of employment also increased a businesswoman's social capital (and that of her employees). Crocheters often subcontracted some of their work to other female relatives, neighbors, and friends who could be relied upon to take on such assignments on relatively short notice. Women on both sides of these arrangements extended their social networks and their camaraderie with other women, which could serve as important sources of support in business and personal matters. Such arrangements also enabled the businesswomen and their employees alike to share designs and techniques in knitting and crocheting with each other.

Through subcontracting, businesswomen in this sample created temporary positions, which did provide income-generating opportunities to other mostly poor and low-income women in Harare and Bulawayo. In addition to assisting in the development of these enterprises, such actions contributed to the growth of human capital as well as poverty alleviation in urban communities.[29]

Innovation was another important factor in this study and one that further not only demonstrates the commitment of entrepreneurs to the growth of their firms, but also demonstrates their creativity and their understanding of the market and, in some cases, illustrates their contributions to the development of material culture. Since the beginning of their enterprises, 68 percent (thirty-nine) of these businesswomen have used new materials and/or introduced new products into their businesses.

Crocheters make a wide range of clothing and other decorative goods for the household. They make sweaters, women's tops, dresses, doilies, tablemats, tablecloths, and bedspreads, among other items. Many women began making only doilies and then expanded their production to include several of these other items. Most of the goods that they make, such as doilies and tablemats, are Western in orientation and are meant to appeal largely to expatriates and tourists in southern Africa. Although these doilies, for example, are identified as the production of Zimbabwean women throughout the region, they are seldom purchased or used by this population.

The majority of crocheters changed the colors and patterns of the goods that they made. These businesswomen used mainly beige cotton in the late 1980s and early 1990s and shifted to more vibrant colors around 1992 and 1993. This was particularly evident in fieldwork visits that I made in 1994 and 1997, when tablemats and doilies were increasingly made in white cotton and in bright colors, such as magenta and turquoise. This is illustrated by a crocheter in Bulawayo who said: "Started with doilies and small things. Got more money and expanded to other goods. It is a way of living; now things are a bit better; $45 for a spool of white; $22.50 for cream. Used beige at the beginning and then able to use white" (interview with Sipiwe Sinole, crocheter, Bulawayo, 1994).

In some ways, it was surprising to find this innovation, considering that many businesswomen had been complaining about the exorbitant prices of white and brightly colored yarn, especially since the establishment of ESAP in late 1990. These women noted, however, that among the tourist and expatriate customers, white and brightly colored items had great appeal. These entrepreneurs also frequently changed the styles of the clothing that they made, with different designs appearing in each hand-knitted sweater.

The most exciting examples of innovation among crocheters, however, were noted in the new items that they began making and/or selling in the mid-1990s. In an effort to increase their sales and to appeal to the tourist market (which appeared to have significant potential for growth with the coming of majority rule to South Africa), crocheters began to make and sell items, such as batiks and Shona carvings, that appeared authentically "African" in addition to crocheted and knitted goods.[30] Batiks were made in very vivid colors with African-inspired designs and, in many cases, often included symbols from southern Africa, such as the Zimbabwe bird. These bright and appealing objects, which can be used as wall hangings, bedspreads, or tablecloths, were hung on clotheslines in the crochet markets, immediately adjacent to the hand-knitted sweaters and crocheted tablecloths. Such artistic creations by these entrepreneurs illustrated some of their contributions to the development of modern material culture in Zimbabwe. In addition, in the first few years after the adoption of ESAP, crocheters began to sell Shona soapstone carvings, an art form which is widely recognized internationally. Shona sculpture from the region consists of carvings of women, men, and children, generally depicted as families, as well as figures of animals. Such sculpture is usually made by men, and until the early 1990s street-corner artists and other men in the microenterprise sector most often sold these works. Beginning with my second fieldwork visit in 1994, I began to notice crocheters increasingly selling soapstone carvings in addition to their other handmade goods. In recent years, businesswomen in crocheting have discovered that these items are in high demand among tourists and have added these to their roster of goods for sale. Such examples of the crossing of gender boundaries with respect to sales in the microenterprise sector became far more evident as Zimbabwe's economic crisis deepened. Shifts in the gender-based division of labor have also been noted in areas traditionally dominated by women, such as market trade, in periods of deepening economic crisis.[31] Several crocheters in this study discussed innovation in their firms in terms of the addition of Shona stone carvings and batiks to the roster of items that they sold:

> I sell stone carvings, hand-knit sweaters, crochet tablecloths, clothes, bedspreads, and doily sets. I started knitting jerseys in 1992 so that I could earn more money. Started selling carvings in 1993 as a back-up when the other things weren't selling so well. The cotton wool is far more expensive now compared to the cost in 1981. In 1985, a ball of cotton cost $15, now it is $35. (Interview with Kunaka, a crocheter, Harare, 1994)

> Started with crocheting only but realized white foreigners wanted more items and so started selling jerseys and other carving items. Now, I sell wood

carvings, stone carvings, jerseys, all crochet work, bedspreads, tops, table-cloths. (Interview with Maud, a crocheter, Harare, 1997).

In 1983, [I was] making crochet dresses only. Added batiks in 1995; five years ago, with money, I added carvings. Sell batiks, jerseys, tops, sets, dresses, carvings, necklaces, wood carvings. Yes, I also change the patterns and colors. (Interview with Kisyedza, a crocheter, Harare, 1997)

One crocheter from Newlands Shopping Center, the largest crochet market in Harare and a major tourist venue, has significantly diversified her production and sales not only by selling Shona carvings, but also by making and selling items appealing to customers with pets. In this regard, when compared with her peers at Newlands, she has certainly made her site in the market more distinctive: "I sell tablecloths, jerseys, stone carvings, dog and cat mattresses, wooden carvings, and bowls. I started in 1990 with jerseys and tablecloths only. This year we began to sell wooden goods. I began selling the stones about three years ago. I began selling the dog mattresses last year. I made these" (interview with Rose, a crocheter, Harare, 1997).

These examples of innovation demonstrate that crocheters were very con-scious of the tastes and demands of their white Zimbabwean customers, tourists to the area largely from Europe and the United States, as well as their black Zimbabwean clients. At the four crochet markets visited in Zimbabwe, two sites were very popular with tourists, namely, Newlands Shopping Center in Harare and the City Hall in Bulawayo. These were the largest sites for crocheters in these cities, and while black Zimbabweans did purchase goods from these business-women, whites from Zimbabwe and the southern African region in general and tourists were the more frequent customers. Crocheters based at City Hall and especially those located at Newlands Shopping Center exhibited high levels of innovation, particularly marked by the addition of batiks and Shona carvings to their roster of goods for sale. These changes made in the operation of their firms further illustrate that these entrepreneurs understood the market, aimed to increase their profitability, and were committed to the growth of their enter-prises. They were operating at a level beyond simple survival. This chapter will now explore how the current phase of globalization, in the form of the structural adjustment program, affected their enterprises.

The Impact of Globalization and the Economic
Structural Adjustment Program (ESAP)

Like many of their sisters in the global South, crocheters in the microenterprise sector have been affected by globalization, namely, in the form of the Economic Structural Adjustment Program (ESAP) established by the Zimbabwean govern-ment at the behest of the International Monetary Fund (IMF) and the World Bank in late 1990.[32] Although the ESAP was designed to stem the tide of the economic crisis that gripped the nation beginning in 1990, the program intensified the crisis, most especially for poor women and children in Zimbabwe. As poor and low-income women, the majority of entrepreneurs in this sample were negatively affected by ESAP.[33] They were astute and could identify as well as understand how this program had negatively affected their firms. They experienced the consequences of this program in both their business and personal lives in the form of (1) increased unemployment in their families; (2) increased costs of raw materials, licenses, and customs duties for their firms; (3) increased competition from more crocheters entering the market and selling the same goods; and (4) increased prices for all basic commodities as well as education, housing, health care, and transportation.[34]

Many businesswomen began by discussing how escalating unemployment in Zimbabwe under ESAP was responsible for reduced sales and profits in their establishments and changes in their quality of life:

> Unemployment . . . when more people are working, more people will buy my work. (Interview with Barbara, a crocheter, Harare, 1991)

> Yes, if people lose their jobs, it affects the business. If people lose their jobs, they will not buy goods to send overseas; and if people lose jobs, we can't get cooking oil, we won't get flour, and we can't cook vegetables without oil. Yes, ESAP does have to do with employment. (Interview with Kusyedza, a crocheter, Harare, 1997)

Another businesswoman noted how "illegal," unlicensed sellers, in this case selling Shona carvings, negatively impacted her sale of crocheted goods: "Yes, unemployment in Zimbabwe does affect the business because too many unemployed people come here running after the customers, selling their things without permission, for example, carvings, and then the people won't buy the crochet goods" (Interview with Lisamiso, a crocheter, Bulawayo, 1997).

Higher customs duties and fees for import licenses often led to shortages of needed raw materials for these entrepreneurs and problems in exporting their goods. In addition, high rates of inflation in Zimbabwe, coupled in some cases with scarcity in the market, led to increased costs for raw materials:

> If we want to sell our things out of the country, we are charged a lot of money in customs duty. (Interview with Tsitsi, a crocheter, Harare, 1991)

> Time when making [my goods] with beads. All plastic—white people don't like plastic ones. Economy made beads not available. (Interview with Sipiwe Sinole, a crocheter, Bulawayo, 1994)

> The municipal authorities are the ones who regulate our activities, making us pay rent here in the open. ESAP has caused the cost of wool/cotton to rise. Even when we increase the prices of our goods, it doesn't help because all

other things are more expensive, and our money buys less. No one wants to buy expensive things either. (Interview with Ndaizioeyi, a crocheter, Harare, 1994)

Perhaps one of the most frequently heard problems associated with ESAP was the increased competition in the market from the growth in the number of women selling crocheted and knitted clothing and household goods. As many Zimbabweans, most especially men, lost their positions in the formal sector, more women attempted to support their families or supplement their partner's or other family members wages (if the latter were employed) through income-generating activities in the microenterprise sector. Crocheting and knitting businesses provided opportunities for women who had these skills, and in this period of economic crisis more women were acquiring these skills with the help of their female relatives. The major growth in the number of crocheters can be noted through observing their site at Newlands Shopping Center in Harare, the largest crochet "market" in the city.[35] The number of traders there increased from about forty in 1991 to more than eighty in 1997. In fact, as noted by Erik Cohen for the production of pottery in Thailand, it was precisely the increased competition from entrepreneurs in the markets in Harare that led to the introduction of new products, such as batiks, at Newlands and other shopping centers.[36] Businesswomen expressed their frustration with the influx of crocheters in the marketplace:

Things are too expensive so too many people are crocheting to sell the same goods, e.g., doilies. There is something wrong. Everything is going up. My husband earns little money; people don't have much money. (Interview with Priscilla, a crocheter, Bulawayo, 1994)

If too many vendors, then fewer customers will come. Think there are too many vendors, so there are fewer customers. (Interview with Margaret, a crocheter, Harare, 1994)

The removal of government subsidies from social services and the end of price controls on staple products led to significant growth in the rate of inflation. These problems were compounded by the massive unemployment and devaluation of the currency that were part of the ESAP. Thus, local residents found it exceedingly difficult to buy crocheted and knitted goods, which were increasingly viewed as luxury items. In a period when many families were struggling to provide the basic necessities, handmade clothing and household items became unattainable:

Prices at other places affect our prices, what people expect to buy my goods at. They have to understand that with transport costs and material costs, my prices are as they are so that I can make a margin of profit. (Interview with Tennyson, a crocheter, Harare, 1994)

Economic Structural Adjustment Program affects our business because our customers are now few because they can't spend money on our goods. (Interview with Maud, a crocheter, Harare, 1997)

Because of ESAP, most companies are closed. So most people are not working, which means that they don't buy as they used to. (Interview with Rhoda, a crocheter, Bulawayo, 1997)

Globalization, particularly in its manifestation in the ESAP, took a negative toll on these entrepreneurs, their businesses, and by extension their families. While most crocheters had certainly realized some growth in profits since the start-up phase, many women had witnessed declines in sales and profits in the mid to late 1990s. Furthermore, both before and during the economic crisis, the state did not assist Zimbabwean crocheters in developing export markets for their goods, which would have increased profits.[37] Despite the downturns in the economic performance of their firms, these businesswomen had achieved some success in their enterprises, developing coping strategies which assisted them in the most difficult periods, and at the time of these interviews were generally optimistic about the future. What strategies did these entrepreneurs use in responding to the crisis?

Coping with the Economic Crisis and Adjustment

Crocheters in urban Zimbabwe exhibited a broad range of strategies in response to the harsh toll that the economic crisis and adjustment were taking on their businesses. The major coping mechanisms that these entrepreneurs utilized were (1) innovation and diversification of production and sales; (2) participation in rotating credit schemes and obtaining loans from banks; and (3) involvement in cross-border trade.

As stated above, crocheters were significantly involved in innovation in these enterprises. Over two-thirds of them made changes in what they produced and sold, in the materials they used, and in production methods since they began their firms. What was perhaps most noteworthy in their efforts to maintain and/or expand their businesses during the economic crisis was their addition of Shona carvings and handmade batiks to the roster of goods that they sold. They clearly recognized and understood the tastes of the tourist market from South Africa, Europe, Australia, and the United States as well as the demands of the local expatriate white populations. The presence of this ethnic artwork that appeared "authentically African" at their worksites held a magnetic attraction for foreign tourists, who were their major customers. The decision to sell Shona carvings also illustrated the empowerment of these crocheters in crossing gender boundaries, since both the production and sale of these goods resided primarily in the hands of men. Such diversification of production and sales enabled these enterprises to move beyond the level of simple survival and to experience some growth, even though limited because of ESAP.

The ability to obtain capital from banks and microfinance groups was another powerful coping mechanism that sustained many of these businesses in a period of economic hardship. Approximately 12 percent (seven) of these entrepreneurs were able to obtain loans from banks and nongovernmental organizations (NGO's), enabling them to purchase raw materials and machines and pay wages in the economic downturn of the 1990s. While the numbers of crocheters who obtained loans appears small, it is noteworthy nevertheless, since a resources gap continues to persist in access to governmental and nongovernmental support for microenterprises in Zimbabwe.[38]

Another important source of capital for women in this study was the rotating credit scheme, or round, as it is frequently called in Zimbabwe. As demonstrated above, while Zimbabwean women in the microenterprise sector continued to experience difficulties in obtaining bank loans, they remained undaunted in the midst of the economic crisis and turned to the rotating credit scheme to maintain their businesses. This action demonstrates that these businesswomen are, indeed, creative and strategic in the decisions that they make about their enterprises and in response to adjustment policies. Rotating credit schemes have been especially important in assisting women in maintaining businesses there as well as in West Africa, the Caribbean, and East Asia.[39] There are over ten thousand rounds in Zimbabwe with more than fifty thousand members, and more than 97 percent of them are women.[40] Such rotating credit schemes (also referred to as *esusus* in West Africa) have been defined as "an indigenous system through which people join hands to save money and help each other to meet credit needs. Esusus involve a group of people coming together and saving a mutually agreed upon amount of money on a predetermined day at regular intervals. The money realized after collection is given on a rotating basis to a member of the group and the process is repeated until everyone in the group has had a turn."[41]

Nineteen percent (eleven) of the crocheters belonged to such groups. These associations were most often organized at their worksites with a woman (or man) at the site serving as banker and collecting deposits from members on a daily or weekly basis. Businesswomen frequently mentioned how the lump-sum payments from these accounts most often assisted them in meeting their business and family expenses. For example, crocheters noted that they were able to purchase raw materials, replenish their supplies of other items, such as carvings, and pay subcontractors with the payments they received from rotating credit schemes. These rounds also enabled them to meet their responsibilities to their children by providing them with needed cash in the form of large lump-sum payments in December or January, in time to pay school fees at the beginning of the academic year. Therefore, rotating credit schemes were notable as coping mechanisms that not only sustained businesses, but also contributed to national development through the expansion of human capital.

Another useful mechanism for coping with the strains of economic crisis and adjustment for some crocheters was participation in cross-border trade. Business-women in Zimbabwe regarded cross-border trade as a significant means of improving the profitability of their businesses, although they also realized the heavy costs associated with such activities. Despite the sacrifices that cross-border trade entails, engaging in this activity illustrates another example of the creativity and ingenuity of Zimbabwean women entrepreneurs in the face of economic crisis. Increasing numbers of crocheters from urban Zimbabwe today transport their goods mainly from Harare to Johannesburg, South Africa, prima-rily to sell to residents of the former black townships, such as Soweto, in addition to black South African customers who pass through Park Station, the major railway station in the city. Other crocheters bring their wares to sell in flea market stalls in the largely white areas of the city, such as at Bruma Lake Flea Market.[42]

Handmade crocheted and knitted goods, most especially the former, are not generally made in South Africa. These goods are more affordable than machine-made goods found in the major department stores for much of South Africa's poor, black population. When visited by Zimbabwean traders at their front doors in the townships or at the railway station, black South Africans can comfortably bargain with their Zimbabwean sisters or exchange used clothing for new cro-cheted or knitted goods. Used clothing has come to play a very prominent role in southern Africa, as demonstrated by the expanding marketplace for such goods in Mbare, the largest black suburb in Harare.

Upon completing their sales in Johannesburg, crocheters most often purchase computer software, other high-tech goods, and/or housewares in South Africa for resale in Zimbabwe. Some women are even involved in broader networks of trade that include buying Zimbabwean- or South African—made blue jeans for sale in Zambia.

Zimbabwean crocheters who sell their goods in South Africa and/or through-out the region also incur many problems. Like black men during the colonial period, they are frequently separated from their children for long periods of time. While extended family members are still a major source of support in caring for their children, the economic crisis has weighed heavily on these families and made such arrangements less stable and certainly more stressful. In addition, black Zimbabwean women are frequently harassed by South African immigra-tion officials upon entering and leaving the country, as well as by the police near Park Station. All too often, these crocheters are fined for trading without appro-priate visas and permits, and their goods are often confiscated by the police. Yet, despite these problems, Zimbabwean businesswomen engaged in cross-border trade still maintained that it was worth it because they earned more money than if they sold their goods solely in Harare or Bulawayo. As the economic crisis intensified, more and more women utilized this creative and strategic coping strategy to maintain their enterprises and their families.

Conclusion

Entrepreneurs in this study clearly illustrated that they were committed to the growth and development of their firms significantly beyond the level of simple survival. They were critically engaged in several business practices to achieve these ends: namely, (1) they were dynamic innovators who diversified production and sales; (2) they introduced subcontracting in their enterprises to enhance efficiency and, thereby, created temporary employment for other women in their communities; and (3) they reinvested profits in their businesses. Through these activities, they contributed to the development of both human capital and material culture and the well-being of their households, families, and communities. They experienced setbacks in their activities due to the economic crisis and ESAP, such as greater competition from the large numbers of women entering the crochet market, high rates of inflation, and shortages of vital raw materials. Despite these problems, these businesswomen continued to strive toward their goals by demonstrating their knowledge of the marketplace and the larger economy, their creativity, and their ingenuity. They were strategic in their responses to the problems posed by the larger national and global economies as exhibited by their participation in rotating credit schemes, their diversification of production, and their involvement in cross-border trade with South Africa.

Unfortunately, since 2000, the intensification of the economic crisis, coupled with the political crisis and the HIV/AIDS pandemic, has more seriously jeopardized the maintenance and future growth of these firms. Constitutional crisis, the seizure of white-owned farms, demonstrations of massive violence against the political opposition, and seriously tainted elections only begin to list the maladies of the Zimbabwean state which have further led it on a downward spiral. Although the international community also bears responsibility for the crises that now beset that nation, the Mugabe government has significantly turned the country into a pariah state on the world stage. Recent reports reveal that emigration has substantially increased, with many residents fleeing to South Africa. In an effort to keep families afloat, more and more women have taken to the streets as vendors and hawkers of goods. Under such political and economic circumstances, it will be very difficult for the businesswomen in this study to realize their dreams. These entrepreneurs, however, have demonstrated that they are, indeed, phenomenal women, so it is likely that many are continuing to resist the vagaries of the state and the global economy!

NOTES

1. Akosua Adomako Ampofo, "The Sex Trade: Globalization and Issues of Survival in Sub-Saharan Africa," *Research Review* 17, no. 1 (2001): 27–43; Gracia Clark, *Onions Are My Husband: Survival and Accumulation by West African Market Women* (Chicago: University of

Chicago Press, 1994); Nancy Horn, *Cultivating Customers: Market Women in Harare, Zimbabwe* (Boulder, Colo.: Lynne Rienner, 1994); Bessie House-Midamba and Felix Ekechi, eds., *African Market Women and Economic Power: The Role of Women in African Economic Development* (Westport, Conn.: Greenwood Press, 1995); Amina Mama, *Women's Studies and Studies of Women in Africa during the 1990s*, Working Paper Series (Dakar: CODESRIA, 1996); Mary J. Osirim, "Negotiating Identities during Adjustment Programs: Women Microentrepreneurs in Urban Zimbabwe," in *African Entrepreneurship: Theory and Reality*, ed. Anita Spring and Barbara McDade (Gainesville: University Press of Florida, 1998), 277–297; Mary J. Osirim, "Carrying the Burdens of Adjustment and Globalization: Women and Microenterprise Development in Urban Zimbabwe," *International Sociology* 18, no. 3 (2003): 535–558; Claire Robertson, *Trouble Showed the Way: Women, Men, and Trade in the Nairobi Area, 1890–1990* (Bloomington: Indiana University Press, 1997); Kathleen Sheldon, ed., *Courtyards, Markets, and City Streets: Urban Women in Africa* (Boulder: Westview Press, 1996).

2. Akosua Darkwah, "Trading Goes Global: Market Women in an Era of Globalization," *Asian Women* 15 (2002): 31–49; Clark, *Onions Are My Husband*; Horn, *Cultivating Customers*; House-Midamba and Ekechi, *African Market Women and Economic Power*; Janet MacGaffey and Remy Bazenguissa-Ganga, *Congo-Paris: Transnational Traders on the Margins of the Law* (Bloomington: Indiana University Press, 2000); Osirim, "Negotiating Identities during Adjustment Programs" and "Carrying the Burdens of Adjustment and Globalization"; Claire Robertson, *Trouble Showed the Way.*

3. Darkwah, "Trading Goes Global"; Kaendi Munguti, Edith Kabui, Mabel Isoilo, and Eunice Kamaara, "The Implications of Economic Reforms on Gender Relations: The Case of Poor Households in Kisumu Slums," in *Gender, Economic Integration, Governance, and Methods of Contraceptives*, ed. Aicha Tamboura Diawara (Dakar, Senegal: AAWORD Book Series, 2002–2003), 13–43; Osirim, "Carrying the Burdens of Adjustment and Globalization"; Mohau Pheko, "Privatization, Trade Liberalization, and Women's Socio-Economic Rights: Exploring Policy Alternatives," in *Africa: Gender, Globalization, and Resistance*, ed. Yassine Fall (Dakar: AAWORD Book Series, 1999): 89–99.

4. Urban women's clubs in Zimbabwe became quite established in the 1950s, and the majority of them were begun by white Rhodesian women with few black African women as members. See Teresa Barnes, *We Women Worked so Hard: Gender, Urbanization, and Social Reproduction in Colonial Harare, Zimbabwe, 1930–1956* (Portsmouth, N.H.: Heinemann, 1999).

5. The current phase of globalization has many aspects. In this chapter, "globalization" refers to economic globalization—the emergence of a world system that strives for the integration of national economies under the auspices of the free market into one unified system. The integration of nations into this system occurs through trade, production, and financial transactions. During this phase of globalization, labor and capital have become more fluid. In the sub-Saharan African context, about forty nations have experienced globalization through the imposition of structural adjustment programs.

6. Peter Evans and John Stephens, "Studying Development since the Sixties: The Emergence of a New Comparative Political Economy," *Theory and Society* 17 (1988): 713–745; Immanuel Wallerstein, *The Modern World System: Capitalist Agriculture and the Origins of the European World Economy in the Sixteenth Century* (New York: Academic Press, 1974).

7. June Nash and Maria Patricia Fernandez-Kelly, eds., *Women, Men, and the International Division of Labor* (Albany: SUNY Press, 1983); Valentine Moghadam, "Gender and the Global Economy," in *Revisioning Gender*, ed. Myra Marx Ferree, Judith Lorber, and Beth Hess (Thousand Oaks, Calif.: Sage, 1999); Saskia Sassen, *Globalization and Its Discontents* (London: New Press, 1998).

8. Valentine Moghadam, *Gender and Globalization: Female Labor and Women's Mobilization*, Occasional Papers, No. 11, Women's Studies Program (Normal: Illinois State University, 2000).

9. Desiree Lewis. "Feminist Knowledge/Review Essay: African Feminist Studies, 1980–2002," *Gender and Women's Studies Africa* (2002), http:www.gwsafrica.org/knowledge/.africa; Patricia McFadden, "Issues of Gender and Development from an African Feminist Perspective," *Women's World*, http://www.World.org/programs/regions/africa/patricia_mcfadden4.htm.

10. McFadden, "Issues of Gender and Development from an African Feminist Perspective"; Charmaine Pereira, "Configuring 'Global,' 'National,' and 'Local' in Governance Agendas in Nigeria," *Social Research* 69, no. 3 (2003): 781–804.

11. Such actions have been noted in response to structural adjustment programs in western and southern Africa as well as in Latin America.

12. Osirim, "Carrying the Burdens of Adjustment and Globalization"; Mary Osirim, "African Women's Entrepreneurship and Cultural Production: The Case of Knitters and Crocheters in Southern Africa," *Contours: A Journal of the African Diaspora* 1, no. 2 (2003): 154–170.

13. Robert Blauner, *Racial Oppression in America* (New York: Harper and Row, 1972); Christine Sylvester, *Zimbabwe: The Terrain of Contradictory Development* (Boulder, Colo.: Westview Press, 1991).

14. The existence of patriarchy in Zimbabwe predates colonialism. In the pre-colonial period, although a system of complementary roles existed where both women and men contributed to the support and maintenance of families and households, women and men were not equal. Zimbabwean pre-colonial society was patriarchal as exemplified in rights over land. Men had the power to allocate farmland to their wives, and the latter controlled the products of such land. In this system, women were also responsible for tilling their husband's fields although husbands controlled the products of their lands. As argued by McFadden, "African patriarchy is the oldest patriarchy known in the human story" ("Issues of Gender and Development from an African Feminist Perspective," 3). However, Zimbabwean patriarchy was significantly exacerbated by British (colonial) patriarchy; see Horn, *Cultivating Customers;* McFadden, "Issues of Gender and Development from an African Feminist Perspective."

15. Horn, *Cultivating Customers.*

16. Carol Summers, "Native Policy, Education, and Development: Social Ideologies and Social Control in Southern Rhodesia, 1890–1934" (Ph.D. diss., Johns Hopkins University, 1991).

17. Elinor Batezat, and Margaret Mwalo, *Women in Zimbabwe* (Harare: Southern Africa, Political Economy Series Trust, 1989); Patricia Made and Myorovai Whande, "Women in Southern Africa: A Note on the Zimbabwe Success Story," *Issues: A Journal of Opinion* 17, no. 2 (1989): 6–8.

18. Some issues that led to the decline of the Zimbabwean economy in this period were a reduction in the prices of primary products on the world market, the problems incurred by South Africa's frequent raids into Zimbabwe, and frequent droughts.

19. Despite the existence of many micro-lending organizations in Zimbabwe, few poor and low-income women in market trade, crocheting, hairdressing, or sewing receive such loans. Men continue to have greater success in receiving business loans. Those women who do receive such funding are disproportionately from higher-class backgrounds than their sisters in market trade. See Mary J. Osirim, "Making Good on Commitments to Grassroots Women: NGO's and Empowerment for Women in Contemporary Zimbabwe," *Women's Studies International Forum* 24, no. 2 (2001): 167–180.

20. Although most businesswomen in this field are engaged in both crocheting and knitting, crocheting is the activity in the region that is most unique to Zimbabwe and the one with which Zimbabwean women are most closely identified. Thus, the term "crocheters" will be used most often in this paper.

21. In the British system of education in the United Kingdom as well as in the British Commonwealth, students were required to take "O-level" (Ordinary level) examinations to receive the lower-level secondary school certificate. These exams are achievement tests in the major subjects studied in high school, such as English, mathematics, the sciences, and history. Students who began school at the age of five and continued without interruptions would generally complete lower secondary school around the age of sixteen. The O-level certificate is required for entry into formal-sector jobs and is an absolute "must" for poor and working-class individuals.

22. In her work on the division of labor among U.S. families, Arlie Hochschild discusses how women bear the major responsibilities for chores that have to be done on a daily basis, while most men have greater flexibility in their household tasks, which most often do not require daily attention. See Arlie Hochschild, *The Second Shift: Inside the Two-Job Marriage* (New York: Viking Penguin, 1989).

23. In Zimbabwe, as in many other parts of sub-Saharan Africa, this is how the gender hierarchy works. Sons remain a part of the natal family and are thus ascribed a role that seems to justify the differential investment in males.

24. The names included in these interviews refer to the interviewees. The respondents were asked to create their own pseudonyms to protect their identities.

25. The crossing of gendered occupational boundaries is also noted in other fields and regions during periods of economic crisis and adjustment. While women historically were involved in food and vegetable vending, more men were participating in such activities during the time of these interviews in the major markets in Harare and Bulawayo. In her earlier work, Gracia Clark also noted that men were increasingly found trading in such commodities during the period of economic crisis and adjustment in Ghana; see Clark, *Onions Are My Husband*.

26. Donald C. Mead, "MSE's Tackle Both Poverty and Growth," in *Enterprise in Africa: between Poverty and Growth*, ed. Kenneth King and Simon McGrath (London: Intermediate Technology Publications, 1999).

27. At the beginning of this research in 1991, US$1.00 equaled Z$2.30. By 1999, US$1.00 equaled Z$37.00.

28. Alejandro Portes, Manuel Castells, and Lauren Benton, eds., *The Informal Economy: Studies in Advanced and Less Developed Societies* (Baltimore: Johns Hopkins University Press, 1989).

29. This is not to suggest that crocheters' subcontracting arrangements were never exploitative of the poor women whom they mainly employed. Certainly, entrepreneurs intended to increase their profits through such practices, paying these women on a piece-rate basis averaging a few cents per crocheted square (or a few dollars per sweater). The finished goods clearly sold for more than the price of the labor that produced them.

30. Batiks made by black Zimbabwean women in the contemporary period can be considered ethnic or tourist art (*turistica*). As noted among scholars studying the tourist market for local crafts in Nepal, Mexico, and Papua New Guinea, ethnic arts such as Zimbabwean batiks are generally made for tourists from Europe and North America. Such objects are distinct from "real" goods that local populations use, but these batiks are still culturally important to the Zimbabweans who produce them. This is especially evident in their incorporation of local symbols in the batiks. Shona carvings, on the other hand, do occupy a space as an indigenous art form for the nation, although much of what is sold in urban markets is tourist art. See R. C. Dougoud, "Souvenirs from Kambot: The Sacred Search for Authenticity"; Graeme Evans, "Contemporary Crafts as Souvenirs, Artifacts, and Functional Goods and Their Role in Local Economic Diversification and Cultural Development"; and Ken Teague, "Tourist Markets and Himalayan Craftsmen," all in *Souvenirs: The Material Culture of Tourism*, ed. M. Hitchok and K. Teague (Burlington: Ashgate, 2000).

31. Gracia Clark has noted the increased presence of men in Kumasi Market in Ghana selling products historically sold by women in periods of economic crisis and adjustment in that nation; see Clark, *Onions Are My Husband*. I have also made similar observations with respect to more men engaged in fruit and vegetable vending in Mbare and Manwele Markets in Harare and Bulawayo, respectively.

32. The second phase of ESAP was instituted in 1997 under the title, "The Zimbabwe Program for Economic and Social Transformation."

33. Osirim, "Negotiating Identities during Adjustment Programs."

34. Richard Kamidza, "Structural Adjustment without a Human Face," *Southern Africa: Political and Economic Monthly* 7, no. 6 (1994): 11–12; Osirim, "Negotiating Identities during Adjustment Programs."

35. While I refer to the crocheters' site at Newlands Shopping Center as a market, it is merely a large patch of dry land rented to individual crocheters by the City Council of Harare. It includes no benches, tables, bathroom facilities, sheds, or other protective covering.

36. Erik Cohen, "The Heterogeneization of Tourist Art," *Annals of Tourism Research* 20 (1993): 138–163.

37. In the late 1980s and early 1990s, however, the state did assist businesswomen in the cooperative sector by establishing export markets for Ndebele beadwork. Of course, export markets exist for Shona carvings that are considered real art. These pieces can be found in art galleries and gift shops in the United States and Europe.

38. Osirim, "Making Good on Commitments."

39. Sena Gabianu, "The Susu Credit System: An Indigenous Way of Financing Business Outside the Formal Banking System," in *The Long-Term Perspective Study of Sub-Saharan Africa: Economic and Sectoral Policy Issues*, ed. R. Agarwala (Washington, D.C.: World Bank, 1990), 122–128; Osirim, "Making Good on Commitments."

40. Constantina Safilios-Rothschild, "Women's Groups: An Underutilized Grassroots Institution," in Agarwala, *The Long-Term Perspective Study of Sub-Saharan Africa*, 102–108.

41. Gabianu, "The Susu Credit System," 123.

42. Given the contemporary political and economic crises that beset Zimbabwe, increasing numbers of Zimbabweans have been migrating to South Africa. Zimbabwean cross-border traders and/or immigrants are now found selling crocheted goods far beyond the city of Johannesburg. In a recent visit to Cape Town, I saw several Zimbabweans selling doilies and tablemats in a major downtown market most often visited by tourists.

PART III

SURVIVING THE GLOBAL ECONOMY

Of Land and Sea

WOMEN ENTREPRENEURS IN
NEGRIL, JAMAICA

A. LYNN BOLLES

Jamaica's colonial motto, "the island, the land of wood and water," hardly describes the incomparable beauty of the island. Nevertheless, those two primary elements, wood and water, still describe this country now in terms of its tourist industry. Tourism is the largest source of revenue for this island nation. Wood no longer refers to lumber but instead to land packages, sightseeing, and services. The sources of water now focus on Dun's River Falls, the sea, sea views, beaches, and water sports. There are many business opportunities on land and sea, with many ways of making a living for Jamaicans, especially women, who work in the tourist industry. This chapter looks at three Jamaican businesswomen whose principal economic activities are based on those two primal elements. Looking at a day in the life of these particular female business owners will help to situate them in Negril, Jamaica, a small tourist town located on the northwestern point of the country.[1] Although each business is distinct, the legacy of female business ownership, the intermesh of tourism work, and the importance of Negril's success as a place in which to live and to work connect these three enterprises.

This work begins with a discussion of tourism as an economic sector critical to the Jamaican national economy, but still lacking in the amount of attention garnered by its citizens, in comparison to its input to the gross domestic product (GDP). Explored, in a historical framework, is the way the gender system orchestrates how women are perceived as workers and as entrepreneurs. Studies of small entrepreneurs in the United Kingdom, the United States, Senegal, and India provide a comparative perspective. Coming afterwards are the accounts of the daily life of three businesswomen who work in the tourist business on land and by the sea. By example, these three women's lives should not be viewed as an exercise of contrast across numerous differences. Rather, the goal here is to show how three types of businesses and the women who own them intermesh to meet the demands of a tourist industry that offers visitors a sense of adventure in this land of wood and water.

In Jamaica, the small businesswoman must be discussed in terms of a cultural legacy. This circumstance is contrary to the microenterprise development model promoted by international donor agencies. Small business is a cultural practice, not a new initiative for women's economic empowerment. Women as entrepreneurs came with the system of slavery. Beginning in the sixteenth century, enslaved West African women carried with them a female social role as market women, called "higglers" in Jamaica. Throughout the days of slavery and post-emancipation, market women contributed to the production, distribution, and consumption of locally grown foodstuffs and sometimes imported small items. Their position in the economy was recognized, but not valued because of the size and social position of those who tended to be market women—usually dark-skinned working-class or poor women. Regardless of the society's perception of market women, they are, in fact, self-employed small business people.

This cultural legacy does share attributes associated with the issues addressed in the micro-development discourse that is promoted by the United States Agency for International Development (USAID) and the International Labor Organization (ILO). Among the overlapping issues are the conflicts of time constraints and a sex-role barrier and a sex-segregated labor force whereby women receive lower pay and fewer opportunities than men. Furthermore, women do not have access to credit, technology, or support services and suffer from a lack of systematic information. Although in Jamaica, as beneficiaries of education and training and other post-independence opportunities, contemporary businesswomen can seize the moment when their entrepreneurship is valued in the economy.[2] The types of businesses in which they are engaged run the gamut from IT (Internet technology) to a broad array of services and small manufacturing. However, given the dictates of gender inequality across many institutions of Jamaican society, like their counterparts, illustrated by case studies from the United Kingdom, the United States, Senegal, and India, the majority of women do not have equal access to long-term financial sources required to sustain a business.

My work in Negril centers on women tourist workers and looks at the differential importance of class, color, and access to opportunity among them.[3] This gendered perspective provides an alternative way of understanding tourism as an economic sector. Here, I examine how a traditional job for Jamaican women is incorporated into contemporary tourism. Small businesses owned by women cut across the social and economic differences that appear in the society. By looking at small businesswomen, I illustrate how Negril's success rests, in part, on the entrepreneurial shoulders of these women. Jamaican women as market women—now an expansive notion—provide necessary services in compliment to corporate tourism. By corporate, I refer to the Sandals, RIU, and Super Clubs genre of resorts located in Jamaica and all found in Negril. Overall, these women are members of the local business community, in small or in big ways. What I argue is that the range of businesses that women own follows the complexity and aura of the sector. Moreover, although tourism is the greatest source of foreign exchange for the country, little is known about it in terms of its structure or of the labor force, except that it incorporates much of the country's domestic service workers. One difficulty in analyzing this sector lies within certain interpretations of what the work activities are for women in tourism. For example, there is the chambermaid factor. Government of Jamaica (GOJ) documents do not separate tourism from other service industries. Therefore, even though service jobs increased by 2.9 percent (189,300 in 1993 in comparison to 195,000 in 1994, the time frame of the study), employment changes in specific job categories could only be inferred, but not exactly, by the demands of tourism.[4] Furthermore, there are other areas of employment and self-employment in tourism, too.

Nevertheless, there is a tendency to focus on the neat boxes of clearly identifiable trends that officials refer to quite easily in their deliberations on tourism. These include the number of cruise ships that come into port, the number of visitors who stay for three days or more and their national identities, and the occupancy rates of hotel rooms. However, tourism is a structurally messy business, and the multitudinous sites of economic activity are for the most part beyond the scope of the national official data. On top of that, I contend that tourism in Jamaica is a predominately female industry in terms of the product and the workforce. In such circumstances, the overdue material gains for women are overshadowed by gender systems that continue to be inequitable in regards to the status of women.[5]

The basic belief of female subordination exists and is reflected in tourism. As a service sector, tourism is deemed low in prestige because it is assumed that the workforce—mainly women—already knows how to perform the tasks required by jobs in the industry. Furthermore, the majority of jobs in tourism are labor intensive. This means the sector requires a high ratio of employees to paying customers; people who come as tourists need and expect a lot of service. The kinds of jobs typed as labor intensive are also unskilled, low skilled, and low cost in terms of wages and benefits. The jobs in the tourist sector are viewed as not only the ones that women know how to do, but also ones that come "naturally" to them. Therefore, jobs such as housekeeping, doing laundry, cooking, serving, and so forth are female dominated, necessary, but with low economic value.

Besides the low-skill jobs, women tourist workers are also employed in a variety of occupations that require a secondary education and/or higher education, technical skills, and advanced training. Some of these jobs are in accounting, bookkeeping, hotel management, recreation, and medical personnel. These, too, are also designated as "female" with the associated low value. The very nature of tourism exhibits characteristics associated with a sex-segmented labor market.[6] In the tourist industry, the majority of women occupy identifiable female labor categories while there are a few who hold jobs usually held by men. Counted among the nontraditional jobs held by women are bank managers, food and beverage managers, and head accountants. There are few women who fill these kinds of positions. Tourism remains under male control, but the majority of the workforce is female.

Regardless of its largely female workforce, tourism is part of a larger gender system that represents the network of power relations. These relations are based primarily on two dimensions, one is ideological and the other concerns access to material resources. The material dimension explains how and why women and men gain access to or are allocated power, status, and material and social resources within the society. However, gender inequality is the ideological dimension that is reinforced through institutions, often in government policies, and in cultural practices all supporting the gender system.[7] While cultures change over time, there are certain elements of gender systems that are difficult to transform, particularly gender inequality and the accompanying attitudes and habits. Furthermore, change comes slowly even when material conditions make it possible for women to have access to greater resources from the society.[8]

Jamaican Women's Work

Historically, working-class women in Jamaica have always played important roles as economic providers for their households.[9] During slavery, black and brown women labored side by side with men in the cane fields while others worked as domestics in the great house. Enslaved and free women of color recognized their own worth in both public and private spheres. It is from this root of Jamaican culture and society that the majority of Jamaican women still see themselves in terms of their economic worth *and* their roles as mothers. This perception has not changed over the years and now crosses class divides.

One clear indication of how women fulfill their role as economic providers is seen in their critical contributions to their families' welfare. Data to support this point is found in the statistics on female labor participation in relation to household organization. Looking at data relevant to the time of the Negril study, 1994 GOJ statistics show that 62.4 percent of women are in the labor force. In addition, women head close to half of the country's households. Subsequently, of the 403,200 employed women recorded, 44 percent of them were heads of households.[10] Therefore, almost half of the entire population depends on the economic activities of women. Middle-class women also adhere to the economic provider/mothering role, too. However, regardless of class position, when a woman's wage is combined with that of her male spouse/partner (who will earn more than her), it creates a dual-income household that often generates greater earnings for that domestic unit.

Before going further, there are things to be said about color, class, and access to education. In the Jamaican context, skin color (race) and class are historically connected, with people of darker hue (the majority) occupying the low strata of society. A proven key toward upward mobility in Jamaica is education.

Accordingly, the number of citizens with an elementary education dramatically increased since independence in 1962, with a secondary education viewed as essential. However, access to the fruits of the society is still limited, and the social system remains highly stratified by class and color. A seminal work on social mobility in Jamaica by Derek Gordon was prophetic when he noted the following: "researchers must confront the paradox of large scale social mobility generated by the opening up of new positions coexisting side by side with gross and perhaps, even widening inequalities of opportunity between the minority at the top and the majority at the bottom of the social order."[11] In sum, class and color do count in factoring mobility; however, these social factors also intersect with gender.

As a host of Caribbean scholars and their feminist colleagues from abroad demonstrate, sexism constrains and limits women's access to opportunities in Jamaica.[12] This is clear when looking at the sex-segregated nature of the labor market. Confined to "classic" female occupations, women work in teaching, nursing, secretarial work, domestic service, and self-employment—the informal sector. Of course, there are women who are visible exceptions to the rule. In the Jamaican context, skin color gradation harks back to the days of slavery but with a contemporary twist. Women considered "brown" can be light skinned with light eye color or dark skinned. In contemporary times the "color bar" lifted as new economic and educational opportunities became available to a larger number of women. "Brown" as a social term also refers to middle-class status. However, the options are fairly bounded for the majority of women. Since these women are poor, working class, and black, then the class/race nexus is further apparent.

Just how strong are the aspects of the gender system? It is born by example of the Jamaican higgler, whose contribution to society is both lauded and devalued. Much of the Jamaican gender system is inherited from its British colonial past. Coming from a British colonial frame of thinking, whereby men were breadwinners and women were homemakers, the wider society considered higglers in a negative light. Collectively, higglers were fixed as being shrewish, loud, boorish, aggressive, and exhibiting behavior associated with low classes of society. In the Jamaican context, this assumed skin color, too. Skin color is a critical factor as the majority of the working class and the poor are dark skinned. Part of the higgler identity also had to do with what was deemed socially acceptable deportment for women. Regardless of their business acumen and keen awareness of trends and financial soundness, higglers were not deemed proper. In recent years, the exceptional abilities of the higgler became subjects of praise by poets and novelists.[13] In addition, feminist social scientists and activists have raised the higgler's status in the eyes of many in the society.[14]

Nonetheless, the contemporary small businesswomen who are not higglers are still tainted by the traditional image of market women. They may engage in other kinds of commercial and business services that are highly technical and capital intensive but still remain in inequitable positions due to the general ideology regarding women in the economy. Of course, there are women who have been extremely successful in business, and Jamaica has quite a number of them. Each of those women's rise to the top included surpassing not only basic obstacles but also those that were gender related, such as proving way beyond reasonable doubt that they were worthy, despite being female. Again, this perception relates to the contradictory nature of inequality inherent in the gender system.

Historical Roots of Jamaican Women Entrepreneurs

Trading has a long history in the Caribbean. West African women brought the concept of "woman as trader" to their enslavement in the Americas.[15] In Jamaica, slaves grew enough food in house gardens to sell or barter some of it to other slaves and white masters. In vibrant Sunday markets, a West African tradition became a part of Jamaican culture—and stayed the domain of women. Over the next 130 years, notes Jamaican sociologist Elsie LeFranc, "higglering," as it is called, changed little.[16] After emancipation in 1838, peasant holdings and small farms grew, as did the trading in produce by higglers, who distribute 80 percent of all domestic agricultural products.

Recently, a new type of higgler emerged, the informal commercial importer (ICI). These women import goods from Panama, Haiti, Curacao, the United States, and other countries to sell in Kingston and Montego Bay. Informal importing expanded in the late 1970s when scarcity and high prices in Jamaica's formal economy brought the traders high profits.[17] ICI's concentrate on manufactured goods, and many of them are men.

Despite this connection between the formal and informal sectors, LeFranc argues that the higglers' main goal is to be independent, as individuals and workers.[18] A higgler determines her own timetable and marketing strategy, uses her own access to capital, makes personnel decisions, and manages her own investments. Similarly, other small businesswomen, who may not be in the produce and microenterprise commerce arenas like the higglers and ICIs, utilize the same goals, business strategies, and managerial skills. Some of these women learned their business skills through their employment in their family business as a wife/partner or a paid or unpaid employee.

Entrepreneurship is valued in Jamaican society, not in terms of being a higgler, but in the sense of making something of oneself as a personal goal. Further, the personal accomplishment aspect has proven to be a useful tract if other qualifications are missing from a person's background. For example, making something of oneself can counterbalance the lack of middle- or upper-class background, advanced degrees in education, and light skin color. Entrepreneurship receives high marks because it promotes one of the fundamental features of modernity whereby individuals are ordained to achieve autonomy. In addition, making something of oneself assumes a masculine gendered identity that is privileged given the prescriptive gender system.

In their study of a group of small businessmen in the United Kingdom, Richard Scase and Robert Goffee noted an ethos that was elementary to their entrepreneurship.[19] First, there was the notion of the "self-made man," which has a strong undercurrent in the United Kingdom and especially in the United States. Small business owners exercise the right of the individual to build the "new society," also known as capitalism. There is the romantic element to this kind of entrepreneurship, including virtues of being enterprising, inventive, and generous with people.

Sara Carter and Tom Cannon conducted a study among a set of women entrepreneurs in the United Kingdom.[20] Finding capital and finding clients were generic to all start-ups. However, reasons for these women starting their own businesses had a lot to do with family commitment and time constraints. The type of businesses some of the women in the study started allowed them to take care of family and work simultaneously in one location. Many of the women who participated in Carter and Cannon's study recognized a gender dimension in some of the problems that arose, despite the fact that many operational difficulties were very gender neutral and had more to do with experience than anything else.

In addition to the research from Britain, women-owned businesses in the United States are on the rise, a product of the changing cultural tide favoring women. These entrepreneurs face hurdles similar to those of their counterparts, especially securing capital/loans, but benefit from government promotion and laws that redress past exclusions. In the United States, it was noted that women own almost one out of three businesses in the Washington, D.C., metro area. California led the states with the greatest number of women-owned firms, seven hundred thousand.[21] Women entrepreneurs say that contracts with the federal government and a welcoming business environment have helped locally, but women still face hurdles in accessing capital and running larger companies. A former bank executive, turned entrepreneur, stated, about the banking business, "We weren't very helpful with women-owned businesses because it was a male-dominated arena." Over half of the women-owned business is in the service industry, including hotel, health, legal, agricultural transportation, and communication services.

Overall, women, like their male counterparts, share the same sense of drive, confidence, risk-taking, and goal orientation. Further, women are motivated to be self-employed to escape from "glass ceilings" or other gendered obstacles put in place by employers. Further, as Carter and Cannon showed, women viewed owning their own business as a way to control resources and management styles, allowing them individual freedom and monetary expansion.[22] As owners of small businesses, women face a variety of constraints when they set up these enterprises. In other parts of the world, women encounter other kinds of problems that impede their empowerment and limit their access to resources even further. However, as the following cases show, this situation is slowly changing for the better in the form of microenterprise strategies for women in development models.

Microenterprise development models are elements of the International Labor Organization's (ILO) core mandate for the promotion of social justice, the protection of women workers, and the promotion of equality between men and women in employment. Gender training in microenterprises affords women training, technical cooperation activities, and employment. In addition to the ILO, the U.S. Agency for International Development (USAID) also takes pride in its training of women in the microenterprises it funds in various parts of the world. One of the essential avenues for success is the technical assistance and training, particularly in the area of savings and credit programming, an area where women face major hurdles. The following two cases demonstrate how microenterprise strategies facilitate this common problem faced by women entrepreneurs.[23]

Prior to the USAID training, the Senegalese Federation of Women's Groups had no formal record of the loans they made and did not know if the group received reimbursement for services by their membership. Although they had the will, the women in the Senegalese Federation of Women's Groups did not have the training to deal with contemporary financial practices that, in fact, could increase their effectiveness and improve the lives of their membership. Two women who received this instruction were involved in the crochet business. They sold their products in their own neighborhoods, but that was the end product. Now, after taking the profit from those sales, the crocheting group received additional loans and invested in livestock. Between the two businesses, the women reinvested the profits of both ventures with the backing of their local branch of the Senegalese Federation of Women's Groups credit union for future investments. The branch office followed up on the progress of the portfolio and the list of investors and monitored its new systems of credit and lending.

In the case of India, the Popular Women's Microenterprises of Manipur focused on three of the most popular activities for women—poultry raising, pig raising, and weaving—and figured out ways that the poor women in the district could conduct this business, be close to home, and still perform their domestic duties. The important factor here is that women's group's access to informal credit and savings was an innovative practice. Of the three income-generating activities, only one, poultry raising, required little investment and could generate a quick return of profit, and the poultry could be sold locally in exchange for other items needed by the family. Pig raising and weaving were either too labor intensive or required too much start-up capital and were not feasible for these poor rural households. Poultry raising is now a mainstay for these women entrepreneurs, particularly because that business generates quick cash for rein-vestment—the key element to success.

Overall, these sets of concepts, ideals, and practices were evident among a group of small businesswomen in Negril. Often beginning on a limited scale, women entrepreneurs in Negril were found in various retail stores; they did catering, owned guesthouses, did professional services such as hair styling, hair braiding, and dressmaking, and made craftwork. The three women whose daily lives are presented here also follow similar senses of drive, risk-taking, and goal orientation toward their businesses, particularly since there is great competition for market shares in Negril. Only one of the three women from Negril, Miss Priscilla May, was involved in similar agricultural ventures. Miss May, also know as Miss Cilla, is perhaps the less driven of the three, given her age and long-term business experience as a higgler. However, she does have tremendous pride as a vendor/market woman and uses this cultural and historical element to her advantage in the way she conducts business. Miss Cilla represents higglering as a true Jamaica way of making a living. The second businesswoman featured here, Miss Hortense Manners, is a confident, goal-oriented, aggressive person who is in direct competition with the bars, small restaurants, and hotels on Negril's seven-mile beach. From behind the counter of her snack bar she sells soft drinks, boxed juice drinks, and beer. But most importantly, she sells beef, chicken, or veggie patties, the traditional fast-food lunch for those on the go in Jamaica. Her clients are visitors who are staying in guesthouses or other properties that do not have food service, those on a budget, and local people who find themselves on the beach as workers, hangers-on, or domestic tourists. The third woman is Mrs. Cuthburt, who owns and manages three cottages on the cliffs. Usually soft spoken in front of strangers and customers, Mrs. Cuthburt is really about taking care of business in this very competitive arena of tourism. Together, Miss Cilla's, Miss Hortense's, and Mrs. Cuthburt's experiences echo issues that arose in the research conducted in the United Kingdom, the United States, Senegal, and India. They all are confident, understand their market, and are goal oriented. When considered within the constraints of the society, these small businesswomen exemplify the range of opportunities available to women in the tourist industry and the ways one circumnavigates obstacles, leading toward a successful venture.

In an earlier research study in Negril, Deborah D'Amico-Samuels found women small-scale vendors in tourist areas engaged in creating economic oppor-tunity in the narrow space between the "rock" of doing poorly paid, scarcely available wage labor and the "hard place" of living in abject poverty.[24] D'Amico-Samuels also observed that middle-class and upwardly mobile working-class women made significant contributions to Negril's successful tourist business. As proprietors of cottages and guesthouses and crucial to Negril's person-to-person ambiance, middle-class women and those who aspired to be so reaped the rewards of doing good business. In between the street vendors and the cottage and hotel owners, there are numerous sites where women are engaged in small businesses as employees and as owners. Miss Cilla, Miss Hortense, and Mrs. Cuthburt represent the profitable side of being a small businesswoman in Negril.

Negril Center, White Sand Beach and Cliffs

Tourism is the primary activity of Negril, and how one participates in that activity is based on one's place in the social system. Negril was designated as a potential site for tourism development in 1956. This prospective tourist area came about from an environmental calamity in which the lethal yellowing disease killed thousands of native tall coconut trees found on the beach and in nearby Rutland Plantation. Beginning in 1942 through to the 1950s, this arboreal disease killed native tall coconut trees and eliminated the major crop of the village, the coconut. Coconut processing and marketing of coconut oil, fishing, and subsistent agriculture were the major sources of livelihood of the region. The resultant vacant seven-mile white sand beach was called to the attention of lawmakers who in 1956 were trying to find ways of bringing pre-independent Jamaica into the world of advanced capitalism. Tourism was one route fostered in other areas of the island, such as Montego Bay. Bare of native tall coconut trees, Negril's pristine beach and the dormant coconut plantation were available lands for investment for tourist development. Negril, with its population of two hundred people, who were mostly members of twenty interrelated, extended families, had no schools, medical services, roads, markets, banks, electricity, or telephone service. Following independence in 1962, the government of Jamaica bought the dormant plantation and an additional three thousand acres of other land parcels and paved a road that replaced the village's small dirt track that followed the water's edge. Within fifteen years, all of the above mentioned missing services were now in place in Negril. The former dirt tract is now Norman Manley Boulevard. Following this road, when it bears to the right at the round-about, it becomes West End Road, which leads to Red Ground and the lighthouse, the westernmost tip of Jamaica. The government built a resort and other Jamaicans built and invested in hotels and guesthouses on the beach and in Negril center. Among those building were also those of working-class Negrilians who constructed guesthouses or structures adjacent to their own homes on the cliffs and Red Ground. This is the area where Deborah D'Amico-Samuels conducted her research.

D'Amico-Samuels interviewed a group of elderly Negrilians who could talk about the loss of the coconut trees as a critical setback for women and their family income. Women boiled the meat of the nuts, rendered the oil, and sold it in markets in large nearby towns. Along with what men earned from fishing and commuting to work on sugar plantation, coconuts were the source for cash income. Cash was needed to pay for clothes, school fees, rice, flour, salt, sugar, and other "shop food" and necessities. Negrilians migrated to Kingston, the United States, and the United Kingdom seeking wage labor. As wage work in the tourist sector took hold of the economy, women sought ways to find their niche in this only game in town. Further, since Negrilians' ethos revolved around a mixed economy, or "occupational multiplicity," they assumed that tourism would be one of their sources of income.[25] Growing a subsistence garden, with the surplus sold to a higgler (who sold the fruits and vegetables in the market to tourists), selling crafts, establishing and maintaining guesthouses, and providing other services were economic activities that truly were natural outcomes. The question is, How did some women find a niche for their sustenance while navigating the social and cultural obstacles of color, class, and gender embedded in the society?

Jamaica's social system took on a local flavor in Negril, one that changes over time as the village becomes more socially complex. Before 1956, Negril had no professional or landed elite class, so social hierarchy was based on another criteria: land ownership. Residential members of native Negrilian families, those whose families resided in the village when its primary economic activities were fishing and coconut oil processing *and* who still own beachfront property, are called "royalty." Over time, those in this group referred to themselves as "brown" (middle class) because when they sold valuable beachfront property or rented it to investors for development they became wealthy. Another mark of distinction rests with those who arrived in Negril in the late 1960s and early 1970s, at the beginning of the tourist industry. Involved in occupational multiplicity men worked in nearby sugar plantations in neighboring Westmorland parish and women had garden plots, and did part-time higglering. When they combined their savings, they built on extra rooms to their homes as rental properties for vacationers. Many of these houses are located in the West End and on the cliffs. Then there are those who came in the mid-1970s and 1980s. This group includes Jamaican hoteliers who first came to Negril as vacationers and saw a niche in the market. These investors set up new businesses such as supermarkets, banks, and other services. Many who migrated to the United Kingdom or the United States sent money home to Negril for investment in family-owned cottages and businesses, too. In addition, there were hippies from North America and Europe looking for a tropical paradise and Rastafarians seeking refuge from the constrictions of "Babylon" who grew ganja (marijuana) for their own spiritual consumption and to supply the tourist trade. They live, too, in Red Ground and other areas in the West End.

These population shifts all coincided with the slow but steady growth of tourism in Negril. The town's contemporary slow-paced atmosphere harks back to its fishing village origins, when everyone knew everyone, and that sentiment also extended to return visitors. However, as the village residential membership grew in complexity, the simple life was stifled by drug-smuggling activities, as Negril became a site for cocaine drop-offs to the United States from Colombia; and for the first time, crime was an issue for the citizens. Finally, there was still another set of families who lived in nearby villages, such as Orange Bay and Sheffield, and commuted to Negril to work in hotels, guesthouses, and the like.

Negril's diverse population connects very clearly with the differences between the three businesswomen featured here. In a society where color, class, gender, and "royalty" are cornerstones of the culture, those elements are very evident here. Within this context, the goal here is to show how three women seized opportunities with those obstacles in place. One circumnavigated some aspects of the gendered social system not by being a member of Negril's royal family per se, but by having long-term roots in the community. The second is a native Negrilian who married into a poor, extended side of royalty. She is partnered with a man whose family has rights to a tiny slip of beach land. The third woman is one of the cottage owners whose access to capital via her husband's full-time employment in the sugar industry made her a success in tourism. How visitors and Jamaicans from elsewhere perceive these three women will be discussed later.

Miss Cilla, a dark-skinned woman, has very little formal education and her family has roots in Whitehall. The family is considered poor, but stable. Her great-grandmother, grandmother, and mother grew subsistence food, were higglers by trade, and also sold coconut oil as additional source of livelihood. Now, Ms. Cilla represents herself as a visualization of a classic or traditional higgler. This representation is less about what her economic activity entails, but is directed toward her customers. Most of her patrons are tourists, and she acts the part of the higgler, including her dress. Miss Cilla's business attire and activity are not quite a historical reenactment, but close enough. Miss Cilla calls herself a higgler, and Jamaicans perceive her as a higgler, too. Miss Cilla was able to skirt impediments such as low social status and a low level of education because she was a part of the fabric of the community before the road was paved. Miss Hortense was educated in the local schools and but never went further than sixth grade. A tall, thin woman, Miss Hortense's mahogany-colored skin and long hair reflect her East Indian heritage. She keeps house with her partner but is not formally wedded into "royal family" as a poor relation. Mrs. Cuthburt was also educated locally but attended secondary school in Montego Bay. She left school early and did not take the Cambridge examinations, the requirement for good jobs and tertiary education. Mrs. Cuthburt's deep-colored eyes and wide smile highlight her sienna-colored complexion. Her route to success was her marriage to a man whose steady job provided a cushion, and they were able to save. The savings were invested into their money-making cottage business.

Following the daily routines of each of the three businesswomen affords an understanding their lives in Negril. Further, as case studies, the narratives can be viewed as representative of others who are also engaged in small businesses. Through detailed descriptions, meanings of history, social hierarchy, and tourist development, I hope to illuminate a critical dimension of gender systems in a modern, global economy.

On the Land: Miss Cilla May, the Traditional Higgler

Miss Cilla May is a classical higgler.[26] She prides herself on being a higgler so much that she is perhaps the most photographed fruit and vegetable vender in Negril. She sits on the side of the road behind a series of crates on which she displays the fruit and vegetables that she has grown herself, bartered for from her network of suppliers, or bought elsewhere. Beside her crates and display are a gill cup which is used to measure dry peas (beans), plastic bags, string, and newspaper. Miss Cilla ties her head with a piece of traditional higgler cloth (plaid of red, black, and yellow colors). A large-breasted woman, Miss Cilla wears a loose top and a deep-pocket apron over a long skirt. On her feet are sneakers worn without laces for comfort. Although her children are all grown and off to work, Miss Cilla usually has a toddler or two in tow who are her grandchildren. Today she is by herself.

Miss Cilla learned her trade as a child as her own mother was a higgler. At that time, Negril produced coconut oil for cooking with its abundance of trees. However, due to the coconut tree blight, the trees died and so did the coconut oil processing and selling trade. Of course, Negril's economy shifted from fishing and coconut oil to tourism. Subsequently, Miss Cilla branched out and included other provisions and fruits to replace the coconuts and the rendered oil. Tailoring her business to a new market strategy, she focused more on fruits than vegetables on a daily basis because tourists buy fruit quite steadily throughout the week. Her ground provisions and vegetables are sold to regular local customers during the end of the week, when most of them do their marketing.

In the mornings, Miss Cilla checks the progress of her "paw paw "(papaya) trees, the ripeness of her bananas, and, during the summer, what mango, *guineps*, and avocado pears are ready to pick. She plants peas, yams, *caliloo*, and carrots. On her way to town, Miss Cilla stops by neighbors' homes to see if they have any fruits to sell her, or if it is a Thursday, ground provisions to sell, all to augment her supply. She puts these goods in crocus sacks (burlap) and stands to wait for the bus that comes by to carry her to Negril. When they are in season, Miss Cilla will buy pineapples in the large market in Sav-La-Mar; then she re-sells them in Negril.

A beneficiary of Negril's expansion, Miss Cilla's business requires that she compute the value of her stock, the pricing, and demand for certain goods by different customers. During a quiet time of the day, Miss Cilla puts a gill of peas in plastic bags that will be sold on the weekends. She explains to a group of Canadians what a sour sop is and slices one for them to sample. Her major outlays of cash come from her buying and selling operations with her supplier-neighbors and the large market in Sav-La-Mar. She marks up these items accordingly, but, for example, all bananas, whether they come from her yard or that of her neighbors, get the same high price. As a primary producer, Miss Cilla is dependent on good yields from her crops and good weather. Another expense is the cost of traveling to Negril and her trips to Sav-La-Mar. And although she does not pay rent, her spot of crates on the side of the road is designated as her own by the court of popular custom. What makes her work vulnerable is the possibility of a major buy, for example, someone buys all her stock of bananas or all of her guineps. She depends on her steady customers for financial stability with her ground provisions because those people will be there even if tourists do not come. However, the major problem is another higgler underselling her, despite the unspoken rule of respect among those in the business. Miss Cilla, who has a third-grade education, can calculate pricing, mark-ups, and the depreciation of stock in a flash without any technological support.

On the Beach: Miss Hortense Manners and the Patty Shack

Hortense Manners runs the Patty Shack, located in the middle of Negril's seven-mile sandy beach. Nestled between two hotels, the shack looks like a rundown tiny house and is shuttered after five o'clock, at the end of the business day. Miss Hortense runs the business, although her common-law husband helps at the counter. Their sons hawk the patties along the beach on the weekends and during school holidays. During the winter months, the lines in front of the patty shack are long as hungry customers wait their turn to buy this cheap but succulent food. A patty is a delicious crescent-shaped meat pie made with highly seasoned minced meat, chicken, or vegetables in a flaky pastry shell. Miss Hortense has run this business for ten years, since her partner claimed a portion of the slip of family land that runs from the road to the beach. There was just enough footage to erect the shack, and clearly not enough for a house or cottage. The small wooden building has two doors. One leads to the back of the edifice and the other is a side door where customers can file in, order, pay, and leave. There are no chairs or places to sit, just a countertop. Patties are bought in Montego Bay very early in the morning and kept warm in the metal oven behind the counter. A refrigerated case keeps drinks cold. There is no menu. One asks if the Red Stripe beer is cold or if there are veggie patties on hand, and that is it. When the stock of patties and coco bread (eaten with a patty for a major carb-loading effect) is depleted, then Miss Hortense starts to close up shop for the day. Because she knows her business, the last of the patties is not sold until almost five o'clock, closing time.

Miss Hortense begins her day very early. Her home is located down the road from Negril in Orange Bay, and she does her domestic chores while her partner goes to Montego Bay. He leaves the house two hours beforehand in his van and travels to the bakery to buy the day's supplies of patties. The shack is not the only source of this food item in Negril, so he must be in line to get his order early. Since it is a mid-July weekday, the order is medium sized (about two hundred patties) with more beef ordered than chicken and veggie. During the winter months and during spring break, when Negril is full of U.S. college-aged tourists, the shack sells more veggie patties than during the rest of the year. Beef is the traditional filling. A patty really is very much a Jamaican food. A bread pastry filled with minced meat, chicken, or vegetables, it is folded over like an empanada and baked. Unlike the bland British version, the filling of the Jamaican patty is spicy and most favorable. Most of all, the patty, coco bread, and juice or soft drink make a fine lunch that comes in a small brown paper bag. On the beach, Miss Hortense sells the combination for US $4.00 (with a Red Stripe beer it costs $2.00 more), a fraction of what a lunch costs in a beachside restaurant or bar. She reaps a 25 percent profit margin. During the high season of the winter months, and especially during the U.S. college spring break month of March, the sheer volume of business increases the profit.

Miss Hortense has little overhead, except for electricity to heat the warming oven and the refrigerated box, to keep the drinks cold. There is no lighting save for the sunlight that stream in from the doors. She does have to pay taxes to the members of the family that own that tiny strip of beach land. Miss Hortense also pays her teenage sons a small wage when they work in the shack and hawk patties along the beach. She works eight hours a day, six days a week, taking off only Sunday, except during the high season.

On this mid-July day, the noontime temperature on the beach is real hot, and most of the vacationers are spending a lot of time in the water as they attempt to cool off. The temperature inside of the shack is almost suffocating, but Miss Hortense stands behind the counter quickly filling orders. She is sweating in the heat as she fills a small paper bag with a patty, hands over an orange box drink, and collects the money from a visitor. Since no one lingers in the heat, customers file in and out quickly. Today, there are a lot of drinks being sold as well as the patties. There are pleasantries expressed, all having to do with the weather. The sons ventured out onto the beach, selling to tourists right in their beach chairs or at the water's edge. The patties are already in the small paper bags, and the "traveling" metal box that holds them is soon empty thanks to good sales. With two points of purchase, customers do not have to walk the hot sand to buy patties and a drink. As the day progresses, Miss Hortense calls out to her partner about the size of tomorrow's patty order and says that the drink supply must be restocked due to customer demand. At five o'clock, she closes up the shack and the business day is done.

On the Cliffs: Mrs. Cuthburt's Cottages

Before it became an international tourist attraction, Negril was the vacation spot for the urban Jamaican middle class, who liked to have a simple holiday in the "country." On the West End Road, running from Negril Center to the Lighthouse, there are cottages for rent that were originally built to satisfy that clientele. Mrs. Cuthburt owns and manages three cottages. She is the sole owner of one cottage, and the other two she co-owns with her husband. Mrs. Cuthburt started out renting cottages to Jamaican middle-class families who vacationed in

Negril in the mid-1960s. She did all the cooking, laundry, maid service, desk work, and "every little striking thing." Mrs. Cuthburt saved her money, as business was good because of referrals from returning guests, some of them Jamaicans, but more from Canada and Europe. She acquired the two additional cottages with her husband's financial contributions, provided by his wages as a low-level supervisor on a nearby sugar estate. Mr. Cuthburt built the cottages one by one after work and on the weekends. Each has a veranda, a bedroom, and a little alcove that accommodates a child's sleeping arrangements. Amenities now include a television and bathing facilities with hot and cold water. The Cuthburt's have five children. All of their children grew up in Negril, and after school and on holidays they played with the guests and the guest's children. The Cuthburt children also helped their mother change linens, clean rooms, water the flowers, sweep the paths, and run errands. Since they are now all grown up, they live either in the United States or in Kingston and have their own children.

Mrs. Cuthburt begins her workday as she has for almost forty years. She prepares an early morning cold breakfast spread for the guests. It consists of juice, coffee, tea, toast, cheese, and marmalade, continental style. After she sets out the trays on a table under the tree in front of the cabins, she checks the register to see if anyone is checking out or coming in. Since most of her clientele are referrals, there is a sense of ease in the business. No voices remind people to check out on time, but to be mindful when the time comes and to ask for assistance if needed. Over the years, Mrs. Cuthburt has gone from doing it all—chief cook, maid, accountant, and the like—to hiring help. Now she employs one woman to help in cleaning the cottages and an older man to do the gardening and handyman work. She still takes care of the books herself. Her careful management has made the three cottages a successful business. As a member of the chamber of commerce, Mrs. Cuthburt worked hard to improve the infrastructure of the West End, including resurfacing the road. Water lines are still listed for the future. When a hurricane came through Negril a few years ago, Mrs. Cuthburt was able to secure a rebuilding loan very quickly due to her relationship with the local bank. She makes daily business transactions with the bank and is known by the manager through chamber of commerce events. Mrs. Cuthburt has investments in a number of businesses in Kingston and Montego Bay. Her children have no interest in the cottages, even though they are profitable. Mrs. Cuthburt hopes that one of the grandchildren will take over when she and her husband retire.

An event that occurred one late June day was the arrival of the credit-card machine. As a small business owner, Mrs. Cuthburt did not think it necessary to have credit-card capabilities for the cottage rentals. However, a growing number of the return visitors wanted the convenience of paying with a major credit card. To obtain the machine, Mrs. Cuthburt had to arrange a line of credit and a secure electrical outlet and be willing to pay the points when something was charged. Only after a discussion with fellow members of the chamber of commerce did

Mrs. Cuthburt agree to try it out to see if the cost of providing the service out-weighed the convenience. Beforehand, Mrs. Cuthburt accepted cash, traveler's checks, and, for a few, bank checks. Since she is the accountant and fiscal manager, Mrs. Cuthburt looks for areas where costs can be beneficial to her business.

Discussion

When tourism is viewed from the vantage point of the wider environment, the gendered and raced systems and processes of this industry can be examined. Further, when these systems and processes focus on the ways tourism affords women the means of making a living, then a range of situations and opportunities can be explored. Such is the case of the small business sector, as illustrated by the three cases studied here. Whether they want to claim kinship to the enslaved African market women who established a history of female entrepreneurship in Jamaica or not, Negril's women who own small businesses have much in common with that legacy.

There are a number of trends that the women featured here represent in the development of tourism in Negril. First of all, there is the sense of history noted here. Negril became a tourist area by evolving from an environmental calamity, the lethal yellowing disease that killed thousands of Negril native tall coconut trees. Without those trees, over a twenty-year period the area was left without a major source of income, particularly for women. Investments by the government, Negrilians, and Jamaicans at home and abroad developed this beach, bare of trees, to be one of the top tourist areas in the Caribbean. The women who established businesses as the infrastructure of the village developed found niches in which they could seize opportunities both great and small. They could do so circumnavigating some of the impediments of the gendered social system. Miss Cilla, the traditional higgler, comes from a family who are higglers. This line of work has not diminished in Jamaica's economy but, in fact, has been reinforced due to the tendency of distributors to keep a roller-coaster effect of inefficiency going. How foodstuffs get to market is still tied to historical means and still accounted for in small quantities. Miss Cilla's business thrives on this situation, and she has been able to make a living, take care of her family needs, and show small-scale profits.

Miss Cilla is well aware of her legacy as a higgler and uses that history in a manner of reenactment for tourists. She dresses in higgler clothes, educates tourists to the new and exotic fruits they encounter in Jamaica, and provides samples for them to taste. She grows, distributes, and sells food in the same manner as her mother did decades earlier. In the larger scheme of things, Miss Cilla is considered a "grassroots" poor person. However, she has hopes for a better future for her granddaughters because they are able to go to school and perhaps "make something better for themselves."

Miss Hortense Manners uses a little bit of expensive land and reaps good-sized profits in her patty business. Selling a bit of Jamaican cuisine right on the beach shows marketing strategies at work. Her partner is the one who has access to this tiny spit of land through his family ties. Their division of labor allows them to be a successful "family" business, although he and Miss Hortense never married, but after seven years they do have co-ownership under the law. Miss Manners and her partner illustrate how those who recognize talent and success in one another can easily sidestep gender inequity.

Mrs. Cuthburt's ownership of cottages on the cliffs is an example of a hallmark of entrepreneurialism in Negril. One of the major failures of small businesses, and particularly those owned by women, is lack of access to long-term financial resources. First, like Miss Hortense, Mrs. Cuthburt works in partnership with her husband. Because of his steady income, they were able to secure loans to build the two other cottages, do the remodeling, and upgrade the services. Mr. Cuthburt never quit his job in the sugar estate. Secondly, Mr. Cuthburt recognized his wife's talents as a manager and her business acumen. They might plan together, but she does the work, viewed in terms of a success for his family. All of their children were sent to secondary schools and went on to receive additional training, and two of them finished college when they migrated to the United States. As a team they also recognize the levels of gender inequality seen most clearly in the banking system. They navigate around those impediments and plan and move forward. Mrs. Cuthburt's kind of business sense is critical for the country if Jamaica is to continue to rely on its natural beauty as a selling point on the world tourism market.

Conclusion

In Jamaica, the United States, and other parts of the world, barriers have been broken that allow women access to a range of jobs and accompanying successes unheard of just three decades ago. Since the mid-1970s, change in support of women's equality has come slowly, and it is not for the lack of trying on the part of generations of women and men who work for gender equality, human rights, and social justice. However, in Jamaica, there are still the links to the past that are kept alive by the economy that benefits and relies on both traditional and technologically advanced sectors. Further, the intermesh of traditional business practices with ones that use technologically advanced equipment within the tourist industry enhances the Jamaican experience for visitors, who will thus return to the island. In the discussions about Negril, Miss Cilla, Miss Hortense, and Mrs. Cuthburt, the intermesh of tourist-related activities fell in line with what the local community had hoped for in the development of tourism. Royal families were rewarded a windfall, as they owned prime beachfront property, and many invested in guesthouses and hotels, even if they had to move from their home site. Families like that of Miss Cilla were able to make a decent living from the tourist trade, despite not owning land or having an education. Miss Hortense does not own the land her patty shack occupies, but it is such a tiny slice that her taxes to her partner's family and a monetary contribution in the form of rent are small enough to make it all worthwhile. Mrs. Cuthburt represents the woman small business owner who has become one of the success stories of Negril. Working seven days a week for years has finally paid off in terms of educated children, vacations in the United Kingdom, Canada, and the United States, and recognition by the local chamber of commerce.

One of the definitions of "tourism" states that it is "about the experience of the place and what happens there."[27] The tourist experience is thoroughly mediated with the appearance of the relationship between the visitor and the host (native, worker, etc.).[28] Miss Priscilla May, Hortense Manners, and Mrs. Cuthburt provide those experiences for visitors through their businesses. Each has a distinct clientele and they service them well.

In sum, when the focus turns to tourism as an economic sector, an overall picture of the gender system materializes. Much like the household division of labor, where women's labor is essential but devalued by the market, tourism relies on women for its image, service, and accountability, but does not fully recognize those contributions because of gender inequality operational in its material and ideological dimensions. Subsequently, the critical element in the tourist industry, the incredible range of women's labor, remains hidden in the large scheme of things. However, it is on that very local level of interaction and business transactions that businesswomen make their contributions to the success of Jamaica's tourist industry and make a living for themselves and their families.

The three cases presented here illustrate the scope of small businesses in which Jamaican women, native born or Jamaican by marriage, are engaged. In tourism, women take advantage of this range of options according to their access to capital, training, and education. The expansion of Negril's role in tourism has made it possible for women to make a living, take care of domestic responsibilities, and, for some, make a profit. This is not a new gimmick, although better access to loans is a contemporary benefit. Further, whether they recognize the link or not, this is Negril's part of the Jamaican legacy of the savvy, aggressive, shrewd businesswoman also known as a higgler.

NOTES

1. As an anthropologist, the primary tool of research is that of participant observation. Not only do you observe, take mental notes (sometimes literary ones), and analyze and interpret (later on) what you witness; but also, more importantly, you participate in this course of events. Just being a bystander gives the anthropologist an edge of familiarity that no survey data could ever capture. This method has been a blessing and a curse for the discipline as abuse, misrepresentation, and unethical practices are included in the history of the discipline. Participant observation means getting a general understanding of how a social organization or institution works by actually being a part of the scene. It requires that the person be not an observing intruder, but someone whose familiar presence does not detract from the course of action on hand. It means that the anthropologist must be explicitly aware of what is going around her or him in a fieldwork context by daily association.

2. Government of Jamaica, *Economic and Social Survey* (Kingston, Jamaica: Planning Institute of Jamaica, 1994).

3. My larger study on Negril's women tourist workers is a work-in-progress. A. Lynn Bolles, "Common Ground of Creativity," *Cultural Survival* 16, no. 4 (1992): 34–38; "Sand, Sea and the Forbidden: Media Images of Race and Gender in Jamaican Tourism," *Transforming Anthropology* 3, no. 1 (1992): 30–35; "9 am to Midnight," paper presented at American Anthropological Association, Chicago, November 1999, mimeo; Christopher Baker, *Jamaica* (Victoria, Australia: Lonely Planet Publishers, 2000); and Polly Pattullo, *Last Resorts* (Kingston, Jamaica: Ian Randle, 1996).

4. Government of Jamaica, *Economic and Social Survey*.

5. Eudine Barriteau, "Theorizing Gender Systems and the Project of Modernity in the Twentieth-Century Caribbean," *Feminist Review* 59 (summer 1998): 186–210.

6. Patricia Y. Anderson, "Conclusion: Women in the Caribbean, Afterview," *Social and Economic Studies* 35, no. 2 (1986): 291–324; Elsie LeFranc, "Petty Trading and Labour Mobility: Higglers in the Kingston Metropolitan Area," in *Women and the Sexual Division of Labour in the Caribbean*, ed. Keith Hart (Kingston, Jamaica: Consortium Graduate School of Social Sciences, University of the West Indies, Mona, 1989), 99–132; and Carmen Diana Deere, Peggy Antrobus, Lynn Bolles, Edwin Melendez, Peter Phillips, Marcia Rivera, and Helen Safa, *In the Shadows of the Sun* (Boulder, Colo.: Westview.Press, 1990); Olive Senior, *Working Miracles* (Bloomington: Indiana University Press, 1990); Cecilia Green, "Historical and Contemporary Restructuring and Women in Production in the Caribbean," in *The Caribbean in the Global Political Economy*, ed. Hilbourne Watson (Boulder, Colo.: Lynne Reinner Publisher, 1994), 149–172.

7. Eudine Barriteau, "Theorizing Gender Systems and the Project of Modernity in the Twentieth-Century Caribbean," *Feminist Review* 59 (summer 1998): 186–210.

8. Lourdes Beneria, "Accounting for Women's Work," in *Women and Development: The Sexual Division of Labor in Rural Societies*, ed. Lourdes Beneria (New York: Preager Books, 1982), 119–148,

9. A. Lynn Bolles, "Anthropological Research Methods for the Study of Black Women in the Caribbean," in *Women in Africa and the African Diaspora*, ed. Rosalyn Terborg-Penn, Sharon Harley, and Andrea Benton Rushing (Washington, D.C.: Howard University Press, 1987), 65–78; Lucille Mathurin Mair, "A Historical Study of Women in Jamaica, 1655–1844" (Ph.D. diss., University of the West Indies, 1974).

10. Government of Jamaica, *Economic and Social Survey*.

11. Derek Gordon, *Class, Status, and Social Mobility in Jamaica* (Kingston, Jamaica: Institute of Social and Economic Research, University of the West Indies, Mona, 1987).

12. Sidney W. Mintz, *Caribbean Transformations* (Baltimore: Johns Hopkins University Press, 1974).

13. Louise Bennett, "Self Parade Peddler," in *Jamaica Labrish* (Kingston, Jamaica: Sangster's Book Stores, 1983), 27; Michelle Cliff, *No Telephone to Heaven* (New York: E. P. Dutton, 1987).

14. Victoria Durant-Gonzalez, "The Role and Status of Rural Jamaican Women: Higglerling and Mothering" (Ph.D. diss., University of California, Berkley, 1976); Dorian Powell, Erna Brodber, Eleanor Wint, and Versada Campbell, *Street Foods of Kingston* (Kingston, Jamaica: Institute of Social and Economic Research, University of the West Indies, Mona, 1900).

15. Elsie LeFranc, "Petty Trading and Labour Mobility: Higglers in the Kingston Metropolitan Area," in *Women and the Sexual Division of Labour in the Caribbean*, ed. Keith Hart (Kingston, Jamaica: Consortium Graduate School of Social Sciences, University of the West Indies, Mona, 1989), 99–132.

16. Ibid.

17. Gina Ulysses's work on the informal commercial importer chronicles this sector in great detail. See Gina Ulysses, "Uptown Ladies and Downtown Women: Informal Commercial Importing and the Social/Symbolic Politics of Identities in Jamaica" (Ph.D. diss., University of Michigan, 1999).

18. LeFranc, "Petty Trading and Labour Mobility," 99–132.

19. Richard Scase and Robert Goffee, *The Real World of the Small Business Owner* (London: Croom Helm Ltd., 1980).

20. Sara Carter and Tom Cannon, *Women as Entrepreneurs* (London: Academic Press, 1992).

21. Sara Kehaulani Goo, "Company Leader? Call Her Madame," *Washington Post*, April 15, 2001, E.

22. Carter and Cannon, *Women as Entrepreneurs*; and Katherine Browne, *Creole Economics: Caribbean Cunning under the French Flag* (Austin: University of Texas Press, 2004).

23. See http://www/ofad/prg/gender, "India-Popular Women's Micro-Enterprises in Manipur"; http://www.makingcents.com.

24. Deborah D'Amico-Samuels, "You Can Get Me out of the Race" (Ph.D. diss., City University of New York, 1986).

25. Lambros Comitas, "Occupational Multiplicity in Rural Jamaica," in *Proceedings of the American Ethnological Society*, ed. V. Garfield and E. Friedl (Seattle: University of Washington Press, 1963), 41–50.

26. The names of the women represented here are pseudonyms. This research was carried out in Negril, Jamaica, over two years, 1993 and 1994. I thank all of the women who let me watch, listen, and learn and answered questions. The study was funded by grants from the Committee on Africa in the Americas; Department of Women's Studies, the Latin American Studies Center; and the Office of International Affairs of the University of Maryland, College Park.

27. C. Ryan, *Recreational Tourism: A Social Science Perspective* (London: Rutledge, 1991).

28. Erve Chambers, introduction to *Tourism and Culture*, ed. E. Chambers (Albany, N.Y.: SUNY Press, 1997), 1.

"My Cocoa Is between My Legs"

SEX AS WORK AMONG GHANAIAN WOMEN

AKOSUA ADOMAKO AMPOFO

Historically, in the country known today as Ghana, women had a variety of gender scripts available to them that were complementary to those of men, and they played important roles not only as mothers, sisters, wives, and queens, but also as chiefs, rulers, counselors, and spiritual authorities. Further, because women and men remained members of their respective lineages after marriage, they retained responsibilities to these lineages that implied a level of autonomy, especially in the acquisition of property. Of the Asante state, Wilks has described the sixteenth century as a time of great ancestresses and argued that oral traditions privileged the role of women in the establishment of the state.[1] This did not necessarily imply gender equity; however, the introduction of Western notions of a hierarchy of (men's and women's) roles between work (public) and home (domestic and private) introduced greater competition into gender conventions and scripts in societies where biological sex, and thus gender, were not the important social stratifiers that they subsequently came to be after the incursion of colonial rule.[2] Consolidating colonial rule required the British to "contain men and women on terms unfamiliar to them, imposing Western notions of household organization and gender on local conceptualizations, and to instill new . . . notions of housewifery."[3] Modernization brought exclusion. Under colonial rule women were not recognized as chiefs, for example, nor as members of the native councils and courts.[4] The change from traditional to modern farming systems enhanced men's prestige at the expense of women's by widening the gap in their levels of knowledge and by introducing changes in production patterns which frequently reduced women's roles to those of mere laborers. Essentially, a sex bias, which was frequently inherent in missionary education as well as in the British administrative system, was reinforced in Ghana. The colonial emphasis was on male education, specifically to prepare them for entry into the civil service. Female education, when girls went to school at all, was often geared toward domestic training (for example, subjects such as home management and cookery) or the caring sectors, such as nursing and teaching.[5] The colonial officials, by superimposing Victorian notions of appropriate gender roles and relations, introduced relations in which men were perceived as and trained to be "breadwinners," while women were expected to "support" men.[6]

Sex work is an (economic) activity where women's dependence on men is starkly manifest, but it is also an area of work that allows some women the opportunity to attain some financial autonomy from a male sexual partner. Because sex has become an increasingly sought after product in today's global marketplace, and because the supply of sexual services usually requires few formal skills and little capital, it presents a viable alternative for many women. Further, the demands of international sex tourists for "exotic" women also make Third World women, especially young women, particularly vulnerable to sex work. This chapter will focus on a discussion of the different forms of sex work among Ghanaian women, ranging from the activities of girls and young women who seek long-term (especially expatriate) "boyfriends" and clients to the formal prostitute situated permanently in her workplace. I rely on data collected in the mid-1990s among a variety of women—stationary prostitutes, women working in hotels and bars, and streetwalkers or "roamers"—as well as data collected in 2004 among teenage girls in Accra to discuss how sex is constructed and experienced as work. In order to provide some insight into sex as work from the women's stories, I situate them in the global and local economies, thereby suggesting some of the reasons for entry into sex work and how prostitution becomes a means of livelihood, a survival strategy, the precursor for new forms of vulnerability and subordination, as well as an opportunity for autonomy.

Women's Changing Economic Opportunities

In this section I discuss of the division of labor, sex-role expectations, and the social obligations that go along with them. I pay attention to informal trade since this is an important activity for many women in urban areas today and because some sex workers link their entry into this activity with the loss of trading capital.

Resource allocations in marriage dictated that the husband would bring his wife the products of his labor: fishermen would give fish, farmers would give staple crops, and so forth. The husband was also responsible for providing the meat and salt for the sauce. While a woman worked on her husband's farm, she also had a smaller (subsistence) plot on which she grew food for the family's meals, as the wife was expected to contribute the vegetable ingredients and the staples to go with the meals. With the introduction of a cash economy, women began to sell some of their husbands' contributions and to accumulate surpluses which they could use to purchase other goods. At the end of a given period, a wife would render accounts to her husband, stating that she had spent so much of the profit from her sales for, say, a new pair of shoes for their son, or on kerosene for the lamp. She would declare how much was left over, and her husband would then say she could keep a certain percentage, or even all of it, for her own economic ventures.[7]

Ghanaian women are well noted for their industry and economic autonomy. Important in this context are the cultural norms that encourage women's participation in the labor force and reward industry. An Akan girl, upon attaining the age of maturity as evidenced by the arrival of menarche, was given some capital to trade with by her father as a means of accumulating independent resources.[8] Since women were expected to engage in productive activities independent from their husbands, the idea of a woman being merely a "housewife" is still frowned upon, and a woman who is not engaged in any economic activity is labeled as lazy. One husband, in a study of Kumasi traders, commented that he would feel ashamed as a father "to satisfy his vanity and convenience by keeping a wife at home to wait on him at the expense of his children's higher education or food supply."[9] Further, inheritance systems did not assure women of economic assets through marriage or the patrilineal system (though in the latter case a woman could more readily expect lifelong support from her sons, if not necessarily from her husband's lineage). Thus it was important for a woman to acquire economic assets of her own.

When cocoa became an important cash crop in the early 1900s, Asante men entered this area of farming in droves because of the high incomes it offered. Fewer women entered cocoa farming, and even when they did their farms tended to be smaller as they did not have access to the same labor pool men did. For Asante men their gender and ethnicity gave them favored access to the type of land required, to lineage loans, and to unpaid labor from male kin, wives, and children. Men also did not have to concern themselves with providing food supplies, as this was women's responsibility.[10] On men's cocoa farms it was women who owned the food crops, however. Further, although women did not feel that they had established a joint concern with their husbands, they did expect to receive compensation for their work on their husbands' farms in addition to these crops, possibly a portion of the farm itself.[11] Among the Anlo Ewe poultry farming remains an important activity, especially for women, and they would usually be involved in the sale of chickens and eggs as well as food crops. Godwin Nukunya notes that these multiple economic activities have made trading an important occupation, especially for women; he cites Westermann, a German missionary in colonial times who observed that "there was hardly any woman who did not trade."[12] Ga women have been involved in trading from as far back as historical records are available. The trade in fish and vegetables was conducted by women, and with the arrival of the Europeans, Ga women began a trade in imported items.[13] Both Ga and Fante women have also long been involved in the fish trade.

Among fishing communities such as the coastal Ga and Fante, a commercial system operates whereby husbands give their wives fish on commission; this is a commercial arrangement in which the business partner is a spouse. Wives collect their husbands' share of the fish on the beach and either sell it directly or smoke it before they sell it. At the end of the fishing season a wife renders accounts to her husband, from which she deducts her *atondze* (sales commission), normally 10 percent, as well as money she may have borrowed for the upkeep of the family.[14] With her share of the profit the woman is expected to trade, although Emile Vercruijsse claims that "the trading capital built up in this way is bit by bit claimed back by the husband during the lean season to be spent on repairs and maintenance as well as on food."[15] George Hagan, writing on the Effutu, argues, to the contrary, that the sale of fish makes the women in the community the ones who control "the husbands' purse strings" and also control the circulation of money in the society.[16] Claire Robertson makes a similar assertion when she argues that in accounts of the relative economic power of men and women in Ga fishing villages "women seem to have been generally better off than men."[17]

However, the colonial officials, by superimposing Victorian notions of appropriate gender roles and relations, introduced relations in which men were perceived as and trained to be "breadwinners" while women were expected to "support" or "help" men.[18] This bias set the tone for certain inequities that remain until this day. New income opportunities for men opened in the formal sector, mainly as white- and blue-collar workers in the civil service and European enterprises. Naturally, there were only a few women in these sectors, and even when they gained entry, restrictions applied. Once they got married, women had to resign from the civil service. Wives of civil servants, whether with qualifications in their own right or not, were not permitted to work in the formal sector either,[19] and female teachers were required to stop teaching once they got married.[20] Thus, marriage under the colonial order brought new levels of dependency for wives. In one study, Ga women traders were found to be more economically dependent on their husbands in the new economic order because of a reduction in cooperative trading with their mothers and husbands.[21] Participation in formal schooling has reduced the extent to which these Accra women cooperate with their mothers in trading ventures.[22] They no longer cooperate with husbands in the fishing business either (i.e., processing their husbands' fish catch) because many men are now artisans and clerks, professions which lend themselves to little cooperation. Western ideologies led to the hierarchical assignment of gender roles and introduced competitiveness into a gender system which had hitherto been much more complementary, with the result that women's progress and mobility assumed a strong association with their relationship to men—husbands, fathers, uncles, brothers, and even sons.[23]

Today Ghana's economy is a mixed one consisting of a large agricultural sector and a smaller, capital-intensive mining and manufacturing sector. Since the late 1980s the service industry has also come to play an increasingly important role in the economy. Agriculture, which provides 51 percent of the gross domestic product (GDP), is made up of mainly small-scale peasant farmers and absorbs 60 percent of the country's labor force. There are several detailed accounts of Ghana's political and economic procession from the 1950s, just before independence, through the 1980s, which saw the introduction of structural adjustment programs (SAPs) and the rise of the International Monetary Fund's (IMF) influence in Ghana.[24] Most of these accounts seem to agree that the period from the 1970s to the early 1980s saw the economy at its worst since independence, with GDP growing at a rate of −0.5 percent between 1975 and 1982. Low agricultural production, poor industrial output, high inflation, declining per capita income, and rising unemployment became almost endemic.

During the period 1984 to 1992 economic policy shifted slowly away from a commitment to self-reliance and popular mobilization, which had been the populist cry of the then military regime and their military predecessors, to liberal structural reforms and the birth of the Economic Recovery Program (ERP) in 1983. The Economic Recovery Program was introduced to stabilize the economy. The ERP was the precursor for the implementation of the IMF's structural adjustment program (SAP). The aim of Ghana's SAP, like most in Africa, was to revitalize the economy. Some of the more important prescriptions made by the World Bank included a "rationalization" of the public sector, "deindustrialization," and "trade liberalization."[25]

There are many useful studies, especially by feminist scholars, noting that the effects of neoliberal structural reforms have not been gender neutral, and I will not repeat those discussions here.[26] It is, however, useful to summarize some of the main arguments made. Public-sector rationalization and trade liberalization led, among other outcomes, to the sale of state-owned enterprises and the massive laying-off of employees in the formal sector of the economy. Often women were the first to be let go, since corporations usually got rid of their least skilled employees. As local industries collapsed under the onslaught of cheaper imported goods, especially from Southeast Asia, small-scale women entrepreneurs, as they faced increasing competition from multinationals, folded up their businesses at the same time that areas such as mining and communications, typically dominated by male foreign investors, received special support.[27] As the reforms continue under new guises such as the HIPC (Highly Indebted Poor Countries) initiative and Ghana's Poverty Reduction Strategy (GPRS), women continue to suffer and their dependency on men is expected to grow.[28] Although Ghana has received millions of dollars into its HIPC account and disbursed these on poverty-related activities under the GPRS, critics argue that these do not necessarily enhance the welfare of the poorest and most vulnerable.

When funding for social services such as health is withdrawn, women are usually the first to feel the pinch; they are responsible for the care of sick household members, they need to take time off to go to the health service or do the care-taking, they provide the funds, and when they themselves fall sick, women wait until their symptoms are really severe before seeking treatment.[29] What seems obvious from qualitative accounts of socioeconomic conditions in Ghana today is that while there may have been overall growth, and perhaps positive changes for a small, elite, and often entrepreneurial class, most ordinary Ghanaians do not perceive that there have been any significant positive changes from SAP or, later, the HIPC initiative and Ghana's Poverty Reduction Strategy under the current government.

Most women in Africa work in the informal sector, usually as farmers or traders, two economic sectors that are very sensitive to changes in policy and structural reforms such as the removal of subsidies and introduction of taxes. Trading for women usually means small-scale, often itinerant, trading such as the sale of cooked food. Men, on the other hand, even if in trading, are usually the store owners and sell hardware such as electrical goods. The image of the wealthy West African female trader (market mammy) is more myth than reality.[30] Yet women traders came under consistent attack during successive (military) governments in the 1970s and 1980s, attack that took both an ideological and literal form.[31] Gracia Clark notes: "The high incomes and prestige available to illiterate women through market trading functioned as a powerful symbol of national degeneracy in 1979. Direct government distribution would return these incomes and positions of power to the educated (male) civil service or the public-spirited (male) military, where they belonged."[32] The public hearings of the National Reconciliation Commission bear testimony to the fact that many women suffered the loss of their trading enterprises during the Armed Forces Revolutionary Council and early New Democratic Congress years.[33] While harsh polemics and policies during this period sought to provide alternatives to female trading, the government could not offer a viable alternative and women remained important players; however, the gender isolation of women traders intensified.[34] SAPs came to conclude what successive governments had failed to fully effect. As Clark puts it, "It was left to structural adjustment to undermine female control of market trading indirectly by sending more men back into trading and by subordinating the locally based economy more deeply."[35] In other words, the expanded free market indirectly exacerbated existing gender inequalities. Under structural reforms market mechanisms and cost competitiveness are given overwhelming emphasis. An increase in employment in areas such as mining, transportation, and communications has not generally benefited women. Many small (cottage) industries typically owned and operated by women, such as sewing and trade in cloth and locally manufactured foodstuffs, have collapsed because they cannot compete with cheap imports or new multinational companies. Female farmers and traders were particularly hard hit in the late 1980s and early 1990s.[36]

The failure of a business, with its accompanying debt, when coupled with women's frustrations around their inability to care (adequately) for their children, can precipitate women's entry into prostitution.[37] For younger women with fewer skills and resources, for whom street vending is usually the most readily sought means of livelihood, a transition from street vending to sex work is not at all uncommon given the precipitous nature of street vending and given that the global demand for sexual services seems to be growing.[38]

"My Cocoa Is between My Legs": Sex as Work

African women's sexuality, and within that area the subject of prostitution and sexual exchange, has interested researchers, especially Western anthropologists, for a long time, often with an emphasis on black women's exuberant sexuality. African feminists have complained about this gazing on the female African body, and some of the more recent works by African scholars, especially African feminist scholars, have responded to the gaze of Western voyeurism by emphasizing women's agency and drawing attention to their own self-perceptions.[39] However, many of these same studies also point to the fact that for many women, and especially girls and young women, prostitution is an economic strategy in the face of increasingly limited economic options. Thus it is important to point to the links between globalization (such as international terms of trade and international sex tourism) and African women's sex work. As one Ghanaian prostitute who was interviewed put it, referring to an important income earner for her country, "My cocoa is between my legs."

A form of institutionalized prostitution existed in so-called traditional Ghanaian societies to meet the sexual needs of unmarried men. Early European references to prostitution among the Southwest Akan of the Gold Coast and the Ivory Coast can be traced back to the seventeenth century.[40] In this form of institutionalized prostitution women, usually slaves, were acquired by the political elite to meet the sexual needs of unmarried men. Essentially these were public women "coerced into what was definitely a social institution designed to alleviate sexual pressures among unmarried men."[41] They were initiated into and confirmed for "sex work" by a series of religious rituals, and their sexuality as well as their earnings were controlled by the state, which provided for their upkeep by allowing them to take food from homes and the market. According to Jean Godot, a French adventurer and voyager writing after a visit to Assini (on the Gold Coast) in 1701, these public women were required to be distinguished from other women by wrapping their heads in white linen.[42] Further, they were obliged to receive every bachelor or face severe punishments. The practice of prostitution by any other women in the community who had not been set apart for this work constituted an infraction and would require purification from the malevolent spirits sure to inundate them, and others, as a result of their numerous contacts with strangers.[43] Godot also claimed that married men accused of having sexual relations with the public women were fined and severely punished. In sum, this institutionalized form of sex work existed simply to provide a service to unmarried men and did not allow for the accumulation of wealth among the women.[44]

With European intervention in Africa, the increasing disenfranchisement of women from traditional means of livelihoods and support, and the introduction of cash economies, women who "sold sex" were able to accumulate assets over which they had sole control, often using these incomes to support rural families.[45] Marjorie Mbilinyi and Naomi Kaihula, in their work in rural Tanzania, show how, following male loss of incomes in agriculture and the formal sector, many rural households now depend on women's incomes and how some women turn to sex work, using this money to expand businesses or build houses.[46]

Nonetheless, prostitution remains a stigmatized line of work. In both Ghana and La Côte d'Ivoire, where the women interviewed were located, the position of a prostitute remains ambiguous. It is not illegal to be a prostitute; however, women can be arrested for "soliciting" or being a "public nuisance."[47] In theory, then, of the categories of women I will discuss shortly, only the work of the stationary prostitute (seater) can be considered as legal since she neither "solicits" nor "opportunes." Public opinion around sex work remains negative, often being constructed in racial terms—greedy African women chasing the dollars of white expatriate men. Thus it is also important to bear in mind the links between globalization—international terms of trade and international sex tourism—and African women's work in the sex industry. Further, the particular vulnerabilities women face cannot be ignored: the legal status of sex work, the potential for abuse, the absence of collective strategies in many cases, and the threat of AIDS. What is important for any analysis of sex work is recognition of the complex social and gender relations involved in prostitution. In the next few sections of this chapter I will focus on aspects of women's lives as sex workers, paying attention to how they came to sex work and how sex work is constructed and experienced as work.

At the risk of over-simplifying or universalizing, prostitution in Ghana can be divided into three rough, though not always discrete, categories, each with its own forms of labor organization and labor time: one, the formal, organized, sedentary women referred to by Adomako Ampofo as seaters;[48] two, women who operate from upscale bars, nightclubs, and hotels patronized by wealthy expatriates and who can be classified as high-class; and, three, roamers, probably the most visible group, who walk the streets where ordinary workers live and work. The fluidity of these categories becomes clearer when we note that "high-class" women "roam" some streets, and many roamers work bars and clubs on the lower end of the market. Also more difficult to categorize are young women and girls who hang out at particular events, such as dances, musical shows, or funerals, in search of clients. Further, many sex workers only work part-time to supplement other earnings. The data I draw on in this chapter come from two studies among Ghanaian women: the first, from a series of in-depth interviews carried out between 1992 and 1994 among 188 Ghanaian prostitutes and single women living and working in Accra and Kumasi, in Ghana, and Abidjan, in La Côte d'Ivoire.[49] The study, which sought to explore understandings of AIDS, disease transmission, safe sex, and sexual attitudes and behaviors, was carried out among 188 women living in Ghana and La Côte d'Ivoire; the data in this chapter refer to the 45 high-class women, 39 roamers, and 47 seaters that I categorized as "sex workers" based on their responses. The second set of data comes from a 2003 study among young people on Accra's streets that sought to examine understandings and experiences of sexual exploitation among 152 girls and boys on Accra's streets. Although sexual exchange was found to be common among the young people, only the conversations with five young women who described themselves as consciously engaging in sex as work are included here.[50]

The Sex Workers: A Brief Profile

Most of the women are under the age of thirty-five (71 percent), with seaters and women in Abidjan slightly older, and roamers younger, than other women.[51] Most roamers and high-class are under age twenty-five (39 percent and 38 percent, respectively), while the majority of seaters are between ages thirty-one and forty-five (about 68 percent).[52] Although a few of the women have some education, this is mainly basic (primary) education, generally incomplete because they dropped out as there was no money to see them through or because they became pregnant.[53] Almost a third of all the women have no formal education, and those who have been to school typically have only had a basic education (generally nine years or less). Even among the high-class, only 11 percent have some secondary school education. In terms of work only a small proportion (less than 3 percent) have never done anything besides sex work. The rest had been traders (45 percent), service industry workers (21 percent), formal-sector/salaried workers (about 4 percent), or farmers (6 percent), and some still trade or go back to their villages to farm occasionally (11 percent). At the time of both field studies less than 10 percent of the women had any regular work or source of income apart from prostitution, although some indicated that they had seasons when they concentrated on trading, using income earned from sex work as capital.

Almost all the women have been married before or have had long-term domestic/romantic relationships with men with whom they have had children. They cite a number of reasons for the breakup of their relationships, including physical separation due, usually, to the man's traveling or disappearance; disapproval of in-laws; the wife's infertility (or presumed infertility); the husband's infidelities; the husband's failure to support his wife and children; all manner of disagreements and quarrels; physical and emotional abuse; and death. Lack of financial support, however, is an import reason for the breakdown of a relationship, especially when linked to the man having other women: a typical refrain is, "He never gave me money to trade with or bought me a cloth. Whenever I asked for something he never wanted to give me; he was tight-fisted and a womanizer." Many women have invested financially in their partners and feel very betrayed when the men do not come through for them: "Men are no good; they have no character! Ask my sister how I suffered before this boy could get this job on the rig. It was less than a year after he got the job that my brother died—I had laid down myself for you but he did not care about the mishap that had befallen me. Do you think this will make me love another man again? You had nothing; everything depended on me, be it food or other meals. When he started working he became like a king. . . . [I]t is rubbish to waste your time for somebody's son only to be shown the 'red card' at the last minute" (Kate, aged forty-two, Abidjan).[54]

Women also complained that men were not serious about formalizing their relationships. Aisha, from Kumasi, a twenty-three-year-old high-class with a young son by a previous lover, complained about her current partner's feet dragging in this regard, a partner, incidentally, whom, she had just discovered, had made a colleague pregnant: "I waited to see if he would go and do what he said, but he didn't. Rather, every time he sees me he wants to go to bed with me. I have also told him that unless he goes to see my parents he shouldn't expect anything like that from me. . . . It's true that I want to get married, but I don't want to be used by any man again and then be left to take care of another child. I don't want a situation where the man will want to sleep with you and after he has had his fill of you he will just break your heart. As for that I won't do it."

What remains for many women is a deep sense of disillusionment and cynicism about romantic relationships and a sense that if they are being exploited sexually in their intimate relations with no emotional or financial returns, then sex for money cannot be such a bad alternative. At the time of the field studies only eight of the women stated that they were married or in a long-term relationship. Fifty-five of the women, including two of the girls interviewed in the 2003 study, mention having boyfriends. However, almost all of them have dependents, either their own children or those of a sister or brother and/or aged parents. The need to take care of these dependents, especially to try and put children through school, emerges as an important reason given for entry into prostitution.

Some women made conscious decisions to enter sex work, for many others the process is described as one that happened almost by default as other alternatives became unavailable or did not provide enough money to meet basic needs. Afia's story provides an example of the process. Aged seventeen, Afia is an attractive, well-dressed young woman who says she left her village and came to Accra because her family is poor and she felt she was a burden to them. She had dropped out of school in class 4 because her parents could not afford to continue paying for her education. Afia was actually encouraged to leave home by her family, who said Accra is a big city and people would buy whatever she had to sell.[55]

Failure of a business, sudden debts, and the need to provide for dependents are the overwhelming reasons offered for entry into prostitution. Almost

70 percent of the women (83 percent of seaters, 58 percent of roamers, and 37 percent of high-class) have at least one living child, and 60 percent also have other dependents:

> I have a child [daughter, aged seven], but at first I was selling *waakye* [cooked rice and beans], but I run into serious debts. It was my mother who went for a loan for me. When I asked my boyfriend [child's father], he refused to give it to me . . . so I started selling *kelewele* [fried plantain], but that also led to more debt. I started selling *tuo* [cooked rice dumplings and sauce] with a second loan from my mother, but that also did not work and so my mother said she won't give me any more money. That is why, when my friends told me about this place, I decided to come here to get some money to start another business. (Aisha, roamer, aged twenty-three, Kumasi)

> The [younger brother's] wife was then pregnant. She had four children with my brother. One day she put the youngest child behind her and went to bring food from the farm, but on her way back it rained and so the bridge was lost in the flood. When she tried to cross she drowned . . . [due to] the weight of the pregnancy and the child behind her . . . and she became weak trying to swim against the tide and so she drowned with the child. The way the woman liked me among all the others, before she was buried I dreamt and she said that I should be given the children, and in whichever way she will help me she will try to do it. (Vida, seater, late thirties or forties, Accra)

Vida now has, in addition to the two surviving children, a son, the daughter of a sister, and a mother to look after, and many women underscore the need to provide for children. And sometimes the imperative to provide goes beyond basic needs:

> I and my children, sometimes even what we will eat is a problem. It so happens that in Kumasi . . . you can get up in the morning and your child will be crying such that someone sitting by will ask, "But can't you buy food for the child." But just think, at least I know that every day I have to feed my child, but that what is needed to buy the food was the problem . . . so I couldn't help it. (Elizabeth, roamer, aged twenty-nine, Kumasi)

> What am I looking for in life? It is for my children. If I don't come here to struggle my way through, my children can't have a good education. (Akor, seater, aged thirty-eight, Kumasi)

> As for me, when I get money I buy cloth and when I find someone going to Ghana I send it to my mother. (Adjorkor, roamer, aged twenty-five, Abidjan)

For young roamers in Accra, the 1990s was a period when municipal authorities frequently sent guards to rid the streets of illegal hawkers. These guards would seize the traders wares and demand heavy fines from them, often higher than the value of the goods. For some, this created a debt to creditors, and sex work seemed to provide an immediate option through which this debt could be repaid: "If these *a-ba-ei* [literally, they are coming] people had left us in peace to do our trading, it would have been better because this work is risky. . . . Today it's the police, tomorrow something else. So what we are asking is now what exactly do they want us to do? If you have money and you decide to trade, no peace" (Akos, roamer, aged twenty-four, Accra).

Women who migrated to Abidjan in the 1980s and early 1990s in search of greener pastures and the opportunities that were absent in Ghana, at a time when La Côte D'Ivoire was a favored destination for unskilled workers in the West African sub-region, soon discovered that finding such work could be quite difficult and the dream elusive: "It was while I was selling that a lady who is from my house said she was coming here [Abidjan], so I decided to follow her. . . . She told me she was working in a bar over here. . . . When we got here I realized it was a lie. She just left me under the pretext of going to look for money to pay the driver (we did not pay our fare on our way here, so the driver agreed that we would pay him when we got here). She sent me to a certain woman who made me begin this job" (Adjorkor, roamer, aged twenty-five, Abidjan).

Afiba, thirty-two, became pregnant when she was nineteen; however, the boy responsible denied his involvement and she had to drop out of school: "I was kind of useless in front of my people; they were always raining insults on me like I have a fatherless child and the way I couldn't complete my education. They were really mad at me, and even if they gave me something they would insult me first. . . . I was really worried; that is why I left for this place [Abidjan]." She could not find work as a housemaid because no one wanted a woman with a baby, so she eventually allowed herself to be persuaded to try sex work: "When I came here [Abidjan] for the first time, I had a child, so I decided to look for a job like a house maid. . . . I never knew this was the kind of work the Ghanaians here were doing. . . . But because I was carrying a little child I couldn't get any house-maid job. There was this woman who suggested that I should 'sit by the way side.' I had not heard of this before; even in Ghana when people do this kind of work we laugh at them. How come I will have to be doing it now? And all they told me was if I don't do it then I would not eat because as for here in Côte d'Ivoire nobody looks for food for another person" (Afiba, seater, aged thirty-two, Abidjan).

This aspect of deception is not uncommon as regards entry into sex work for Ghanaian women in La Côte d'Ivoire. Ama, thirty-six, explained, "You see, the person who brought me here did not speak the truth. She said there was work here, but when we came here that was what she introduced us to." In some cases it can best be described as a form of indentured brothel labor under "queen mothers" who have financed the trip to Abidjan and who run the houses where

the women live. They keep the young women's incomes until the initial investment for travel and settling in is paid off.[56]

While for some women entry into sex work is described as one among few
alternatives, there are others for whom sex work was more consciously chosen as
a way to meet needs and desires that the conventional jobs they had the skills for
could not provide, or to supplement their regular incomes. "There was this girl
who will always go out in the evening. And she kept buying things almost every
day, so I wanted to know how she got her money. So one day after we had both
had our bath in the evening she called me and said we should go for a drink and
I agreed. That was when she told me what she did. She brought me here. . . . In
fact, the first day I felt very embarrassed. . . . I got a client that day anyway. After
that we kept coming" (Adwoa, roamer, aged twenty-two, Kumasi).

The desire to live the "good" life is reflected most among the high-class.
When nineteen-year-old Akosua was asked why she entered sex work since her
mother was a well-to-do trader, she explained: "I traveled to see whether I would
be able to 'make it' [become successful]. My big sister [also a prostitute] is now
somebody in life, so I also want to be somebody. . . . I want to have a car. . . . I
want nice things. I want to look 'luxe' [luxurious]. . . . Yes, I want nice things, go
to nice places, have a nice room. I have expensive and nice things. . . . I want a
husband. I want someone who has money, . . . one who would give me money
for my upkeep and life. . . . I don't care about anybody; mine is to get money."
Thus a woman's sexuality is viewed as a concrete resource to be traded in the
marketplace. Amina had the most apt imagery: "When you sell 3,000 cedis worth
of toffee you earn a profit of only 200 cedis, and this would not be enough to
cater for myself and the children. I would therefore have to steal, but I cannot do
that. You know God has given me cocoa which is between my legs, so if I go into
prostitution it is my own body" (Amina, high-class, Accra). In this marketplace
some looked out for big-spending clients and were thus willing to tolerate less
pleasant acts, like Akosua: "As for me I collect the big amount, . . . sometimes
gifts. . . . It is because of what I do for them, . . . like I suck them. . . . If I like you,
I let you do what you want [like hold my breast], and after that they pay well."

In viewing sex as a tradable good in the marketplace, women take a prag-
matic and sometimes cynical approach to sex work. Early in life they learned to
view sex as an exchange commodity offered by a female to a male, especially
when she has no other means of returning a kindness or service:

> From the way he has been assisting me I could not refuse when he asked for
> [sex] because I wanted him to meet my needs. (Afia, roamer, aged seventeen,
> Accra)

> He [first sexual partner] told me that—you know, at first our school uniform
> was light and deep red. . . . The seam came off and I used black thread to sew
> it—he promised to buy me a new school uniform and pay my fees. So after he

had sex with me he went to pay it [fees], and I told him I needed books and he bought them for me and gave me money. (Yaa, young roamer, Accra)

[Laughing] As a girl, when you come of age you will by all means meet a man who will express interest in you, and if you happen to need some little things then you follow him so he can help you. I thought that it is not everything that I can ask [my brother] for; it is because of this that I agreed to move with this man . . . in order to have the things I really need. (Ama, young roamer, Accra)

For Afia, Yaa, and Ama, the move from paying a kind benefactor with sex to more formal sex work with clients was ultimately a short step. Older women were more cynical, arguing that irresponsible and unresponsive husbands and lovers had been sexually (ab)using them "for free," so, in a bid to never be "cheated" again, why not earn money for sex? Further, argues Adjorkor, a roamer in Abidjan, sex work not only provides for basic needs, it also provides autonomy and freedom from abusive employers that other forms of work do not: it is better than working for someone who will insult you.

Sex work enabled Adjorkor to be independent and, according to her, to maintain a certain level of dignity that being employed would never provide, especially since Adjorkor has only two years of schooling and could only expect to be employed to do menial work. The bottom line for most women involved in sex work is the issue of livelihoods. Sex work provides an income in the face of perceived zero options; for others sex work provides a better income than the one they had or could expect, but ultimately most women think about supporting children and family members, especially elderly relatives. Yet sex work is hard work and comes with a number of risks which are not immediately evident to most women. Once they discover these, and the challenges of negotiating the terrain, this informs not only their strategies, but also the ways in which they ultimately construct their work. In the next section I outline some of the hazards of working as a prostitute.

"As for This Work, Your Body Aches": Working Too Hard for Money

Adjorkor may be right that sex work provides autonomy; however, the challenges and hardships involved in sex work cannot be ignored, and some women are realistic about the risks they face. Esther, a forty-two-year-old seater, explained how physically demanding sex work has been for her: "As for this work, the frequency with which men lie on top of you, your body aches!" Having sex several times a day is, simply put, hard work! Hence most women (ab)use a variety of prescription and nonprescription drugs, including analgesics and antibiotics. Other risks include STDs and pregnancy.

In Abidjan especially, women were found to rely heavily on the use of herbal enemas to prevent STD infections and pregnancy. In Abidjan it was common for women to describe abdominal pains, pain when passing urine, vaginal itches, sores, and discharges. Abuse of drugs and alcohol was common, especially among women in Abidjan, partly because they experienced their work as both emotionally and physically demanding. Some clients demand sex that the women find demeaning, such as oral and anal sex, or dangerous, such as sex without condoms. Sometimes women feel compelled to oblige to earn more or because they have not earned anything or enough that day. Afia, a twenty-seven-year-old roamer in Abidjan, explained, "[Cocaine] helps me against getting sick. . . . The thing is once you get hooked to it if you don't get it you fall sick. . . . It helps me perform [sex] well." Nineteen-year-old Akos, who had earlier explained that she is in sex work to make money and "become somebody," later said that she smokes marijuana: "to get over my problems, and to think of myself and how other friends are getting on in life with me in this position." Clients and colleagues also often introduce women to street and prescription drugs.

In addition to the hardship of sex as work itself, there is the ever-present threat of abuse from some clients. For most clients the condition for payment is ejaculation. For sex workers, on the other hand, income and profits are calculated around the time spent, whether a short time or the whole night. Thus, prolonged sex acts often lead to quarrels and even physical violence when women demand payment and clients who feel unsatisfied refuse to pay. While there are many accounts of "respectful" and "gentle" clients, stories of the problems created by clients and circulated among the women are also legendary. In Abidjan a lot of complaints surrounding nonpayment by clients are lodged with the police, especially among seaters, who generally have fixed prices. Sometimes clients rob the women or even beat them up. There are the clients who refuse to pay, those who refuse to use condoms, others who want particular sexual styles that women consider inappropriate or demeaning; some are abusive, and others come surreptitiously in groups: "Some of the men don't come alone. They come with friends and . . . they switch off the lights and when they have finished somebody else comes to have sex with you" (Boba, roamer, in her early twenties, Accra).

Although public officials such as city guards and police officers can become important allies and even confidants and boyfriends, the police were also accused of undue harassment, rape, and theft: "Even some of the policemen come and arrest some of the girls and, instead of taking you to the police station, they take you somewhere else, sleep with you without giving you anything. I feel if we had been left in peace to do our trading it would have been better" (Akos, roamer, aged twenty-four, Accra). "There are times, too, the policemen, when they arrest the women, he'll intentionally wear his uniform and come here to arrest you and then take you home and sleep with you" (Elizabeth, roamer, aged twenty-nine, Kumasi).

In Abidjan, coupled with the fact that Ghanaian women are foreigners, most also speak little French when they arrive, making them even more vulnerable in the social milieu in which they live and work. Sometimes they are arrested, harassed, beaten, imprisoned for a few days, have their heads shaved, or are even raped. Nonetheless, although sex work is constructed as being about livelihoods, and despite the pragmatism of some of the women, none constructed sex work as an ideal profession. Tina, who occasionally works in a hotel, said, "As for this place I only use it to supplement my money, so that I don't depend too much on my capital (for trading) for me to lose it." Sex work is thus legitimated as a means of ensuring that a woman can continue to earn a living in a culturally approved manner.

Seaters are the only group of women who construct their work as a formal profession and who practice openly, sometimes even to the knowledge of family members. Organized into associations, they consciously see their work as an option for women who have lost access to more acceptable means of support via marriage, and they do not see it as temporary or as a stepping-stone to other opportunities for they have already come to the end of their road of opportunities. Auntie Martha, who described herself as the national president, explained that their association dates back to the Gold Coast era, "when Nkrumah came to power."[57] She even described the role of the association almost as a social support or welfare group for older women with few skills for whom alternative employment is hard to find:

> We don't allow young girls here. As you [interviewer] are sitting here now, if you come to me I won't take you because I wouldn't like you to come here and waste away since you don't have a child. Unless the woman has been married before and has had all her children, or women who have been abandoned by their husbands and don't have anyone looking after them, . . . those are the ones we accept here. Or let us say that you are a widow. . . and have not capital to work with, there we will consider you. As for the work we are doing here, it is some sort of charity work to help those who may be indebted or have lost their husbands but don't have anyone.

Indeed, Atta B, the late, legendary seaters' leader in Kumasi, is purported to have claimed that sex work provided an important service to the community by keeping men who had no other sexual outlets from raping young women, for example. This conceptualization fits in neatly with the traditional form of sex work practiced by the public women of historical times, and contemporary seaters made references to this history as they romanticized their own work in the past and compared it to that of the modern sex worker: "Now it's only dirty work they are doing here in Abidjan. There are women who are penetrated from behind. First, ours was the best; we called it 'life.' Now they call theirs 'life,' but the work is not as vibrant. As I sit here I know what they do in Abidjan, and if I get somebody from Ghana, a 'big' man who can clear all these girls, I would like it" (Ghanasah, high-class, aged fifty, Abidjan).

Possibly, such comparisons allow women like Ghanasah to make sense of their lives by juxtaposing them against an "other." Twenty-one-year-old Akua, a roamer in Abidjan, also talked about prostitution in the old days with nostalgia, comparing it to a less-profitable form of contemporary sex work: "First when our mothers came here there was money. . . . We had not dreamt of coming here, but it was when we came that we realized that this place too was fun." Others, as noted above, see sex work as better than begging, stealing, or being bound to an abusive employer or partner. They also recognize the financial autonomy that prostitution provides. The majority, however, viewed sex work in less positive colors:

> In fact, I don't like this kind of business, but it's all due to harsh conditions. (Abena, seater, aged thirty-two, Accra)

> It is not good; ideally a woman should be doing a more respectable job, get married and be responsible. (Adwoa, roamer, Kumasi)

> Whenever I come here I always say that this is a rotten life that I find myself in. If God takes me out of this bad life I'm in, I don't have anything with which to thank him. . . . I will rather lie on the ground and just roll to give God the glory. . . . My coming here is not out of will, but it's due to financial difficulties. (Elizabeth, roamer, aged twenty-nine, Kumasi)

> It is nasty work. (Afia, roamer, aged twenty-one, Abidjan)

In addition to providing hope that enough capital can be earned to enable a woman to end her life as a prostitute, for some women sex work also presents an opportunity to find their Prince Charming with whom they can live happily ever after. It is perhaps not surprising that young girls such as seventeen-year-old Afia, who sells oranges and sex on the streets of Accra, have as their goal to "have a good husband and have a nice place to stay." More surprisingly, perhaps, is that although most of the women have had unhappy marriages and love relationships that did not work out, or partners who proved to be irresponsible and financially unsupportive, finding true love and a "good" marriage to a "kind-hearted" or "responsible" man remains the ultimate goal for many, with the exception of the seaters. "The beauty of this world is marriage. For a woman, even if you should have everything and yet have no husband, you have not tasted of the joy of the world. . . . But when you have experienced it and have known what love is, you will know that love is the joy of the world. A woman's glory is marriage. That, as a woman you'll get married and be staying with your husband so that at the end of the month he will give you chop money and give you something as capital" (Elizabeth, roamer, aged twenty-nine, Kumasi). This seemingly unrealistic expectation is fuelled by the fact that many women can narrate stories of colleagues who got married to a foreign (white) client and were spirited away, supposedly to a life of relative ease and financial security in the West.[58] Of course, women rarely get to hear how these relationships play out. "If I get a white man to marry [he will take me out of the country]" (Boba, roamer, in her early twenties, Accra).

Closing Thoughts

In this chapter I have attempted to show the varying forms of sex work among this group of Ghanaian women, the paths that led women into this line of work, and the ways in which they constructed sex work as work. While the lines between casual sex and prostitution can be very blurred, and some even argue that marriage is a form of sex work, the fact remains that availability of opportunities to choose from a variety of options seems rather limited among the women in this study. Essentially, entry into sex work is perceived as a survival strategy and one option among only a few usually less viable alternatives. In fleeing poverty, unemployment, debt, or a failed relationship, for many women sex work provides an opportunity for financial autonomy and the ability to care for dependents, which is an important responsibility in Ghanaian society. Paradoxically, while financial autonomy from a male partner is achieved, autonomy within the line of work is limited in terms of when, where, how, and with whom to have sex. It seems to me that for most women the scale weighs heavily on the side of sex work becoming the precursor for new forms of vulnerability and subordination as women give in to clients' demands or are subject to abuse. Indeed, the very nature of sex work opens some sex workers up to new forms of exploitation and abuse with partners because these latter relationships become an important alternative and hoped-for safe space as an alternative to the indignities of sex work. Thus, in these romantic relationships some women tolerate the same kinds of abuse or dominance that they escaped from into sex work in the first place.

Sex work may provide opportunities for economic independence. And certainly the older respondents especially were satisfied that they were able to pay school fees for children and send money to aged mothers. However, they are not able to escape the stigma and indignities that come with having to provide a service that, despite their cynicism about love and marriage, they still attach to an intimate relationship. With the exception of the seaters, almost all the women still look to marriage—hence presumably some loss of economic independence—as an alternative to sex work. Given Ghana's economic situation as a "highly indebted poor" nation, women's own declining status within that economy, and growth in the global sex business, the likelihood that many poor women will continue to enter this line of work seems probable. The way out of this gloomy prognosis lies primarily with the Ghanaian government, which needs to initiate some structural changes by creating an environment in which so-called small- and medium-scale enterprises (SMEs) can survive and thrive. This requires changes in banking laws and practices such that SMEs can have access to loans, and at low interest rates, not the current 20 to 30 percent required by most lending institutions. Additionally, the state will need to introduce some level of protectionism for SMEs so that they can establish themselves without fear of onslaught of cheap imported goods. At a more fundamental level, sex work thrives in contexts where women's bodily integrity is not guaranteed, where public discourse, the media, and cultural practices encourage men and women to see women in sexual terms. When sexual harassment, rape, and even defilement of minors is reported and received as unfortunate but normal, and in the absence of stiff penalties, the environment remains one in which the provision of sex by women to men is seen as women's duty, and men's entitlement to sex in whatever circumstances is seen as legitimate.

In April 2006 the Cabinet of Ghana's government approved the Domestic Violence Bill, which would criminalize all forms of violence between domestic partners and people living in domestic relationships. However, the document that is being sent to parliament for passage into law has removed from it the repeal of Section 42(g) of the Criminal Code 1960 (Act 29). The repeal of this law has come to be known as the "marital rape clause," even though marital rape is not mentioned in the bill, because its repeal would legitimize the concept of marital rape and make it a criminal offense. This old law, inherited from the British, states, inter alia, that consent given by a husband or wife at marriage for the purposes of marriage becomes null and void as a result of divorce or legal separation.[59]

NOTES

1. Wilks, quoted in Emmanuel Akyeampong and Pashington Obeng, "Spirituality, Gender, and Power in Asanto History," in *African Gender Studies, a Reader*, ed. Oyeronke Oyewumi (New York: Palgrave, 2005), 23–48.

2. Akyeampong and Obeng, writing about power in the Asante state, note that "patriarchy" originated in particular economic conditions, primarily to ensure the means of subsistence by organizing the recurrent activities that cultivation involved, and that its growing coherence was associated with accumulation of wealth (Akyeampong and Obeng, "Spirituality, Gender, and Power in Asanto History").

3. Karen Tranberg Hansen, "Introduction: Domesticity in Africa," in *African Encounters with Domesticity*, ed. Karen Tranberg Hansen (New Brunswick, N.J.: Rutgers University Press, 1991), 5.

4. Agnes Akosua Aidoo, "Women in the History and Culture of Ghana," *Research Review*, n.s., 1, no. 1 (1985): 14–55; Kwame Arhin, "The Political and Military Roles of Akan Women," in *Female and Male in West Africa*, ed. Christine Oppong (London: George Allen & Unwin, 1983), 91–98.

5. It should be noted, however, that the more elite girls' schools, such as the famed Wesley Girls High School, often had their own agenda to prepare girls to compete with men in the workforce, albeit never neglecting to prepare them to be suitable wives as well.

6. D. G. Azu, *The Ga Family and Social Change*, African Social Research Documents 5 (Leiden: Afrika Studiecentrum, 1966).

7. George P Hagan, "Marriage, Divorce, and Polygyny in Winneba," in Oppong, *Female and Male in West Africa*, 192–203.

8. Peter Sarpong, *Girls' Nubility Rites in Ashanti* (Tema: Ghana Publishing Corporation, 1977).

9. Gracia Clark, *Onions Are My Husband: Survival and Accumulation by West African Market Women* (Chicago: University of Chicago Press, 1994), 339.

10. Christine Okali, *Cocoa and Kinship in Ghana: The Matrilineal Akan of Ghana* (London: Kegan Paul International, 1983).

11. Okali, *Cocoa and Kinship in Ghana*. She notes from her study in Asante that many men did, in fact, bequeath cocoa farms to their wives.

12. Westermann, cited in Godwin K. Nukunya, *Kinship and Marriage among the Anlo Ewe* (London: Athlone Press, 1966).

13. Claire Robertson, "Ga Women and Socioeconomic Change in Accra, Ghana," in *Women in Africa: Studies in Social and Economic Change*, ed. Nancy J. Hafkina and Edna G. Bay (California: Stanford University Press, 1976), 111–136. In 1911, when the first attempt to record women's professions was made, 75 percent of the four thousand women in the Accra district were traders.

14. Hagan, "Marriage, Divorce, and Polygyny in Winneba," 192–203; Emile Vercuijsse, "Fishmongers, Big Dealers, and Fishermen: Co-operation and Conflict between the Sexes in Ghanaian Canoe Fishing," in *Female and Male in West Africa,* ed. Christine Oppong (London: George Allen & Unwin, 1983), 179–191.

15. Ibid., 181.

16. Ibid., 195.

17. Robertson, "Ga Women and Socioeconomic Change," 122.

18. Azu, *The Ga Family and Social Change.*

19. Personal communication from Professor George Hagan, May 1999.

20. George Hagan cites the case of his own parents as an example of such discrimination: his mother had to give up her teaching position when she got married to his father, also a civil servant. He adds that his mother was actually better educated than his father (personal communication, May 1999).

21. Robertson "Ga Women and Socioeconomic Change."

22. Akosua Darkwah, in this volume, shows that such mother-daughter enterprises still exist, thrive, and, perhaps, given current economic conditions, may indeed be a re-emerging option even for "educated" daughters.

23. Ellen Bortei Doku, "Theoretical Directions in Gender Relations and the Status of Women in Africa," in *Gender Analysis Workshop Report; Proceedings of the Gender Analysis Workshop (DAWS) Institute of African Studies, University of Ghana, 14–16 July 1992*, ed. Takyiwaa Manuh and Akosua Adomako (Legon: Institute of African Studies, 1992), 53–63.

24. See J. H. Frimpong-Ansah, *The Vampire State in Africa: The Political Economy of Decline in Ghana* (London: James Currey, 1991); Paul Mosley, Jane Harrigan, and JohnToye, *Aid and Power: The World Bank and Policy-Based Lending* (London: Routledge, 1991); Bade Onimode, ed., *The IMF, The World Bank, and the African Debt,* Vol. 1: *The Economic Impact* (London: Zed Press, 1989); Douglas Rimmer, *Staying Poor: Ghana's Political Economy, 1950–1990* (Oxford: Pergamon Press, 1992), for the World Bank.

25. This meant reducing fiscal and balance-of-payment deficits and external debt arrears, stabilizing wage bargaining, reducing the role of the state in economic activity, and enhancing conditions for foreign direct investment.

26. See, for example, Kojo Sebastian Amanor, *Land, Labour, and the Family in Southern Ghana: A Critique of Land Policy under Neo-Liberalism*, Research Report no. 116 (Uppsala:

Nordiska Afrikainstutet, 2001); Lynne Brydon and Karen Legge, *Adjusting Society: The World Bank, the IMF, and Ghana* (London: Taurus Academic Studies, 1996); Gracia Clark and Takyiwaa Manuh, "Women Traders in Ghana and the Structural Adjustment Programme," in *Structural Adjustment Programs and African Women Farmers*, ed. Christina H. Gladwin (Gainesville: University of Florida Press, 1991), 217–236; Patience Elabor-Idemudia, "The Impact of Structural Adjustment Programme on Women and Their Households in Bendel and Ogun States, Nigeria," in Gladwin, *Structural Adjustment Programs and African Women Farmers*, 128–216; Diane Elson, "Gender and Adjustment in the 1990s: An Update on Evidence and Strategies," background paper for Interregional Meeting on Economic Distress, Structural Adjustment, and Women, June 1991, Commonwealth Secretariat; Rodreck Mupedziswa and Perpetua Gumbo, *Women Informal Traders in Harare and the Struggles for Survival in an Environment of Economic Reforms*, Research Report no. 117 (Uppsala: Nordiska Afrikainstutet, 2001); Grace Ongile, *Gender and Agricultural Supply Responses to Structural Adjustment Programmes: A Case Study of Smallholder Tea Producers in Kericho, Kenya*, Research Report no. 109 (Uppsala: Nordiska Afrikainstutet, 1991); Ingrid Palmer, *Gender and Population in the Adjustment of African Economies: Planning for Change*, Women, Work, and Development Series (Geneva: ILO, 1991); and Philomena Steady, *Black Women, Globalization, and Economic Justice* (Rochester: Schenkman Books, 2002).

27. For the past two decades Ghana's budget has shown a bias toward industries such as mining.

28. Akosua Adomako Ampofo, "The Sex Trade: Globalisation and Issues of Survival in Sub-Saharan Africa," *Research Review* 17, no. 1 (2001): 27–43; Akosua Adomako Ampofo, "Women and AIDS in Ghana: 'I Control My Body (or Do I)?' Ghanaian Sex Workers and Susceptibility to STDs, Especially AIDS," in *Women's Position and Demographic Change in Sub-Saharan Africa*, ed. Paulina Makwina-Adebusoye and A. Jensen (Liege: Ordina Editions, 1995), 233–251. Some countries are so poor, yet so indebted, that even with the full application of traditional debt restructuring mechanisms and the provision of concessions they cannot "service" their debts (pay the interest on the accumulating debt); i.e., their total debt burdens are in excess of GDP and export earnings. Essentially, income earned is used to pay off debts rather than service the economy, and thus new debts continue to accrue, although, for Ghana, actual debt-service debt has declined from an annual average of $392 million between 1998 and 2000 to an average of $149 million per annum from 2001 to 2003. Debt relief for 2004 was estimated at $268.5 million (*Daily Graphic*, July 16, 2004). The HIPC initiative was a response, largely, to agitations by civil society groups such as Jubilee 2000, calling for a cancellation of Africa's debt, and emerged out of a 1996 meeting of the twenty-four finance and development ministers who make up the Development Committee and who represent the 181 member countries of the World Bank and the International Monetary Fund. The HIPC initiative is not about outright debt cancellation, but rather about lowering debt to so-called sustainable levels, and it involves debt restructuring, the provision of grants, and some debt relief. The initiative was modified in 1999 to provide faster relief and a stronger link between debt relief and poverty reduction. Ghana became the fourteenth country to join after Benin, Bolivia, Burkina Faso, Ethiopia, Guyana, Mali, Mauritania, Mozambique, Nicaragua, Niger, Senegal, Tanzania, and Uganda.

29. Sherill Sellers, Akosua Adomako Ampofo, and Susan Frazier-Kouassi, "Stress, Coping, and the Health of Ghanaian Women at the Crossroads of Change," paper presented at the Global Health Forum, Mexico City, Mexico, September 2004.

30. No doubt, there are some very prosperous African market queens, especially in the Makola and Keijetia markets in Accra and Kumasi, respectively; however, the majority of female traders are small-time.

31. Akosua Adomako Ampofo, "Controlling and Punishing Women in Ghana," *Review of African Political Economy* 56 (1993): 102–111.

32. Clark, *Onions Are My Husband,* 329. Before the military coup that removed one military regime and brought another, the AFRC (Armed Forces Revolutionary Council), into power in 1979 on a "house-cleaning exercise" to rid Ghana of corruption, some of the wives and consorts of high-ranking soldiers had become powerful and wealthy. Nonetheless this power was frequently predicated on male patronage.

33. The New Patriotic Party (NPP) government won elections in 2000, taking over from the NDC (New Democratic Congress), led by Jerry Rawlings. Apart from a brief period of constitutional rule between 1979 and 1981, Rawlings had been head of state since 1989: first as the chairman of the AFRC, then the PNDC (Provisional National Defense Council, 1981–1992), which ousted another elected government, and later, as president under the democratically elected NDC-led government (1992–2000). One of the early projects of the NPP government was to set up a National Reconciliation Commission to investigate human rights abuses from the early post-independence years until 1992. The majority of complaints were brought by "ordinary" Ghanaians who had suffered the loss of a loved one, torture, or the loss of a business or means of livelihood as a result of abuse by state officials. Many of the complainants were business women and female traders who, during the AFRC period, had been made scapegoats for the country's economic decline (Adomako Ampofo, "Controlling and Punishing Women in Ghana," 102–111).

34. Lawrence A. Adeokun, "Catering in Ile-Ife: Case Study of Male Entrance into Traditionally Female-Dominated Occupations," in *Sex Inequalities in Urban Employment in the Third World,* ed. Richard Anker and Catherine Hein (New York: St. Martin's Press, 1986), 57–62.

35. Clark, *Onions Are My Husband.*

36. Richard Anker and Catherine Hein, "Introduction and Overview," in Anker and Hein, *Sex Inequalities in Urban Employment in the Third World;* Clark and Manuh, "Women Traders in Ghana and the Structural Adjustment Programme," 217–236; Elson, "Gender and Adjustment in the 1990s"; Palmer, *Gender and Population in the Adjustment of African Economies.*

37. Adomako Ampofo, "Women and AIDS in Ghana."

38. Akosua Adomako Ampofo, "Nice Guys, Condoms and Other Forms of STD Protection: Sex Workers and AIDS Protection in West Africa," in *Vivre et Penser le Sida en Afrique/Experiencing and Understanding AIDS in Africa,* ed. Charles Becker, J. P. Dozon, C. Obbo, and M. Touré (Paris: Codesria, IRD, Karthala, PNLS, 1999), 559–590; Adomako Ampofo, "The Sex Trade"; Akosua Adomako Ampofo, Josephine Beoku-Betts, Mary Osirim, and Wairimu Njambi, "Women's and Gender Studies in English-Speaking Sub-Saharan Africa: A Review of Research in the Social Sciences," *Gender and Society* 18, no. 6 (2004): 685–714.

39. Adomako Ampofo, "Nice Guys, Condoms and Other Forms of STD Protection"; Adomako Ampofo et al., "Women's and Gender Studies in English-Speaking Sub-Saharan Africa"; Marjorie Mbilinyi and Naomi Kaihula, "Sinners and Outsiders: The Drama of AIDS in Rungwe," in *AIDS, Sexuality, and Gender in Africa: Collective Strategies and Struggles in Tanzania and Zambia,* ed. Carolyn Baylies and Janet Bujra (London, New York: Routledge, 2000), 76–94.; Bethlehem Tekloa, *Narratives of Three Prostitutes in Addis Ababa,* Centre for Research Training and Information on Women in Development (Addis Ababa: Addis Ababa University, 2002).

40. Emmanuel Akyeampong, "Sexuality and Prostitution among the Akan of the Gold Coast c. 1650–1950," *Past and Present,* no. 156 (1997); and Adam Jones, "Prostitution, Polyandrie oder Vergewaltigung? Zur Mehrdeutigkeit Europaeischer Quellen uber die Kueste Westafrikas zwischen 1660 und 1860," in *Aussereuropaeische Frauengeschichte: Probleme der Forschung,* ed. Adam Jones (Hamburg: Pfaffenweiler, 1990), 27–97.

41. Akyeampong, "Sexuality and Prostitution among the Akan," 146.

42. As cited in Jones, "Prostitution, Polyandire oder Vergewaltigung?"

43. Akyeampong, "Sexuality and Prostitution among the Akan."

44. When they became too old to work, the women received a pension from the king and were allowed to "live the rest of their lives in peace" (Jones, "Prostitution, Polyandire oder Vergewaltigung?" 132).

45. Adomako Ampofo, "The Sex Trade"; Mbilinyi and Kaihula, "Sinners and Outsiders"; Tekloa, *Narratives of Three Prostitutes in Addis Ababa*.

46. Mbilinyi and Kaihula, "Sinners and Outsiders."

47. In Côte d'Ivoire, Article 3 of the Martha Ritchard decree states that anyone who, by gestures, words, in writing, or by any other means, shall publicly solicit or attempt to solicit any person of either sex for immoral purposes shall be liable to a prison sentence. Article 2 provides against passive soliciting as a second degree felony, which consists in "adopting behavior on the streets which leads to immorality" (G. Kouassi, *La prostitution en Afrique: Un Cas Abidjan* [Abidjan: Les Nouvelles Editions Africaines, 1986]). In Ghana, despite amendments to the 1960 criminal code in 1998 that affect a range of sexual offenses, the laws governing prostitution remain unchanged. "Any female loitering or importuning wayfarers for the purpose of prostitution in any public street . . . or any place of public resort . . . shall be guilty of an offense and may be arrested" (Criminal Code 1960).

48. Adomako Ampofo, "Women and AIDS in Ghana"; and Adomako Ampofo, "Nice Guys, Condoms and Other Forms of STD Protection."

49. The three cities were chosen because all are highly urbanized commercial centers. All three have also had small settlements of prostitutes since colonial times, and their commercial basis has seen the emergence of other kinds of sex work in recent years. Abidjan was included in the study for three additional reasons. Firstly, there is some evidence that Ghanaian women have been working as prostitutes in that city from as far back as the 1940s (Kouassi, *La prostitution en Afrique*). Secondly, more recent studies and anecdotes suggest that Ghanaian women feature prominently among prostitutes in Abidjan. Thirdly, at the time of the study travel between Ghana and Abidjan was common and the border corridor had been described as an important vector for the transmission of the HIV virus into Ghana.

50. I would like to gratefully acknowledge the support that the two studies received, the first from the World Health Organization's Special Programme of Research, Development and Research Training in Human Reproduction, and the second from UNICEF Ghana.

51. All names are pseudonyms.

52. Traditionally, seaters have been older women, either divorced or widowed, who have completed their childbearing and entered prostitution later in life when they no longer entertained ideas about having a romantic relationship.

53. Although basic education in Ghana is free (i.e., tuition), parents have to provide school uniforms and books and pay other levies to schools. Even these nominal amounts can present a financial challenge to some parents.

54. In soccer a referee gives a player a "red card" for a major transgression or after having received two prior yellow cards for more minor fouls. A red card means the player leaves the field for the rest of the game.

55. Incidentally, Afia had also fled a sexual approach from an elderly man, and when she reported the incident to her family, they did not take it seriously because, according to her, they "liked the man" and viewed him as a suitable suitor.

56. Kouassi, *La prostitution en Afrique*. An Ivorian police officer confirms the role of procurers and madams, and Nerquaye-Tetteh (no date) notes that girls are taken from Ghana and sold to brothel owners in La Côte d'Ivoire.

57. Kwame Nkrumah openly courted the seaters, and they formed an important constituency during the elections that brought his CPP party to power (Akyeampong, "Sexuality and Prostitution among the Akan").

58. Some of my own findings from work in Dakar, Senegal, and Amsterdam, the Netherlands, suggest that all too often such marriages are extremely abusive.

59. This law was repealed in the United Kingdom in 1990.

Work as a Duty and as a Joy

UNDERSTANDING THE ROLE OF WORK IN THE LIVES OF GHANAIAN FEMALE TRADERS OF GLOBAL CONSUMER ITEMS

AKOSUA K. DARKWAH

Written records from visitors to the then Gold Coast in the nineteenth century, many of whom were European, noted the active role that women in the Gold Coast played in the public sphere. Coming themselves from a Victorian background where ladies were supposed to stay at home and see to the domestic needs of the family, these writers must have been struck by the fact that in Ghana quite the contrary perspective existed; women were expected to take on responsibilities in both the domestic and the public sphere. Work in the public sphere for women of that time period was seen in a purely instrumentalist fashion; Ghanaian women, like their male counterparts, worked to provide for their basic needs. As individuals, men and women had obligations to their families of socialization which they were expected to fulfill. In addition, as parents, they each had obligations toward their children. Indeed, there was a gendered division of labor with respect to the provision of the needs of family members. During the subsistence era, the provisioning of food for children was shared by both parents; mothers provided the carbohydrate component of food while fathers provided the protein component of food. With time, this has been translated into a situation where women are expected to provide a large proportion of the family's living expenses while men are expected to take care of major cash expenditures such as rent, school fees, and the acquisition of kitchen appliances. The financial responsibilities of a mother toward her child take emotional precedence over the physical care of a child so that the very idea of a stay-at-home mother seems ridiculous in the Ghanaian context. As a woman interviewed by Gracia Clark puts it, "Everyone likes children, so they would not let them stay hungry or hurt themselves, but no one would work for them the way I do."[1]

Work in the traditional context was also valued beyond its instrumentalist function of providing an individual with economic resources. This appreciation of the intrinsic value of work is reflected in Ghanaian greetings. In the Ghanaian context, when an individual comes upon a group of people working in the fields or on a construction site, the greeting rendered, *adwuma, adwuma,* translated literally as "work, work," is an endorsement of the value of hard work, which the workers affirm in their response to the greeting with *adwuma yie,* translated loosely as "work is valuable."[2]

Based on the traditional importance of work for instrumentalist purposes as well as its intrinsic value, Ghanaian women were found working on a daily basis to be able to provide for the needs of their families of socialization and procreation as well as for the sake of work itself. Ghanaian women typically engaged in one of two economic activities: agriculture and trade. Women traveled long distances trading initially in agricultural products and, as time went on, consumer products such as textiles.

In what follows, I explore the multiple meanings of work for Ghanaian women in contemporary times. It moves beyond the importance of work as a means of generating income to show the ways in which work for some Ghanaian women in contemporary times is both a duty and a joy. Work is a duty in the sense that traditionally it is an obligation for individuals to work so they can have access to economic resources. However, in recent times, I will argue that work for a particular segment of the population can also be described as a joy in the sense that work, in and of itself, has intrinsic value. Beyond the economic benefits that one gains from working, this chapter highlights the ways in which work provides a particular segment of the Ghanaian population with the unique opportunity to engage with the world outside of Ghana in ways that are not open to the majority of Ghanaians. While few of such women explicitly acknowledge the unique opportunity that their jobs provide and, indeed, engage in this activity first and foremost for its economic benefits, I seek to highlight the ways in which, in undertaking their activities for purely economic reasons, these women are put in the unique position of impacting the lives of Ghanaians both at home and in the diaspora as well as citizens from many other parts of the world.[3]

The analysis focuses on female traders of global consumer items, a group of women whose numbers have increased dramatically since the introduction of trade liberalization policies as part of structural adjustment reforms in the country in the 1980s. These women travel to places as far off as Dubai and Beijing to bring back global consumer items for sale. The consumer items that these women sell are light industrial goods, produced outside the shores of Ghana, which can be found in supermarkets in cities all over the world. The majority of the Ghanaian businesswomen sell three general categories of light industrial goods. The first are items of beautification such as nail polish, makeup kits, and hair products. The second general group of items they sell are items for children, specifically, children's wear, toys, and various items for infants. Finally, the women sell kitchen items such as crockery and cutlery. In essence, the women sell items that reinforce the stereotype that women are in charge of children and the kitchen. Interestingly enough, while women are seen as being in charge of the kitchen and as such sell many kitchen items, this only rings true in so far as non-electronic kitchen items are concerned. Women in Ghana, for the most part, do not sell standard kitchen appliances even though kitchen appliances are generally seen as the preserve of women. Here, the logic seems to be that even though women are the ones who use kitchen appliances, they are not technologically savvy enough to be able to assess the various kinds available in foreign markets.[4]

I define these light industrial goods as global consumer items in reference to both the means by which they are acquired and the cultural significance of purchasing these goods, hence I draw on both economic and cultural definitions of globalization. These light consumer goods are acquired through a process by which the traders undertake journeys all over the globe to different sites of production. These economic trading routes have been made possible with the increasing removal of restrictions on the importation of goods into the Ghanaian market, a process that was put in place as Ghana sought to integrate its economy into the world economy more fully. The Ghanaian border thus places little restrictions on its citizens so far as the acquisition of consumer items is considered. Beyond these items being global in the economic sense, their acquisition also provides purchasers with a sense that they are plugged into the world of Western consumerism; although not located in the Western world, they are a part of the Western world in that they share common tastes with citizens of the Western world because they purchase similar products.

Contextualizing the Research Subjects

According to the most recent Ghana Living Standards Survey conducted in 1999, the second largest source of employment in Ghana is in trade with 18.3 percent of the population in this line of work.[5] These are the people who ensure that goods are available in shops and markets all across the country. The Ghanaian distribution system consists of two distinct segments. The first is the formal, large-scale private sector, which is dominated by South African multinational retail chains such as Woolworth. Relatively large chain stores such as Melcom, owned and run by a third-generation Ghanaian family, originally Lebanese, also offer consumers access to a variety of low-cost consumer items. This segment of the distribution chain is relatively small and accounts for a small portion of all the global consumer items that are traded in the Ghanaian economy.

The second segment in the distribution system is predominantly informal, owned primarily by Ghanaians, each of whom has a shop that is much smaller than an average shop that operates as part of the formal-sector distribution system described above. The majority of Ghanaian citizens rely on this informal segment of the distribution chain for their global consumer items.

Ghana's informal retail sector is dominated by small-scale businesses largely managed by women, who have a long history of trade activities. In 1988, 91 percent of the female labor force was self-employed and working in the informal sector. Indications from the 1997 Human Development Report suggest that the picture has not changed much since the 1980s.[6] The trade liberalization policies implemented by the government over the course of the last two decades simplified the procedures for importing goods, making the whole process less cumbersome than before. As such, trade liberalization has fostered a steady increase in commercial activity in the capital city. Commercial activity takes place in three locales: market stalls and shops, retail shops and stalls outside the market, and, for those without the resources to obtain fixed premises, along the streets of the markets in the capital city and other major urban centers.[7]

The female traders discussed in this essay work in the first two locales. They are located at the apex of the indigenous trading hierarchy. These are women of a high social standing with the resources to own and operate a shop. These women wholesale and retail both goods that they themselves have gone outside of the country to purchase as well as those provided by suppliers and/or friends who may have gone outside of the country for a variety of reasons and chose to bring back some items to sell on a trial basis or have items originally acquired as gifts that they would rather sell.

Known in Ghanaian circles as businesswomen, these women represent a veritable extension of West African female trade that is such a part of many a West African woman. Their shops are registered with the Attorney General's Office and they pay income taxes. On average, these women command working capitals of anywhere between 45 million and 180 million cedis (between \$5,000 and \$20,000). These women have bank accounts, usually both foreign and local ones, and have a long history of savings with a formal credit institution, a requirement for transit visas to various countries for purchasing trips. Their association with the formal banking system also provides them with the opportunity to avail themselves of loans from those banks if they so desire.

Work as a Duty

For the Ghanaian women engaged in the trade in global consumer items, work, as it was in times past for their ancestors, is a duty. It is a duty because these women grow up knowing that one of the roles they have to fulfill as adults is that of working individuals. Work is considered of paramount importance in Ghanaian society. The idea of an adult depending on others for financial support is abhorrent in this environment. No matter how little an individual earns, it is important that an individual be seen as working to secure his or her economic fortunes. Working is considered equally as important as parenting. In fact, Clark argues that while the role of parenting can be taken on by a surrogate parent, usually a female sibling of the child's mother, without much ado in traditional Ghana, a mother who is seen idling at home, unable to provide for the financial needs of a child, is seen as lazy and good for nothing. The emotional aspects of mothering can be shared, but the financial needs of a child should be provided first and foremost by the parents of a child. Parents unable to do so despite their best efforts are excused, but parents who fail to do so, choosing instead to idle about at home, are seen as irresponsible. The traders of global consumer items therefore work because it is expected of them.[8]

As has been noted by Christine Oppong in the traditional Ghanaian context, the choice as to which type of income-generating avenue to pursue was determined in large part by the vocation of one's parents. Sons took after their fathers while daughters took after their mothers, be it carpentry, iron smithing, gold smithing, *kente* weaving, or farming. This is no less true of women who take up trading in consumer items. For two-thirds of the women I interviewed, trading was an occupational choice that had already been made by their mothers. The role of mothers in shaping the occupational choices of their daughters is evident in the words of their daughters. Agyeiwaa offered her reasons for deciding to trade in the following words: "It's something I learnt from my Mum. I used to help my Mum whenever I was on [school] holidays. Through my involvement in my Mum's business, I developed the interest in trading."[9]

Other women I interviewed who had chosen other career paths felt themselves pulled back into trading as their mothers got older and the question of what to do with these shops became apparent. As Takyiwaa put it in explaining her decision to quit her job as a legislative research assistant to run her mother's clothing accessories shop: "My mother has owned this shop in this very spot for as long as I can remember. In fact, she started this business before I was born and I am the oldest of her children. I have such pleasant memories of afternoons spent in this shop. I would hate to see the shop turned over to some other family once my mom gets too old to run it herself. My other siblings have careers in medicine and engineering. They will not give it up for this. I decided that if I wanted to keep this shop in the family, then I was going to have to take over the shop myself." For other women, the decision to trade was made much earlier on in their lives and shaped the educational paths that they took. In the words of Asantewaa, "It is the norm that a mother passes on her trade [trading skills and business] to her eldest daughter, and I happened to be the one. Knowing this as a duty, I didn't find it necessary to continue with my education."

One might be tempted to think from the foregoing discussion that these women lack agency in determining whether to work or not to work and what kind of career to pursue, such that they may be stuck in jobs in which they have little interest. I will argue, however, that the very nature of trade in global consumer items makes it a real joy to work in this sector, first, because it provides substantial incomes in the Ghanaian context. Secondly, it allows the women to join both the small group of elite Ghanaians who take on a cosmopolitan worldview as they travel across the world and the small group of citizens the world over with a transnational identity. In addition, trading in global consumer items allows these women to express their creative sides through the items they choose to purchase for the Ghanaian market as well as the advertising strategies they develop to convince Ghanaians to purchase particular brands of global consumer items with which they are not familiar.

The Economic Joys of Work

Private-sector employees in Ghana, such as female traders of global consumer items discussed here, earn more on average than employees in the formal public sector. These traders, in particular, are perceived as unusually wealthy. This perception is not unique to Ghana. In neighboring Togo, these traders are referred to as Mama Benzes, ostensibly because they own Mercedes Benzes. Indeed, there is some basis to this perception. George Amponsem, in his work on a similar group of women, noted that all the traders with spouses in the formal sector earned far more than their spouses. There are, however, large disparities in the incomes that these women earn. Ghanaians are generally reticent to talk about their earnings. To get a sense of how wealthy my informants were, therefore, I used the amount of property, specifically, cars and houses, as a proxy. In Akan culture, joint property between couples is extremely rare, so it was an ideal way of assessing the earnings of the women.[10]

Using cars and houses as a proxy for wealth has its limitations since it gave me no idea of how much money these traders have invested in stocks, bonds, or anything of that nature. However, there was no way I could find out that information without them volunteering it, and none of them did that. Despite the shortcomings of the method I used, it gave me some sense of the financial worth of the group of women I interviewed. Twenty percent of the women interviewed had no cars; 48 percent had one car; 24 percent had two cars each; and, finally, 8 percent of my informants had five cars each. A similar story is evident when one looks at the number of houses these traders owned. Thirty-six percent had not yet built houses; 64 percent had one house; and 4 percent each had three and four houses.

The money that these female traders could conceivably make served as an incentive for some of them to go into trading as their full-time job. This was particularly true of the highly educated women whom one might have thought would have been more comfortable working in offices where they could put the skills they acquired in school to use. Afariwaa, who had a bachelor's degree in sociology, in response to my query as to why she had chosen to trade instead of work in the formal sector, had this to say: "In 1992, I was doing national service at a public institution where I was paid forty thousand cedis ($40) a month. On Saturdays, I helped my sister out at her shop and discovered that she could make a profit of forty thousand cedis ($40) in one day. At that point, what more could I ask for? The choice was quite clear to me. It made far more economic sense for me to trade than to continue working at that office."

The profits that these traders of global consumer items make are dependent on the vagaries of the global economy with respect to the rates of devaluations of various currencies. Traders make more profit if the Ghanaian cedi stays stable while the currency of the country from which they purchase the consumer items they sell devalues. The Asian financial crisis of late 1997 through early 1998 was, therefore, a particularly good earning period for the traders of global consumer items. With the Ghanaian cedi stable against foreign currencies and the Asian currencies devaluing at an alarming rate, the traders who purchased consumer items from Asia for resale in Ghana made huge profits that year. Afariwaa, who sold clothing items purchased from Thailand, recounted the fortunes she made that year with a sense of great joy: "I made so much money that year. I was getting married in December that year [1998] and I was able to buy all the heavy electrical gadgets and the furniture for our future home with the profits I made from the two trips I took that year. Since then, my profit margin has not been that great, but it is enough to survive on."

The Non-economic Joys of Work

Trading in global consumer items provides these female traders with another set of benefits that are not monetary. Indeed, perhaps because these benefits are not financial, traders rarely offered these benefits as reasons for taking up this particular line of work. Yet, these traders are in a unique position. The work they do helps set them apart as members of the small group of Ghanaian elite. There are four ways in which these traders are unique. The first of these is the opportunity that these traders get to become a part of the relatively small elite circle of transnational citizens, in general, and transnational Ghanaians, in particular.

Transnationalism is defined as the various processes by which immigrants "forge and sustain multi-stranded social relations that link together their societies of origin and settlement." Aided by the time-space compression brought on by the various technological advancements in transport and communication, such as the information superhighway since the 1970s, there are now distinctive differences in the manner in which migrants of today are able to keep in constant touch with both their adopted homes and homes of origin.[11]

The traders in question here are not migrants in the layman's use of the word. Funk and Wagnall's standard dictionary provides two definitions of the verb "migrate." The first is "to move from one country, region, etc. to settle in another," while the second is "to move periodically from one region or climate to another, as birds or fish." The idea then is that when we use the term "migrants" in reference to human beings, we use it in the context of people moving from their country of origin to settle *permanently* in an adopted country, while periodic movement is typically associated with nonhumans. Scattered through the scholarly literature on migration, however, are concepts that assume that human migration can be periodic in nature. Cyclical migration and transnationalism are two such concepts.

The traders of global consumer items are, therefore, migrants if we use the term "migrant" to refer to a movement from one region to another for a purpose, be it temporary or permanent. With their feet firmly planted in Ghana, their home country, the traders forge social relations in whatever country they purchase their items as they transact business with different groups of people over a period of time. The traders' social relations with people abroad, both Ghanaian and non-Ghanaian, underscore their status as Ghanaian elite with contacts in places both far and near.

I refer to the social relations that the Ghanaian female transnational traders forge and maintain as transient nationalistic networks. I use the term "transient nationalistic network" to refer to the social network created by transnational traders and migrants from their homeland who are based in the foreign countries where they go to purchase their global consumer items. The basis for the creation of this network is the bond of national origin, although the class and ethnic barriers that prevail in Ghana are for the most part maintained. However, these barriers are not as rigidly maintained as the barrier between Ghanaians and non-Ghanaians. In other words, a trader in a foreign city will forge a link with a Ghanaian of a different ethnic background rather than create a link with a non-Ghanaian if there is no Ghanaian of a similar ethnic group in that city.

The Ghanaian traders' preference for individuals from the same national origin is due to the trust that migrants who share a sense of bounded solidarity have. Alejandro Portes and J. Sensenbrenner define "bounded solidarity" as a sense of solidarity shared by members of a particular immigrant community who "find themselves affected by common events in a particular time and place." Since the members of the Ghanaian community in these foreign towns often share similar experiences as migrants, the community is often quite close knit. As such, it is almost impossible for any one of these migrants who work for the transnational traders to abscond with monies given them. If they did, it would come to the knowledge of the other traders and their reputations as workers for transnational traders would be ruined, making it difficult for them to earn the incomes they would otherwise derive from such endeavors, a situation that they would loathe to encounter, particularly since for a number of these migrants their work with transnational traders provides them with their only source of consistent earnings. Just as the tight web of social ties—or what James Coleman refers to as "closure" among Jewish diamond traders in New York City—minimizes the amount of malfeasance among them, so also do the close-knit relationships among Ghanaian migrants in foreign lands prevent malfeasance. In the words of Portes and Sensenbrenner, it allows for "enforceable trust." Economic transactions between the Ghanaian transnational traders and Ghanaian migrants abroad are undergirded by a certainty that neither party will fail to abide by their part of the bargain.[12]

In a transaction between a transnational trader and a migrant, each of them "behaves according to expectations not only because they must, but out of fear of punishment or in anticipation of rewards." Transnational traders who remunerated the migrants poorly were unlikely to find migrants the next time around who were willing to render services to them. Likewise, migrants who could not be trusted would find it difficult getting transnational traders to employ them. A migrant who attempts to abscond with the financial resources of a transnational trader will simply not live it down in the Ghanaian community there and can be sure that no one else in the Ghanaian community will bring him or her other income-generating opportunities. Secondly, since these migrants find themselves in an environment where either their legal status or poor skills prevents them from accessing opportunities outside the Ghanaian community of which they are members, they are by their very dependence on the resources of their community bound to behave in a manner that is consistent with both the Ghanaian transnational traders' and immigrant communities' expectations.[13]

These networks are transient in the sense that the members who constitute the network keep changing. Transnational traders may change their purchasing destinations just as others join the network of transnational traders to a particular country. In addition, migrants in the foreign countries who constitute the other major component of the network may move on to jobs in the formal sector of the country in which they are located or move out of the country to a more favorable destination. This is particularly the case with Ghanaians engaged in what Kwadwo Konadu-Agyemang refers to as "step-wise migration," the process where Ghanaian emigrants desirous of living in higher-status countries of their choice, such as the United States, Canada, Japan, and Australia, migrate first to a "lower status, easy visa" acquisition country from where they hope to eventually relocate to the "higher-status" country of their choice.[14]

These transient nationalistic networks are also gendered in the sense that the traders who constitute one-half of the network are either predominantly male or female, depending on the specific part of the world in which the network develops. This is so because of the fact that male and female traders sell different items and, therefore, travel to the different districts that specialize in the sale of the items that they are interested in buying. As a result, the Ghanaian migrants who constitute the other half of the network interact primarily with traders who are either male or female, depending on the specific location of the migrants and the kinds of consumer items that are readily available in their locality.

This transient nationalistic network is primarily economic in nature and offers both the Ghanaian transnational traders and migrants benefits that they would not get if they sought or offered their services to non-Ghanaians. Typically, the Ghanaian migrants abroad provide the transnational entrepreneurs with services for which they receive material rewards in return. The services are of various kinds and of crucial benefit to the transnational traders. While Ghanaians abroad might first offer these services to traders when they are on a business trip, over time, the traders can count on their compatriots abroad for such services even when they are not on business. The services include chauffeuring the traders around in a privately owned car for about half the cost of a cab, serving as a tour guide and translator where necessary, to take the traders to various commercial centers and so on. In this regard, these Ghanaian migrants abroad serve as cultural brokers who play an important part in ensuring the financial success of the female traders of global consumer items. In a few cases, the transnational traders are the ones who provide the migrants with services for which the traders receive cash payments, services such as transporting Ghanaian food items to the various countries. While these relationships start off for economic reasons, a good number of them take on non-economic characteristics in the long run.[15]

Anthropologists have long documented cases of personalized economic relationships that exist between traders and particular customers in markets around the world. Known by various names, such as *pratik* in Haiti, *onibara* ties in Nigeria, or *suki* ties in the Philippines,[16] these relationships are best defined as "long lasting dyadic ties formed between individuals operating in the market place. At a minimum, they imply the existence of regular transactions between the individuals. They may also involve extension of credit, concessions in quantity, reduction in price, and multiplex social ties."[17] A member of a transient nationalistic network may become the godparent of another's child, or the trader can oversee the construction of a house in Ghana for a member of the transient nationalistic network located abroad. Notwithstanding the benefits, the traders who are members of this network share the unique opportunity to build social relations with fellow Ghanaians who live abroad, a privilege that few other Ghanaians share. These social relations are, however, gendered. Females will build social relations with a different set of Ghanaians than those with whom male traders build social relations, based primarily on the fact that these networks are developed in the specific locales where the items that are considered culturally appropriate for males and females to sell are located.

Yet another advantage of trading in global consumer items is that the traders, in traveling the world to purchase their items, become cosmopolitan in outlook, by which I mean that they come to acknowledge the fact that there are different human ways of being evident in various places around the world. Conversations with these female traders suggested the extent to which their perspective on life was shaped by a multiplicity of experiences gained from their exposure to life in different parts of the world. They could draw on facts gleaned from personal experience in various parts of the world to make their points. For example, Gyamfuaa had a lengthy discussion with me about the various uses to which cars could be put; she lamented that unlike in Ghana, where cabs are usually old, relatively cheap cars, in Germany a decent-looking Mercedes Benz could very well be a cab.

These traders gained their cosmopolitan perspective from their extended periods of stay in various countries. Traders usually travel twice a year to coincide with the Easter and Christmas seasons, when most Ghanaians are likely to purchase global consumer items for the festivities. Each of these trips lasts about a fortnight. Each year, then, many of these traders spend a month in a particular country. Over a number of years, they end up building relationships with citizens of these countries, particularly the subcontractors and suppliers with whom they work, who could then invite them into their homes. As a result, the traders have a much more authentic understanding of life in these countries than can be obtained from visiting these countries as a tourist. The traders think of themselves as being very international and worldly and, of course, compared to many of their fellow Ghanaians, they are. Particularly with regard to fashion trends, these traders are clearly more aware of the array of fashion possibilities out there in the world at large than the majority of Ghanaians. These female traders by virtue of their trade join the ranks of the world's few who get to travel around the world and incorporate the sights, sounds, and sometimes perspectives of different locales into their world view.

A third benefit that accrues to the traders of global consumer items is the power they have to shape the fashion trends in Ghana. As the individuals who purchase items en masse for sale in Ghana, the traders serve as the medium between the fashion trends in the West and East and the Ghanaians who do not have access to these goods either through personal travel or friends/family who travel abroad to pick and choose from the broad array of items available in the world outside of Ghana. For such Ghanaians, their sense of fashion is defined within the limits set by the traders of global consumer items. For the Ghanaians who are unable to travel, the traders define everything from the newest trends in clothing, shoes, cosmetics, bags, and so on for them. If the traders do not purchase something for sale in Ghana, these Ghanaians will not have access to it. What the Ghanaians wear or use then is basically what the traders think of as fashionable and in vogue. Adwoa, a lady in her late thirties with an above-average-sized store filled with a variety of clothing items, comments as follows: "What would all these young women do without me? Some of the products I bring in are very unique; it's very difficult to find them in other shops. I feel very good knowing that I am impacting on how young women dress at the university. Even though I did not finish secondary [high] school, I have some power over these highly educated women. Really, what would they do without me and all other such traders like myself bringing in all these items from all over the world?"

As with shops in the West that advertise their new arrivals, in their shops these traders also learn to advertise their products in uniquely Ghanaian ways.

Here again the traders get to exhibit their creative sides as they think up innovative ways of advertising the items that they consider to be what Ghanaians should be purchasing. The unique manner in which the traders are able to advertise their goods is yet another non-economic benefit they derive from engaging in this business. The traders do not restrict themselves to the conventional means of showcasing one's products using the mass media such as television or radio. While some traders do exactly that, many others resort to the use of more personalized forms of advertising in which the traders play an active role in advertising the products they have for sale. Transnational traders draw attention to the items they sell in a variety of ways. The most common strategy is for the trader to choose an item that is not selling quite as quickly as the others, often because it is new on the market, and wear it at the shop themselves. In wearing the item on their bodies, the traders get to invent or emphasize a particular way of utilizing a product. A lady's purse that looks quite formal can be made informal by a trader who chooses to utilize it in an informal manner in the shop as an advertising strategy. The idea here is that if somebody sees her and makes a comment about how nice she looks, she can then announce to the person that the item is for sale in her shop. To enhance the likelihood that the advertising strategy will increase sales, these women often go on to name the item that they are introducing onto the market. The names are usually derived from a characteristic of the item to be named, so that a skirt made with a bit of Lycra that clings to one's body might be named "clingy." Once an individual is convinced to buy such an item, she will then go on to advertise the particular item by the name the trader imposed upon it. Soon, other buyers will flock to the shops looking for the item so named. I have seen this strategy reap results on a number of occasions.

Conclusion

Living in a cultural environment where the idea of work among women is deeply entrenched, Ghanaian women work first and foremost as a duty. Having an activity that one concentrates on day in, day out is seen as an essential part of being human. Ghanaians work then because work has intrinsic value. They also work because they have families who depend on them for their daily sustenance. Working therefore fulfills instrumentalist needs in addition to its intrinsic value. However, there can be no guarantee that work will be enjoyable. Indeed, to be able to engage in an economic activity that is enjoyable and pays well is a privilege that the majority of women around the world do not have.

In the case of the female Ghanaian traders of global consumer items described here, work clearly has intrinsic and instrumentalist value. They work because it is expected of them. Their choice of trading as their life's work is because, for a fair number of them, their mothers were also traders and thus passed on skills, contacts, and sometimes businesses to them, expecting that they would work as traders in their adult lives. As traders in global consumer items, their jobs are very lucrative compared to the many other kinds of jobs available in a developing country. Traders of global consumer items earn incomes that are far above the average income of Ghanaians. As such, these traders are able to provide quite well for their families. They thus fulfill their duty to work in an admirable fashion. These traders were very well aware of the intrinsic and instrumentalist reasons that shaped their decisions to work and articulated that quite easily.

It was, however, very difficult for them to appreciate the uniqueness of their position as traders in global consumer items and to conceive of that as a non-economic benefit that accrued to them as traders in those items.

These women cannot be classified technically as professional women for they have not undertaken specialized training in the art of trading. All of them learned on the job in an informal setting and work in the informal sector of the economy. Yet, like specific groups of workers in the formal sector such as career diplomats or army personnel who get sent all over the world in the course of their professional lives, these traders are well traveled. As such, they join the ranks of the few Ghanaians and individuals worldwide who get to share a cosmopolitan and transnational perspective on life because of their professional experience in different countries.

In addition, these traders who maintain relationships with individuals both Ghanaian and otherwise in places as far flung as China in order to be able to sustain their businesses break down the barriers of race, class, and ethnicity, however temporarily, as they move easily from one context to the other for economic purposes. Suppliers in various parts of the world whose interaction with Ghanaian traders is confined initially to business may, over the long period of time as business associates, develop a non-economic relationship that, no matter how fragile, cuts across racial lines. So also do these transnational networks provide an opportunity for traders and migrants of Ghanaian origins to interact across class and ethnic lines for business purposes.

While both males and females who trade in global consumer items are well traveled and get to break down barriers, female traders, by virtue of the fact that trading is gendered, are in the unique position of being able to define fashion trends in Ghana. For the individuals without access to consumer items either through personal travel or as gifts from friends or family members who travel, their only access to fashionable items is determined by these female traders in global consumer items who select a range of items from the much wider selection available outside the country for importation into the country. The selection a trader makes is largely dependent on her own personal taste. Once a trader discovers upon arrival in the country that these goods are not selling quickly, she resorts to a personalized form of advertising to encourage Ghanaian consumers to break out of their straight-jacketed tastes so they can own an item determined as fashionable by the female trader who imports and sells it.

Work then, as shown here, can have a myriad of benefits. While it is first and foremost undertaken for the instrumentalist reason of providing an individual with economic resources, in the case of female traders of global consumer items, engaging in work allows them to join the ranks of the few in the world who can claim a cosmopolitan, transnationalist existence while helping to shape the consumerist landscape in Ghana.

NOTES

1. Brodie Cruickshank, *Eighteen Years on the Gold Coast of Africa, Including an Account of the Native Tribes and Their Intercourse with Europeans* (London: Hurst and Blacket, 1853); William, F. Daniell, "On the Ethnography of Akkrah and Adampe, Gold Coast, Western Africa," *Journal of the Ethnological Society* 4 (1856): 1–32; Gracia Clark, *Onions Are My Husband: Survival and Accumulation by West African Market Women* (Chicago: Chicago University Press, 1994), 360.

2. Kwame Gyekye, *African Cultural Values: An Introduction* (Accra: Sankofa Press, 1996), 102.

3. The data presented here was collected between June 2000 and December 2001 using both participant observation and unstructured interviews. The participant observation was undertaken in Makola market, Ghana's largest consumer goods market. Thirty-two unstructured interviews were also conducted with female traders of global consumer items over the same period. These women, who were aged between twenty-six and fifty-six, came from five different ethnic groups in the country.

4. Ernest Aryeetey, "Private Investment under Uncertainty in Ghana," *World Development* 22, no. 8 (1994): 1211–1221.

5. Ghana Statistical Service, *1999 Ghana Living Standards Survey IV* (Accra: Ghana Statistical Service, 1999).

6. United Nations Development Programme, *Human Development Report 1997: Human Development to Eradicate Poverty* (New York: Oxford University Press, 1997).

7. Ibid., 1218.

8. Gracia Clark, "Negotiating Asante Family Survival in Kumasi, Ghana," *Africa* 69, no. 1 (1999): 66–86; Christine Oppong and Katharine Abu, *The Seven Roles of Ghanaian Women: The Impact of Education, Migration, and Employment on Ghanaian Mothers* (Geneva: International Labour Office, 1987).

9. Christine Oppong, *Growing up in Dagbon* (Tema: Ghana Publishing Corporation, 1973).

10. George Amponsem, "Informal Cross-National Trade in Ghana," Working Paper, No. 212 (Bielefied: Max Planck Institute, 1994), 10. Even then, nine out of the thirty-four women I interviewed declined to tell me about how many of each they owned, if any. Their argument was that this bore no relationship to my research question. Christine Oppong, *Middle-Class African Marriage: A Family Study of Ghanaian Senior Civil Servants* (London and Boston: G. Allen and Unwin, 1981).

11. Linda Basch, Nina Glick Schiller, and Cristina Szanton Blanc, *Nations Unbound: Transnational Projects, Postcolonial Predicaments, and Deterritorialized Nation States* (Langhorne, Pa.: Gordon and Breach, 1994), 7.

12. Alejandro Portes and J. Sensenbrenner, "Embeddedness and Immigration: Notes on the Determinants of Economic Action," *American Journal of Sociology* 98 (1993): 1327 and 1332; James. S. Coleman, "Social Capital and the Creation of Human Capital," *American Journal of Sociology* 94 (1988): S99.

13. Portes and Sensenbrenner, "Embeddedness and Immigration," 1332.

14. Kwadwo Konadu-Agyemang, "Travel Patterns and Coping Strategies of Ghanaian Immigrants in Toronto," *Ghana Studies* 2 (1999): 13–34.

15. Janet MacGaffey and Remy Bazenguissa-Ganga, *Congo Paris: Transnational Traders on the Margins of the Law* (Oxford: James Currey, 2000). Here, they note a similar phenomenon among Congolese traders from both Zaire and Brazzaville and their fellow citizens in Paris.

16. Robert Stephen Pomeroy, "The Economics of Production and Marketing in a Small-Scale Fishery: Matalom Leyte, Phillipines" (Ph.D. diss., Cornell University, 1989); Maria Szanton, *A Right to Survive: Subsistence Marketing in a Lowland Philippine Town* (University Park: Pennsylvania State University Press, 1972); Lillian Trager, "Customers and Creditors: Variations in Economic Personalism in a Nigerian Marketing System," *Ethnology* 20 (1981): 133–146.

17. Trager, "Customers and Creditors," 133.

Gendering Sugar

WOMEN'S DISEMPOWERMENT IN
SRI LANKAN SUGAR PRODUCTION

NANDINI GUNEWARDENA

As one of the world's first transnational commodities, sugar has the indubious distinction of holding a place in the political economy of global production and consumption as one that has fueled subordination, servitude, and impoverishment. The valuation of sugar as "white gold" destined to satisfy the consumption desires of a privileged few epitomizes its place in building imperialist modes of power, domination, and subjugation, deployed historically dating back to the colonial era in both the Americas and the Old World (East Africa, Asia, and the Pacific). After all, it was the consumer desire for sugar in Europe and the massive response to that demand that prompted the initial efforts to dominate the mercantile market in sugar—providing the impetus for the trans-Atlantic slave trade. Sugar production is thought to have provided one of the original means and motivations for European expansion, colonization, and control of the New World, while similar processes are replicated with few alterations in contemporary sugar cultivation and production in many other parts of the world.[1] From the enslavement of African populations imported to meet the labor needs of New World sugar plantations, the subsequent importation of indentured labor from many parts of the world, and the coercion of farming populations to work on sugar plantations in the Dutch East Indies (i.e., mainly Java in Southeast Asia) to the proletarianization evident in contemporary sugar production (in East Africa, South Asia, and elsewhere), the legacy of sugar is marred with violence, destitution, and hegemony.

This role of sugar as a commodity that has set in motion historical forms of servitude such as enslavement, labor indenture, and a shift from subsistence to wage labor invests sugar with a formidable symbolic burden in the history of global commodities. As documented extensively by many scholars, the cultivation, processing, and marketing of sugar has entailed related processes of racial, regional, and geopolitical subordination, where previously autonomous populations have been subordinated and exploited in the process of commodification of labor in transnational sugar production. Yet, our knowledge of the ways in which sugar is implicated in gender subordination is still inadequate. Women's role in sugar production, along with the gender-differentiated incorporation of labor and the differential terms and conditions of work for women and men in the transnational sugar economy, is a subject that has received insufficient attention. In the voluminous literature on sugar and its intertwinement with power, the gendering of the sugar subaltern remains an under-investigated topic (due to the absence of gender-specific studies and gender-disaggregated data), attesting in part to the general invisibility of women's work in commercial agriculture, complicated by the heavy reliance on male labor for sugar production in the colonial Americas.[2] Paradoxically, within the brief span of time that the island nation of Sri Lanka has been involved in commercial sugar production (a thirty-year period dating back to the 1970s),[3] transnational sugar companies have recruited a predominantly female labor force for field work, resulting in a disintegration of the gender parity previously existent in subsistence-farming communities and an erosion of women's social status and economic autonomy. In this chapter, I discuss the related processes of social and economic disempowerment experienced by women in the sugar economy of Sri Lanka, set in motion by the labor ideologies and practices of the largest sugar plantation in the country, the Pelwatte Sugar Corporation.

My aim is to document the ways in which traditional forms of gender parity in rural Sri Lanka have become transformed with the incursion of the sugar economy and the simultaneous processes of gender subordination it has fueled as gender became instrumental in labor deployment and control on industrial cane estates. Drawing upon a case study of the foremost industrial sugar estate in the southeastern region of Sri Lanka,[4] the Pelwatte Sugar Corporation (PSC), I will discuss how a trend toward a declining social and economic position of women has been set in motion by the way gender roles began to be reconceptualized in this capital-intensive agricultural enterprise. Referencing the concept of "women as the last colony" advanced by Edna Acosta-Belen and Christina Bose, I borrow from the Gramscian notion of the subaltern;[5] and I suggest that in a post-colonial era, where agriculture has become subsumed to the dominance of transnational, global capital, women workers in modern sugar industries experience a dual process of disempowerment: first, via their invisibility as labor of value and, second, via their exploitation and subordination in the processes of labor extraction. While proletarianization is an inherent part of the commercial sugar economy, my concern is more to examine how women's disempowerment is implicated in the introduction of sugar as an agro-industry. I suggest that the proliferation of gender hierarchical notions, ideologies, and practices espoused by PSC's strategies in labor recruitment and utilization is responsible for the disempowering shifts in women's lives. Their marginality is further exacerbated as rural communities mimic and embrace the newly configured gender organization of labor on the sugar estate. In order to highlight the manner in which such

processes of gendered disempowerment have occurred, I discuss two case studies that illustrate the parallel experiences of settler women on PSC land and
wage workers on the PSC sugar plantation. The story of Karuna (pseudonym)
represents the former and is discussed next, while Seela's story represents the latter and is recounted further along in the chapter. Through their stories, I weave
in the voices of other women sugar workers who narrate common experiences
of transformations in their lives as they became incorporated into the sugar
economy of Sri Lanka.

Karuna's Story

I encountered Karuna one mid-morning at the height of the dry (*Yala*) season, in
August 1994 (seven years since my first round of field research at PSC), as she fran-
tically made her way to her 2.5 hectare cane plot at PSC, upon receiving the news
that her ready-to-be harvested cane land was on fire. She was just returning from
the nearest district hospital at Buttala, where her husband, a night watchman on
the sugar estate, was warded the night before after an accidental injury. As we
approached the scene, water trucks were already attempting to douse out the rag-
ing fire, leaving billowing clouds of smoke wafting over the landscape. A crowd
had already gathered at the scene—mostly Karuna's neighbors, who had summoned the water trucks hours earlier when they had noticed the first sparks catch
ablaze. In the frenzy of shouts of concern and exchanges of side remarks, there
was a clear registration of discontent by the PSC settlers over their positioning in
the sugar economy. Visibly angry men commented on the delay in the arrival of
the water trucks and explained to me that even a stray spark could start a fire in no
time, given the dry, windy conditions and that the underbrush was dried to a crisp
at this time of the year. Some even ventured to heap blame on the PSC for alter-
ing climatic patterns, noting that the clearing of the vast jungle tracts to make way
for the sugar estate had eliminated so much of the forest cover, enough to further
reduce the sparse rains in the Yala (dry) season. They bemoaned the lack of crop
insurance available to them and elaborated on what they perceived to be the
extortive practices of PSC, such as charging them for the annual land preparation
by company-owned bulldozers (a factor they further attributed to the "hardening
and compacting" of the soil, leading to lower soil fertility), for seed cane, and for
chemical inputs (e.g., fertilizers, pesticides, and weedicides).

Karuna was besides herself, unable to comprehend the loss, and kept repeat-
ing why her husband was not around, clarifying almost monotonously that he
had fallen in the pitch dark the previous night on his way back from the night
watch and injured his head on a nearby boulder. Muthu, an outspoken elderly
woman, launched into a tirade about the underdeveloped conditions in the settlement villages—the dust on the unpaved roads (and the resulting upper-
respiratory ailments, particularly among children), the absence of street lighting
(and the personal security risks it posed), the lack of much needed amenities like

safe drinking water and sanitation (and their vulnerability to epidemics of water-borne illnesses and malaria). As the water trucks managed to abate the fire, Karuna's thoughts turned to the sobering reality of recovering what little unburned crop might be left. Holding back her tears, she turned to me, more to raise a worry than to expect an answer about how they would manage for the rest of the year without the income they depended on from their cane harvest. "What shall we do now!" she exclaimed. "We toil all year long to raise this crop and it is our only source of income. The salary my husband brings in as a night watchman is not enough even to white wash our house!"

As the anthropologist engaged in routine observations, I had become con-verted now to a witness of an injustice. "At least with *chena*, in our former vil-lages," she continued, referring to the local term for shifting agriculture,[6] "even if our main crops—maize and millet—were destroyed by wild boar or elephant herds, or by the occasional severe drought, we had a variety of vegetables and fruits we could rely on, not to mention the home garden crops that I used to plant, like sweet potatoes, other yams, pumpkin, bananas, and so on. Because we were unable to pay off our loans to the company last year for the charges for land clearing, seed cane, fertilizer, and all that, this year we planted tobacco on our home garden. Several settler families have done that," she trailed off.

In a subsequent interview with a young settler couple who had converted their infertile cane land into more hardy tobacco fields, the subsistence insecuri-ties settler families faced in the sugar economy were clarified to me in a similar manner. "We have to purchase the rice and other staples we need now from the store," Seetha, the wife, explained. "That means that we are subjected to the price fluctuations in the market—making our daily meals unaffordable," her hus-band, Vije, a high-school graduate who fell short of two points on the college entrance exam (and thus was compelled to return to agricultural pursuits) chimed in, presenting his argument in well-articulated economic terms (no doubt indicative of his sound preparedness for college, despite his exam results).

"Karuna, sister, you need to go to the main office and ask them to harvest the remainder of your crop right away," another older woman at the scene of the fire interjected. "Now what good will that do? They will think that we deliberately set fire to the cane," Karuna retorted, referring to the perceived lack of credibility and bargaining power settlers felt vis-à-vis the sugar company. As further clarification, Neela, a younger woman worker who had been harvesting the adjacent cane plot and had rushed to the scene of the fire, wiping away the beads of perspiration that had collected on her brow, whispered quietly to me that Karuna was hinting at the rumors of her husband's involvement in protest activities against PSC years back. This was in reference to an incident that occurred several years previous, part of the burning of cane tracts and other more direct confrontations by settlers armed with cane-cutting machetes against PSC's managerial staff as a strategy to negoti-ate a fair price for their cane and improved labor conditions on the estate.

As noon approached and the heat of the fire and the blazing tropical sun became unbearable, I continued to record the tense discussions among the settlers, recalling a similar scene in 1986 during my initial field research at PSC. On that occasion, a thin wisp of smoke had curled skyward on the horizon early one morning; that smoke I had suspected to be from a camp of workers heating their morning tea. By mid-morning, however, it had turned into a fire that consumed the entire cane track. Trapped at a PSC field office encircled by the fire, I had watched helplessly as the soot and heat began to burn my eyes and skin, while half-singed deer, rabbits, and wild boar scampered desperately through the underbrush in search of an escape. Although it could never be proven, the talk in the settlement villages at the time was that it was, indeed, an act of protest by local youth belonging to the Marxist political organization Janatha Vimukthi Peramuna (People's Liberation Front, JVP) against the sugar company, which they perceived to be a capitalist and exploitative enterprise—an early precursor to the island-wide insurgency the JVP launched within a few years.

"Why not try, Karuna?" I urged, keen to learn more about other hesitations she might have that might reveal more about the shifting constructions of gender and her own perceptions on the subject. "I don't know how to interact with these officers or this bureaucracy. I am only a housewife. . . . It is my husband who usually attends to these things," she replied, with uncustomary resignation. Her comment was rejoined by nods of assent from many of the other women at the scene. In subsequent interviews with groups of women, I sought further clarification on these perceptions. I was particularly concerned with their self-representation as "housewives," a characterization that contravened their plainly visible intensive contributions to the household's production activities (on their own cane fields, in field labor on PSC-owned cane tracts, and on their homestead plots). This characterization also represented a marked contrast to the views and gender norms of the subsistence-farming communities in the region where I had conducted research prior to this site (as discussed below).

Field Site

This chapter draws upon eighteen months of comparative field research I conducted at two locations in the district of Moneragala,[7] in the southeast of Sri Lanka, from 1985 to 1986, and in subsequent bouts of field research over the past decade at the Pelwatte Sugar Corporation (PSC) and in the subsistence-farming communities immediately surrounding the sugar estate as well as in more interior, remote locations. The purpose of undertaking such comparative research was to determine how varying degrees of engagement in commercial farming affected the gender constructs at each location given that the traditional, subsistence-farming communities of the region evidence high degrees of gender parity in terms of the division of labor, decision-making practices, and social as well as economic valuation.

The district of Moneragala is the most impoverished district on the island, along conventional indices of poverty such as income and consumption measures, and is also underdeveloped in terms of infrastructure (i.e., roads, communication networks) and services (health, education, banking). Part of Sri Lanka's Dry Zone,[8] the southeast is largely rural, sparsely dotted with kin-based subsistence-farming communities that are primarily Sinhala ethnics, Buddhist, and claim ancestry to the indigenous populations of the island.[9] These communities were established by founding ancestors who cleared parts of the extensive jungle tracts and settled in caste-homogenous hamlets. Given the harsh eco-climatic conditions of the region, they have been eking out a living primarily from shifting agriculture based on the staples of maize and millet, supplemented by seasonal rain-fed rice (paddy) farming.

Commercial sugar production in Sri Lanka was targeted exclusively for the southeastern quadrant of the island, considered ideal because of its arid, dry, agro-ecological conditions.[10] As the largest agro-industrial complex in Sri Lanka, the Pelwatte Sugar Corporation (PSC) is considered the primary commercial sugar production site in Sri Lanka, boasting of generating employment for over three thousand employees and an additional field labor force of over six thousand seasonal/casual workers. PSC was slated to meet 74 percent of the sugar production capacity of the country, although this meant that it was still only able to meet a fraction of the sugar consumption needs of the country—approximately 15 percent. When sugar production was introduced to the southwestern part of the island, it was under multinational ownership: 52 percent government ownership and 48 percent ownership by the British sugar giant, Booker Agriculture International of the United Kingdom, jointly with another U.K. firm, Kerry Engineering Company Ltd.

The land required to establish PSC had been occupied primarily by ethnic Sinhala subsistence-farming communities that, as noted above, for generations had cleared and cultivated the land,[11] practicing shifting cultivation in nearby jungle tracts while growing fruit and vegetable crops on their homestead land. Partially classified as crown land owned by the state, part of it was leased from the body of monks (sangha) affiliated with a central place of worship for Buddhists and Hindus alike in Sri Lanka—the Kataragama shrine (devale). PSC effectively ousted this subsistence-farming population by referring to the technical clause of "crown" land as belonging to the state (and therefore not legally owned by the public) and classifying them as "encroachers." Meager monetary compensation was offered to them for the land, leading some families to retreat deeper into the nearby jungle, while others, unwilling to agree to the insufficient compensation, were evicted as unlawful squatters. In addition, the calculation of value for the land they had occupied entailed a great deal of duplicity and manipulation. Fruit-bearing home garden crops, including coconut, papaya, mango, lime, etc., that were a source of seasonal supplementary income for this population were assigned meager and arbitrary values and assessed at Rs. 250 (approximately two dollars) each, when their market value was at least four times that. Assessors entrusted with the task of assigning a value to home garden crops often negotiated or pressured the occupants to agree to commissions (suggestive of their resort to coercive practices), a strategy that further reduced the compensation while serving as a reminder of the latter's vulnerability to the power represented by PSC. "Encouraged" to take up sugar cultivation on the premise of its more lucrative returns as compared to traditional subsistence crops, they were incorporated thereafter as "settlers" and resettled on homestead plots of half an acre and a two-hectare plot meant for sugarcane. Many of those resettled complained of the stony, virtually uncultivable land they were allocated, unsuitable for any form of farming. By contrast, the former bed of an ancient irrigation reservoir,[12] which clearly contained the most fertile land on the site, was chosen as the location of PSC's nucleus estate, where experimental trials and the optimal inputs assured a constant supply of cane to ensure a production flow. Essentially converted into a wage labor force, these farming households were compelled to acquiesce to a division of labor imposed by PSC authorities—one that ignored local conceptualizations and arrangements of the gender division of labor.

Research Methods

This chapter draws upon ethnographic research that relied primarily on the methods of participant-observation at both research sites, supplemented by interviews with women members of the respective communities, occasional interviews with their husbands and other male kin, and open-ended, unstructured focus group interviews with women workers in the cane fields, with ritual and administrative specialists of the subsistence communities, and with the cadre of field officers and upper-echelon managerial staff of PSC. My year-long residence at the first field site, the subsistence-farming community that I call Kande Village (pseudonym), enabled me to establish a high degree of trust and rapport not only with members of that community, but with the population across the district as word spread via kinship and other significant networks about the nature of my research.[13] A subsequent residence of six months at PSC allowed me to conduct interviews with women settlers and women workers on PSC's cane land.[14] For a number of culturally critical reasons, Kande Village proved to be a strategic location that facilitated my entry into the settler communities at and adjacent to PSC. It was, for one, the home of the head monk for the District of Moneragala, and the close relationship I had cultivated with his mother, who soon assigned me the fictive kin relationship of "daughter," conferred me "insider" status. It was also home to a well-loved and respected political leader, the first cousin of the head monk, who had met an untimely death from a venomous cobra bite a decade prior to my research. As the only "stranger" in this remote location, my long-term residence, participant-observation of their daily lives, and close affiliation with these socially important families eventually shifted my location as an outsider, granting me access to their emic perspectives on critical issues.[15]

The Place of Sri Lankan Sugar in the Global Market

Given the prevalence of long-established sugar giants in the world (i.e., Brazil, China, India, Thailand),[16] and the relatively low comparative advantage of Sri Lanka as a sugar producer, the decision to embark on sugar production is, indeed, a mystery.[17] Before the 1970s, sugarcane was grown solely as an occasional delicacy on a non-commercial basis in home gardens, particularly in the arid southeastern regions of the country. Its introduction as a commercial crop was part of the strategy adopted by the government for building national food self-sufficiency. Despite its late incursion into the local economy, commercial sugar in Sri Lanka is similarly implicated in the destitution, impoverization, and subordination of local populations, similar to the impoverishment of transplanted/enslaved/migrant populations in the New World. Even at its inception, the inordinate cost to the consumer (not to mention the producer) was evident by the mere fact that the world market price of sugar was about Rs. 12 per kilogram while the consumer in Sri Lanka was obliged to pay about Rs. 30 per kilogram. After two decades of unsuccessful attempts to produce enough sugar to meet local consumption needs, two of the commercial sugar production schemes (at Hingurana and Kantalai) have closed, while sugar production at the other two sites (Sevanagala and Pelwatte) only meets a bleak 10 percent of total consumer demand in Sri Lanka,[18] compared to 19 percent in the early 1990s, with the current sugar recovery rates at these two sites at about 8.5 percent and a government loss estimated at Sri Lankan Rupees 65 million (U.S. $813,000) in 2000.[19] Labor disputes have plagued the sugar industry in Sri Lanka, resulting in decreases in output,[20] the closure of several sugar factories, and the reallocation of smallholder sugar (subsistence farmers') lands to rice and other irrigated crops.[21] The decline in international sugar prices has also had an adverse impact on local sugar production ($U.S. 291 per metric ton in 1998 as compared to $U.S. 163 per metric ton in 2004).[22] The government's response to protect local sugar producers by imposing a duty tax on sugar imports (which has raised the cost of imported sugar to U.S. $500 per metric ton) has imposed a burden on the average consumer. Meeting the sugar consumption needs of the country (estimated at an average of approximately 511,700 tons annually) costs the country Rs. 18 billion in foreign exchange.[23] The current (2004) retail price of sugar in Sri Lanka is Rs. 33 to Rs. 36 per kilogram.

Subverting Gender Parity: The Displacement of *Karata-Kara* in the Sugar Economy

The subsistence-farming communities in Sri Lanka that practice shifting agriculture (*chena*) show a high degree of gender parity in marked contrast to the gender hierarchical ideologies and practices evident elsewhere in the island. Such gender parity is evidenced in several social norms and practices: complementary gender roles (rather than hierarchically organized) in agricultural pursuits, the explicit valuation of women's contributions to household production activities, joint decision-making in household affairs, joint household headship, exclusive assignment of household fund management to women, equal property inheritance rights for women and men, and a woman's right to an independent income from her land even within a marriage. As documented extensively in the anthropological literature, such systems of gender parity are evident in most swidden (shifting) farming systems, unlike the more hierarchical gender patterns that prevail in intensive agriculture systems.[24]

One local arrangement that well captures this gender parity in Sri Lanka is the complementary relegation of tasks in agricultural work between a conjugal pair embodied in the term *Karata-Kara,* which literally means "shoulder-to-shoulder." It refers to the gender division of labor that assigns and specifies parallel responsibilities between a husband-wife pair in sustaining the production/livelihood needs of the household. Karata-Kara is also imbued with symbolic significance in recognizing the economic contributions women make to the production activities of the household. It also embodies the idea of partnership in household decision-making as a joint task. A related arrangement, joint household headship and management, is reflected in the term *maha denna* (two household heads) assumed by a conjugal couple, common among shifting farming communities in Sri Lanka. A woman's role as an equal partner in household decision-making is inscribed in the notion of maha denna, explicitly acknowledging her role in a significant realm of activity—without any degree of gender privileging. A further indicator of gender parity in chena farming communities is that women typically assume the management of household finances, including the allocation of separate funds for various expenditures and savings practices. This role allocation rests on a general belief that women are more thrifty and, therefore, more conservative managers of money than men, who are considered to be spendthrifts in the local gender ideology. Vestiges of these traditional gender constructs that allow for gender-role complementarity in the division of labor, in decision-making, and in money management still prevail among many subsistence-farming populations who are primarily shifting cultivators, as revealed in the extensive field research I conducted.

By contrast, the gender constructs in other contexts of Sinhala Buddhists in Sri Lanka reflect notions and practices that are a marked departure from the latter type of gender parity. As Gananath Obeyesekere, Malathi de Alwis, and others have documented,[25] this variation is attributable to three distinct influences: Sanskritic gender norms (via the cultural exchanges with India prior to the colonial period),[26] Victorian gender codes (via the experience of colonization), and what I term "neo-Buddhist" gender ideals that emerged as a result of the nationalist Buddhist revivals launched in the 1800s. Although the southeastern region of Sri Lanka remained for the most part outside the ambit of these dominant constructions of gender, the incursion of the sugar economy has contributed to dramatic shifts over the past three decades. The outcome has been that pre-existing arrangements that ensured gender parity have been subverted via a gender-hierarchical labor structure associated with a feminization of the field labor force and resulting in power disparities that culminate in an overall process of disempowerment for women, as discussed in the next section.

Gendering the Work of Sugar

Contravening the complementary allocation of work roles evident in subsistence-farming communities (epitomized by the notion of karata-kara), a nearly exclusive female labor force is employed for the arduous and lower-status work of planting, weeding, and harvesting cane at PSC and other commercial sugar plantations in Sri Lanka. Men, on the other hand, have been incorporated into more diverse and higher-status occupational categories in field labor, work in the sugar factory, and administrative work. For example, male labor is exclusively deployed in supervisory positions in the cane fields, as machine operators and tractor drivers, in intermediate "technical" tasks such the spraying fertilizer and the distribution and collection of cutting knives to women harvesting cane, in the lower echelon of field administration (manning the field offices responsible for land clearing, timely harvesting, and other tasks that ensure the smooth operation of the annual cycle of cane production), and the middle- as well as higher-level administrative roles. While a handful of local women are recruited for clerical and secretarial work in the administrative offices, as sugar packers, and as part of the cleaning crew in the sugar factory, men dominate the occupational hierarchy in the field, in the factory, and in the administrative offices of PSC. The large-scale industrial production of sugar in present-day Sri Lanka also evinces another kind of gender paradox: the clear assignment of male labor for the handling and operating of machinery. Similar patterns are evident elsewhere in the world with agricultural modernization, as documented three decades ago by Ester Boserup and others since then.[27] In sum, although women's labor is crucial on estate cane fields, it has become de-valorized as unskilled, unproductive, and secondary and, as a result, under-remunerated and newly subordinated to regulation by male supervisors.

Striking distinctions in the work atmosphere on the cane fields on the industrial sugar estates versus those owned by subsistence-farming smallholders bear further witness to the gendered shifts in labor conditions. A tense silence prevails on the former, punctuated by the commanding tones of supervisors, while a cacophony of voices fills the latter. The silence on estate sugar fields is only interrupted by the sound of the wind swishing through the cane grass, the distant whir of the mechanical arm of a cane-loading machine lifting the bundles of cane, cut by women wage workers, into a conveyance bin, and the occasional instructions barked out by an impatient supervisor. While family and kin labor deployed in the latter fields lends to the conviviality of the worksite, on the sugar estates, the presence of a supervisor severely curtails any such exchanges. Monitoring the pace of work, often directing stern admonishments to the women workers, supervisors effectively discourage talk as a distracting device, making field work on the sugar estate fraught with tension.

By contrast, on the cane fields in the subsistence-farming communities, the work day is filled with chatter, sprinkled with the friendly "hoo hoo" call to a neighbor on an adjacent plot, a shout to a child to stop chewing on cane stalks or to fetch a pot of water for a thirsty crew, and the occasional sound of raucous laughter among women exchanging wild jokes to break the tedium. The difference in the gender composition of the labor force adds the final stamp of distinction between these two sites. Village-grown cane draws in whatever available laborers regardless of gender, while on the sugar estate it is primarily impoverished women who labor as wage workers in the tasks of planting, weeding, and harvesting cane and are supervised exclusively by male overseers.

At PSC, throughout the fourteen-month cultivation cycle of sugarcane, groups of women workers bent over digging sticks, hoes, and scythes are visible on the cane fields, positioned within viewing distance of a lone male whose singular responsibility appears to be the direction and supervision of the female workers. Why it is presumed that these women need such supervision and how such a need is rationalized reveal the gendered control that has emerged in the industrial production of sugar. This is particularly paradoxical since the women workers originate in subsistence-farming communities where they are quite accustomed to and have intimate knowledge of and familiarity with the cultivation practices and the use of simple equipment in planting, weeding, and harvesting, given their active involvement for generations in the agricultural pursuits of the community. Hence, it appears that this new pattern informs us more of the ways that commercial sugar production as a capitalist venture effectively reproduces the colonial notion that authority and disciplining—policing if you will—is an essential ingredient even in the control of "free labor" (unfettered, that is, in the sense that these are not enslaved or indentured workers). I suggest that this is rooted in the reasoning that without coercion an unwilling workforce is likely to be errant, unproductive and lax, and that it reflects the contemporary continuities in the colonial notions of the lazy native. As such, a novel power hierarchy, one that is associated with male power (vested in the authority of males placed in higher occupational categories in the labor structure of the sugar economy), has been introduced at PSC.

Gendering the Labor Contract and Impoverishment

The labor contract for women field laborers is tenuous in that it offers no work security or permanence, as compared to males, most of whom are not in field labor and hold salaried positions. Hired as seasonal casual laborers, women form the core of the unskilled, non-mechanized, back-breaking, tedious, and repetitious jobs like planting, weeding, and harvesting (as noted above), which are lower in the occupational hierarchy but essential for sugar cultivation. The authoritarian role of a male supervisor is summoned as the primary tool to extract maximal productivity. Their payments are made per unit harvested, weeded, or cleared, individualized tasks that isolate them from each other—a distinct difference from the team harvesting systems in traditional villages. Traveling into fields at dawn from adjacent villages, women field workers are given their implements (cutting knives, hoes, etc.) and expected to return them at the end of the day in exchange for a signature on a time card that assures them of their meager monthly pay. Their discipline and control is predicated on the argument surrounding the importance of timing in cane operations, and the exploitative tactics such as low wages rest on the socially "marginal" status of women.

Women are drawn into the field labor force on the sugar estates from the ranks of the landless farmers in the nearby countryside. Their landlessness derives either from being ousted from the land they occupied without a title deed, as PSC took over common state-owned land considered crown land, or from being previously rendered landless due to a combination of lost or damaged harvests and the cycle of indebtedness to usurious moneylenders. Women who are widowed, "divorced,"[28] or originate from dissolved households (separation, divorce, etc.), and hence economically marginalized and vulnerable, form another category of labor. In particular, changes in the social organization of production set in motion by the expropriation of land by PSC have played a pivotal role in compelling non-settler women residing in the villages adjacent to PSC to become wage laborers on company-owned sugar land. Loss of their landholdings and the resultant poverty then is the primary reason that women from subsistence communities are compelled to engage in wage labor, as Seela's story below illustrates. Although Seela's economic situation, and that of most women in the subsistence communities adjoining PSC, is somewhat different from that of PSC's women settlers like Karuna, as discussed earlier (i.e., smaller landholdings and greater subsistence insecurity as they are tied into the wage economy), both groups of women experience similar processes of subordination and disempowerment in the new ways they are placed in the social structure of the sugar economy and the ways they are incorporated into the labor structure of the sugar economy. While Karuna found herself ill-equipped to navigate the bureaucratic labyrinth of PSC because of its gender ideologies that diminished her credibility and capacity to negotiate the outcome of her burnt cane, Seela by contrast finds that the contours of her life are increasingly constrained by the cycle of wage work on the sugar lands of the PSC. As both women face similar predicaments in their livelihood struggles (albeit in different ways), we witness the manifestation of the culmination of their social subordination with their economic marginality.

Seela's Story

Seela is a widowed woman in her fifties who is a daily wage-worker in the PSC cane fields. Her life is dictated by the cane cycle and the rhythm of work pre-scribed to her. Her daily routine is to awake at 3 a.m. to prepare the daily meals for herself and her children, after which she walks approximately half a mile, long before sunrise, to a pick-up point where she boards a locally operated lorry that takes her, along with other women workers, to the PSC cane fields. As a habit, before she leaves her home compound in a village bordering the PSC estate, she lights a lamp at a devotional altar, invoking the blessings of the Buddha and reciting a chant that seeks good merit (*pin*) to alleviate the suffering (*dukkha*) she feels she is enduring in this life. Drawing on the Buddhist notion of karma (*karume*), she explains to me the nature and causes of her suffering—the untimely death of her husband five years ago and the imprisonment of her two grown sons two years hence because of suspected anti-state political activities (and membership in the JVP), leaving her to seek wage work in the cane fields. "I have to find food and shelter for my two daughters somehow," she clarifies. "Otherwise, they will have no future or dignity," she hints, alluding to the need to secure some form of dowry for the girls and the intensification of former under-standings of dowry simply as a mechanism for ensuring a woman's standing in the marriage rather than a transfer of wealth to the groom.

"It is not that I am not used to working in farming activities," she adds. "When the children's father was alive,[29] we worked karata-kara, growing our own maize, millet, bananas, and the usual vegetables. We also had lime trees that brought us a good seasonal income. But, of course, we were dispossessed of part of the land we had worked on for twenty-five years when the estate came," she notes, referring to PSC, "because they told us we did not have proper legal title to the land. What a karma! We thought that this land belonged to the Kataragama devale when we first settled here all that time back when we got married," she sighed.[30] "But, I suppose even the devale never gives out land to the public—we just didn't think about the possibility of being ousted because this was such thick jungle in those days. And we never did have any paper work—now we are reduced to this compound that only holds our little hut, the bathing well in the back, and that old mango tree in the front," she trails off.

While the moon is still visible in the pre-dawn sky, Seela, ready to leave for work, grabs an old long-sleeved shirt that belonged to her late husband, explain-ing to me that despite the heat the long sleeves are a protection against the spin-dles at the end of the cane leaves that cut into the skin. She lights a bundled sheath of palm leaves to make a *cadjan* torch that will light her way along the village roads sans electricity to the lorry pick-up point. There she boards the lorry, crowded in with other women workers who come from even greater distances, some further than the Kataragama temple (itself located about twenty miles fur-ther south), hugging her woven reed basket that contains a flask of tea and some cookies ("biscuits," as they are referred to locally) for her morning break and her lunch packet of rice wrapped in a banana leaf. The lorry reaches the cane fields at sunrise, a splendorous splash of golden orange and pink that holds no hint of the blazing heat that will soon overtake the morning. Together with other women in her crew, Seela stands in queue to collect a cutting knife and follows the directions of the supervisor to the assigned tract, where she resumes the harvesting work begun earlier that week.

During the scheduled tea break that is timed to the minute by a trouser-clad supervisor who seems to take his duty even more seriously in the presence of the outsider/anthropologist, we resume the interview. "Some of them are younger than me, and some are distantly related to me—those supervisors," Seela explains, motioning her head toward the supervisor and anticipating the questions embedded in the extensive scribbles on my field notepad, questions that she correctly suspects are about the nature of supervision. "But they bark orders as if they don't know me, or as if they think I don't know how to hack off the cane stalk!" she muses, adding a note of humor to the irony in her voice. "Some of the women argue with them, but I don't have the energy to." Pausing to sip from her tea, she continues, "I am too destitute to risk losing this work, even though you see how parched and dry my skin is, like the cracked and thirsty earth beneath us this Yala season, when we haven't seen a drop of rain in months." "What about other kinds of work?" I query cautiously. "Who will hire me in a store in the town center, tell me. I only studied to sixth grade, and I can't read or write or count properly. My girls have to add my pay packet to make sure they didn't cheat me. By the time my elder daughter finishes her O-levels, maybe she can get a job in the new garment factory they are bringing into the next town. But they only want to hire young girls in those factories too."

The above narrative and subsequent interviews revealed the predicament of poverty and powerlessness encountered by Seela and women like her who were drawn into the PSC wage labor force. They provide insights into the factors in the personal/family histories as well as the structural features of the labor arrangements at PSC that have led to the shifts from gender-role parity to hierarchies. As the next section elucidates, this shift rests on a new twist, not only in the assignment of women's work as secondary in value and importance, but also in the naturalization of women's work as an extension of their work in their proper domain—in domestic work—despite the extensive work they undertake in the cane fields.

The Naturalization of Women's Work: Capitalist Rationale for Smallholder Production

Historically, in the sugar plantations of the Americas, the typical strategy for securing the extensive labor needs of sugar production was to import slave or indentured labor. As abolition of both these systems came into being, colonial sugar plantation owners sought alternate sources of cheap labor. Tenant farming was considered the best solution, since it allowed for a degree of control, while ensuring the cane supplies necessary to keep up the uninterrupted pace of sugar-milling operations. This system prevailed in Fiji, as documented by several scholars.[31] It was also adopted in colonial sugar production in Kenya and in Queensland.

The modern version of tenant farming evident in Sri Lanka is the "resettlement" scheme—a device that enabled PSC to avert the huge outlay of expenditure for hired labor. This strategy rested on an understanding that the settler family would recruit household labor for producing its sugarcane and thereby ensure a steady supply of cane to feed the factories at PSC. This meant the utilization of the labor of all household members, including women and children, as available. It also entailed a naturalizing ideology about women's labor contributions as an inherent component of family labor arrangements of the settler household. Promotion of this naturalizing ideology about women's labor lent itself to the invisibility of women's productive contributions. Ultimately, it resulted in the under-valuation of women's economic contributions (in stark contrast to the value attached to women's work in the subsistence-farming communities that practice chena/shifting cultivation) and became another route to women's disempowerment.

Subsequently, male discourses began to emerge about women's inability to work in the cane fields—another route to disempowerment for women. Drawing upon emergent notions of women's physical inferiority (i.e., capable only of work in the domestic sphere, increasingly justified as better suited for them), these discourses demarcate women's work on the cane fields as an extension of their domestic work (i.e., subsistence-farming work). Thus, despite the preponderance of women in the cane fields, laboring long hours in the hot sun, and the contributions such labor makes to the household fund, local discourse about cane work has begun to construct women as secondary earners, physically vulnerable and incapable of bearing the drudgery of work in the cane fields. Depicting a picture wholly contradictory to the visible presence of women toiling in the cane fields, women sugar workers are characterized as incapable of bearing the tedium of laboring in the cane fields and as vulnerable to the dangers from elephant encroachment and predatory human beings in cane groves that are far from human settlements, as elaborated upon below.

Gendered Discourses about Labor Capacities: Constructing Notions of Female Vulnerability

"Women are not fit for this work," one male settler, Ari (pseudonym), commented to me during an interview exploring settlers' ideas of the gender division of labor in the PSC cane fields. "Sometimes, the cane is taller than me, and the ground is parched dry like a barren desert," he mused. "It is difficult terrain, and who knows what is on the other side of the cane rows—man or beast.[32] A female won't be able to deal with that kind of danger, and that is why I say this work is not for women." While he was alluding to the structuring of the settlement communities that departed from the kin-based composition of subsistence villages that offer women a high degree of physical security, this comment clearly reflected the shifting perceptions of women's capabilities associated with the new vulnerabilities that defined their lives.

Contravening the visible evidence of women workers toiling in the estate cane fields year-round, this emergent discourse constructs women as physically weak and unable to protect themselves from the dangers inherent in cane work. In this discourse, cane fields are constructed as dangerous terrain unsuitable for helpless women who need the protection afforded by male kin with superior physical strength. Hence, the domain of sugarcane has come to be a site for privileging male physical power, superiority, and strength, effectively rendering women's work invisible and marginal.

Constructing women as helpless subjects on the cane fields has had a spill-over effect to the domestic arena. Women's financial contributions to the household economy and their household fund management capacities are also increasingly dismissed as insignificant by males who claim sole household headship—a complete departure from the pre-existing pattern in subsistence-farming communities (as discussed above). These ideas extend also to a reduced participation in household decision-making by women as men claim that domain, too, as a strictly male domain and deride women's ability to make effective decisions pertaining to household matters.

In interviews I conducted with a sample of settler households on PSC land, the consistent response to my question on the assignment of responsibility for household decision-making and fund management is that it is the task of the male head of household, a pattern in stark contrast to that in the subsistence-farming communities in the region. It was clear that to claim otherwise would be an assault on the masculinity of the husband. In one focus group interview with a settler family, an indignant husband, Raney (pseudonym), questioned the very basis of my inquiry. He was irked by the fact that implicit in the mere inquiry about the gender assignments in decision-making and fund management was a questioning of what he took to be the natural allocation of these roles as a male domain. "Without me, how can these women folk manage money?" he demanded in an annoyed tone, going as far as to deride the capacity of women to handle this task. "As the head of the household, it is I who makes these decisions. Women don't know how to do these things," he added, indicating the extent to which the mere question appeared as a personal affront to him. Since the interview had been scheduled for the evening hours when he and his wife, Kusuma (pseudonym), had returned from working in the cane fields, I posed a follow-up question to both on her income contributions. "What is the use of the mere two or three hundred rupees she brings in?" he spoke first, asserting further, "It is the male who brings in the significant income that helps the family advance financially." Although Kusuma, seated beside him, held her silence, at various points in the conversation she interjected matter-of-factly about the kind of work she did as a wage laborer on the PSC cane fields (planting, weeding, and harvesting), without contradicting him about the valuation of her economic contributions. As he continued to make additional statements associating masculinity with household headship and decision-making, she would intermittently clap her hand over her mouth and suppress a laugh, amused partly at her husband's self-righteous anger and how his need to subscribe to this new patriarchal ideology was being challenged by the interview questions.

For the most part, women's responses to these new discourses about the insignificance of their economic and labor contributions were to avoid attaching any significance to them since they were secure in the knowledge that they did continue to bring in an income. Their strategy was to allow the males to present this public front as a means of maintaining a shred of dignity in the context of increasing impoverishment and the social subordination of local, low-income males in the social and economic hierarchy of the sugar economy. Publicly, they refrained from contradicting the dominant discourses that allude to their secondary status, while, in private, they resorted to humor to comment on how men are increasingly invoking notions of masculinity to construct their superior status. Some women found it convenient and perhaps advantageous to go along with the depictions of vulnerability, as Karuna did, and used this designation to call upon male kin to take on key household production decisions and activities, like approaching a field manager about information, seeking a loan from a financial institution, and other public encounters with the sugar company or local officials. Alternately, other women found it strategically prudent to avoid direct confrontations, as Seela did. These tendencies may not be read as a mere collusion in their subordination, however, but more as strategic protective measures designed to avert further economic and social vulnerability, not unlike the physical protection afforded to women by the veil in Middle Eastern society.[33]

Women's responses to these emergent discourses, nonetheless, register variations from distancing to a complete internalization of the new representations of subordination. The internalization of notions of physical inferiority and the devaluation of their economic contributions has meant, on one hand, that women too have begun to perceive themselves as secondary earners while they have begun to subscribe to the discourses about their economic and labor contributions as insignificant in sustaining the livelihood needs of the household. Increasingly, more women are beginning to characterize themselves as mere housewives, as Karuna did, a move that is perceived as a socially protective measure but ultimately robs them of the capacity to intervene in their own economic interests. The emergence of this gendered discourse on differential work capacities and production contributions has also represented a dilemma for low-income house-holds hovering at the edge of poverty, in extremely precarious economic situa-tions. In no position to withhold women's labor in wage work because of the financial contribution it makes to the household, they confront the disjunctures of conflicting gender ideologies. As settler households improve their incomes, the tendency has been to pull women out of the field labor force, prompting the estate management to seek women's labor from distant, more impoverished villages.

Ironically, the managerial staff on the sugar estate prefer women field work-ers because of an alternate (but equally patriarchal) construction of women workers as easy to manage (responsive to discipline and control) and more com-pliant (submissive). In fact, the militancy of male workers in the cane fields early on (reportedly in the early 1980s), including a stand-off with management by gangs of machete-toting male workers, was the turning point for estate manage-ment to recruit greater numbers of female field workers. Managerial discourses that construct women as a docile group that can be subjugated easily add to the local discourses that construct women as powerless. These parallel discourses prevail in a delicate tension and inform us of how women subjects are consti-tuted to reflect relations of power. The powerlessness attributed to women is doubly instrumental—in justifying male superiority/dominance and in imposing the inequitable terms and structure of the labor contract. Gender-based wage inequities offer further information on how this process exacerbates women's exploitation in the sugar economy of Sri Lanka.

Gendered Exploitation via Wage Inequities in Commercial Sugar

Wage inequities are one aspect of the gender-differential patterns of labor exploitation in sugar production. Women workers in the sugar fields of PSC earn substantially less, partly because they are classified as field hands, whereas men occupy supervisory positions. Even in the rare instances when men participate in cane cutting, however, men's wages average 175–200 rupees per day (the equiva-lence of approximately U.S. $2.00–$2.50), far above women's wages of 100 to 150 rupees (approximately $1.00–$1.50) per day. This pattern is historically evident elsewhere, not only in sugar work in the colonial Americas, but also in contem-porary sugar production in many parts of the world,[34] rooted in the general pat-tern of gender-based wage disparities in agricultural work across the world and partly due to the specific strategies of labor recruitment and deployment in sugar production.[35] On Tanzanian sugar plantations, for example, women are concen-trated in low-pay and subordinate field tasks, while men are hired for higher-placed and better-remunerating jobs as supervisors and headmen.[36] In Jamaican sugar plantations, although women constituted 70 percent of the cane cutters, they were paid half the wages of men.[37] Similarly, in Guyana, several scholars have commented on the exploitative labor conditions experienced by women workers, including wages that amounted to between 50 percent and 66 percent of the wages of male workers.[38] Despite the institution of a fixed daily minimum wage for Indian indentured laborers working the sugar fields, albeit a gender disparate one (25 cents for males and 18 cents for females), women were paid far below the minimum wage—typically between 48 to 60 cents a week. Moreover, as Moses Seenarine notes, pregnant women workers in Guyanese sugar plantations were provided food rations in lieu of their salary. These food rations were calculated as an accumulating debt they incurred, to the extent that many women, despite working a full day, received no wages for the course of their pregnancy and subsequent pregnancies, while they faced the challenge at the end of their pregnancy of repaying the debt they had accumulated.[39]

Aside from the basic injustice of inequitable wage standards and the neglect of minimum daily wage stipulations in practice, the dependence conferred to women by such wage practices is a noteworthy issue. Reversing their previous standing as valued contributors of critical labor power in chena (shifting) cultivation (subsistence crops), the newly conferred economic dependence of women on the larger wage packet earned by a man has effectively eroded women's sense of autonomy. This process has also contributed to the emergence of a notion of women's social dependence and an ideology of women's inability to fend for themselves, as Karuna emphasized in describing her inability to negotiate with PSC officials the matter of harvesting the remainder of her burnt cane. The sense of economic and social vulnerability that settler farmers report with the shift to and exclusive reliance on sugar income as their only source of a livelihood has aggravated the subjective inadequacies women experience.

Conclusion

This chapter has argued that the re-definition of gendered capacities and revised demarcations of the social boundaries of work have been ushered in by the institutional operation of a new form of gendered power on the sugar estates. New constructions of male power have emerged in the region, deriving from a subscription to the hierarchical gender notions espoused by those in dominant positions in the sugar estate/industry/economy (i.e., PSC), where PSC represents the institutional site that embodies gender hierarchies. Sugar, in other words, has rendered rural spaces incorporated into the sugar economy as social sites where newly constructed symbolic, discursive, and ideological meanings of masculinities have begun to circulate, making invisible women's work, household economic contributions, and participation in decision-making, and thereby naturalizing their subordinate positioning vis-à-vis men. I have documented how women's positioning within the household and family has deteriorated among settler households incorporated into the commercial sugar estate at PSC (as compared to subsistence communities in the region) by the internalization of these new gender ideologies and their replication within the domain of social reproduction. These patterns reflect the dynamics and potency of the power invested in the sugar agro-industries as representatives of modernity, progress, and development.

This chapter has documented the shift in agricultural labor relations in sub-sistence-farming communities in Sri Lanka that evidenced a high degree of gen-der parity to the gender-hierarchical configuration of capitalist production relations exemplified in commercial sugar enterprises. Despite the relatively high degree of gender parity that was pre-existent in this region,[40] dominant concep-tualizations of gender and notions of social hierarchy, mobilized and manipu-lated in the sugar economy, have set in motion a transformation of local gender and labor relations and women's social position.[41]

The discursive production of distinctly gendered forms of power that privi-lege males in the sugar economy may be traced to the structuring of the sugar industry as a male-dominant enterprise. As a corporation, PSC was structured along a strictly male-dominated occupational hierarchy in its headquarters in Colombo as well as in the field headquarters in the town of Buttala. Outside of the local politician's endorsement of PSC and the conversion of land to sugar-cane fields, the first interface that villagers in Moneragala District had with PSC was via its male officers charged with the task of promoting the project and coax-ing villagers to accept the project. Subsequently, male settlement officers were entrusted with the task of coaxing villagers to settle on the sugar estate land, some charged with the responsibility of assessing the value of tree crops existing on each farmer's homestead. Upon the establishment of PSC, extension officers who provided information on the cultivation practices appropriate for sugarcane were exclusively male, as were the administrative staff members of PSC's field offices. The practice of employing a strictly male staff by PSC in all its higher level administrative functions and much of its field functions has, in effect, led to the privileging of males in the sugar industry. The tendency of such male admin-istrative staff was to interact primarily with male representatives of settler house-holds, to the extent that a pattern of endorsing and enforcing male "superiority" emerged in the sugar economy. Women, too, began to internalize their margin-ality on the PSC estate, as evidenced, for example, by claiming that they were unable to negotiate with the administrative staff of PSC. The knowledge and power vested in these male representatives served as a discursive field for estab-lishing a new form of gendered power relations that has emerged in this part of the country. The associated discourses constructed only partial truths about local social/gender arrangements and cultivation practices, normalizing males as the preeminent holders of agricultural knowledge, subsequently leading to women's increasing marginality, contrasted to men's growing centrality in the sugar econ-omy. Ironically, rural populations across Sri Lanka seeking to overcome their marginal social status have resorted to emulating the practices of urban and middle-class Buddhist Sinhala populations. Gender notions that construct women along lines of domesticity and respectability (notions circulating among the latter population) occupy a central place in the conceptualization of gender in the society.[42] These hegemonic notions and associated practices are subscribed to increasingly by rural populations in their attempts to shed their stigmatized social positioning in this deeply class and polarized society.[43] This nexus is the route through which a transformation of the pre-existing gender parity has been made possible and the disempowerment of women has begun to take place.

The feminization of agricultural labor in the context of neoliberal policies considered a positive trend merely because of women's increased access to work.[44] The growth in women's employment is perceived as an opportunity for women to secure financial and, thereby, social autonomy. Yet questions surrounding the persistent wage differentials between male and female workers, their differential placement in the agricultural labor hierarchy, and the declining decision-making power of women present challenges to this thesis. Lucia Da Corta and Davuluri Venkateshwarlu's work on women agricultural laborers in Andhra Pradesh, India, documents how women's greater participation in agricultural work did not bring about a corresponding improvement in their power in household decision-making—something they refer to as the "women's empowerment paradox."[45] Similarly, in Kenya, where women from independent "outgrower" households do not contribute any labor to the cultivation of sugarcane, as Eileen Kennedy and Bruce Cogill document, the percentage of female-controlled income is significantly less than that in non-sugar-producing households. Although the income of sugar-producing households is higher than those producing other crops, the proportion of income controlled by women is lower.[46] In the present case, we not only see a reversal of the gender parity pre-existent among shifting agriculture communities, but a newly introduced gender hierarchy that conceptualizes women's work as insignificant for the sugar economy, with a corresponding devaluation of women's financial contributions to the household being prevalent at PSC and elsewhere on the sugar estates in Sri Lanka.

Contrary to the neoliberal claim that participation in commercial agriculture (capital moderated by the market principle) would provide women a source of independent income, thereby serving as an empowering mechanism for women, the introduction of sugar as a capital-driven agro-industry into Sri Lanka's previously subsistence economies of Moneragala has had a detrimental effect on women. Despite the significant contribution women make to the household income through their work in the cane fields, there is an increasing devaluation of the cash they bring into the household; it is seen as insufficient. Males claim that household decision-making is entirely within their purview and that women must seek their permission in all matters. We may surmise, then, that mere access to a source of income is insufficient for empowering women, given the structuring of gendered wage differentials that introduce new forms of dependence and notions of subordination. Moreover, looking toward income as the sole source of autonomy and empowerment is insufficient since this effectively bolsters the processes of labor commodification that capitalism relies on for the generation of profit. Instead, as this case study reveals, the nexus of gender- and class-based exploitation needs to be addressed in tandem with economic marginality in order to avert and reduce women's disempowerment.

NOTES

1. Sugarcane was introduced to the New World by the Spanish in 1493. In demand since the Crusades, sugar had been under the control of Arab producers and traders. Realizing its value as a commodity, the Spanish became interested in the commercial production of sugarcane, but it was only in 1516 that the Spanish had a sugar mill in the New World. See Chelsie Vandaveer, "How Did the Arabs Break Spanish Control of the Sweet Spice?" in Plants That Changed History Web site, http://www.killerplants.com/plants-that-changed-history/20011106.asp (accessed November 6, 2001).

2. See Michael Tadman, "The Demographic Cost of Sugar: Debates on Slave Societies and Natural Increase in the Americas," *American Historical Review* 105, no. 5 (2000): 1534–1575.

3. Formerly occupied by three colonial powers, the Portuguese (sixteenth century), the Dutch (seventeenth century), and the British (eighteenth century through 1948, when independence was granted), Sri Lanka is more renowned as the world's foremost exporter of commercially grown tea.

4. In the district of Moneragala, the most impoverished district outside the conflict-torn northern and eastern regions of the country.

5. Edna Acosta-Belen and Christina Bose use the concept of "women as the last colony" as a metaphor to understand how the power relationships inherent in colonialism positioned women and colonies in similar forms of subordination to European colonizers, and continue to be perpetuated in contemporary times. Edna Acosta-Belen and Christine E. Bose, "From Structural Subordination to Empowerment: Women and Development in Third World Contexts," Special Issue: Women and Development in the Third World, *Gender and Society* 4, no. 3, (September 1990): 299–320. Antonio Gramsci's mention of the term "subaltern" appears first in the *Prison Notebooks* and is his euphemism for the proletariat, the economically dispossessed, but also, by virtue of economic dispossession, the socially marginalized. See Antonio Gramsci and Joseph A. Buttigieg, *Prison Notebooks* (New York: Columbia University Press, 1991).

6. Meaning slash-and-burn farming practices or horticulture.

7. Moneragala District was a thriving rice-cultivating region at one point in history (1800s). Despite inadequate rainfall in the region to support wet-rice, thousands of small irrigation reservoirs commissioned by reigning monarchs in an earlier time permitted the population to produce at least one rice crop. The native agricultural communities of the region alternated this crop with shifting cultivation (locally referred to as *chena*), growing mostly pulses, tuber crops, and vegetables as well as fruit trees that provided them a sufficient sustenance. Due to gradual disrepair, encroachment by the jungle, and the effects of three hundred years of colonization, these reservoirs were abandoned, with the population relying more and more on clearing the nearby jungles for chena crops. As the seat of a ruthlessly crushed rebellion against the British in 1848, the people of Moneragala are hailed for their strong inclinations for independence, their spirit of resistance. Moneragala is poor, poor for geographical reasons and also because of bureaucratic and political negligence. However, the ancient history of this part of Sri Lanka tells a different story. In present-day Sri Lanka, Moneragala District records the highest unemployment, malnutrition, and associated poverty rates in the country.

8. The Dry Zone covers 70 percent of the island and receives only a scant, but concentrated rainfall (between thirty and seventy inches a year, falling primarily during one of the three months of the rainy season—in October).

9. The ethnic Sinhala population represents 74 percent of the population of Sri Lanka, and they are mostly Buddhist (except for approximately 5 percent, who converted to Catholicism during the era of Portuguese colonialism in the 1500s and other Christian faiths during subsequent periods of missionary activity).

10. For example, low rainfall, several continuous months of bright sun that permit glucose formation, and flat, well-drained soils.

11. Considered "crown" land, meaning land belonging to the state, and interpreted traditionally as accessible freehold to the public.

12. Archaeological remains attest to the prevalence prior to the twelfth century of large irrigation reservoirs (also referred to as "tanks") and other irrigation canal systems commissioned by the royalty of Sri Lanka throughout the rain scarce Dry Zone in order to ensure that the agricultural populations of this region could meet their subsistence needs sufficiently.

13. At Kande Village, I conducted ethnographic research based on the techniques of participant-observation, working with women on their daily household chores and agricultural activities, including work on their cane fields. I supplemented this type of research with focused interviews with the adult women of the forty families residing there. This research included repeat interviews with individual women, groups of women, and key males in the community (village headman, the registrar of births and deaths, the county administrative official, and the ritual specialists) on key indices, such as the gender division of labor and women's economic contributions, decision-making, household fund management, and symbolic and ideological notions (e.g., purity/pollution) associated with women.

14. These were opportunistic samples, based on who consented to and had time to participate in an interview. They were, nonetheless, representative samples, given the random manner in which the interviewees were identified and the consistency of their responses. Adhering to the open interview method in ethnographic research, I did not use a survey instrument but focused on the key indices of gender noted above (women's household and public decision-making, household fund management, valuation of economic contributions, and physical mobility). Household demographic data (gender and age composition, educational status, occupation and income levels) was consistently collected from all Kande Village interviewees, and most of those interviewed at PSC, based on consent.

15. The rapport and enduring relationships based on fictive kin arrangements established at the first field location enabled me to gain the trust of settlers on PSC, who were generally mistrustful of any one that appeared to be "official." The settlers had gained an understanding that my research took an empathetic perspective in documenting their plight and as such they were eager to share their stories. I am truly indebted especially to the women who participated in the research for the openness with which they revealed the difficult conditions under which they lived.

16. In 2005/2006 Brazil produced the largest volume of sugar (27,910 metric tons) and exported 16,488 metric tons; the European Union produced 21,735 metric tons and exported 8,004 metric tons, while India (the third-largest producer of sugar in the world) put out 19,891 metric tons, although it only exported 1,087 metric tons. Ilovo Sugar Web-site posting of International Sugar statistics, http://www.illovo.co.za/worldofsugar/international SugarStats.htm (accessed September 14, 2006).

17. According to a report by the Asian Development Bank, even at the onset, Sri Lanka's sugarcane operations were considered to be uneconomic (Asian Development Bank, *Report on the Second Agriculture Program* (2002), http://www.adb.org/documents/PERs?IN241-01.pdf).

18. Per capita sugar consumption is estimated at twenty kilograms in 1988 and thirty kilograms in 1997.

19. Asian Development Bank, *Report on the Second Agriculture Program*.

20. Output was 71,000 metric tons in 1994 and 61,000 metric tons in 1998.

21. Asian Development Bank, *Report on the Second Agriculture Program.*

22. OXFAM, "Dumping on the World: How EU sugar policies hurt poor countries," OXFAM briefing paper (United Kingdom: OXFAM, 2004).

23. Lionel Yodasinghe, *Daily News Sri Lanka,* April 6, 2004, http://www. dailynews.l,/2004/04/06/bus01.html.

24. Clifford Geertz, for example, discusses the complementary roles in swidden agriculture assumed by men and women in Java, Indonesia, as intrinsically a part of swidden systems. Clifford Geertz, *Agricultural Involution: The Processes of Ecological Change in Indonesia* (Berkeley: University of California Press, 1963).

25. See, for example, Malathi de Alwis, "'Respectability,' 'Modernity,' and the Policing of 'Culture' in Colonial Ceylon," in *Gender, Sexuality, and Colonial Modernities,* ed. Antoinette Burton (London, New York: Routledge, 1999), 177–192; Gananath Obeyesekere, "The Fire-Walkers of Kataragama: The Rise of Bhakti Religiosity in Buddhist Sri Lanka," *Journal of Asian Studies* 37, no. 30 (1978): 457–476; Gananath Obeyesekere, "Pregnancy Cravings (dola-Duka) in Relation to Social Structure and Personality in a Sinhalese Village," *American Anthropologist* 65 (1963): 323–342.

26. The term "sanskritic" was first used by the Indian scholar Srinivas, who coined it to refer to the influence of the Brahmanic scale of values. Here I use it to refer to the influence of Brahmanic gender codes upholding ideals of women's chastity (with the expectation of virginity at marriage), subordination to males (with the expectation of deference behaviors toward males and social and economic dependence on males), and women's relegation to the domestic/private sphere (with the specification of limited mobility in public spaces, and assigned only reproductive responsibilities).

27. Ester Boserup, *Women's Role in Economic Development* (London: George Allen & Unwin Ltd., 1970). See also Judith Carney and Michael Watts, "Disciplining Women? Rice, Mechanization, and the Evolution of Mandinka Gender Relations in Senegambia," *Signs: Journal of Women, Culture and Society* 16, no. 4 (1990): 651–681; and Ann Whitehead, "Food Crisis and Gender Conflict in the African Countryside," in *The Food Question,* ed. Henry Bernstein et al. (New York: Monthly Review Press, 1990), 54–68.

28. Since many conjugal unions were not formally registered in this region of the country, I have inserted the word "divorce" in quotation marks to signify the dissolution of a long-term relationship where the woman is left with the responsibility of providing sole maintenance of the offspring of that conjugal relationship.

29. The use of the phrase "children's father" to refer to one's husband is a typical expression in rural Sri Lanka, and her words have been translated verbatim.

30. Kataragama devale is the main center of worship and temple complex that had been given charge of the surrounding land by the royalty of the region several centuries previously.

31. See, for example, Sue L. Carswell, "A Family Business: Women, Children, and Smallholder Sugar Cane Farming in Fiji," *Asia Pacific Viewpoint* 44, no. 2 (2003): 131–148; Michael Moynagh, *Brown or White? A History of the Fiji Sugar Industry, 1873–1973,* Pacific Research Monograph Series, No. 5 (Canberra: Australian National University Press, 1981); Shaista Shameem, "Sugar and Spice: Wealth Accumulation and the Labor of Indian Women in Fiji, 1879–1930" (Ph.D. thesis, University of Waikato, Hamilton, New Zealand, 1990).

32. Elephant encroachment on the sugarcane fields has been the perennial dilemma of cane growers since, as popular lore holds, elephants love sugarcane and will resort to any means to get to a cane field, even going to the extent of throwing a dead tree trunk across the electric wire fencing the estate sugar land, which then enables them to cross the fence and feed on the cane stalks.

33. While mainstream liberal feminists had long argued about the confinement and oppression that the veil represented, new scholarship has begun to point to the ways in which women use the veil to their advantage as a way of shielding and protecting themselves.

34. In Brazil, for example, average rural sector wage is R$257.97 for men and R$144.40 for women. See Leila Linhares Barsted, *Genero e legislacão rural no Brasil: A situaçao legal das mulheres face a reforma agraria—Relatório Final* (Brasília/Roma: INCRA/FAO, 2002).

35. Lorenzo Cotula, *Gender and Law: Women's Rights in Agriculture* (Rome: FAO Legislative Study, 2002), 76.

36. M. Mbilinyi, "Gender and Employment on Sugar Cane Plantations in Tanzania," Sectoral Activities Programme Working Papers (Geneva: ILO, 1995).

37. Rhoda Reddock, "Freedom Denied: Indian Women and Indentureship in Trinidad and Tobago: 1898–1960," *Economic and Political Weekly* 20, no. 43 (1985): 75.

38. See Janet A Naidu, "Indian Women of Guyana: Reflections of Their Existence, Survival, and Representation," *Guyana Journal* 10, no. 7 (2005): located online at http://www.guyanajournal.com/current.html. See also Reddock, "Freedom Denied."

39. Walter Rodney, *A History of the Guyanese Working People, 1881–1905* (Baltimore: John Hopkins University Press, 1981), 41, quoted in Moses Seenarine, *Recasting Indian Women in Colonial Guyana: Gender, Labor, and Caste in the Lives of Free and Indentured Laborers* (Saxakali Publications, 1996), http://www.saxakali.com/Saxakali-Publications/recastgwa.htm.

40. Evidenced in this region of the country, as noted above, by child preference that favors females or the absence of a preferred gender, high valuation of women's labor, marriage and residence arrangements that permit women continual affiliation with their natal household, the absence of dowry and associated expectations of virginity and purity, women's participation in household decision-making and a key role in household fund management.

41. I am referring to the concept of "local" at this juncture to denote its distinctness in comparison to imported gender ideologies embedded in Western capitalism, but I am maintaining the notion of local gender constructs as those which have been formulated with the influence of sanskritic value systems, as clarified in a previous endnote.

42. See de Alwis for a more detailed elaboration of this construct: Malathi de Alwis, "'Respectability,' 'modernity,' and the policing of 'culture' in colonial Ceylon," in *Gender, Sexuality, and Colonial Modernities*, ed. Antoinette Burton (London, New York: Routledge, 1999), 177–192.

43. While ethnic and political polarities are additional axes of the social hierarchy in Sri Lankan society, I refrain from including these in the present analysis, given that the subject of this research is an ethnically homogenous group.

44. See the following document for a sound discussion of the impact of neoliberal policies on women's work in agriculture and other sectors: United Nations Research Institute for Social Development (UNRISD), *Gender Equality: Striving for Justice in an Unequal World* (New York: UNRISD/UN Publications, 2005).

45. See Lucia Da Corta and Davuluri Venkateshwarlu, "Unfree Relations and the Feminisation of Agricultural Labour in Andhra Pradesh, 1970–95," *Journal of Peasant Studies* (1999): 71–139.

46. Eileen Kennedy and Bruce Cogill, "Effects of Cash Crop Production on Women's Income, Time Allocation, and Child Care Practices," Working Paper #167, East Lansing, Michigan State University, Office of Women in Development, 1988.

Contributors

AKOSUA ADOMAKO AMPOFO is an associate professor at the Institute of African Studies and head of the Centre for Gender Studies and Advocacy (CEGENSA) at the University of Ghana. Adomako Ampofo's scholarship focuses on power and decision making; constructions of masculinity and femininity; gender-based violence; the sex industry; gender, race, and ethnicity; and women's mental health. Her recent publications include articles in *Gender and Society*, *Jenda*, *African Journal of Reproductive Health*, and *Ghana Studies*. Since 2003 she has been working on a project that examines the lives of non-Ghanaian women living in Ghana and is particularly interested in the inter-generational processes by which women contest or re-inscribe sexist and racist ideas and behaviors. Currently she is also collaborating with Takyiwaa Manuh and Aloysius Denkabe, both of the University of Ghana, on a CODESRIA-funded work, "Masculinities and the Making of the Ghanaian Nation."

A. LYNN BOLLES, who received her Ph.D. in 1981 from Rutgers University, is a professor and the director of graduate studies in the department of women's studies and an affiliate faculty member in anthropology, African American studies, comparative literature, and American studies at the University of Maryland College Park. Her research focuses on the African diaspora, the Caribbean, and the political economy of women. Before coming to Maryland, she was the director of Africana Studies at Bowdoin College. Her work appears in *American Anthropologist*, *Caribbean Studies*, and *Transforming Anthropology*, among other journals. Bolles authored *We Paid Our Dues: Women Trade Union Leaders in the Caribbean* (1996) and *Sister Jamaica: A Study of Women, Work and Households in Kingston, Jamaica* (1996) and two monographs. She also co-authored *In the Shadow of the Sun* (1990). For nine years, Bolles was an editor of *Feminist Studies*. Very active in her profession, she is past president of the Association of Black Anthropologists, the Association for Feminist Anthropology, and the Caribbean Studies Association, the oldest interdisciplinary academic organization in the region. At Maryland, Dr. Bolles revitalized the Africa and Americas Committee, now the David C. Driskell Center, and served twice as interim chair of the African American Studies Department. She is the recipient of the UM Presidents Outstanding Minority Faculty member award and numerous teaching honors. Bolles is a fellow of the American Anthropological Association and the

Society for Applied Anthropology. In 1989, she was honored by Syracuse University with the Chancellor's Citation for Distinguished Achievement in Education.

AKOSUA K. DARKWAH is an assistant professor in the department of sociology at the University of Ghana, Legon. Her research interests are quite varied. In addition to her interest in the area of gender and work, she has written in the areas of religion, gender, and sexuality. She is currently working in collaboration with another colleague at the University of Ghana to conduct a study on adoptions in the Ghanaian setting.

CAROLE BOYCE DAVIES is an active scholar in African diaspora and related studies. Publications include *Migrations of the Subject: Black Women, Writing Identity* (1994); *Ngambika: Studies of Women in African Literature* (1986); *Out of the Kumbla: Caribbean Women and Literature* (1990); a two-volume collection of critical and creative writing, *Moving beyond Boundaries*, vol.1: *International Dimensions of Black Women's Writing*, and vol. 2: *Black Women's Diasporas* (1995); *The African Diaspora: African Origins and New World Identities* (1999); *Decolonizing the Academy* (2003). She is writing a series of personal reflections called "Caribbean Spaces: Between the Twilight Zone and the Underground Railroad" and is preparing three projects on the Caribbean feminist activist Claudia Jones: a book on Jones, an edition of the writings of Jones, and a Web site on Jones. Some of her academic positions have been Herskovits professor of African studies and professor of comparative literary studies and African American studies at Northwestern University; director of African–New World Studies and professor of English at Florida International University; and professor of English and Africana studies at SUNY-Binghamton. She has served as president of the African Literature Association and of the Association of Caribbean Women Writers and Scholars and was founding president of the Women's Caucus of the African Literature Association.

EVELYN NAKANO GLENN is professor of gender and women's studies and of ethnic studies and founding director of the Center for Race and Gender at the University of California, Berkeley. She teaches undergraduate and graduate courses: Social Structural Theory and Methods, Transdisciplinary Methods, Gender and Work, and Comparative Structures of Gender. Glenn's research interests focus on race and gender especially as they are co-constituted structurally and discursively in various arenas, including immigration, labor, and citizenship. Her writings have appeared in such journals as *Social Problems*, *Signs*, *Feminist Studies*, *Social Science History*, *Stanford Law Review*, *Contemporary Sociology*, and *Review of Radical Political Economy*, as well as in numerous edited volumes. She is the author of *Issei, Nisei, War Bride: Three Generations of Japanese American Women in Domestic Service* (1986) and *Unequal Freedom: How Race and Gender Shaped*

American Citizenship and Labor (2002) and co-editor of *Mothering: Ideology, Experience, and Agency* (1994). Glenn's chapter for this volume is based on research for a larger historical project that traces the race and gender construction of caring as a form of coerced labor.

NANDINI GUNEWARDENA is a practitioner anthropologist who has worked professionally on gender justice issues for over a dozen years. Her research on the sugar economy dates back to her dissertation field work in the mid-1990s and subsequent ethnographic work since then. She is currently affiliated with the University of California, Los Angeles, department of anthropology and the international development studies program.

SHARON HARLEY is chair and associate professor of the African American studies department at the University of Maryland, College Park. She is recipient of numerous scholarships and fellowships, including the 2003 Woodrow Wilson Center Fellowship, the Smithsonian Postdoctoral Fellowship, the Rockefeller Fellowship for Minority Group Scholars, the American Association of University Women, and the Ford Foundation. She is the editor of *Sister Circle: Black Women and Work* (2002), an interdisciplinary volume exploring the role of work in black women's lives, to which she also contributed a chapter. She also has a chapter in *Sisters in the Struggle: African-American Women in the Civil Rights and Black Power Movements* (2001). She is the co-editor of the widely read *Afro-American Woman: Struggles and Images* (1978) and *Women in Africa and the African Diaspora* (1987), contributing scholarly chapters to both volumes. She was the co-director of a Ford Foundation–funded project grant, "The Meanings and Representations of Black Women and Work," which produced the book *Sister Circle,* and is currently the principal investigator and project director of the Ford Foundation-funded "The Meanings and Representations of Work in the Lives of Women of Color" seminar. This faculty research seminar was awarded the Rockefeller Foundation's International Bellagio Study and Conference grant for an August 2004 conference of national and international women-of-color scholars.

NANCY A. HEWITT is a professor of history and women's and gender studies at Rutgers University, where she also directs the Institute for Research on Women. She is the author of numerous publications related to women's activism in the United States and to American women's history more generally. More recently she has published *Southern Discomfort: Women's Activism in Tampa, Florida, 1880s–1920s* (2001) and edited *A Companion to American Women's History* (2002). She is currently writing a biography of nineteenth-century abolitionist-feminist Amy Post.

EVELYN HU-DEHART is a professor of history and ethnic studies and director of the Center for the Study of Race and Ethnicity in America (CSREA) at Brown University. She has published three books on the Yaqui Indians of Northern

Mexico and Arizona, one in Spanish, and numerous articles and book chapters on her current research on the Chinese diaspora in Latin America and the Caribbean. She is the editor of *Asia and Latin America,* a special 2006 issue of *Review,* a journal of the Americas Society, and co-editor of *Voluntary Organizations in the Chinese Diaspora* (2006). She is published on five continents, in English, Spanish, Chinese, and Zoque Mayan.

MARIA L. ONTIVEROS is a professor of law at the University of San Francisco School of Law. In addition to co-authoring a leading casebook on employment discrimination law, she publishes on the topics of workplace harassment of women of color, farmworkers, organizing immigrant workers, and contemporary applications of the Thirteenth Amendment. She has an AB in economics, with general and departmental honors from the University of California; a JD, cum laude, from Harvard Law School; a Masters of Industrial and Labor Relations from Cornell University; and a JSD from Stanford Law School.

MARY JOHNSON OSIRIM is a professor of sociology and a faculty diversity liaison at Bryn Mawr College. She is the former co-director of the Center for Ethnicities, Communities, and Social Policy, chair of the sociology department, and coordinator of Africana studies at Bryn Mawr College. She received her AB and PhD degrees from Harvard University in social studies and sociology, respectively, and received the MSc degree from the London School of Economics and Political Science in sociology. She has many publications in these areas, including articles in *International Sociology* and *Gender and Society.* She is currently writing two books: "Enterprising Women: Identity, Entrepreneurship, and Civil Society in Urban Zimbabwe" and "African Voices on Gender Research and Activism in Africa," co-edited with Akosua Adomako Ampofo, Josephine Beoku-Betts, and Wairimu Njambi. She has received several awards and fellowships, including grants from the National Science Foundation, a Pew Faculty Fellowship in International Affairs, and a Carter G. Woodson Fellowship at the University of Virginia. In 1995, she received the Rosalyn R. Schwartz Teaching Award for model classroom teaching, creative course development, and campus leadership. In April 2001, she was the minority scholar-in-residence in women's studies and sociology at Illinois State University. For 2002–2003, she received fellowships at the Radcliffe Institute for Advanced Study and the Woodrow Wilson International Center for Scholars, the latter which she accepted.

VICKI L. RUIZ is a professor of history and Chicano/Latino studies at the University of California, Irvine. Her monograph *From out of the Shadows: Mexican Women in Twentieth-Century America* (1998) was named a Choice Outstanding Academic Book of 1998. She is also the author of *Cannery Women, Cannery Lives* (1987). Ruiz also co-edited with Ellen DuBois the influential U.S. women's history reader *Unequal Sisters* (1990), with a fourth edition on the way. She is the co-author of a U.S. history textbook, *Created Equal: A Social and Political History of the United States* (2002), with Jacqueline Jones, Peter Wood, Thomas Borstelmann, and Elaine Tyler May. She and Virginia Sánchez Korrol recently co-edited *Latina Legacies: Identity, Biography, and Community* (2005) and they are also co-editors of *Latinas in the United States: A Historical Encyclopedia* (2006). In addition, she and Donna Gabaccia are co-editors of *American Dreaming, Global Realities: Re-Thinking U.S. Immigration History* (2006). Finally, she and John R. Chávez are the co-editors of *Mapping Memories and Migrations: Locating Boricua/Chicana Histories* (forthcoming). Ruiz is the president-elect of the American Studies Association. She is also immediate president of the Organization of American Historians and the Berkshire Conference of Women's Historians. In 2006, she became an elected fellow of the Society of American Historians.

Index